First Light

Morning Conversations with God

WILLIAM S. STODDARD

MULTNOMAH

Portland, Oregon 97266

Cover design by Multnomah Design Group

Edited by Larry R. Libby

FIRST LIGHT
© 1990 by William S. Stoddard
Published by Multnomah Press
Portland, Oregon 97266

Multnomah Press is a ministry of Multnomah School of the Bible, 8435 N.E. Glisan Street, Portland, Oregon 97220.

Printed in the United States of America.

Library of Congress Cataloging-in-Publication Data

Stoddard, William S.
  First light / William Stoddard.
    p. cm.
  ISBN 0-88070-327-X
  1. Devotional calendars. I. Title.
BV4811.S85   1990
242'.2—dc20   89-48780
                                                   CIP

90 91 92 93 94 95 96 97 98 99 - 10 9 8 7 6 5 4 3 2 1

This book has no meaning apart from
God's love and faithfulness
and is dedicated to

Henrietta

who has shared with me that love and faithfulness
for half a century

Isaiah 30 : 15 —

" In returning and rest
     shall ye be saved,
in quietness and confidence
     shall be your rest."

(S. C. W) '90

Acknowledgments

Prayer is the vital center of spiritual well-being. For this reason the heart of this book is found in the written prayers of a grateful pastor. They were written across three decades of my actie ministry for no hearing except that of our Heavenly Father and for no other purpose than to receive His blessing and to give thanks for mercies already received.

In these prayers (many of them written at "first light"), light from the *written Word* has led to praise and obedience to the *living* Word. All of the prayers as originally written are offered in that spirit.

But now there is the additional hope that, in sharing them, other disciples of the Way will find strength and guidance for the demands of daily living. To make this possible I am indebted to Multnomah editors, Al Janssen and Larry Libby, who first saw the need and the potential of such a wider sharing. They challenged me to make these intimate and deeply personal prayers understandable and useful to a larger reading public. Without their insight and confidence, this book as a shared blessing would never have made it.

I am thankful for the support of my wife, Henrietta, and our four children and their families who have been deriving help from these prayers and who kept insisting that I try to share them with other families. Cherished friends and associates, too numerous to mention, have read these prayers from time to time with appreciation for their spiritual worth. This has helped me to keep on putting my prayer-thoughts into words.

I would also express my indebtedness to Dr. Edward Howell Roberts, Dean of Princeton Theological Seminary and long since in the Father's nearer Presence, who encouraged me more than fifty years ago to write something original and creative every day. This is what really led to the writing out and now the preservation of these prayers.

But most of all I acknowledge the favor and wisdom of our loving Father who has given me the health, the energy, and the time in retirement to produce this work. I was ordained to the ministry of the Word exactly a half-century ago in June of 1940. As this ministry will soon extend beyond my sphere of influence and my span of life, I say now as I said then, "To God be ALL the glory." The circle is complete. The blessing goes on. It never needs to end. Praise the Lord!

*"Just as the day was breaking,
Jesus stood on the beach"*

(John 21:4).

IN THE BEGINNING, GOD

"In the beginning God created . . ." (Genesis 1:1).
"In the beginning was the Word . . ." (John 1:1).

Read: **Genesis 1:1-2; John 1:1-4;** Hebrews 1:10-12.

WHAT IS GOD SAYING?

God was in the beginning. He transcends all created things because by Him all things were made. The Word that became flesh, our Lord Jesus Christ, was with God in the beginning. In fact, He was God and is God. He is the Source of all life and the life He gives is the light of men. The fact of creation and the gift of light are closely associated. He who was in the beginning is the source of all light and true life now.

HOW DOES THIS APPLY TO US?

God, who was in the beginning, can take the disorder and emptiness of our lives and create something entirely new. He created. He can recreate. He is the God of all beginning and of all *beginning again.* Jesus Christ, who was in the beginning THEN, can provide for us a new beginning NOW. Each day with Him is a new beginning. Let us come to prayer with tip-toe eagerness to see what God has for us in new adventure and joyful discovery today.

Pray with Me

O God, who in the beginning was, I affirm that in the beginning of this year, You already are. Your hand opens the door, Your presence gives me courage, Your voice calls me on and up. "In the beginning God created . . . ." O God of infinite power and endless love, at the beginning of this year—and always—create in me a clean heart. Let all the follies and failures of the past be erased. Let the thoughts which have stained my mind and the desires which have corrupted my heart be removed. Let them be replaced by such thoughts of Your holiness and such desires for Your Kingdom as shall give no quarter to the attacks of darkness, however subtle and persistent they may be.

"In the beginning was the Word . . . ." Reveal Yourself to me, O God, in the transforming radiance of Your Son. He is Your Word. He is Your way of making contact. He is Your purpose revealed and Your love made clear. Let this be a year which, from the beginning to the end, shall be lived in the conscious presence of Jesus Christ, the Alpha and the Omega, the Beginning and the End, the Author and the Finisher of our Faith, who said, "Surely I am with you always, to the very end." God of all beginning and all beginning again, make this beginning Your beginning. As You have created, recreate. As You have spoken in Jesus Christ, speak again. May the breathless beauty and the reverent hush of this dawning spent with You linger with me through this year's most common tasks and give me living hope and strength through every trial.

In His Name, Amen.

MOVING ON IN THE LIFE OF PRAYER

We should keep going back to the God of all beginnings. He can get us started right. He can keep us going right. He can see to it that everything ends right. And when we say "Amen," let it be with the glad conviction that Jesus is the Author and the Finisher of our faith. He who begins a good work in us won't stop His work until it is finished. Can we say "Amen" to that? Is it possible that our "Amens" have worn thin through custom? "Amen" should NEVER be said carelessly or thoughtlessly. In 2 Corinthians 1:20 we read, "For all the promises of God find their Yes in him. That is why we utter the Amen through him, to the glory of God." No wonder we say "Amen" at the end of our prayers. So . . . in the beginning, God. In the end, God. In between, the privilege and the power of prayer.

Day 2
ANGELS? REALLY?

"But while he thought about these things, an angel of the Lord appeared to him . . ." (Matthew 1:20).

Read: **Matthew 1:20; Acts 12:5-17; Psalm 19:14,** 39:3, 104:34, 91:11; 1 Timothy 4:15 (KJV); Acts 27:23; Hebrews 1:14.

WHAT IS GOD SAYING?

Angels are for real. God sends them to help us. They are meant to "keep" us and to "guard" us in all our ways. Not here and there, not now and then, but always and in all our ways.

Peter was in prison. An angel of the Lord said "Get up quickly" and the chains fell off his hands. Belonging to God and serving God (Acts 27:23) means that God has an angel standing by us. It comes with the territory.

Joseph saw the angel of the Lord when he was in great perplexity. Guidance from that angel came in his deepest hour of need. God often sends a ministering angel when we reach the end of our rope—or the end of our hope, for that matter.

HOW DOES THIS APPLY TO US?

Psalm 91:11 reminds us that we cannot go any distance FOR God without the presence and help of a ministering angel FROM God. The world may scoff at this thought, but believers draw strength from it. They trust and oftentimes prove that in true meditation the angels of God stand nearby. And when an angel of the Lord tells us to get up and get going, we are given the freedom to do it. Peter's experience in prison demonstrates that when we are held in bondage to anything, God can and will (if we believe) lift us up and set us free.

Pray with Me

O God, I thank You for all great and glowing thoughts. As every good and perfect gift comes from You, so all thoughts of pure love and unblemished beauty are Yours to give . . . and ours to enjoy. Forgive me that too often I have seen right and thought wrong, I have seen beauty and thought ugliness, I have seen Your faithful provision and thought anxiety, I have seen Your gift of a second chance and thought revenge.

Help me to see Your thoughts expressed in all that is good and true and beautiful, and beyond all this give me the grace of some ministering angel to turn my thoughts toward the right and to shield my thoughts from the wrong.

Yes, with Joseph, even in times of perplexity and deep concern, may my thoughts be so centered on Your unfailing goodness that meditation shall be a heavenly "ladder" down which angels of light and mercy may come.

O God, keep my thoughts so holy and loving that the appearing of angels may not seem strange nor their message go unheard.

In the Name of Jesus who also knew the grace of ministering angels, Amen.

MOVING ON IN THE LIFE OF PRAYER

In Copley Square, Boston, stands a statue that gives a silent but eloquent witness. It portrays Phillips Brooks, great preacher of the last century, looking out across the busy circle of traffic. In the shadows behind him there is a slightly elevated figure which can be easily identified as the Christ, and one hand reaches out to rest gently on the shoulder of His faithful servant, Phillips Brooks. In a similar fashion there is a nearby angel who ministers to us, guards us, and sometimes, as with Peter, "strikes" us to get us up and going.

When things go well and life is at its exhilarating best; or when things are very humdrum and life is painfully commonplace; or when we have reached the end of our rope, perplexed, bewildered, and void of hope, *think about it.* God has an angel for *you,* to keep you in *all* your ways. Remember: While Joseph "thought," the angel appeared. Pray faithfully. Angels are nearer than we think and never too busy or too late.

Day 3

THE FACE OF GOD

"The Lord make his face to shine upon you, and be gracious to you" (*Numbers 6:25*).

Read: **Numbers 6:22-26; Genesis 16:6-12;** Psalm 31:14, 80:3.

WHAT IS GOD SAYING?

God sees us. He makes His face to shine upon us. In Genesis 16, Hagar was fleeing from the angry jealousy of Sarai. Then an angel found her alone and forsaken in the far wilderness. In her distress she became aware of the compassion of God. She acknowledged the heavenly grace that sees and cares about human need. God was looking out for her. When other faces were turned away, she said, "Thou art a God of seeing." How well she could have echoed David's thought (Psalm 27:10)

.e, then the LORD

?s of the great and
and keep you, the
vid, who knew well
., lifts his voice in
? again there is the
, with steadfast love
s.

Us?

ds to turn us around
)oking the right way,
:alize that no matter
l compassionate. His
face d...   ; to see Him who sees
us! We want to experience rus g..... compassion. But we
must be willing to be turned around. The way we are often
headed . . . in the fog of indifference and sin . . . hiding behind
our safe, hard shells of pride . . . feeling no need of repentance,
we cannot see the shining face of God's favor and blessing. If we
want the face of God to shine on us, we must turn toward Him,
even if it means 180 degrees.

Pray with Me

Lord, You are a God who sees. Your face is always turned
toward me, even when my sins, like a thick cloud, have risen to
make You seem more distant; even when comforts and luxuries,
like a subtle anesthesia, have made You seem nonexistent; even
when hardship and trial, like the Devil's Advocate, have made
You seem uncaring. Nevertheless, Your face is always turned
toward me.

May this day be one when through all clouds and darkness
there shall come the vision of Your face. For when I see it truly, I
shall see it shining.

Your face shines with the grace of understanding. In the
face of Jesus Christ I see a God who cares. In Him I see a God
who listens to the faintest cry and heeds the wordless anguish of
unuttered prayer.

Your face shines with the grace of salvation. Let me rest in
this healing peace, because Your hand is not shortened. The
shining of Your face and the triumph of Your hand belong
together.

Your face shines with grace of hope. By the resurrection of
Jesus Christ, by all the glory that streams from His empty tomb,
by the splendor of His ascending into Heaven, by the promise

that He is there even now making intercession for those who draw near to God, by His own pledge that He will come again, we are born anew to a living hope.

All this I see in the shining of Your face. "In the light of a king's face there is life." In the light of the face of my risen King there is understanding and salvation and hope. In the light of His face there is life eternal.

To the praise of His holy and deathless love, Amen.

MOVING ON IN THE LIFE OF PRAYER

We should live in the confidence of God's shining face. It is not hidden behind clouds of fear around a throne of rigid, unapproachable judgment. Not for those who have embraced Jesus Christ, and have received by faith the gift of salvation. Look, the sight is glorious. "For it is the God who said, 'Let light shine out of darkness,' who has shone in our hearts to give the light of the knowledge of the glory of God in the face of Christ" (2 Corinthians 4:6). Lay hold of that truth. Face God with hope every morning, see His shining face in blessing through every day, and close each day still looking on His face. It is still shining on you with the grace of understanding, salvation, and hope.

Day 4

THE POWER OF THE RESURRECTION

"For I know that my Redeemer lives" (Job 19:25).

Read: **Job 19:25;** Psalm 130:7-8; Isaiah 44:22-23; Titus 2:13-14; Acts 4:33.

WHAT IS GOD SAYING?

Job is presumed by many to be the oldest book in the Bible. And the oldest of books has to do with the oldest of problems: "Why do the righteous suffer?"

Up to this verse in the story of Job, he is asking questions. Tough ones. "But man dies, and is laid low; man breathes his last, and where is he?" (14:10). "If a man die, shall he live again?" (14:14).

They were unanswerable questions that rose from a perplexed and anguished heart. But with his cry of faith, *"I know that my Redeemer lives,"* he is on solid ground. He is led of the Spirit to make the statement that has conveyed assurance to believers down through the centuries. He says, "I know." He points with certainty to the fact that the solution to all problems, the ultimate answer to all questions, whether they be old and persistent or new and passing, lies in knowing that the Lord, our Redeemer, lives. God in Christ is on top of it all. He lives. He has conquered the last great enemy which is death. He is "declared to be the Son of God with power . . . by the resurrection from the dead" (Romans 1:14, KJV).

How Does This Apply to Us?

In spite of every argument to the contrary, we may know that our Redeemer lives. Furthermore, to live successful Christian lives we *must* know that. God's plan for the believer is that, by the testimony of the Holy Spirit and by opening one's eyes to see the innumerable evidences of God's power and authority in the world of nature and history, we may come to a place where we can say we *know*. God's agenda for us is that we come to know. That is why the Bible was given to us. "I write this to you who believe in the name of the Son of God, that you may know that you have eternal life" (1 John 5:13). KNOW. Not guess, not suppose, not wish, not wonder, but KNOW.

Pray with Me

Lord, to meditate upon this magnificent truth brings glory to my soul and a peace that remains unshaken amidst the shattered dreams of a Christ-rejecting world.

I know that my Redeemer lives. The bond between us is personal and close. I am not a number on a long list of data that has been fed into a celestial computer. I have a name and You know it. I need a living Redeemer that I can call my own and You are that Redeemer.

I know that my Redeemer lives. God be praised for the ability to know, with knowledge as clear and as sure as Your own word. There is no vagueness in Your promises, no wondering if You really mean it, no wandering about in the wastelands of philosophical speculation.

I know that my Redeemer lives. I am delivered from the bondage of the fear of death. I am free because I am possessed by One who has power to lift me up and hold me above the entangling alliances of sin and the bitter harvest of eternal, spiritual death. He is real to me, I know Him. He is my great eternal Redeemer because He lives. His voice is rich and warm, not a dead echo of superstition nor the faint whispering of wishful thinking. His hand is strong and His eyes are kind. He lives, and to eternity I shall praise Him that "because He lives, I too shall live."

In the Name of Him who ever lives to make intercession for me, Amen.

MOVING ON IN THE LIFE OF PRAYER

"You ask me how I know he lives,
He lives within my heart."

That is the great finale to a familiar and cherished hymn. It is also the experience of the steadfast Christian. In his or her heart the Christian *knows* that Jesus is alive and in control and that He will come again, as He promised, to receive us to Himself. The secret of joyous living lies in *knowing* that whatever happens, Jesus Christ is real; He is really ours and we are really His. Do you KNOW that your Redeemer lives? Then, by your life, SHOW that your Redeemer lives!

Day 5

IN TO GOD FOR OTHERS, OUT TO OTHERS FOR GOD

"For there is one God, and there is one mediator between God and men, the man Christ Jesus" (1 Timothy 2:5).

Read: **1 Timothy 2:1-6a;** Deuteronomy 4:5; Hebrews 12:22-24.

WHAT IS GOD SAYING?

In this 1 Timothy passage, Paul offers simple instructions for living in a complex world. He opens with an emphasis on prayer which lays the foundation for relationships with others and tells us how to enter the life that is "good and acceptable" to God. He stresses that we are not to have favorites in our prayer life. All persons are important to God. He is not willing that any should perish (2 Peter 3:9). "He desires all men to be saved and to come to the knowledge of the truth." Everyone is eligible for our prayer list and no one should be turned off by our lifestyle. Could it be any clearer? Our lives are to be quiet and peaceable, godly and respectful in every way. This is a large order . . . but we have a strong Master in Jesus Christ and a great Enabler in the Holy Spirit.

Consider what this passage says about the unity of the Godhead and the deity of Jesus Christ. Here Jesus is called "God the Savior, the one God and the one Mediator" and still "the man Christ Jesus." With respect to His being the Mediator, don't miss the significance of the contrast found in Hebrews 12:24 (NKJV), "the blood of sprinkling (His blood shed for us) that speaks better things than that of Abel." The blood of Abel cried out for revenge, and that was right. The blood of Jesus, the Mediator of the New Covenant, cries out for forgiveness and mercy. That's far better. That's "amazing grace."

How Does This Apply to Us?

Instead of being troubled by competing views or worried that we might appear too narrow, we ought to be thankful. We can rest in the assurance that there is one God and one Mediator, one perfect answer to life's many problems, one door into the sheepfold of abundant life and meaning (John 10:9-10), one Master to serve in a quiet and peaceable life. Don't run away from *this* narrowness. It is the narrowness that leads to life abundant and eternal. Believing, loving, and serving one God makes us a greater blessing to all whom God loves in the world, in our city, in our neighborhood, and in our family.

Pray with Me

O God, I thank You that I have seen Your solitary splendor. I have seen the glory that You will not share with another. I have seen Your throne above all thrones. You are not "many gods" that my heart should conjecture and be confused. You are "one God" that my heart may be certain and at rest. I thank You that in the living reality of Jesus Christ, I can be lifted into Your healing Presence.

"One God . . . one Mediator . . . ." Far from being troubled by the narrowness of such belief, I am grateful for it. I need not knock on many doors, fearing that perhaps not even one will open to me. The joy of salvation may be grasped by simple faith. The assurance of eternal life may be possessed for sure and forever because of the faithfulness of a covenant-keeping God. The satisfaction of being in the company of Him who holds the key to the meaning of the universe is not the culmination of a long search. It is the beginning of a good and useful life.

Father, I thank You that I do not need to struggle blindly with a multiplicity of ideas. I do not need to dabble wastefully in a variety of opinions. I do not need to become lost in a maze of possible solutions. The narrowness of the faith You have given is its glory. The simplicity of Your revealed will in the love of Jesus Christ makes it possible to lay hold on Heaven's sweetest mysteries and richest treasures. How wonderful to know that there is "one God and one Mediator!"

With singleness of heart I accept Jesus Christ, the one Gift that embraces all good gifts. With simplicity of devotion I would live to His eternal and singular glory.

In the Name of the one and all-sufficient Mediator, Amen.

Moving On in the Life of Prayer

Jesus, the one God and the one Mediator, gave Himself as a ransom *for all.* Is it asking too much that we should pray *for all*? Pray for others and live for God. In to God for others and out to others for God. Let others see in your life that you have been with Jesus, the one God who cares and the one Mediator who saves.

Day 6

Always with Us

"I have been with thee whithersoever thou hast walked" (1 Chronicles 17:8, KJV).

Read: **1 Chronicles 17:17-14;** Genesis 28:15; Exodus 33:14; Isaiah 43:1-2; Philippians 1:6; Matthew 28:20.

What Is God Saying?

God is with us always. David was brought from the humble duties of a shepherd to the awesome responsibilities of a king. He started by "following the sheep." He rose to "leading a nation." He was a chosen vessel to sing the praises of God in words that will last to the end of time. His sweetest songs rose from the awareness that wherever HE was, GOD was. He was God's choice against all odds to be elevated to the highest position in the land. He was a man after God's own heart. All the way from a cipher to a scepter, God was with him. There were times when David must have been inclined to believe that God had forgotten him. Yet he went on, in faith, to discover that God was always with him, in all circumstances and in all places.

He is with all His children in whatever place, in whatever circumstance (Isaiah 43:1-2). He is with all who put their trust in Him, even when their trust has waned, even when they have proved themselves untrustworthy (Isaiah 41:10). He is not going to give up on the work He has begun in the making of a Christian. ALL who do His will can count on His presence. This is the last promise that Jesus made on earth (Matthew 28:20).

How Does This Apply to Us?

It is important for us to remember that God was at work not only in biblical times and with biblical leaders. Here and now He is working out His purpose in *us*. We may not be special to the world but we are special to Him, and when God calls, He also enables. Remember, too, that when God starts a work in our lives, He intends to finish it. That is the point that Paul makes to the Philippians.

In Philippians 1:6 . . . The work begun will become the work completed.

In Philippians 1:9 . . . Love will abound—not a little blossom of promise or a little drop of blessing now and then, but abounding more and more—and more.

In Philippians 2:13 . . . God is not only with us, He is at work in us. This is His promise—a promise we must claim as our own.

Pray with Me

O God, I am constantly thrilled by Your mercy. Your mercy blends with goodness and follows me all the days of my life. Your mercy is steadfast. It doesn't vacillate in response to my behavior. It doesn't change according to the level of my faithfulness.

What I have deserved and what I have received are often at opposite poles. Pride and willfulness have drawn my steps into Vanity Fair. But even there You have walked with me. You have shielded me from that which would wound and sear my soul.

Your steadfast mercy is at work even more when my willfulness takes over. Sometimes, through the pain of chastening grace, You hold back my steps in order that I may walk in paths of freedom and light.

May each passing year find me more aware of this steadfast mercy. May I never cease to be grateful for the love that will not let me go. And when this earthen vessel has run out its earthly value, take it redeemed, refined, remade to Your heavenly mansions. There I shall say with more understanding and love than I could ever say it now: "I thank You, Lord, for being with me, whithersoever . . . ."

In the Name of Christ, Amen.

MOVING ON IN THE LIFE OF PRAYER

God is with us "whithersoever" we walk. We must make sure we are going for Him whithersoever He wants. We should pray that we will be shown the *place* where we are to serve, the *way* we are to serve, and *whom* we are to serve for His sake today. This is the way to find more vitality, joy, and power in prayer.

Day 7

THE RACE BEFORE US

"Let us also lay aside every weight, and sin which clings so closely, and let us run with perseverance the race that is set before us" (Hebrews 12:1b).

Read: **Hebrews 12:1-2;** John 13:14-15; 1 Peter 2:21-23.

WHAT IS GOD SAYING?

Life is well defined as a race. It calls for discipline, determination, and above all, perseverance. We must be willing to lay aside every weight and the sin that clings so closely. We must lay aside the garments that would hamper our progress or even cause us to stumble. We must make any necessary sacrifice. If we think the race is important at all, it must become important above all. He who would travel far must travel light. But we do not go it alone. Our inspiration comes from two sources: First, from those who have gone before, such as the heroes of the faith described in Hebrews 11. Their faith was tested and it did not fail. Their example and their victories should spur us on. Second, and above all, we are inspired by the example of Jesus Christ. We look to Him for the pattern of His life, the way He was willing to serve (John 13), and the manner in which He triumphed over suffering (1 Peter 2).

HOW DOES THIS APPLY TO US?

Jesus doesn't TELL us how to run the race, he SHOWS us how. That is why we need to look to Him. He doesn't TELL us we must be willing to serve others and take care of the humble necessities of life that others might be blessed. He SHOWS us. He doesn't TELL us that our love should suffer long and be kind. He SHOWS us how, when reviled, not to revile again. He SHOWS us how, when treated unjustly, we may rise above it all and continue to live for Him and with Him, having hearts filled with His love and guarded by His peace. He is saying, "You can do it. You will be glad if you continue to run the race with patience, for you will finish the race with joy." He even endured the Cross for the joy that was set before Him.

"Look to me," Jesus is saying, "I did it for you. Now you do it for Me and for the others who may be looking to you and will be affected by the way you run the race."

Pray with Me

Loving Father, of all the blessings with which my life is filled, I count this the greatest: "Looking to Jesus. . . ." It is my greatest privilege. It is also my constant need. May this be a day that finds me living in the continual triumph of faith because I have found the secret of looking continually to Jesus.

Looking to Jesus is my greatest need. When I turn my eyes from Him, small trials seem great and large ones seem impossible. My heart is filled with a hunger that can never find satisfaction until Jesus becomes the supreme object of my desire. When I look to Jesus, I see myself and others in the true light. When he fills my vision I cannot be worried about self or annoyed with others.

Life is wonderfully changed when He is the One to whom I continually look. I can lay aside the weight of repeated failure. I can lay aside those selfish concerns that cling so closely. I can take up the burdens of others. In sorrowing hearts I can awaken the slumbering chords of faith. All this, and more, I can do when I make it my continual business to look to Jesus.

"Looking to Jesus . . ." It is more than desperate necessity, it is abundant blessing. It is more than the must of duty, it is the plus of beauty. It is more than a necessary yoke to bear, it is a boundless joy to share.

"Looking to Jesus . . ." Spirit of God, I thank You for Your Word to me today. It has changed weary and burdened walking into an unencumbered race of victory.

To the glory of Him who is the Pioneer and Perfecter of my faith, Amen.

MOVING ON IN THE LIFE OF PRAYER

Jesus' life was and is an example and we would do well to follow it diligently. But we are also privileged to look continually to Him for encouragement and strength. I remember a sermon I preached fifty-two years ago. I remember it with great clarity and emotion. I don't have to search through old file folders, yellow and brittle with time, to jog my memory. It is as fresh as yesterday. I remember that sermon, born of great travail and delivered with even greater labor in a seminary class. It was the third sermon of my pulpit ministry and it was on this text. I was looking to Jesus then and I am still looking to Him as the Author and Finisher of my faith. Jesus is set before the runners (any and all Christians) as the example on whom they are to fix their eyes. His living, loving, and understanding presence is still my greatest encouragement. His example is still my highest goal. His life is still my shining ideal. I still "look to Him." I always will. Won't you join me in this? "Looking to Jesus" is not only our greatest need, it is our most abundant blessing.

Day 8

TROPHIES FOR GOD

"David took the shields of gold which were carried by the servants of Hadadezer and brought them to Jerusalem" (1 Chronicles 18:7).

Read: **1 Chronicles 18:1-11.**

WHAT IS GOD SAYING?

David was a warrior and a devout believer. Today the Christian is faced with this dilemma: How can one follow Jesus, turning the other cheek and praying for one's enemies, and still countenance the horrors and injustice of war? The practice of returning evil for evil, retaliation, and getting revenge fills the daily newspapers and consumes much too much of the evening news on TV. But it is usually done by those who have not taken seriously the words of Jesus who commands us to PRAY FOR our enemies and not to PREY ON them.

In the time of David, however, the conquering of enemies and the taking of spoils from them was the name of the game. David brought the vast treasure (imagine, shields made out of gold) which he had gained by his own skill and courage, and set it apart for the Lord's use. Altars do seem a better use for gold than shields. Dedicated booty is not rare in history. The Mosque of St. Sophia in Istanbul has the marble pillars that once stood in the Temple of Diana at Ephesus. Saint Mark's Basilica in Venice has many articles taken from pagan temples and Eastern ruins. While David thought of his victories as being in line with the will of God and while he dedicated the costly spoils to the glory of God, he paid dearly for his warlike deeds. Read 1 Chronicles 28:2-3.

HOW DOES THIS APPLY TO US?

There is a better way. There are trophies of love, there are rewards of discipline, there are riches that come to our hearts through sacrifice (Mark 10:29-30). God will be no man's debtor. He will give us bounty from enemies we conquer in that spiritual warfare in which we must of necessity be engaged. "And let us not grow weary in well-doing, for in due season we shall reap, if we do not lose heart" (Galatians 6:9).

Pray with Me

Lord, I have not seized great treasure as prizes of war. Things are different now. We wage other kinds of war. And the spoils of this other kind of warfare never show up as vessels of gold and silver and brass.

Nevertheless, when I am quiet enough to reflect upon it, I am receiving other things every day. These prizes of war come to me even from my enemies, even while the warfare is still going on, even when victory seems a long way off.

There is the gold of heavenly friendship on earth. There is the silver of purity in myself and in those I love. There is the brass of confidence which others place in me. There is the golden glow of health. There are the silver tones of music. There are the brazen shields of moral courage.

Some of these I have seized, some I have received, and all will be kept for You. Use them as You will. If it is necessary, cast them into the fire until they are refashioned according to Your plan. Turn every prize of war into a tool for peace. Turn every prize from an enemy into a gift to be returned with love and in Your name to all my enemies. Bring this to pass, Lord, that my enemies may never feel subdued except by Your love. May they never feel indebted to anything except to the very same grace that has conquered me.

That is how I want to dedicate life and all its gifts and prizes . . . to You . . . and to others for Your glory.

In the Name of Him who when He ascended led a host of captives on high and gave gifts to men, Amen.

Moving On in the Life of Prayer

The kind of war we wage for Christ and in His name may be with a different set of weapons but the trophies of victory are just as real and far, far better. Continue to pray in confidence and to live in obedience to the commandments of Christ and you will receive something far better than gold or silver or bronze . . . love and peace in your heart now, and a place in the Father's House forever.

Day 9

HIS POWER TO SAVE, HIS RIGHT TO RULE

"Now the salvation and the power and the kingdom of our God and the authority of his Christ have come" (Revelation 12:10).

Read: **Revelation 12:10-11; Philippians 2:5-11;** Matthew 28:18; Isaiah 45:17-22.

WHAT IS GOD SAYING?

Jesus Christ is our Savior. He truly tasted death but His love is deathless. He died in humiliation and shame, but rose in power and will return in glory. His enemies thought they had stilled His voice and ended His rule. They soon found it was just beginning.

"O behold the Man of sorrows, O behold Him in plain view; Lo! He is the mighty Conqueror Since He rent the veil in two." He is Savior AND Lord. The Cross is no minor incident or tragic accident. Max Lucado writes: " . . . And according to Paul, the cross is what counts. My, what a piece of wood! History has idolized it and despised it, gold-plated it and burned it, worn it and trashed it. History has done everything but ignore it. That's the one option that the cross does not offer."[1]

If we have received Him as Savior, we must yield to Him as Lord. "Now the salvation of our God and the authority of His Christ have come."

HOW DOES THIS APPLY TO US?

We must remember that the One who rescues us from the kingdom of falsehood and evil is the One who has authority to rule over us in the kingdom of truth and righteousness. To know the saving power of Christ is to yield to the ruling power of Christ. He not only saves, He rules. Think of Jesus as Friend. Thank Him as Savior. Obey Him as Lord. The One who saves is the One who rules. Or does He?

Pray with Me

O loving and mighty Savior, You have redeemed my soul at infinite cost. You have saved me from the destiny that my sin

---

1. Max Lucado, *No Wonder They Call Him the Savior,* (Portland, Ore.: Multnomah Press, 1986), p. 13.

deserves. Now I want to live each day in the awareness that the power that has rescued is also the power to rule.

I have not been saved to live in antiseptic apartness. I am not a glass-encased display. I am not a lifeless mannequin of still and angular propriety. Neither have I been saved to wander in a wasteland of undisciplined license. I have been saved because I have been counted worthy of being ruled.

To know Your saving power is to yield to Your ruling power. Owning You as Savior must mean having You as Lord. Let me never try to separate what has been united in a changeless decree: "The salvation of God and the authority of His Christ."

Not only are You the Lord of my life, O Christ, You are the Lord of all life. It is no small thing to cast down the Accuser from my heart. But You have cast him down from heaven. I will work and wait, I will run and rest, I will toil and tarry in this assurance: however great may be the claims of my soul's enemy, I am, through the Lord of all, more than conqueror. He now rules my heart through willing consent. One day He will rule all things in universal love and authority. All evil shall be gone for all time. Until then I gladly serve Him who by His grace has saved and in His power shall always rule.

To the praise and honor of immortal Love, which in saving rules and in ruling saves, Amen.

MOVING ON IN THE LIFE OF PRAYER

The One who has authority over us commands us to share His love with others. The greatness of the privilege is equaled only by the greatness of the responsibility. There is a story I read somewhere that tells how Jesus said to Peter: "Go and preach." "Preach, Lord, to the men who drove the nails?" "Yes, Peter, and to those who cursed, say that I have a song for them; and to the soldier who pierced my side, say that there is a nearer way to my heart than that." Keep the faith, yes, but also give it away. His love is to be cherished but not hoarded. We are saved to tell others. Too much? Too hard? Too busy?

"Love so amazing, so divine, demands my soul, my life, my all."

Day 10

THE CHRISTIAN'S JOY

"The exulting of the wicked is short, and the joy of the godless but for a moment" (Job 20:5).

Read: **Job 20:4-5; Psalm 73, 16:11; John 15:11.**

WHAT IS GOD SAYING?

With a friend like Zophar, who needs enemies? His words in today's reading are part of a tirade launched against Job— and it is as if he were throwing another log on his friend's fiery trials. He "comforts" Job by suggesting that he has brought it all on himself. He is saying, "You got what was coming to you. So sorry." Or is he? Zophar is speaking *ex cathedra,* like a self-appointed spokesman of God. With heartless cruelty he tells Job to get his act together. Then things will fall into place.

But in the midst of this brutal lecture from a high pulpit, Zophar has some "right-on" thoughts. Poorly timed, perhaps, but accurate. After telling Job that he should have known this, and that reasonably intelligent people have known it for a long time, he informs him that "the exulting of the wicked is short, and the joy of the godless but for a moment" (Job 20:5).

HOW DOES THIS APPLY TO US?

There is a great difference between the short-lived "joy" of the godless and the deeply grounded joy of those who know Christ. One depends on "the way the ball bounces"; the other is built on a rock, the Rock of Ages. One is but a fleeting illusion of well-being; the other a calm assurance that "in everything God works for good with those who love him, who are called according to his purpose" (Romans 8:28). The joy of the godless is only the interval that comes between periods of unhappiness; the other is learning with Paul, "in whatever state I am, to be content. I know how to be abased, and, how to abound; in any and all circumstances" (Philippians 4:11-12).

We can grow restless and even become envious of the wicked who are "always at ease and increasing in riches." Trying to understand why it happens is well-described by the psalmist (Psalm 73:16) as a "wearisome task." But see it as God sees it from the vantage point of eternity and you will have it in true perspective. ". . . until I went into the sanctuary of God; then I perceived their end. Truly thou dost set them in slippery places . . . they are destroyed in a moment." (vv. 17-19).

Pray with Me

Eternal God, only in Your presence is there fullness of joy. Only at Your right hand are there pleasures forevermore. Help me always to see through the ephemeral and shallow "triumph of the wicked." It is down that path that so much is promised and so little delivered. That road is lined with artificial flowers that have neither fragrance nor root nor value. "The joy of the god-less" is but a mask with a painted grin, a covering for a tearstained face, a pretense that all is well when all is hell.

In contrast to this, O living God, I seek only the triumph of Christ: His triumph over me and His triumph through me. This is the satisfaction that endures. This is the hope that never disappoints.

In contrast to this, O Lord, I choose to lay hold on the deep-rooted and unfading joys of a righteous life. Such joy is not for the moment. It is moment by moment forever.

I have no claim upon such triumph. I have no reason to hope for such joy. It is mine only through Your righteousness, given by grace and received by faith.

I have no other hope. I make no other claim. I affirm that the exultation and the joy of those who are in Christ will endure forever.

To the glory and through the love of Jesus Christ, my Lord, Amen.

MOVING ON IN THE LIFE OF PRAYER

The recording "Don't Worry, Be Happy" won a Grammy award this past year. And the composer doesn't need to worry and can be happy THIS year. But what about next year, or next month? He may prescribe happiness as the cure-all for your problems, and not a few gullible people—who don't know where else to look—will swallow the placebo. His remedy is to push the right button. Worry will vanish and happiness will appear. Happiness is something you can turn on as with a switch or catch with a song.

But for the Christian, joy is not something we *do* but something Christ has *done*, something that He is, and something that He wants to share to the full. For the Christian, joy is a foundation that will be holding us up tomorrow, and tomorrow . . . and tomorrow. For the Christian, joy is based on a relationship that will carry over beyond tomorrow to eternity—and will carry US over to eternity.

"The joy of the godless is but for a moment." The joy of the Christian is forever.

Day 11

THE FRUIT OF TRUE REPENTANCE

"Bear fruit that befits repentance" (Matthew 3:8).

Read: **Matthew 3:1-10;** Ezekiel 18:31; Romans 3:23; Luke 13:1-5; 2 Timothy 2:25.

WHAT IS GOD SAYING?

The Pharisees were no doubt on the fringe of the crowd that day, but they were soon center stage when John the Baptist pierced them with pointed remarks. John was not interested in winning friends and influencing people. It is highly irregular to stand before a gathering of people and call them a "brood of vipers fleeing from wrath," a picture of snakes slithering away in haste from a field being harvested or on fire. *Who warned you? Why did you come? What good will it do you with your mindset to hear what I have to say?*

They came out of curiosity—and also some concern. After all, *they* were the religious experts. They needed to know what this wild-eyed denizen of the desert was all about. What made him tick? This voice out here in the wilderness, this character who was robed in an unwashed and scratchy garment of camel's hair. This first-century health nut who sustained himself on locusts and wild honey. He had so little going for him. Yet he was getting the crowds and stirring them up. He should be looked into. We must put our followers straight. Don't they count on us for religious expertise?

HOW DOES THIS APPLY TO US?

We may not be card-carrying Pharisees. In fact, we pride ourselves on being more humble than they. Not to go overboard, mind you, but we *are* a country mile ahead of them! Could this be the parable of the Pharisee and the publican in reverse, the publican nursing in his heart a little pride for not being so proudly self-righteous as the Pharisee?

We want no part of their stuffed-shirt religious propriety. BUT—are we all that excited about having done with the past and moving on into the future that Christ has for us? Don't we cozy up to an indulgence or two? Don't we see our shortcomings as being not so good but really not all *that* bad? We have ALL sinned (Romans 3:23) and we ALL need to repent. Be sure to read Luke 13:1-5.

Pray with Me

God, You are absolute truth and goodness. Give me a constant awareness of Your wrath against all untruth and hypocrisy.

I read of Your righteous anger against the lies of the Pharisees. Let this not fall in vain on my ears, lest while hating Pharisaism, I may first grow accustomed and then succumb to its subtle and dangerous errors.

To fill my heart with Your peace and joy, to turn my night of broken dreams into a day of bright fulfillment, to open the door to the Kingdom which is right "at hand," You are only waiting until my repentance is real . . . something more than a mumbled, empty ritual. It cannot be muttered under my breath as a resented obligation. It cannot be murmured as a half-sincere and shallow gesture.

It must be really meant or it will mean nothing really.

Lead me, Lord, until I loathe empty words, easily spoken. Help me to take the difficult step, at any cost to pride, down any road of humiliation, in utter disregard for personal comfort and advantage, until I bring forth fruit that befits repentance.

Against You, You only, have I sinned. To You, You only, do I look for liberating grace and pardon. Your reconciling love in Christ assures me that You will understand and support my feeblest, honest effort to repent.

In the Name of Him who has perfectly shown the kindness of God which is meant to lead us to repentance, Amen.

MOVING ON IN THE LIFE OF PRAYER

John said in no uncertain terms: "Repent and shape up." And the message is valid. Jesus said, "Repent and believe in the Gospel" (or receive the Good News). As the Gospel is something that is given, so repentance in the New Testament sense is a gift of God (Acts 5:31; 11:18; Romans 2:4; 2 Timothy 2:25). When repentance is wedded to the Good News (and it always should be) we are *given* the power to change. Not only off with the old, but on with the new. Not only dead to sin but alive to God in Christ Jesus (Romans 6:11). Not only sorry we failed in the past but now, as a new creation in Christ, ready to come out on top as the road stretches into the future.

Kneel down in repentance, then get up and go on faith.

Day 12

ONE REASON TO BOAST

"But far be it from me to glory except in the cross of our Lord Jesus Christ" (Galatians 6:14a).

Read: **Galatians 6:11-14;** 1 Corinthians 1:17-18; Ephesians 2:14-16; Colossians 1:19-20, 2:13-14.

WHAT IS GOD SAYING?

Religious rules can easily get out of sync with truth—and often do. We can end up keeping certain customs simply to "look good." We may even find ourselves insisting that others march to the same drumbeat—or taking pride in our "correctness" while looking down on those who don't "measure up."

But Galatians 6:14 reminds us we should not boast in *any* religious ritual. The Cross—all that it has done and can do—should be our boast, our only glory. The very symbol which was meant to demonstrate man's defeat of God has become the sign and assurance of victory: God's victory for us, received by faith, not works. The Cross was meant to put an end to Christ, His words, His troublesome meddling, His persistent love. Instead it becomes the ground of our boasting, the symbol of Love's triumph, God's way of dealing with the condemnation that sin deserves through forgiveness and grace.

Compared to that, boasting in petty religious rules pales into insignificance.

HOW DOES THIS APPLY TO US?

The world says: "The Cross? Far be it from me!" The Christian says: "Far be it from me to boast EXCEPT in the Cross."

The Cross becomes, for the Christian, a symbol of victory and a source of encouragement and strength. The Cross is universal in its influence and power. Jesus said, "And I, when I am lifted up from the earth, will draw all men to myself" (John 12:32). The Cross is also deeply personal and individual. By looking in its direction, we are reminded how much Jesus loved us to do what He did. With that assurance, we are encouraged to pray with boldness and confidence.

Pray with Me

Gracious God, let the sorrow of Calvary and the love of Your Son be to me as a glory and a covering. Let the Cross stand between my true self and that other self which strives to have the upper hand. If I ever thought that God was too big to bother with me and too distant to care very much, that thought has been removed in the wonder of Your love outpoured on the Cross.

There was a time when I would have said, "Far be the Cross from me. It is ugly, shameful, and cruel." But now, in the healing shadow of that very Cross, my prayer is, "Far be all pride from me."

Far, so far, that in moments of weakness and insecurity I shall neither care nor even remember to glory in anything but the Cross of Jesus Christ. Far from me be all thought of pleasing the flesh. Far from me be all thought of pretending to be something important except as an instrument in Your hand. Far from me be all pride in the efforts of self-will.

My heart is strengthened when I see my Lord's victory on the Cross. Through that narrow gate, You have opened to me an eternity of blessing.

No merit I can earn, no accomplishment I can produce, no record I can show will ever make me deserving of Your Heavenly Kingdom, here or there.

Therefore, again and again, and with deeper wonder each time I say it, this is my prayer: "Far be it from me to glory except in the Cross . . ."

In the Name of Jesus Christ by whose Cross the world has been crucified to me and I to the world, Amen.

MOVING ON IN THE LIFE OF PRAYER

Boasting in Christ's victory, we will never have to be worried that our good works are not good enough. Pointing others to Christ's love and praying for others in the name of that love relieves us of the necessity of judging them. Getting rid of that heavy burden is one of the good by-products of seeing the Cross in the right light. New life and energy, great joy and power surge into our souls when we come to the place where we point only to the Cross and boast only of the love that was there displayed.

Day 13

STAND STILL

"Now therefore stand still, that I may plead with you before the LORD concerning all the saving deeds of the LORD which he performed for you and for your fathers" (1 Samuel 12:7).

Read: **1 Samuel 12;** Psalm 46:10; Exodus 14:13.

WHAT IS GOD SAYING?

The chapter in which the aging and beloved Samuel pleads with Israel to stand still and to consider the saving deeds of God follows immediately after the chapter in which Saul is acclaimed the first king of Israel. It was a time of foreboding change. The people were restless and agitated. They had been insistent upon having a king who would raise them to the status of other nations. Although he knew there would be trouble, Samuel reluctantly gave his assent.

One thing remained to be said, "Now that you have a king, don't forget the Lord. He is your true King." He is saying, "Your king, for all his great promise and striking appearance, is only human. He can falter, he can fail you (and he did), but only God can perform saving deeds. He did and He will. Stand still while I tell you about it."

HOW DOES THIS APPLY TO US?

Our life and times seem very remote from that ancient era of unrest and turmoil. But we, too, are living in restless, chaotic days. If we do not stand still and listen to the still, small voice of God we could be swept away by the earthquake, wind, and fire of our violent times.

The person who goes snorkeling wears a face mask to see clearly below the choppy surface. The same thing happens for the Christian who will stop amid the pressures of activities and the clamor of competing voices to see and to hear the deep truths of God's Word.

Be still and listen. Be still and pray. Then you will discover that God has peace for your hearts, calmness for your mind, and beauty for ashes. He still performs His saving deeds. We have only to stand still and we will see.

Pray with Me

Lord, fretting is only too natural for me! When I move away from the restraint of Your wise and loving disciplines I become restless. When my thoughts are free to flow down well-worn channels of habit, I become worried.

Help me to "stand still!" *"In quietness and confidence shall be Your strength."* It is only by standing still that I can see You as You are. It is only in stillness that I can discover and enjoy the unlimited treasures of a life hidden with Christ in God.

Let Your Holy Spirit find in me a still heart, a calm, listening mind, and a quietly receptive spirit.

When the dust of my own rushing about has settled I can better understand the saving deeds of the Lord. When the clamor of my own demands are silenced, I can hear more clearly the pleading of Your love.

Lord, I am thankful, too, for the knowledge that You have performed "saving deeds." Your greatness is in the record. Salvation is not something promised. It is something performed. Redemption is not a shimmering mirage or a glistening "perhaps." The kingdom and the power and the glory of God are accomplished facts.

Because my faith rests on saving deeds and not on empty promises, I pray that I shall have, moment by moment, the grace of "standing still." Then I shall see and know and always trust the saving deeds of my Lord and my God.

Through Him who on Calvary performed Love's greatest deed, Amen.

MOVING ON IN THE LIFE OF PRAYER

"The Quiet Time." That is the phrase we heard often and truly welcomed in those summer camps of long ago. It was a time to get away from frenzied activities and roughhousing. It was a time when you didn't have to holler for the butter in the mess hall or be on your guard against the character who was about to shove you into the pool against your will.

It was great to be quiet: to rest, to read or write letters, to get refreshed for the next round of exhilarating yet exhausting fun.

We don't have to be one of that happy bunch back at summer camp to crave and welcome—and need—that "Quiet Time." Won't somebody please enforce it on us again? Cultivate stillness, and prayer will have more meaning. "Be still and know that I am God." Be still and listen. Be still and think deeply of your own need. Be still and pray for others who are beside waters that are not so still right now and for whom "green pastures" are only a taunting memory.

God has so much to share with us if we let Him. Prayer is standing still: to ponder the needs of others, to get our own bearings, to hear what God wants to do with our lives. We can't really see the salvation of the Lord without standing still.

Day 14

THE PERIL OF OVERFAMILIARITY

"Is not this the carpenter?" (Mark 6:3).

Read: **Mark 6:1-6;** John 1:11, 12:48.

WHAT IS GOD SAYING?

It was not too strange that the people of His own village did not accept Him. They knew Him so well that they didn't know Him—really—at all. They said, "Anyone who grew up in our village and played with our children and worked in his father's woodshop can't be all that wise or work that many wonders. There has to be something wrong here. He's a *carpenter.* We've known him for years."

They knew Him so well . . . yet hardly knew Him at all.

As Jesus Himself said, pointing out a recognized fact of that day as well as this, "A prophet is not without honor, except in his own country, and among his own kin, and in his own house" (Mark 6:5) It is possible to know a multitude of facts *about* Jesus and miss the truth of who He is and why He came. The result of knowing Him "too well" was that *"He could do no mighty work there."* Unbelief is no trivial weakness or mild annoyance. It is powerful. Here it even stayed the hand of God. Never underestimate the power of unbelief. Nothing can subdue it but faith in the fact of who Jesus really is and what He can really do.

HOW DOES THIS APPLY TO US?

There are many good people who have been led through so many Sunday school lessons and sermons and Bible studies they run the danger of becoming overfamiliar with the Sublime. We need to ask the Spirit of God to keep us from knowing more and more ABOUT Jesus while learning less and less of who He really is—and how much He can do for us and in us.

Pray with Me

Lord, keep me from knowing more about You if it keeps me from knowing You more. May You never become an object of academic interest or the subject of an interesting debate. Help me to go beyond such facts as Your earthly occupation, Your place of residence, and even the things You did. Lead me to the wonder of who You are and to the discovery of what You want to accomplish in me.

The people of Your boyhood knew You only as carpenter. Overfamiliarity kept them from the greater discovery. They were blinded to the glory of Your divine perfection. God forbid that I should ever come to know so much about You that I fail to worship that in You which is always beyond my comprehension.

Yes, You were the Carpenter. You have known the burdens of common and ceaseless toil. Yours was the calloused hand which duty molded to the handle of "plane and saw." You knew the aching of a long-bent back. You understood the importance of a straight line and a clean cut. You knew the strength of good wood and could bring out its beauty.

But, Carpenter of Nazareth, You are more. I pray that You will fashion my soul until it is fit for Your heavenly dwelling. By the miracle of Your forgiving and restoring grace, make my life useful to God and man.

In Your Name, O Carpenter, Builder of life divine, Amen.

MOVING ON IN THE LIFE OF PRAYER

Never cease looking upon Jesus with breathless wonder. When John, in Revelation, saw Him "as the sun shining in full strength and fell at his feet as though dead," he was face to face with the very power and glory of God. Yes, He was still John's familiar and deeply loved Companion. But He was much more and totally other.

As "one of us" He can do the compassionate thing. He understands. As Son of God He can do the impossible. Isn't that why we pray in His Name? We pray to One who is forever beyond us and yet a very present help in trouble. We pray to One who not only cares, but who can.

Day 15

REJOICING SHOULD BE NO SECRET

"And the sound was heard afar" (Ezra 3:13).

Read: **Ezra 3;** Deuteronomy 16:9-11; Psalm 5:11; Romans 5:2; Philippians 4:4; 1 Peter 4:12-13.

WHAT IS GOD SAYING?

Great emotion surged through the people of Israel when they laid the new foundation for the house of the Lord. It was a time of celebration, the opportunity to give vent to long pent-up feelings. Some (the older ones who had seen the first house of the Lord many decades before) wept. Others shouted for joy and the joyful sound could not be distinguished from the sound of people weeping. Either way it was genuine and uninhibited emotion—like the opening of an escape valve. They could not contain themselves and "the sound was heard afar."

How Does This Apply to Us?

Rejoicing, in the Bible, is the Christian's privilege. It is also his trademark.

"We rejoice in our hope of sharing the glory of God" (Romans 5:2). That's not something to keep under our hat or hide under a bushel. When Paul says "rejoice in the Lord always" in Philippians 4:4, he isn't listing it as an option. It's a command . . . not just when things go well, but even when things are not going well. Peter takes up the theme and shows that rejoicing as we share in Christ's suffering leads to the greater rejoicing that will be ours when He comes again in glory.

These passages encourage us to live in constant awareness of His grace and power. We have been redeemed. We live with a purpose. We have a greater destiny than the silence of the grave. We have reason to rejoice. Come to think of it, we can't *help* rejoicing. Others will know we are Christians because of our irrepressible joy. If it is real, the sound of it will be heard far away—and also near at hand.

Pray with Me

Lord, I need to ask myself how far the sound of my praise and the soundness of my life really carries. I have reason to wonder how far the radiance of my life as a Christian really shines. At times it seems like a flickering candle or a dying ember. I have reason to wonder whether someone has to be very close to me to see the light and to feel the warmth of the Savior's love. I must even ask if those who are close to me know that You are real to me. Do they know that You alone are the object of all my affection, the Lord of all my actions, the source of all my hope?

I pray that the influence of my life, or far better, the influence of Christ through me may increase. Let the sound of its rejoicing and the soundness of its testimony reach farther than I could dare to dream.

Lord, trim my lamp and fan these embers until my life sends a brighter, warmer, farther glow.

Let souls that are near and souls that are far off be led to Christ because they have seen His radiance in me. May no one perish because the word I should have spoken went unsaid. May no one be lost because the example I should have set was wanting. May no one take the wrong path because the light that should have been in me was too weak or too dim to be seen.

Let the influence of Christ in me and through me be as a sound heard far away and near.

To reveal His glory and for His honor, let it be! Amen.

MOVING ON IN THE LIFE OF PRAYER

When we leave the closet of prayer and go out to live and work with others, they will know we are rejoicing by the radiance on our faces and the joy we give in thoughtful deeds and timely words of love and encouragement. Don't keep your rejoicing to yourself. Make it a consistent part of your prayer life and it will become the "real you" seen by others.

Day 16

HOW TO BE AT PEACE

"Agree with God, and be at peace" (Job 22:21).

Read: **Job 22:21-29;** John 16:33; Colossians 1:20.

WHAT IS GOD SAYING?

The question is, "Can you agree with God or can't you? Will you agree with God or won't you?" All of life is affected by how we answer that question. This passage in Job tells us how to go about giving the right answer, the answer that leads to peace so deeply desired by all of us and so constantly missed by so many of us.

Consider these verses: Verse 22 urges us to "receive instruction from His mouth," that is, the Word of God. We are to let this instruction find its way through our minds to be stored up in our hearts. Verses 23-25: Let God be God. Not gold or silver, for the Almighty is your gold and your precious silver. Verse 26: He is the Source of your pleasure. Delight yourself in Him. Verse 27: Let His will be done. You find that through prayer. Verse 28: You will reap the harvest of peace. You will make the right decisions and you will make them stick. You will see where you are going and why. The lesson of this portion of Job is that we are to look beyond the wisdom of men and seek the wisdom of God. "Agree with God, and be at peace."

HOW DOES THIS APPLY TO US?

It is so simple, it is so beautiful, it is so clear, and yet, tragically, it is so often missed. You can agree with God always and always be at peace. You can agree with God sometimes and sometimes be at peace. You can agree with God never and never be at peace. The formula never varies. All the hostility, all the wasteful tension, all the irrational passions that ever raised their stench from this good earth—from the time of Cain and Abel to this moment—can be traced to this one thing: Man, out of agreement with God, cannot be at peace with himself or with anyone else.

Pray with Me

To agree with God is to be on the road to peace and to be at peace on the road. Let this agreement, Lord, be deep and real. A casual, easy, hasty agreement will not do. Give me a deep conviction, Lord, that in merely intellectual agreement with you, half-given and half-withheld, there is no assurance, and, in fact, no possibility of peace.

To agree with God is to say that You are right—right in Your assessment of my problem, right in Your offer of a solution, and right in Your ultimate purpose for my life. Deliver me from the folly of seeking peace in any other place, in any other way, or under any other terms.

I thank You that You have made the way to agreement with You so plain. Your will is found in Your Word. Your love is seen in Christ. The guidance of Your Holy Spirit is always theirs who ask.

Have patience with me, Lord, that so often I find it hard to agree. Have patience with me that so often I fail to acknowledge that You are always right and always loving.

Give me the will to will Your will. Give me the honesty to accept Your judgment. Give me the wisdom to recognize Your amazing grace. Then I shall be at peace with myself, with all others, with my world, and with God.

I will bless You, O God, for this wonderful peace so long as a breath remains in my body. Through eternity my spirit will rejoice in the perfect peace which will then come from perfect agreement.

Through Christ who agreed with the Father's will that I might be at peace forever, Amen.

MOVING ON IN THE LIFE OF PRAYER

Is your prayer directed toward the finding of God's will for your life? Is everything you say and think and ask in prayer focused on the supreme desire to be in agreement with God? It should be. That is the way prayer becomes powerful as an effective tool in life. Whether we are to live in disciplined freedom or in undisciplined chaos; whether we are to live a full, unfettered, expansive life or a pinched, selfish, and cramped existence; whether we are to be in a never-abating, enervating, stupid state of war with everything and everybody or "at peace" depends on how that question is answered. If you can say, "Yes, I choose to agree with God," if you can say, "Yes, I will accept His verdict, apply His solution, adopt His plan, and follow His direction"—in a word, if you can say, "Yes, I will go WITH God and not AGAINST Him" . . . if you can say that, then the rest of the verse, "be at peace," belongs to you. The great secret of prevailing prayer is to find the will of God and then bring yourself to AGREE that He is right.

Day 17

THE WORD OF GOD AND THE POWER OF GOD

" . . . *You know neither the scriptures nor the power of God*" (Mark 12:24).

Read: **Mark 12:18-27;** Jeremiah 4:22, 5:21; Psalm 62:11-12.

WHAT IS GOD SAYING?

The Sadducees claimed to know the Scriptures. They respected the Mosaic law. They could see no evidence for immortality or heaven in the early books of the Bible. Talk about "resurrection" seemed ridiculous to them. To support their position they sought to trap Jesus, this new Teacher who was gaining in the popularity polls. In order to prick His balloon, they brought forward a hypothetical case of seven brothers who died. Each successive brother took to wife the childless widow of his preceding brother. "Now tell us, great Teacher, whose wife will she be in this Heaven you are always talking about?" Jesus answered by saying that they had a mistaken idea of Heaven, a false understanding of Scripture, and were total strangers to the power of God.

Jesus is saying, "You say you know the Scriptures. But you don't. God said in the very Scriptures which you think you know, 'I am the God of Abraham, of Isaac, and Jacob.' Does that sound like One who is the God of the dead? No, you are wrong. He is the God of the living."

God is preparing for us a place that is far beyond the crassly materialistic puzzle posed by the Sadducees who would rather quibble than believe, who would rather test the Teacher than accept His words.

How Does This Apply to Us?

This seven-brothers-for-one-bride question seems so ridiculous. Particularly when the questioners had no belief in the resurrection anyway. But the fact still shines out of this passage. "If we don't know Scripture, if we don't respect it as God's loving and wise communication with us, if we are just hearers of it and not doers, *we will miss the power of God.* Not knowing the Scriptures—not listening, caring, or accepting—means we forfeit the experience of God's power in our lives.

Pray with Me

Dear Lord, by Your Spirit You have made known to us Your perfect desire and plan. We may read it clearly in the written Scriptures and in the living Christ. I thank You, Lord, for showing this to me over and over again: The power of God and the Word of God always go together.

To search Your Word is to find Your power. To receive Your Word is to accept Your power. To believe Your Word is to be filled with Your power. To obey Your Word is to move with Your power. To speak Your Word is to persuade with Your power.

O God, it is wonderful to know where Your power is to be found. It is wonderful to know how, through faith and obedience, Your power becomes my power. There have been times when my heart has been open but the Book has been closed. There have been other times when the Book has been opened but my heart has been closed. From now on, Lord, I shall count on this: power always comes when the Book and the heart are open.

Jesus condemned the earthly-minded Sadducees because they did not know the Scriptures and, for that very reason, did not know the power of God. Let me not fall into the same error . . . hearing but not doing, reading but not heeding. I don't want to be simply acquainted with the living, powerful Word of God, I want to *experience* it.

Since in Jesus Christ the Scriptures come to life, and since through Jesus Christ, I may know the power of God, my prayer is in His Name, Amen.

Moving On in the Life of Prayer

Make sure that when the Book is open, your heart is not closed. Make sure that when your heart is open, the Book is not closed. As we continue in prayer we must ask for better understanding of the Word. Power in prayer and power in life go hand in hand with knowing the Scriptures.

Day 18

THANKSGIVING FOR WHAT GOD HAS DONE

"I will praise You forever, because You have done it" *(Psalm 52:9, NKJV).*

Read: **Psalm 52;** 1 Samuel 20-22; Luke 17:14-16; 1 Corinthians 15:57; 2 Corinthians 9:15.

WHAT IS GOD SAYING?

The historical basis for this Psalm deals with Saul's enraged pursuit of David. The young David was forced to flee for his life and find protection by hiding in the Cave of Adullam. Without really asking for it, David was gaining popularity with the masses of the people. Saul could feel his throne tottering under him and in an insanely jealous rage, he dispatched his minions to put a stop to this young upstart. Their acts of treachery and murder were heinous and uninhibited. Many lives were lost and David was deeply pained.

The Psalm denounces the wicked who love evil more than good and declares the sure and ultimate blessedness of those who make God their refuge. The wicked may boast of their own clever devices and powerful treachery, but as stated in verse 6, the righteous will literally have the "last laugh." The wicked will be uprooted from the land of the living. The godly will be like an olive tree, fruitful and abundant, because they trust in the steadfast love of God (v.8). David gives thanks to the God who has done and who will do great things.

HOW DOES THIS APPLY TO US?

We are not fleeing from an angry, jealous king. But we do have enemies bent on getting us down. There are forces that assault us from a world at enmity with God. There are hurtful thoughts and desires that reach out to us from our old, sinful nature. We face family worries, financial struggles, failing health, and job insecurity. We have all faced our Caves of Adullam.

But we have a God who *does*: He does care, He does send miracles, He does get involved. He is the God of the impossible and he will never forsake His own.

Let our prayer rise on a tide of thankfulness to Almighty God for all that he has done. Concentrate on Him who through His great love redeemed us, to be free from yesterday's mistakes, to have strength for today's needs, and to have the hope of glory in the life that is forever. Yes, "I will praise You FOREVER because You have DONE it."

Pray with Me

God of all grace and truth, my heart is filled with the joy of thanksgiving. And the joy of my thanksgiving is like a stream growing into a river, a river flowing into the sea. It can only keep on going in ever fuller measure until it becomes one with the unshadowed bliss of Heaven.

"I will praise You forever." This will be the theme of my heart—a heart filled with hope and redeemed from sin. I shall sing a song of gladness and eternal victory. Never again the dismal sob of a dejected spirit.

"I will praise You forever because You have done it." I look back upon the Cross, that great standard raised against the flood. I no longer need fear the flood. I will not be afraid of the accusations of a guilty conscience.

I will not dread the memory of wasted years. I will not dwell on the debris of broken promises. I will not hold helplessly in my hand the ashes of undisciplined passion. All these, like the thundering surf, break helplessly against the Rock of Ages. In Christ, I am beyond the reach of sin's destructive force. "There is therefore now no condemnation for those who are in Christ Jesus."

No thought of yesterday's failure and no fear of yesterday's evil will restrain the joy of my thanksgiving. Today, tomorrow, and forever, I will praise Him who once died, the Just for the unjust, the Innocent for the guilty, the Creator for the creature, the Master for the servant, the Free for the condemned.

You have done it, Lord. Forever I will live. Forever I will be thankful. Forever I will live for You.

To the praise of Him who is the same yesterday, today, and forever, Amen.

MOVING ON IN THE LIFE OF PRAYER

Base your confidence in prayer on the fact that *God does things.* It is not biblical to say that "God helps those who help themselves." It IS biblical to "fear not, stand firm, and see the salvation of the LORD." It IS biblical to believe that "the LORD will fight for you, and you have only to be still" (Exodus 14:13-14).

CLEANNESS

"I will; be clean" *(Matthew 8:3).*

Read: **Matthew 8:1-3; Psalm 51;** Isaiah 59:2; 2 Corinthians 7:1; 2 Timothy 2:21.

WHAT IS GOD SAYING?

If we could transport ourselves back to the time and situation described in this portion of Matthew's gospel, we would view it as one of the most dramatic scenes in the Bible. Here a leper encounters the compassionate Christ. No one else would come near to him. Certainly no one else would touch him. Yet he came to the great Healer with confidence. He knew if he had come to an orthodox scribe or a rabbi he would have been repelled, perhaps even stoned. See how he makes his request: "If you will, you can make me clean. I am so tired of saying 'Unclean, unclean' everywhere I go. I want to be clean. You can do it if You will." It's not a question of *could* You, just *would* You?

HOW DOES THIS APPLY TO US?

This should encourage anyone who feels incurable in body or too far gone spiritually for Jesus' healing and cleansing touch. If you put yourself in the place of a first-century Jew, you could not imagine anything more astonishing than the fact that Jesus should reach out his hand and *touch* the man. The incident underscores the painful ostracism of leprosy and the amazing love of God.

That's how it is with Jesus Christ: the leper or the sinner is not a loathsome spectacle or a menace to the community. He is a human being in need of help.

Sin is spiritual leprosy. It affects a person in similar ways. Leprosy was the most dreaded disease of ancient times. And people who say sin can't be all that bad have swallowed the Devil's lie. "The wages of sin is death," and as with leprosy, that death comes by inches. It separates us from others, it separates us from our own true selves, and of course, it separates us from God. That is the horrible and ultimate price of sin. (Read Isaiah 59:2.)

"All have sinned." We ALL need to be cleansed of sin. We need to be cleansed of ALL sin. David's prayer in Psalm 51 uses the word, "clean," many times. God wants our hearts to be clean. His intent for all creation is cleanness. His will for us is cleanness. Before we ask for other blessings, and there are so many, we must pray as David did, "Wash me thoroughly from my iniquity, and cleanse me from my sin!" (Psalm 51:2).

Pray with Me

O God, what You give is clean! Rain that falls from the recycling of nature . . . air that moves in, unladen with dust, from the tumbling expanse of the sea . . . stars that sparkle on a clear night "forever singing as they shine, 'The Hand that made us is divine.' "

Cleanness is what You give and cleanness is what You will have: "I will; be clean!" Help me to know this day that Your will for me is cleanness. By the invincible strength of Your will, I shall be clean.

Only as I have doubted Your plan for my life and chosen to follow the errant demands of *my* will have I known that contact with sin which soils and sickens.

Give me the grace of submission that I may pass through the gates of obedience into the green pastures of unblemished joy and vibrant spiritual health. I want to be rid of the stain and the misery of sin and I rejoice that, by Your will, I may know the same freedom as the leper who in Your strength and by Your healing grace was able to walk away from the loathsome thing.

O God of all cleanness, as You command it, so give it, that in the freedom of a life renewed and cleansed in every moment of real obedience, my walk with You may be filled with joy and my work for You be true.

In Your own powerful and ever blessed Name, Amen.

MOVING ON IN THE LIFE OF PRAYER

God is willing to make us whole and clean. We need to recognize our need and simply place ourselves under the healing rays of His love, His mercy, and His truth. As the sun reveals and heals, so God in truth and love shows us our need and provides the solution. "I will," says the One who is able, "be clean!"

Day 20

IN THE LIGHT OF GOD'S MERCY

"Seeing that thou, our God, hast punished us less than our iniquities deserved . . . shall we break thy commandments again?" (Ezra 9:13b, 14).

Read: **Ezra 9;** Nehemiah 9:17-19, 31; Psalm 103:10-11; Titus 3:5.

WHAT IS GOD SAYING?

Israel had been punished greatly. Verse seven leaves no doubt about that. The words fall like a blizzard of flaming arrows: "Given into the hand of the kings of the lands, to the sword, to captivity, to plundering, and to utter shame." Then God made it possible for a remnant to return to rebuild His holy place in Jerusalem and reestablish the Jewish community. They realized that while the suffering was great during those years of captivity, it could have been worse. Ezra says it for them all: "Our God has punished us less than our iniquities deserved."

To Ezra the issue is clear. Intermarriage with those who practice abomination, getting close family ties with those who not only lacked belief in the God of Israel, but who actively opposed Him—that would be a giant step backward. Was that any way to treat God who had been so merciful? Ezra thinks not, and urges his people to do the difficult thing, break with the foreigners, abstain from intermarriage and demonstrate by keeping His commandments that they have not received the mercy of God in vain.

HOW DOES THIS APPLY TO US?

Intermarriage with the foes of God is hardly our pressing problem today. But there are other ways that we can compromise our witness. There are other ways we can allow our hearts to become divided in loyalty. There are other relationships that drain off our enthusiasm for the things of our Lord. None of us, I think, would deny that we have received less than our sins deserve. When Ezra asks, "Shall we break your commandments AGAIN?" How do we answer that? Remembering, with the psalmist, that "[God] does not deal with us according to our sins, nor requite us according to our iniquities," is there any answer but one? "Having received less punishment than we deserve we would henceforth, by Your mercy, keep our feet from stumbling and our hearts from wandering."

Pray with Me

Loving Father, whenever I wonder why I am not getting all that should be coming to me, help me to remember and to be very thankful that I do *not* get all that is coming to me. Truly You have "punished us *less* than our sins deserve."

I am humbled by the remembrance of Your longsuffering love. Like a father pities his children, like a father has hope through all his children's mistakes, so You have been patient with me. I rejoice that Your anger is slow and Your mercy so abundant.

Lord, You gather me up with patient forgiveness and healing love when I wander away. You bear with me though I often break Your commandments and seem determined to break myself. You turn me around, sometimes with the force of circumstance, sometimes with the force of prayer from the lips of a friend, but always with the force of love.

Forgive me for presuming on Your fatherly love. You have not "dealt with us after our sins nor rewarded us according to our iniquities." Fix this on my mind. Engrave it on the tablets of memory. Sink it deeply into my heart where sin gets all its encouragement and where careless living has all its roots.

Then the memory that I have truly received less than my sins deserve will guard me from evil and guide me toward good. Having received less than my sin deserves, help me to return more love, more obedience, more service, and more thanksgiving than I have ever deceived myself into thinking was enough!

In the Name of Him whose grace is more than just enough, Amen.

Moving On in the Life of Prayer

Certainly Ezra and Nehemiah (as the great Restorers they can hardly be thought of separately) were Gibraltars of courage, fearlessly honest and impartial. Above all they were men of prayer. They poured out their hearts before God on behalf of the people; there were no greater intercessors in the Old Testament. Their prayers are marked with transparent sincerity and utter surrender to God. What they thought, they prayed. What they prayed, they lived. What they shared with God on their knees, they showed to men in their lives. Can you think of a better way to "Move On in the Life of Prayer"?

GOD'S INVINCIBLE POWER

"For the LORD of hosts has puposed, and who will annul it? His hand is stretched out, and who will turn it back?" (Isaiah 14:27).

Read: **Isaiah 14:24-27;** Psalm 37:23-24; John 10:25-29; Matthew 19:26.

WHAT IS GOD SAYING?

In this portion of Isaiah, Israel is face to face with the brutal hatred and swaggering power of Assyria. They must have felt a little like a VW being tailgated by an eighteen-wheeler, or a tiny rowboat in the path of an aircraft carrier. It was clearly a case of bad news and worse news.

They needed to be reassured that God was on the throne and that He was still equal to the task. They needed to believe in the invincible power of God. They needed to know that He still cared and that He still could! Did the God of Israel still have a plan for the good of Israel? At this point they were given these words: "The Lord of hosts has sworn: 'As I have planned, so shall it be, and as I have purposed, so shall it stand . . . For the LORD of hosts has purposed, and who will annul it? His hand is stretched out, and who will turn it back?' "

They needed to hear, "If God be for us, who can be against us?"

HOW DOES THIS APPLY TO US?

What are the Assyrians up to in your life these days? If the enemy—any enemy of what is right and true and good—seems to be gaining the upper hand, we need to discover or rediscover the reality of God's invincible power. We need to know that while many adverse circumstances can and do come upon us, we know that "in everything God works for good with those who love him" (Romans 8:28). In that spirit of faith and confidence, let us pray.

Pray with Me

Lord of hosts, be the Lord of my heart! I would expose to You every thought and every desire. I would bring all my plans under the light of Your will. I would hold every dream under the light of Your purpose.

The light of morning fills a whole room even though it comes through a single open window. So fill my whole being with Your presence.

Set up Your throne in my heart, O Lord of hosts. Then I shall live each moment convinced that I am in tune with One whose purpose cannot be thwarted and whose outstretched hand cannot be turned back. I shall be with You in prevailing strength. I shall not be against You in foolish resistance.

When I have been subdued by Your conquering grace, I will share in the victory of the Resurrection.

I have tried in the past to turn back Your hand when it reached out in love. I have fancied through secret compromise that Your will could be thwarted. But now, Almighty Lord, persuaded by Your love in Christ, I see the beauty and the rightness of Your purpose. I see in Your hand as it reaches out, nail wounds that speak eloquently of One who, having loved His own, loved them to the end. This hand I will never turn back. This purpose I will not seek to thwart. To walk in the path of that will is my only hope. To rest in the shelter of that hand is my only glory.

Through Jesus Christ, in whom Your perfect will and the redeeming power of Your outstretched hand is perfectly known, Amen.

MOVING ON IN THE LIFE OF PRAYER

Trust in God, pray to Him in faith and all stumbling blocks will become stepping-stones, all apparent defeats will become real victories, and all trials will lead to triumphs. Let God's hand stretched out in love and power have its way in your life: to support, to guide, and to bless.

Day 22

HOW TO DEAL WITH SIN

"The ax is laid to the root of the trees" (Matthew 3:10).

Read: **Matthew 3:1-12,** 7:16-20; John 15:1-8.

WHAT IS GOD SAYING?

The Pharisees were models of respectability. They had a flawless dedication to respectable religion, and they would practice their respectability no matter who was hurt. Who could call *them* sinners in need of repentance? Why should they straighten up and fly right? They were in the top ten percentile of perfection—and the amount by which they fell short didn't matter much anyway.

They even had religious genes. Who could ask for anything more? They were descendants of Abraham. Their family tree was flawless: nicely shaped, good leaves, strong branches, a showpiece in the first-century Eastern Mediterranean neighborhood.

There was one trouble: These flawless trees were *fruitless* trees. No, it would have been better if they *had* been fruitless, for the fruit they did produce was bitter, without nourishment, even poisonous. There was only one remedy, and John didn't shrink from declaring it: "The ax is laid to the root of the trees; every tree therefore that does not bear good fruit is cut down and thrown into the fire."

How Does This Apply to Us?

Real life for the Christian does not consist of looking nice and being admired. It consists of bearing fruit for mankind's good and God's glory. Like the Pharisees, we cannot hold our faith in the name of our ancestors—even the great ones. We cannot coast along on the stream of life on the momentum of rowing done by our parents and grandparents. We must look more to the roots of our lives than to the roots of our lineage. We need to examine what kind of roots in our lives are producing what kind of fruits. There are times when the only treatment to cure the problem of tasteless, bitter, poisonous fruit is to "lay the ax to the roots." Time for prayer?

Pray with Me

Dear Lord, in Your wisdom and love, come upon my heart to sever at its roots any disobedient impulse or rival passion. In the depths that lie beneath my conscious will, in the places that only Your Spirit can reach, in that part of me that cannot be shown or known to others, do the radical and merciful surgery.

All the ways of the Lord are a combination of mercy and truth. That is why I want to stop running away from the truth which, in the end, is mercy.

Willingly I lay bare the deepest root that cannot bear fruit to Your glory. Lay the ax to the root. Life cannot expand to its fullest and joy cannot fill my being until the blow is struck.

Strike the blow that will set me free. I want to be free from the burden of wasting physical or mental energy on unwanted roots. I want to be free to focus the best of my time and strength on roots that will bear fruit to Your glory and the blessing of others. I want to know the freedom that comes when all selfish thoughts are cleanly severed and utterly dead.

Show no mercy at the root of every evil thought. Show no mercy at the root of every wayward desire. Show no mercy at the root of every subtle discouragement. Then You will be showing great mercy in a life that is both abundantly blessed and abundantly blessing.

Let this become reality, O God, for the sake of Him who does not need man's testimony about man, for He knows what is in a man . . . and in me. Amen.

MOVING ON IN THE LIFE OF PRAYER

If you feel that there are things in your life that ought to be uprooted for the sake of your own physical and spiritual well-being, ask the Spirit of God to lay the ax to the root. If that seems too much to ask or too hard to do, confide in a mature Christian friend or counselor and pursue it together. It's too serious a matter to procrastinate!

Day 23
THE POWER OF GOD'S WORD

"God said . . . and it was so."

Read: **Genesis 1:6-30;** 1 Samuel 3:1-9; Romans 8:18-23.

WHAT IS GOD SAYING?

Genesis is the book of beginnings. It opens with those very words, "In the beginning." It is awesome to contemplate the power of God simply speaking the universe into existence. No detailed and complicated explanations, no plunging into depths over our heads, no tossing around on rough seas of involved and interdependent equations, no inundating with unfathomable scientific jargon. God simply says, and it is so. Science, for all its technicalities and complications, is simply discovering, step by step, what God planned from the beginning.

HOW DOES THIS APPLY TO US?

It has always been so, from the beginning through all ages, in this present hour, and down all the millenia that will come if the Lord tarries: "God says, and it *is* so." This is the power sensed by the centurion whose servant was paralyzed and in great distress. He said to Jesus, "Only say the word, and my servant will be healed" (Matthew 8:8). At a single word from God, all the powers of darkness fall back. Sin and sickness are no match for that recreative, cleansing, and conquering Word. The same Word that brought generation can bring regeneration. The same Word that brought about creation and the first beginning can bring about recreation and a new beginning. God began it all. His Word brought order out of chaos, light out of darkness, and something out of nothing. That Word has never lost its power. He can and will say that Word over the chaotic mess that many of us have made out of life. He can and He would, by that Word, overcome the darkness of doubt and depression and discouragement. If His Word could once bring purposeful order out of meaningless void, does it not still have the power to heal the sick, bring freedom to the enslaved, give hope to the weary, and show the way Home to those who are lost? "God said, and it was so."

Let it be so now, for all of us. His help is *very present* and His Word is *very powerful.*

Pray with Me

God of creation, from far beyond the silence of space You have spoken. In the chambers of meditation where I am alone with myself and with my Lord, You are speaking. "God said." God is ever saying. It was so. It is ever so.

Still within my heart all pride that is determined to speak when You are speaking. Help me not to insist on being heard when I ought to be hearing. Still within my heart the cry of rebellion that echoes man's first great blunder, saying: *God said, but it isn't so.* Still within my heart the faithlessness that fails to reckon with the power of God's simple Word: "It is so."

Help me become aware of the fact that nothing in all creation, except man in his senseless rebellion, can refuse to heed Your sovereign voice. You speak and the heavens are formed. You speak and that which was nothing exists. You speak and dawn creeps over the darkened world.

As Your voice brought forth the first creation, and as neither chaos nor void nor darkness could thwart Your plan, so bring forth in me at the start of this new day Your new creation. If You but speak, the dark tyranny of past sin will not rob me of the calm that is mine today. The suspicion that I might fail tomorrow will not hold me as a slave if I walk with You and heed Your Word.

Hear the voice of my surrendered heart. Help me hear the voice of Your perfect will.

Through Him who said, "Not My will but Yours be done," Amen.

Moving On in the Life of Prayer

It is a wonderful discovery to see what God can do by the word of His power when we are willing to listen and obey. "Speak, Lord, for Your servant is listening." That's the first step. But there is more. Trust the power of His creative Word. Go out in the faith that since what God said HAS been so, what God says WILL be so.

Day 24

THE PROVIDENCE OF GOD

"As for you, you meant evil against me; but God meant it for good, to bring it about that many people should be kept alive, as they are today" (Genesis 50:20).

Read: **Genesis 50:15-21;** Deuteronomy 4:39; 1 Chronicles 29:10-12; Romans 8:28; 2 Timothy 4:18.

WHAT IS GOD SAYING?

This moving story contains one of the most memorable examples in Scripture—or in history—of how God rules and overrules. The devices of men, even though spawned in a climate of jealousy and hatred, cannot have the upper hand in the end. Horatio Alger's assorted "rises" to fame and success are not in the same ball park with Joseph. Sold by his jealous brothers into slavery, he rose to incredible responsibility and power as the right hand man of Pharaoh, archenemy of the despised "shepherds" of Israel.

This story gives the raw details of the worst in humanity. It traces without flinching the depths to which the sin of jealousy can take us. It reveals the unhealthy pride of Joseph, with his shameless airs, rubbing salt into deep wounds as he paraded before his brothers in his special robe, flaunting his father's favoritism. It was enough to awaken the worst in Joseph's brothers.

But God was in control, as He always is. He put it in the heart of Reuben to save Joseph's life and the story with such a sordid beginning ends with the tender beauty of forgiveness and love in spite of all intended and actual wrong. Once again love covers a multitude of sins.

HOW DOES THIS APPLY TO US?

God's providence is often mysterious—but always right.

We must guard against envy no matter how easy it is to become its prey. People make it easy by flaunting their superiority in skills and talents, their affluence, their robust health, or their uncanny ability to come out on top. Yet we are fortressed by a far greater promise than the temporal and passing trophies so prized by others. We know that "in everything God works for good with those who love him, who are called according to his purpose" (Romans 8:28). For now, be assured of this and pray in the confidence that God is still on the throne. Everything meant to do us evil is another rung on a ladder that lifts us until we see that God means everything—even this—for good.

Pray with Me

God, Your love never wavers. Your wisdom is without flaw. Forgive me that I have at times questioned Your mysterious providence. With Israel I have said: "My way is hid from the LORD, and my right is disregarded by my God" (Isaiah 40:27).

The spiritually dead seem to live. The clever impostors seem to get away with it. The dishonest brothers seem to have their way. They seem to be on top of things. Joseph is sold into slavery and sent away.

Is justice really blind? Does honesty really pay? Is love only the refuge of the weak? In doing good is one done in? It must have seemed so to Joseph, many times.

But in the end Joseph could see that man-intended evil can become God-intended good. So from the perspective of Heaven I shall see that "in everything God works for good with those who love him." And even now, when all is still and I am deeply trusting in Your Word, I know this is true.

I affirm in faith the fact that nothing escapes Your overruling providence. Things change, times change, friends change, I change. But Lord, You do not change.

Nothing can stray into my life, or weigh on my heart, or prey on my mind, or stay my determined step without Your knowledge and permissive will. I trust in Your love. I want to walk in Your paths of righteousness. Then everything that comes into my life, even when "meant for evil," will be woven into the final pattern of everlasting good.

Through Jesus Christ, who endured the cross to wear the crown, Amen.

MOVING ON IN THE LIFE OF PRAYER

When things look and feel their worst, and when everything is going against us, it is time to pray for a quiet acceptance of God's will and a deep trust in His wise providence. He understands . . . and He overrules.

Day 25

THE WAY TO KNOW GOD

"No one knows the Son except the Father, and no one knows the Father except the Son and any one to whom the Son chooses to reveal him" (Matthew 11:27).

Read: **Matthew 11:25-30;** Job 11:7; 1 Corinthians 1:18-31; John 7:28-29, 8:54-55, 10:15, 17:25-26.

WHAT IS GOD SAYING?

God cannot be known through many of the ways given priority by the world. Scientific research has its place, but it cannot fathom the unfathomable nor define the undefinable. God is above the facts that science—with all credit to diligent scientists—is discovering. The door to the knowledge of God does not open to the one who dangles from his belt the keys of cleverness and super-intelligence. "I will destroy the wisdom of the wise, and the cleverness of the clever I will thwart" (1 Corinthians 1:19). In today's passage from Matthew, Jesus directs His remarks against the pride and boasted wisdom of the religious leaders who are rejecting Him. The humble listeners who have faith are light-years ahead of these cynical authorities. As William Barclay writes, "It is not cleverness which shuts out; it is pride. It is not stupidity which admits; it is humility. Jesus is not connecting ignorance and faith; He is connecting lowliness and faith. A man may be as wise as Solomon, but if he has not the simplicity, the trust, the innocence of the childlike heart, he has shut himself out."[1]

Then follows the greatest claim that Jesus ever made: He alone can reveal God to man.

HOW DOES THIS APPLY TO US?

Jesus shows where to find the true key to the knowledge of God. He, the Son, and He alone, can reveal the Father. Faith in Him, listening to His words, following His example of love and compassion, seeing in His ultimate sacrifice that which has torn apart the veil of the temple to let repentant sinners come into the presence of the Holy God . . . this is the way to know God. All other knowledge of everything worthwhile branches out from that one basic truth. The better we know Jesus, the better we know God. He wants to let us know God the Father. He wants us to know how much the Father loves us. That is why He came. It

1. William Barclay, *The Daily Study Bible*, Matthew Vol. II, (Edinburgh: The St. Andrews Press, 1957), p. 15.

is the heart of Christianity. He is the Way, the Truth, and the Life. No one comes to the Father but by Him (John 14:6).

If we want guidance through this bewildering world, if we want to see the light at the end of the tunnel or the candle in the window that says, "This is Home where you belong," we must, in humility, look for the answers in the person, works, and words of Jesus Christ.

Pray with Me

Jesus, blessed Son of God, I want to know our Father according to Your perfect revelation. I cannot be content to know Him as a misty silhouette cast upon the curtain of speculation. I want to know Him clearly and deeply through You and the Word which You have spoken.

As You are the only One who knows the Father, You are the only One who *shows* the Father. This was the purpose of Your coming. Immanuel, God with us, in Your mercy, "choose to reveal" the Heavenly Father to me.

Let this truth dawn on the nighttime of my soul. Let it give guidance to my often bewildered spirit. Loving You, I love God. Hearing You, I hear God. Obeying You, I obey God. Knowing You, I know God.

Man, with his vain traditions and empty philosophies, has often obscured these things. Yet how simple, after all, is the Way: Coming to God means coming to Christ. Coming to Christ means coming to God.

I come to You in faith. I come to You in the fresh, glad morning. I want to walk beside You through the common duties of this day. When the day is far spent and our fellowship is still unbroken, I want to be able to say: "Did not my heart burn within me, while He talked with me by the way?"

In Your own blessed Name, Amen.

MOVING ON IN THE LIFE OF PRAYER

Let each day be an adventure of faith. Are you having trouble getting through to God? Does He seem remote, distant, at times indifferent? Does the Bible seem archaic and irrelevant for your pressing needs? Beware of Satan! He has the power to scramble messages broadcast from other well-meaning sources. But the static of his lies cannot plague your reception when you are tuned into Heaven's wavelength, Jesus Christ. Let us listen to the instruction on that, our true "emergency band." Let us go out in trust and obedience. Then we will have a growing knowledge of God and, discovering His will, find both perfect peace and triumphant, lasting joy. That's worth praying about again and again, and in the Name of Jesus Christ.

Day 26

CAN WE BE A FRIEND OF GOD?

"The LORD used to speak to Moses face to face, as a man speaks to his friend" (Exodus 33:11).

Read: **Exodus 33:7-17;** Numbers 12; Isaiah 41:8-10; 2 Chronicles 20:7; James 2:23.

WHAT IS GOD SAYING?

God spoke to Moses in a special way, as a man speaks to his friend. The text suggests that it could have happened many times—an ongoing conversation. Moses was very special in the plan God had for His people. A man of constant prayer, Moses must have often listened for the Lord's voice to give him directions in carrying out his singular responsibility. But there is a sense in which this passage makes a general reference to spiritual communication.

It speaks of the relationship possible between God and man that can be best described as "friendship."

In Jeremiah 3:19, it is the relationship of Father to children. In 2 Chronicles 20:7 and John 15:15 it is the relationship of Friend with friend. In Psalm 123:2 and Isaiah 41:9 it is the relationship of Master to servant. But it is all a matter of communion with God in prayer. God, in Christ, is very approachable. Jesus taught us to think of God as Father, and except for His cry of desolation on the Cross, never addresses Him by any other name.

HOW DOES THIS APPLY TO US?

We must not bring the total otherness of God down to the level of a "Pal in the skies" or "the Man upstairs." If we want to distort reality and, indeed totally miss the message of God, we have only to bring Him down to our level and down to our size. That's akin to making God in our own image and if ever there was a blind alley, that is it.

God wants us to be as children to an infinitely loving Father. Jesus came to show that He was that. And to get hold of that fact is life transforming.

But there is also that awesome Otherness, that total Transcendency, that incomparable Majesty. Lose that and all communication breaks down (Isaiah 55:8-9). Still our relationship with God has other aspects. He wants to communicate with us as a Friend would communicate with a friend. Abraham is called "the friend of God." Let us assume that God wants that kind of communication with us. It will be the purpose of our prayer today to explore those areas of "friendship with God" which can make our daily lives rich with meaning and steadfast in purpose.

Pray with Me

Cleanse me, O God, in heart and in desire, in hand and in deed, in mind and in thought, until, with every barrier down, You can talk to me "as a man speaks to his friend."

A man speaks to a friend and does not have to weigh his words carefully for fear of offending. Speak to me, Lord, as One who neither takes nor gives offense apart from the truth—and only then in love.

A man speaks to a friend and knows that the friend needs no persuading to see things from the speaker's point of view or for the speaker's advantage. Speak to me, Lord, as One who seeks first and only the kingdom of God and His righteousness.

A man speaks to a friend and trusts that he will understand. So I would dedicate myself to the yearnings of Your heart as it is burdened for mankind.

A man speaks to a friend and trusts him to bring his message to others. So I would bring to others the facts of Your judgment on sin and Your love for the sinner.

A man speaks to a friend and trusts him with his dearest plans and highest hopes. So I would have a mind to grasp Your will and a heart that responds with obedience.

Then I shall see Your face, and, seeing Your face, I shall see Your smile . . . the smile of a Father forgiving, a Master approving, and a Friend that will never forsake.

Through Him, whom having not seen, yet I love, Amen.

MOVING ON IN THE LIFE OF PRAYER

Without assuming that we can come to Him with easy familiarity, we may come to the Lord freely and spontaneously. Let us hear what He has to say in His Word and then resolve that our lives will become adjusted to His purpose. Prayer then becomes far more than a way of persuading God to change His mind. It becomes God's way of persuading us to change our lives.

Day 27

LIFE AS GOD INTENDS

"There he [God] put the man whom he had formed" (Genesis 2:8).

Read: **Genesis 2, 3;** Isaiah 45:9; Jeremiah 18:1-7.

WHAT IS GOD SAYING?

God formed man. The verb used in verses 7 and 8 is the same as that which describes what a potter does to clay when he shapes it into a vessel. The idea of a vase or a pitcher begins in the mind of the creating artist. He knows what he wants before he puts his hand to the job. He knows the purpose to which it will be put. He knows the kind of material he needs. He brings it all together. Then, when all is ready—the raw clay, the potter's wheel, and water to keep the clay workable—the idea that started in his mind takes shape beneath the caressing, careful and caring touch of his fingers. So man was "formed." An idea of God. An idea of something, someone, who would be perfect took shape as a vessel on the Potter's wheel.

The man so formed was given the breath of life and he became the greatest of God's creation, its crowning glory. God's perfect idea. God's perfect work. And he was put in a perfect place.

Then came Satan, subtle, deceitful, persuasive; the temptation, the disobedience, the sin. And that which was formed had now become deformed. The beautiful became ugly. The perfect became flawed.

HOW DOES THIS APPLY TO US?

We are all touched by the consequences of sin. We all long for another chance. Across our minds flash visions of what might have been. Can it still be? Is there a plan for that? Yes, God who formed man perfectly can take the vessel that is broken and reform it. "If any one is in Christ, he is a new creation" (2 Corinthians 5:17). The God of creation is also the God of recreation. Could it be said more clearly than in Jeremiah 18:3 and 4? "So I went down to the potter's house, and there he was working at his wheel. And the vessel he was making of clay was spoiled in the potter's hand, and he reworked it into another vessel, as it seemed good to the potter to do."

Let our prayer today concern itself with what God can do with the vessel of our life. Broken, perhaps, but reworked IN His hand, a vessel to be used BY His hand for His glory and for our joy. Not perfect yet, but, in Christ, on the right road.

Pray with Me

O God of all creation, God of the perfect plan, You formed a perfect man and put him in a perfect place. Through pride and rebellion, the man You formed chose his plan over Your plan and preferred the heady sense of short-lived liberty to the deep bliss of steadfast obedience.

And now, across the wreckage of a world that might have been, I reach out for life as You planned it. Out of the shambles of my own willfulness, I want to retrace my life on the pattern of Your perfect design.

Yet like a thick cloud, my transgressions obscure my vision. I cannot look on that perfection which You have intended. The dread paralysis of sin keeps me from moving toward that perfection which You have purposed.

Now, therefore, Lord of the perfect creation, be to me the God of recreation. Though I am not able to take a single step, lift me all the way up and bring me all the way back to life as You first intended it. Bring me in to the serene calm of Your sheltering love. Lead me in paths of righteousness for Your name's sake. Restore me to the joy of Your approving smile. Let me rejoice again in the strength of Your cultivated companionship.

Through the recreating power of Jesus Christ, may I become the man of Your first and only plan. Then keep me, Lord, in this sin-blighted world, as the one that You have formed again!

For Jesus' sake, Amen.

Moving On in the Life of Prayer

The God who formed us and placed us here is still working on us. We keep frustrating His perfect plan by our disobedience and willful pride. Yet through faithfulness in prayer we will discover what He wants to do in us and what He can do through us. Pray without ceasing.

Day 28

WALK IN THE SPIRIT

"Walk in the Spirit" (Galatians 5:16, KJV).

Read: **Galatians 5;** Romans 8:26-27; John 14:13.

WHAT IS GOD SAYING?

The Christian fights an unrelenting spiritual battle. In this chapter the good and the evil, the flesh and the Spirit, the right and the wrong, the road that leads to life and the roads that lead to death are clearly identified. The battle lines are drawn. "For the desires of the flesh are against the Spirit, and the desires of the Spirit are against the flesh; for these are opposed to each other, to prevent you from doing what you would" (v. 17).

These verses brim with both stern warning and great encouragement. We can be sure that the fruit of the Spirit will quietly, abundantly, and certainly overcome the works of the flesh. In this constant battle, the one way to get on the winning side and stay there is to "walk in the Spirit."

HOW DOES THIS APPLY TO US?

What a great chapter lies before us, especially as we seek to cultivate a life of prayer. Here are the best and the worst in open confrontation. How do we handle the perpetual battle against evil? How do we grow more constantly towards God's ideal for our lives? It is all right here before our eyes. Go over the chapter again and note these truths: Stand fast in freedom (v. 1). Wait in hope (v. 5). Fulfill the law of love (v. 14). And walk (continual forward progress, not running, not stumbling, just walking) in the Spirit (v. 16).

Pray with Me

Lord, so often I have walked in my own strength. I have rebelled against Your will—fearing it might be dark with sacrifice. I have held back—fearing Your way would shut me out from joy and shut me in to boredom. I have not trusted the "fences" of Your grace intended to keep evil out and blessings in. I have ignored the deeper truth that Your way alone is the way to full life.

Now, Lord, I want no more of that walk which is preoccupied with me. I want to leave all that caters to carnal pride. I will walk in the Spirit. I will value what He gives. I will believe what He says. I will follow where He leads. I will be quiet to hear Him and quick to obey Him.

I will walk in the Spirit, for this will lead me into places of helpful ministry. I will walk in the Spirit and enjoy unhurried communion with God.

I will walk in the Spirit to be shielded from sin and all that issues in death. I will walk in the Spirit as He leads into paths of righteousness and all that issues in life.

I will walk in the Spirit, for this will help me major on eternal values. I will walk in the Spirit that I may minor in things that have within them the seeds of their own decay.

I will walk in the Spirit to the glory of God . . . and to the eternal satisfaction of my soul.

In the Name of Christ, Amen.

MOVING ON IN THE LIFE OF PRAYER

The Holy Spirit is the promised Comforter, the One called alongside as Friend, the trusted Counselor, the One commissioned to "guide you into all truth" (John 16:13).

Let us pray in the Spirit. Let us be sure of His presence "who intercedes for us with sighs too deep for words" (Romans 8:26-27). Let us pray in the awareness that He is the Counselor who is always there and the Companion who always cares.

Day 29

GOD'S WILL OVER ALL

"All the trees of the field shall know that I the LORD bring low the high tree, and make high the low tree, dry up the green tree, and make the dry tree flourish. I the LORD have spoken, and I will do it" (Ezekiel 17:24).

Read: **Ezekiel 17:24;** Psalm 18:25-27; 1 Samuel 2:1-10; Luke 1:52-53; Matthew 11:27.

WHAT IS GOD SAYING?

Not only is "God's will over all" a major theme of Scripture, it is a fact supported by history. Civilizations, once proud and defiant in their godless ideologies now are dead and buried. Their hollow voices speak across the millions of weathered and tilted tombstones in cemeteries long neglected and forgotten. Out of the long dead past they cry out: "This is the end of 'everything that exalts itself against the knowledge of God' " (2 Corinthians 10:5, KJV). God is still in control. His will alone is supreme. However tall and flourishing may be the trees of the proud and wicked, God brings low the high tree and dries up the green tree. He also gives height to the low tree and makes the dry tree flourish (Ezekiel 17:22-24).

To Ezekiel there is a Messianic significance in the small sprig taken from the top of the great cedar (17:22). It is prospering but doomed. Israel now suffering and enslaved by the Babylonians, would rise again to God's intended greatness and to fulfill God's intended purpose.

It is also of interest to note that this description of the cedar tree (in Ezekiel 17) is the probable source upon which Jesus based His parable of the mustard seed (Mark 4:30-32).

How Does This Apply to Us?

God provides the strong foundation upon which believers may stand with an assurance that reaches on through mortal life and into eternal life. "The eternal God is your dwelling place and UNDERNEATH are the everlasting arms" (Deuteronomy 33:27). But the will of God which is underneath to give us assurance is also over all with power to bring down the proud and to lift up the humble.

How wonderful it is to come to prayer with this thought on our mind: "God's will over all." "Humble yourselves therefore under the mighty hand of God, that in due time he may exalt you" (1 Peter 5:6). It is no mere coincidence that the next verse in Peter's first letter is, "Cast all your anxieties on him for he cares about you." Let us come often to God in prayer since we know that He who is always in control is the One who always cares.

Pray with Me

Lord, Your spoken Word is accomplished fact. I acknowledge Your holiness and power. I pray that I may see all things in true perspective.

I would see myself as being capable of good and destined for joy. I would see that all things that are opposed to the will of God are surely doomed.

The high tree is brought low. The low tree is made high. In the misguided logic of human pride, the low tree is despised. But You, Lord, have chosen what is low and despised in the world, even things that are not, to bring to nothing things that are. Keep me from becoming a victim of the cheap and the obvious. There is a secret which can only be discovered by those who are meek in spirit: "God will destroy the wisdom of the wise and the cleverness of the clever."

Then, Lord, there is the temptation to find nourishment from wells of carnal pleasure. There is the satanic delusion which argues that life cannot be a fulfilling experience unless the desires of the flesh go unchained and unchallenged. Help me rather to see, O God, that You can make the green tree dry and the dry tree flourish. It is the dry tree that flourishes. God, rich in mercy—even when we are dead through our trespasses—can make us alive together with Christ. He who has the Son has life!

My heart shall be a low tree until in Your wisdom it shall be made high. My life shall be a dry tree until by Your life-giving Spirit it shall be made to flourish.

To the glory of Christ whom to know is life eternal, Amen.

MOVING ON IN THE LIFE OF PRAYER

Do we need encouragement in our prayers? Do we need patience when the answers seem slow in coming? Do we need to see the larger picture when our lives become enmeshed in the worthless trivia of much that is daily life? God is over all. His will and only His will counts in the end. Our thrust in prayer should be to echo Jesus' words in the hour of His greatest crisis: "Thy will be done." God's will is the way to glory. God's will is the assurance of victory. God's will, done, leads to perfect peace. "God's will over all." Let us pray to know it, to accept it, and then to do it. Then just see what can happen. Certainly it is the way for "the dry tree to flourish" and "the low tree to stand tall."

Day 30

THE PLACE OF REPENTANCE IN PRAYER

"*. . . Let them cry mightily to God; yea, let every one turn from his evil way*" *(Jonah 3:8)*.

Read: **Jonah 3:8;** 2 Chronicles 7:14; Hosea 14:2; Psalm 51:17; Acts 2:38; 2 Corinthians 7:10.

WHAT IS GOD SAYING?

The situation in Nineveh called for drastic action. God's judgment on unrepented sin was about to fall on that "great city." Jonah was to be God's messenger to the city but he hated to have his number called up for this mission. So he went AWOL. He went as far and as fast as he could—in the opposite direction. It even took a whale to stop him in his tracks and to bring him to his senses. God's mercy can often seem harsh.

But he who was straying started in to praying—earnestly. The place of his prayer was no cushion-pewed chapel with stained glass windows, but the need was evident and the time was right. Jonah prayed for a second chance and by the word of the Lord he was beached by the whale, humbled and broken, but safe and sound, and very, very grateful.

Now he had a second chance. This time he went to Nineveh and "cried out" the message he should have brought in the first place. There was enough God-given eloquence in Jonah's message and enough hard-earned sincerity in this voice to bring conviction to a whole city. Behind the leadership of the king who was also under conviction, the people followed his example and obeyed his command. They "cried mightily" for forgiveness and turned from their evil ways.

HOW DOES THIS APPLY TO US?

Nineveh, in a city-wide revival, cried mightily to the Lord. It was not a few accustomed rituals or some quiet mumbling in the proper time and in the proper manner lest someone other than God might hear. They cried. The cry of conviction, the cry of earnestness, the cry of desperate need. It was reality surfacing. It was steam escaping from a valve. It was the cry of the lost to be found and of the helpless to be rescued.

Repentance does not usually call for "crying mightily," but it does call for sincerity and deep conviction of need and an honest decision to be right with God who through Christ has made it possible. Hosea says in chapter 14, verses 1 and 2: "Return, O Israel, to the LORD your God, for you have stumbled because of your iniquity. Take with you words and return to the LORD; say to Him 'Take away all iniquity.' " There is a place and a time for "crying mightily" to the Lord. Not necessarily audibly but certainly with sincerity. Shakespeare expresses this need in *Macbeth* as Malcolm prods Ross, lately come from Scotland, not to hold back the tragic news of his family there:

"Give sorrow words: The grief that does not speak
Whispers the o'erfraught heart and bids it break."
(4.3.209-10)

When we need to cry, mumbling won't do. So we come to prayer with deep calling unto deep. The depth of our need calling on the wideness of God's mercy.

Pray with Me

God of infinite mercy, You had pity on Nineveh when her people repented. Let me have complete assurance that You always hear the cry for mercy from penitent hearts. "A broken and a contrite heart, You will not despise, O God." Once again in Your Word I have seen what is required in repentance: not only the cry for help but the turning from evil.

Repentance is a cry, and true repentance is a mighty cry. It is a person's owning up to the fact that he cannot save himself. It is not the casual banter of shallow conversation nor the empty mouthing of self-sufficiencies.

Repentance is a cry. It is deep calling unto deep. It is the lost hoping to be found. It is the sinking one reaching out for a hand. It is the hungry begging for bread. It is the burdened needing release. But, Lord, Your Word has also said that repentance is more than crying.

It is turning from the evil way. Give me grace to do more than lift my voice. Help me to turn my feet. Let me ask for Your help, Lord, but let me also act by Your help. Not only will I mourn for failures in the past, but even more I will move into victories that lie ahead.

I will confidently expect those great triumphs that are waiting only for the walk of obedience and faith.

In Your mercy hear my cry and in Your wisdom guide my steps. For the sake of Him who has called us out of darkness into His marvelous light, Amen.

MOVING ON IN THE LIFE OF PRAYER

Have we brought words that tell of our sorrow for sin? There is one further thing that needs to be done before repentance is real and prayer has power: We must turn everyone from his evil ways and then we will find that beyond the sorrow for all we have done wrong there is the inexpressible joy of doing right. And we can do that in the strength of Christ, for He says, "my power is made perfect in weakness" (2 Corinthians 12:9) Take your needs to God in prayer. Then get on the road for God in service.

Day 31

THE HOLINESS OF GOD

"Who shall not fear and glorify thy name, O LORD? For thou alone art holy" (Revelation 15:4).

Read: **Revelation 15:3-4; Exodus 15:1-19;** 1 Samuel 2:2; Psalm 99:3, 9; Acts 9:31.

WHAT IS GOD SAYING?

The song of Moses in Exodus 15 was familiar to all devout Jews. It still is. It contains the elements of Moses' praise, thanksgiving, and triumph in God when, having crossed the Red Sea on dry land, he and his people were safe on the other side. At all synagogue services, the *Shema,* or the Creed of Israel, was recited and followed by two prayers, one of them based on this Song. As Jewish people still commemorate their greatest deliverance, the way God saved them at the Red Sea, so the faithful in Revelation—all faithful Christians of all time and in all circumstances—will sing the same song. They will sing that song in substance and with deep emotion because they have been brought safely through all their fiery ordeals to the promised land of Heaven.

How Does This Apply to Us?

What does this song mean to us right now? Can we sing it in our present trials and triumphs? We have not yet given our life in martyrdom. We have not finished the course or fought the good fight of faith to the end. We have yet to cross the finish line (even though some of us can see the glory that shines beyond it). Our summons to join the faithful martyrs has yet to come.

Can we sing this song and say this prayer? Yes, we can and *should* as we consider how the fear of the Lord and the awareness of His holiness can affect our life and prayer right now—and tomorrow—and tomorrow. Make the song of the triumphant martyrs yours today. But do it in the fear of the Lord. Never fail to respect the strength, beauty, and glory of God's holiness. That's an all-important first step in prayer.

Pray with Me

O God, only You are holy by nature and only from You comes the gift of holiness. Keep me, therefore, in that fear of Your Name which is the beginning of wisdom.

Help me to respect the strength of Your holiness. God-given holiness is the secret of spiritual joy. The world is controlled by corruption and guided by easy compromises. The gift of Your holiness is my only sure defense . . . the very life of my soul. Let Your holiness protect me as a shield, and support me as a foundation.

Help me to sense the beauty of Your holiness. I would accept the holiness that can transform my life from useless existence into the beauty of purposeful living. I would worship You in the beauty of holiness.

Help me to pause in silence before the glory of Your holiness. I would wait in patience, in holy stillness, and in expectant wonder. Then my life, for all its imperfections, will glow with radiant testimony to the holiness that Your grace alone can give. My life will be bathed with glory as the clouds that wait in unhurried silence over the splendor of a setting sun.

"Who shall not fear thee, O Lord?" Who? Only those who, having light thoughts of sin, cannot respect the strength nor sense the beauty nor pause before the glory of Your holiness.

Lead me away from such folly. Let the vision of Your holiness turn me toward You now in grace, lest the day should ever come when the vision of Your holiness will turn me away in the certain judgment of the Final Day.

To the glory of Christ by whose holiness I am shamed and by whose love I am saved, Amen.

Moving On in the Life of Prayer

In Acts 9:31 we read, "So the church throughout all Judea and Galilee and Samaria had peace and was built up; and walking in the fear of the Lord and in the comfort of the Holy Spirit it was multiplied." Let us remember that fearing God and being comforted by the Holy Spirit go hand in hand—in life, as well as in this text. They belong together. The fear of God is not dread or fright. It *is* awe and wonder; it *is* respect and appreciation; it *is* giving honor and glory to the Source of our Life, the Provider of our needs, and the One who is faithful and just to forgive our sins. That is the foundation of real prayer. That is the way to receive the comfort and strength of the Holy Spirit for daily life.

Day 32

God's Love, Pure Gold

"And the gold of that land is good" (Genesis 2:12).

Read: **Genesis 2:8-14; 1 Peter 1:18.**

What Is God Saying?

Across the centuries gold has been coveted by men with a great passion. The possession of it has been the source of pride *and* uneasiness. The lack of it has been the cause of wars and countless crimes of violence. Those who have it are often filled with pride. Those who do not are often filled with jealousy and hate. It is a precious metal. It is scarce. It can be hoarded and it can be stolen. It gleams in the pan of the prospector as he works from dawn to dusk in a river bed. It has caused men to leave home and family and to endure untold hardships of harsh weather and unfriendly terrain. It has destroyed the characters of those who lust for it, making them creatures that grub in the ground for it or sell their very souls to possess it.

Anything for gold. The best medal to win in a competition is gold. The cry that urges Olympic contestants to excel and press beyond normal endurance and strength is, "Go for the Gold!" The shining symbol of the most precious bond of love in all of life, marriage, is a ring made of gold. Fifty years of such a relationship is universally known as the Golden Anniversary.

When God wants to convey to us the great price of our redemption, He compares the precious blood of Christ, that which is incomprehensibly costly, with gold which for all its value is perishable. God wants us to have the gold of His bountiful love, the riches of His blessing, and the gold that He gives is good . . . not mixed and cheapened, a compromising alloy. Pure gold and in endless supply. Such is the love of God. And it is good.

How Does This Apply to Us?

We find this gold by living in the land of abundance that God provides—not a geographical piece of land, not a coveted vein in a limited motherlode that is hard to get and harder still to hold. The gold of God's intention for our life is endlessly available. It is inexhaustible and priceless beyond all reckoning. Let us live in the land of God's blessing and discover the gold He has for us. Let's go for it.

Pray with Me

Lord, I am often mystified and pained by the origin of evil. Its meanings lie beyond my struggling and limited reason. Nevertheless, I have no doubt about the origin of good, for *You* are the Giver of every good and perfect gift.

When I live in the land You have provided, and when I walk in its paths of pure and selfless living, it is always my joy to discover that "the gold of that land is good."

Thank You, Lord, for letting me live in a land where the gold is good. Thank You for blessings that cannot be bought with gold. Thank You for mercies that are not acquired through struggle and pain and labor. Thank You for the joy of knowing that the gold of the land of Your blessing is something I may obtain by Your grace and can never attain by my merit.

Time and again I have risen to the bait of sin's glittering gold only to find it has no value. I have been lured by that which is neither gold nor good only to find that, promising much, it yields but little. Take my heart, O loving Father, for I will trust You to guide me to the land and to keep me in the land where the gold is good. You will direct my steps into that land, into that kingdom, into that life, where value promised is value received beyond all I could ask—or even dare to dream.

In the Name of Him who has redeemed us by that which is far more precious than gold, even the blood of an eternal covenant, Amen.

MOVING ON IN THE LIFE OF PRAYER

Let us turn down the cheap substitutes. "The blessing of the LORD makes rich, and he adds no sorrow with it" (Proverbs 10:22). We should seek and find the pure gold of God's blessings on the deeper levels of prayer. Let us not be content with occasional flecks of gold in the sand of a shallow stream. There are great nuggets, ours for the taking. We can never exhaust God's riches. Never! "And the gold of that land is good."

Day 33

THE PERIL OF RIVAL GODS

"I will cut off . . . those who bow down and swear to the LORD and yet swear by Milcom" (Zephaniah 1:4-5).

Read: **Zephaniah 1;** 1 Samuel 7:3; 2 Kings 17:33; Luke 16:13; 1 Corinthians 10:21; James 1:8.

WHAT IS GOD SAYING?

The Lord is saying through Zephaniah that there are things that really do matter. The people were beginning to think that "anything goes." It really doesn't make any difference. If you go in for that kind of thing, you can worship Baal and run with the crowd. Then, if you feel like it, you can bow down and swear to the Lord. You've got all the bases covered. How can you lose? It was the mood of the times. "I will search Jerusalem with lamps," says the Lord, "and I will punish those who are thickening upon their lees [the wine needs to be stirred up, poured from one vessel to another; otherwise it will thicken and lose its strength], those who say in their hearts, The LORD will not do good, nor will he do ill" (Zephaniah 1:12). A lackadaisical attitude toward the priorities God had established was no small thing to the Lord.

But if and when the Lord's own people give themselves wholeheartedly to the Lord, without any rival affections or divided loyalty, "on that day it shall be said to Jerusalem: Do not fear, O Zion; let not your hands grow weak. The LORD, your God is in your midst . . . he will rejoice over you with gladness, he will renew you in his love" (3:16-17). The sun still shines in radiant fullness behind clouds of their indifference and faithlessness. God's love never fails, and it is expressed in lines which are scarcely equaled for tenderness and beauty anywhere in the Bible: "He will rejoice over you with gladness, he will renew you in his love."

How Does This Apply to Us?

Zephaniah speaks to the mood of our times. Time-proven principles are neglected. Standards of decency evaporate as if into thin air. Guidelines for moral behavior, like traffic-worn divider strips on the highway, grow so faint as to be useless and "every one does what is right in his own eyes" (see Judges 21:25). This is the prelude to social tragedy. It is also the atmosphere in which personal and spiritual disaster is only an accident waiting to happen. *Divided loyalty is not a matter of indifference.* Jesus Christ must be the Lord of all or He is not Lord at all. His words flash like lightning across the dark landscape of the slumbering soul: "No servant can serve two masters; for either he will hate the one and love the other, or he will be devoted to the one and despise the other. You cannot serve God and mammon" (Luke 16:13). This imperative speaks without reservation to every follower of Christ. We must choose.

Pray with Me

Lord, be in this moment and from this moment, my only hope, my only desire, my only God. In Your mercy You have warned against the peril of divided loyalty. The vinedresser must cut off the fruitless branch. Because You care so much You must do the same.

You are willing and able to rescue all Your children in mercy, yet Your voice has spoken: "I will cut off . . ." You are not willing that any should perish. You have gone to the depths of hell in the rescue of men. Still there comes the stern word, spoken in love: "No man can serve two masters!"

So let there be for me no rival gods. Let there be not a single passion that cannot stand up under the light of the Father's knowledge. Let there be not a single loyalty that cannot square with the Father's will. Let there be not a single ambition that cannot receive the Father's approval. Let me not think of You as a far-off goal, a hoped-for plus, a fringe benefit, when in reality I am dependent on the kindness of other people or the wheel of fortune or the strength of my own will.

I would not go on hesitating between two opinions. I would build my life on the words of the psalmist who sang in his victory song: "Some boast of chariots, and some of horses; but we boast of the name of the Lord our God. They will collapse and fall; but we shall rise and stand upright."

Create in me a clean heart, O God, a heart free from entangling alliances and from restless fears. With Your self-giving love in Christ always before me, create in me also a clean break, O God, until I trust only in the Lord with all my heart.

To the praise of your own all-sufficient grace in Jesus Christ my Lord, Amen.

MOVING ON IN THE LIFE OF PRAYER

Let us keep on giving God the best of our hours, the best of our energy, the best of our abilities and talents . . . and certainly the love and faith of our hearts in prayer.

Day 34

RICHES WE CAN TRUST

"In one hour all this wealth has been laid waste" (Revelation 18:17).

Read: **Revelation 18;** Psalm 23:5, 102:25-26; 2 Corinthians 4:15-16; 1 John 2:15-17.

WHAT IS GOD SAYING?

Left to his own instincts, man prizes most highly the things which he can *possess*. If he can put it in a bank, build a fence around it, brand it with his name, or engrave his social security number on it, it has value. To see material things in their true light is to see that in one hour's time it will all be laid waste. The passage in Revelation speaks of "Babylon the great," the pinnacle of material affluence, the proud symbol of all that man has or can achieve in his own power and for his own glory. Rome, referred to as Babylon the great, was the wealthiest and most magnificent city of antiquity. "Fallen, fallen is Babylon the great . . . the fruit for which thy soul longed has gone from thee, and all thy dainties and thy splendor are lost to thee, never to be found again!" (Revelation 18:2, 14).

God knows we have need of material things to exist in these material bodies and in this physical world. He knows, He cares, He provides (read Matthew 6:32). There is only one safeguard against the heartbreak of material loss, and that is to live for Him who *is* forever and who *gives* forever to those who seek first His kingdom and His righteousness.

HOW DOES THIS APPLY TO US?

Because this material world presses in on us in such demanding ways, we need all the more to center our thinking on spiritual realities. This applies not only to making the right distinction between the riches of the spirit and the riches of material abundance. It also has to deal with the danger of becoming unconscious victims of a prevailing atmosphere in a world at enmity with God—a world where self-gratification has become the very essence of life. Living a life of sacrifice for the things of His kingdom and for the welfare of others in the spirit of God's love is hard to maintain. It is a non-goal in our world ruled by pride and envy and selfish lust. Our prayer should, therefore, focus on things that cannot be laid waste in one hour, such as the riches of God's love for us, and ours for Him.

Pray with Me

Lord, You are the Creator-God, the Source of all good. You are the Owner of all things. I would separate myself today from those who with frenzied and insatiable urgings give themselves to seeking and hoarding material wealth.

"In one hour all this wealth"—for all its fascination and vaunted excellence—will be "laid waste."

Therefore I would quiet my heart and see everything in the light of eternity. From that vantage point even the wealthiest fortunes are insignificant compared to that Pearl of Great Price: a soul redeemed and homeward bound for God.

The Christian has riches that will not be "laid waste" in one hour or one year or one century. Forever is not time enough to exhaust the riches that are mine in Christ, beginning now and ending never.

These are the riches I will prize. In these riches alone I will place my trust. These are the riches Christ brought to me in His nail-pierced hands. These are the riches He holds for me. Thieves cannot break through and steal. Moth and rust cannot corrupt. Inflation cannot consume. War cannot lay in ruins the fortune I have received and shall keep on receiving in Christ.

Holding only to those riches that will keep for eternity, help me to remain unchained to all other riches, for "in one hour" they will be "laid waste."

In the Name of Christ in whom are the wealth of redeeming love and all the riches of glory, Amen.

MOVING ON IN THE LIFE OF PRAYER

"Turn your eyes upon Jesus,
Look full in his wonderful face
And the things of earth will grow strangely dim
In the light of his glory and grace."
—Helen Howarth Lemmel

In prayer, all the clamorings of the body and spirit are stilled. We see how wasteful and wrong are the things for which the world struggles in its search for pride and recognition, for power and position. It is then we can see how eternal and eternally right are the virtues of love and the fruit of the Spirit. We lose our desire for things that can be laid waste in one hour and take on a new agenda of things that will last forever— beginning now.

Day 35

GOD GIVES MORE THAN WE ASK

" 'If I have found favor in thy sight, show me now thy ways . . .' And he said, 'My presence will go with you, and I will give you rest' " (Exodus 33:13, 14).

Read: **Exodus 33:11-15;** Deuteronomy 20:1; Isaiah 41:10, 43:2; Matthew 28:20; Ephesians 3:20.

WHAT IS GOD SAYING?

God gave Moses an overwhelming assignment. He was to lead an entire nation away from the relative security of slavery and through a hostile environment where there was little safety and many hazards. There would be opposition and resentment within the ranks. There would be those who would say and get others to agree that Egypt wasn't all that bad: "O that we had meat to eat! We remember the fish we ate in Egypt for nothing, the cucumbers, the melons, the leeks, the onions, and the garlic; but now our strength is dried up, and there is nothing at all but this manna to look at" (Numbers 11:4-6). It was an impossible task. Moses, as anyone else would have been, was in over his depth. His was an understandable cry: "If thy presence will not go with me, do not carry us up hence." God had an answer that was more than that for which Moses, in his desperate need, had asked: "My presence WILL go with you AND I will give you rest."

HOW DOES THIS APPLY TO US?

Time and again the Christian experiences the joy of God's answers. God's best is always better than our most daring petition. Our petitions may seem to us to be oh-so-big, but to the Lord they may be oh-so-small. Moses asked to be shown the way and in his time of trial, he asked for God's presence. But God did more. He gave Moses His presence *and* He gave him rest in the midst of the turbulence and unrest of a constantly complaining mob. If we pray for the right blessing, God will give us

the larger blessing. Let us enter into prayer with a new awareness that God is "able to do far more abundantly than all that
we ask or think" (Ephesians 3:20).

Pray with Me

O Lord of my life, You pour out Your wisdom to those who
seek it. Your power is at work in the lives of those who do Your
will. When my heart is right and I pray for one blessing, You
always give more—more than I dare to ask, more than I am able
to imagine.

When Your servant Moses asked to be shown Your way,
You said, "I will give You more—My presence and My rest will
go with you in the way I show you."

Lord, help me to pray for the right blessing. Then I shall
receive the larger blessing. Praying for grace to conquer temptation, I will find the joy of an uncondemning conscience. Praying
for genuine love for others, I will experience the flood tide of
Your love in my own heart. Praying for the needs of others, I will
find my own wants being satisfied in Your goodness and mercy.
Praying for resignation to Your perfect will, I will find the key to
undreamed-of treasures.

Turning away from an obsession with trinkets, I will have
empty hands to receive Your gold. Turning away from the
bondage of sin, I will find the freedom of righteousness. Turning away from all my urgent askings, I will find the surprising
bliss of quiet receiving.

So, Lord, having asked for the right blessing, I will make
room in my heart for the larger blessing. Having sought to know
the right way, I will make room in my heart for the greater good.
I will make room for Your *presence* in which there is fullness of
joy. I will make room for your *rest* in which there is fullness of
peace.

Through Jesus Christ my Lord, Amen.

MOVING ON IN THE LIFE OF PRAYER

Let us put it to the test in the coming weeks. We will ask
God for great things—then revel in how far His answers exceed
our requests. We will rejoice in God's pluses. We will pray in the
confidence that He gives more strength than we need, more joy,
more beauty, more blessings than we could even think to ask.
Let us take this adventure in prayer. We will ask for the right
blessing and receive the larger blessing. It works every time.

GOD SAYS WHAT HE MEANS AND MEANS WHAT HE SAYS

"Did God say?" "God said" (Genesis 3:1, 3).

Read: **Genesis 3:1-13;** Revelation 12:7-9; 2 Corinthians 4:3-4; Matthew 13:19; Ephesians 6:11.

WHAT IS GOD SAYING?

From beginning to end in the Bible, Satan is the Great Deceiver. Scripture reveals his subtle tactics in its opening pages. And in its closing pages he is called "that ancient serpent . . . the deceiver of the whole world" (Revelation 12:9). He never sows doubt as to the existence of God. He proceeds on the basis of encouraging our first parents in the Garden to doubt that God really means what He says. "He can't be so mean as to mean that! What a cruel trick He is playing on you! Why should He do such a thing? It doesn't make sense. He has given you all this. Certainly it is unreasonable that He would demand obedience concerning one tree in the Garden. Go ahead. It won't kill you."

HOW DOES THIS APPLY TO US?

God knows what we need for true life. "There is a way that seems right to a man, but its end is the way to death" (Proverbs 14:12). When there is a choice (and we *are* free to choose) between a way that seems all right to us but which God says is all wrong, let us not allow Satan to deceive us into thinking that God doesn't really mean it. When we are tempted to let down our guard, it has little to do with doubting God's existence or His right to rule. It has everything to do with "How can God be so unkind as to deprive me of anything when He has given me everything?" When the Deceiver whispers in our ear, "Did God really say that?" We should answer, "Yes, He really said that. I will take His word for it. He means it and He means it for my good."

Pray with Me

O God, Your Word never fails in truth, in right, in blessing, and in all good. Help me through the gift of a steadfast and living faith to overcome that first and worst temptation . . . "Did God really say?"

"Did God say?" is the doubt which our subtle and never resting adversary would cast as a shadow across this day's path.

He would sink that question into my heart as an opening wedge to break my fellowship with You. He would destroy the trust and obedience which are prerequisite to Your fullest blessing.

He would not try to make me doubt that You *are*. The evidence of Your being is too convincing to deny. He would try, instead, to make me doubt that You mean what You say. He would have me believe that the God of power cannot be a God of love. He would have me believe that if You really mean what you say, You are being mean in what You say.

He would suggest that this cannot be God speaking. "God loves you too much to be so severe. It is unreasonable to act in such blind obedience to such a possessive Master and in such an inconsequential matter. Did God really say . . . that?"

May I recognize this question for the hell-inspired thing that it is. I will answer with Heaven-bound confidence and earth-free faith: "God has said!"

This is all the light I need to live this day. This is all the light I ask. But I do need it and I do ask for it.

In the Name and for the glory of your living and perfect Word, Jesus Christ, Amen.

MOVING ON IN THE LIFE OF PRAYER

This is the main thesis of our book: First listening, then praying. Our prayers will be strong and prevailing when we know in our hearts that God means what He says and, regardless of our first reaction or any subtle temptation to think otherwise, that God means it for our ultimate good and for the blessing we can be to others.

Day 37

BELIEF AND UNBELIEF

"I believe; help my unbelief!" (Mark 9:24).

Read: **Mark 9:14-24,** 5:35-43; Luke 17:5; 1 John 5:4.

WHAT IS GOD SAYING?

For the inner circle of Christ's followers, the ones who were with Him in those transcendent moments on the Mount of Transfiguration, this experience down in the valley was like coming to earth with a thud. Such vision, completeness, and perfection above . . . and now such imperfection, trouble, and deep distress: a father looking on helplessly as his son rolls about on the ground and foams at the mouth. What great contrasts! Disciples wanting to help but lacking power. The spiritual elation on the mountaintop; the agonizing distress in the valley. The father saying to Jesus, "If you can do anything"; Jesus saying to the father, "If *you* can believe." The father saying, "I believe. I want to believe. I must believe, but I can't! Please help me in my unbelief."

How Does This Apply to Us?

Jesus wants to show us that we can continue to have the joy of the mountain top in the unpleasant emergencies of the valley. He wants to answer the question we direct to Him: "Lord, if *You* can" by saying to us, "Not if I can but if *you* can—in fact ALL things are possible to him who believes." He wants to emphasize, as He does when He is alone with His disciples, that the effective treatment of problems down in the valley is only handled through prayer—believing, earnest, constant prayer. So it is that we can nourish BELIEF and stifle UNBELIEF in our times of prayer. We need to recognize that there is an endless battle between Belief and Unbelief. Prayer helps us to tilt the balance in favor of Belief.

Pray with Me

Lord, Belief and Unbelief are having it out in my heart. My life is checkered with intermittent hope and fear, joy and gloom, sunshine and cloud, light and shadow, faith and doubt.

Bring me along that road, dear Master, where there will be less and less variableness in my life of faith, less and less shadow caused by turning, less and less introspection and fear and self-preoccupation.

Lord, I want to be confident in the knowledge of Your love, even though there are nagging circumstances that make me doubt. Lord, I want to stand fast in the liberty of my first love for Jesus, even though there are many convincing voices that suggest this liberty is really bondage.

So I come to You, Lord, for the resolution of this interminable battle, this wearisome tug-of-war. Let me see that as light has its origin in You, so darkness has its end in You. Let me see that as light is Your nature to possess, so faith is Your gift to bestow.

I would turn from the peril and paralysis of unbelief to receive the security and to enjoy the freedom of a trusting faith. I would turn, simply turn, for the habits of long unbelief make me powerless to fly or run or even walk to you.

I face the Light. I do believe in that. I do believe in You. I do believe!

In giving light, You remove darkness. In giving faith, You remove doubt. To the degree that I cherish the gift of faith, You

will enable me to disavow the authority and sway of unbelief.
Lord, I believe . . . help my unbelief!

In the Name of Him who said, "All things are possible to
him who believes," Amen.

Moving On in the Life of Prayer

We should not be distressed by moments of unbelief.
When we are confronted by the monstrous contradictions of a
world engulfed by evil, it is easy to yield to the persuasive tactics
of the Deceiver. But in prayer we can live with joy and peace in
the Savior's presence through both the "highs" of a transfiguration and the "lows" of sickening setbacks in the valley. Jesus
gives light—He is the Light of the world—and the instant light
comes, darkness goes. When faith grows, doubt withers. Let us
keep on praying, "Lord, I believe," and see how he keeps on
helping us with the nagging problem of unbelief.

Day 38

Life from the Dead

"Shall the dead arise and praise thee?" (Psalm 88:10, KJV).

Read: **Psalm 88;** Proverbs 21:16; Ephesians 2:1; Colossians 2:13;
Romans 8:6, 6:5-11; James 1:15.

What Is God Saying?

Death for many people is synonymous with "It's all over."
So it is in Psalm 88: "Like one forsaken among the dead, like
the slain that lie in the grave, like those whom thou dost
remember no more" (verse 5). There is a sense in which Death
does mean it's all over. The psalmist is correct in not glossing it
over with flowery phrases and honeyed sentiments. Death is
real—and a real enemy. It is, indeed, the last great enemy to be
destroyed by Christ, who is equally real—and much more powerful. Now we who are Christians can shout in the gladness of
certain victory, "O death, where is thy victory? O death, where is
thy sting?. . . But thanks be to God, who gives us the victory
through our Lord Jesus Christ" (1 Corinthians 15:55-56).

How Does This Apply to Us?

Those who have not experienced the New Birth through
faith in Jesus Christ are dead—dead to spiritual realities, dead
to the stirrings of pure love, dead when God calls to a life of
liberating service, dead to the peace of God's forgiveness, and
dead to the joy of fruitful living. It is important to read Romans

6:5-11 in this connection. Because of *Him*, we, though not dead, should consider ourselves dead to sin and alive to God in Christ Jesus. Whatever our condition or outlook apart from Christ, we can become alive to God. By His grace we can arise from the dead and praise God. When we are dead to sin, a whole new world opens up to us as we become alive to God: strength to overcome, security from and victories over the world, the flesh, and the Devil. Let us pray as those who have been raised from the deadness of an aimless existence and given a new life of productive purpose.

Pray with Me

O God, I have experienced Your saving grace. I see the evidence of Your power at work in the lives of men and women. Therefore I can answer the psalmist's question with a strong and unqualified, "Yes!"

I have been rescued by a strength and a love too wonderful to understand . . . but too real to deny. I can give glad testimony to the real power of the real Resurrection of the real Lord.

I want to tell all those who are forlorn of spirit that there is a Love stronger than death. I want to tell all those who are destitute of hope that there is a Light that cannot be drowned by the darkness of sin.

The world lies in the grip of death. All its pastimes and "busyness" are painted masks that ill conceal the fear of death. From those who are brazenly indifferent or openly defiant or wistfully searching, comes this common cry, spoken or unexpressed, "Shall the dead arise and praise thee?"

Leaning on Your grace, I want to give a glad and certain answer. Help me, Lord, to see that my best answer is in a life devoted to Your praise and service. A prisoner, released from long darkness, is unashamed to embrace sunlight and freedom and new opportunity. So my life, reclaimed from the power of sin and darkness shall give forth a convincing "Yes!" in answer to the question, "Shall the dead arise and praise thee?"

In the Name of Him who said, "I am the resurrection and the life . . ." Amen.

MOVING ON IN THE LIFE OF PRAYER

Saved from the bondage of sin, we can pray to discover more of the inexhaustible blessings of our freedom in Christ. We can pray that others may rise from the dead, even when they think they are alive, and come to know Him whom to know is life eternal.

Day 39

LIVING ABOVE OUR FEARS

"He who flees from the terror shall fall into the pit" (Jeremiah 48:44).

Read: **Jeremiah 48:44;** Amos 5:19; Proverbs 29:15; 1 John 4:18.

WHAT IS GOD SAYING?

Moab was one of Lot's sons, and his descendants rejected the God of Israel, choosing as their god-protector a rival god named Chemosh. Perpetual enmity simmered between the neighboring communities of Israel and the Moabites, and Jeremiah is foretelling the doom of any nation that exalts itself against Jehovah. Lifting verse 44 out of its immediate context—generally *not* the best way to approach a study of Scripture—highlights a lesson we need to learn. If for nothing else, we can at least thank the Moabites for calling forth this potent image from the pen of Jeremiah: *If we run away from what frightens us, we will only run into greater trouble.*

HOW DOES THIS APPLY TO US?

The Christian need not dread what fear can do *to* him because he is certain of what Christ can do *through* him. When Fear knocks at the door, Faith goes to answer it—and the caller is not there! When Faith floods the room with light, Fear has no place to hide. The Christian may be and should be equipped with "the whole armor of God, that [he] may be able to withstand in the evil day, and having done all, to stand" (Ephesians 6:13). In the cataloging of this "armor of God" in Ephesians 6, there is not a single piece to cover the back. This simply means we are never to flee when terror comes or when things get rough. We are to stand our ground, and we can do it in the ever-available strength of our Lord Jesus Christ.

Pray with Me

Since I stand and conquer in the strength of Jesus Christ, O God, help me always to shun the folly and danger of yielding to fear. Help me to face fear without dread of what it can do *to* me since I may calmly rely upon what Christ can do *through* me. Armed for the conflict by the invincible weapons of faith and love, may I go on to face all my fears this day.

May I not flee from the fear of what *things* can do to me, since I am in the loving, omnipotent care of the Creator of all things.

May I not flee from the fear of what *others* can do to me, since I have been taught to love my enemies, and perfect love casts out fear.

May I not flee from the fear of what *my own deceitful heart* can do to me, since that heart belongs to Christ and has no desire, no will, no glory but His.

May I not flee from the unsettled accounts of *yesterday* since I may be fully assured that, "My sin, not in part, but the whole, Is nailed to the Cross and I bear it no more, Praise the Lord, Praise the Lord, O my soul. . . ."

May I not flee from the duties and responsibilities of *tomorrow* though they seem heavier than my shoulders can bear, since accepting the yoke of Jesus means that He is helping me far more than I am helping Him. Through Him I can do and bear all things.

Then, by Your grace and on Your promises, O God, I will not fall into the pit of discouragement and defeat but I shall be lifted to the high, strong rock of vision and walk in the joy of unshadowed and eternal victory,

Through Jesus Christ, my Lord, Amen.

MOVING ON IN THE LIFE OF PRAYER

Read James 4:7-8. Notice this as we come to prayer. Resist the devil and he will flee. Draw near to God and he will draw near to you. In prayer we have no reason to flee. We have only to draw near to God and He will draw near to us. Have this always before you when you kneel before Him. It is the way, the why, and the blessing of prayer.

Day 40

KINDNESS IN
THE IMPERATIVE MOOD

"And be kind to one another . . ." (Ephesians 4:32).

Read: **Ephesians 4:22-32;** Romans 12:10; 1 Corinthians 13:14; 2 Peter 1:5-7.

WHAT IS GOD SAYING?

This chapter of Ephesians makes clear the characteristics that ought to accompany the new life. Here are the fruits that should grow in abundance when a Christian, having been born again, puts down his or her roots in the truth and love that is Jesus Christ. "Put off your old nature . . . put on the new nature, created (that is the new creation in Christ) after the likeness of God in true righteousness and holiness" (Ephesians 4:22). The apostle doesn't list these distinguishing qualities as optional "extras." They are basic ingredients. These spiritual qualities are natural to the Christian. It is the old nature that is now unnatural. "The fruit of light is found in all that is good and right and true" (Ephesians 5:9). Nowhere in the Bible is there a more concentrated list of things that Christians ought to do and to be. We cannot walk through this passage without knowing that God has some specific needs in mind with our names attached. Notice how many times these words appear: "Be," "Do," "Do not," "Put away," and not least, "Be kind."

How Does This Apply to Us?

This passage has deep meaning to the one whose life has been changed by the kindness of God—and knows it. It has little or no meaning to the person who is blind to the kindness of God. When we have received "the immeasurable riches of his grace in *kindness* toward us in Christ Jesus" (Ephesians 2:7), and when we see that our salvation is not our own doing at all but entirely a gift of God (2:8), then we know what kindness is and what kindness does. Let us think of God's kindness in coming to us and we will more readily understand our need and our privilege to be kind to others. If kindness does not come naturally, we need to make it a matter of prayer.

Pray with Me

Lord God, Your kindness to me is beyond all expression. Like the ocean, it cannot be exhausted. It shines with the radiance of the morning sun. It fills the night with stars of hope and promise. It gives joy to the commonplace as flowers splash the drab earth with color.

Yet surrounded by Your kindness and having been assured of Your love in Jesus Christ, I am not always ready to show kindness to others.

Your Word does not suggest or advise kindness to others. It *commands* it. By Your grace, I will show Your kindness. By Your grace I will be Your kindness.

Let my life not be a *receptacle* that only receives Your kindness. Unshared abundance can become stagnant. Uncirculated blessings can lose their freshness and joy. So let me rather be a *channel* through which Your kindness flows. Let me become emptied in order to become full. Let me become full only to be emptied. Let my life carry on the pulsating rhythm of Your unceasing kindness.

Forgive the self-indulgence that has allowed cholesterol to form in the arteries of Your kindness through me. May the threatened risk to spiritual health be removed by an extra portion of your grace . . . until Your kindness flows again through me.

Through Him whose infinite kindness did not shun, for our sakes, the Cross, Amen.

MOVING ON IN THE LIFE OF PRAYER

Receiving the kindness of God leads to sharing the kindness of God. The more we allow kindness to take root in our hearts, the more effective and profitable our time of prayer will be. It won't be a burden or an obligation so much as a privilege. The kindness of God is our greatest reason for praying, for by that kindness we are forgiven, by that kindness we are heirs of immeasurable riches, by that kindness we have eternal life. Sharing that kindness is one of the choicest secrets and one of the strongest encouragements to pray.

Day 41

CLEAVING OR LEAVING

"But ye that did cleave unto the LORD . . . are alive" (Deuteronomy 4:4, KJV).

Read: **Deuteronomy 4:1-14;** Numbers 25:3-5; Psalm 106:28; 2 Timothy 4:18; Hebrews 13:6.

WHAT IS GOD SAYING?

The story of God's jealous anger against those who forsook Him to worship the Baal of Peor does not make pleasant reading. Those who ceased to cleave to Him, who played fast and loose with His commandments and thought compromising wasn't all that bad, met with death. So great was the impact of this faithlessness upon Israel that it is specifically cited in other portions of Scripture. Hosea refers to the time when some in Israel "consecrated themselves to that shameful idol and became as vile as the thing they loved" (Hosea 9:10). Psalm 106, verse 28, tells how they attached themselves to the Baal of Peor and provoked the Lord to anger. But while there were many who followed Baal on a trail to death, there were others who did cleave to the Lord (held on for dear life) and lived to tell the story.

HOW DOES THIS APPLY TO US?

Not many who cross our path today will be tempted to give the Baal of Peor the time of day. That doesn't seem to be a huge problem for us in these late years of the twentieth century. But we do recognize that there are idols, some of them shameful, who are competing with God for our time, interest, and energy. We cannot avoid the subtle and deceitful lures of evil unless we stay close to God, love His Word, seek to know Him better, and do His will wholeheartedly. That's what it means to cleave to Him. And that's why to cleave to Him is to live. That is why leaving Him is to head down the path whose end is death. Cleaving to God is best accomplished by "listening and then praying." Cleave to God in prayer or leave Him in prayerlessness. The way is clear and the choice is urgent.

Pray with Me

Spirit of God, I would follow Your leading and I would accept Your grace that I may know the unbroken joy of "cleaving" unto the Lord!

Forgive me, Lord, that in weakness I am sometimes more ready to "leave" You than to "cleave" to You. I often insist that my way is better. I hold back in hesitancy and indecision when I have the choice of following the way that leads to life.

My yearnings for the way of Your pure and selfless love are too feeble. My desire for Your abiding fellowship is too sporadic. I am too willing to drift into that pleasant and easy way in which there is neither life nor freedom of spirit.

Let there be disappointment on the human level, if it means fulfillment in Your eternal kingdom. Let there be loss in material things, if it means gain in riches that can never be lost or stolen or wasted away. Let me submit to Your temporary "No" if it be the key to Your eternal "Yes."

Deal with me, Lord, in Your perfect wisdom. Let Your kindness become stern discipline, if it brings me to You. Let Your love come in the guise of pain, if it wakens me to Your better plan.

Make me willing to be willing to *cleave* to You and be alive.

Make me willing to be unwilling to *leave* You for the enticing ways whose end is death.

In the Name of the True Vine in whom I would always abide, Amen.

MOVING ON IN THE LIFE OF PRAYER

Let us keep on cleaving and enter the wide and wonderful world of God's unlimited and unfailing blessings. Let us accept His discipline as well as His love and see how much better His plan is than ours. Through prayer we can learn to accept His perfect will and walk in the way that leads to life. He loves us too much to let us go without a restraining hand. In prayer the Hand that restrains is the Hand that sets us free.

WISE AND WILLING

"Willing heart . . . wise heart" (Exodus 35:5, 10, KJV).

Read: **Exodus 35:4-10 (KJV)**; 1 Chronicles 29:9; 2 Corinthians 8:1-12, 9:6-11.

WHAT IS GOD SAYING?

This passage speaks of those who offered their skills to equip and adorn the Tabernacle. An incredible journey called for incredible sacrifice. And only those who were willing and wise (or skilled) were called upon to give of their possessions and talents. Willing hearts and wise hearts are the ones that God wants to touch to accomplish His work. It is consistently true in Scripture that giving must be of one's free will. God owns it all— and He may well require it all as in Luke 12:16-21. But the standard for giving when God wants a job to be done is found in the passage before us and backed up by such New Testament lessons as found in 2 Corinthians 8:12 and 9:7. Wise hearts are willing when it comes to the work which God needs to have done.

HOW DOES THIS APPLY TO US?

The important factor in the believer's free-will offering of time, treasure, and talent is the freedom of choice. God allows us to be stewards of His grace. We can choose to hoard what He gives and find ourselves starving in the midst of abundance. Or we can choose to share what He gives, believing that there is more where that came from. Like a river being supplied by an inexhaustible spring, our lives remain full and free and constantly renewed. Do we have a willing heart for sacrifice and a wise heart for service? Let that become the essence of our prayer.

Pray with Me

Dear Lord, You command obedience and submission from every part of Your creation. Yet You are pleased to give free and responsible choice to man, Your last and greatest creation. It is the glory of man that in Your plan and by Your permission he is free to choose.

This freedom is not given to the elements, to the mountains, to the seas, to the shining light, or to the wheeling stars. Freedom of choice is not given to animals whose existence depends on instinct and the will to survive. Man alone is given the power to weigh the facts, consider the consequences, and make decisions.

Therefore I *choose* to have a heart that is "wise and willing." I want to be among the "wise-hearted" who offer service to the Lord. I want to be among the "willing-hearted" who offer substance to the Lord.

Your Word assures us, "If there is first a willing heart, it is acceptable according to what a man has, not according to what he has not."

May I trust and act upon this promise until it carries me beyond inert principle into dynamic practice.

Give me, dear Lord, the wise heart of service. Give me the willing heart of sacrifice. May I be wise in knowing where service is needed. May I be willing to see what sacrifice is needed.

In the Name of the wisest and most willing Friend, my Lord and Savior, Jesus Christ, Amen.

MOVING ON IN THE LIFE OF PRAYER

Let every prayer begin with the wise choice of giving God a willing heart. Let every word and the desires of our hearts that lie so deep they cannot find expression in words be offered in the full awareness that it is wise to be willing. God receives and rewards the petitions of willing hearts. Prayer brings down Heaven's blessing on those who are willing to share what they receive. So prayer is like breathing—inhale and exhale, take in and give out. Prayer is never static. It moves up to God and out to others. Prayer is not a reservoir to take from God and store for our own use. It is a channel from God, through us, to others.

Day 43

THE GOD WHO SAVES IS THE GOD WHO STAYS

"And they shall know that I am the LORD their God, who brought them forth out of the land of Egypt that I might dwell among them" (Exodus 29:46).

Read: **Exodus 29:42-46;** Genesis 28:15; Isaiah 43:2; Matthew 28:20.

WHAT IS GOD SAYING?

The Tent of Meeting had special significance to the people who were making their way through what must have seemed an endless journey. The environment was bleak and constantly hostile. There were enemies before them, around them, and behind them who would have been very glad to see them erased from the face of the earth. The Promised Land had an annoying habit of getting farther and farther away. God knew they needed the encouragement of His presence. He had delivered them from the land of bondage. They needed to know through the Tent of Meeting that the One who had delivered them once would not only keep on delivering them, but wanted to stay with them always. It was the kind of assurance the Christian receives when Jesus says: "Lo, I am with you always, to the close of the age."

HOW DOES THIS APPLY TO US?

Think of the ways we have been delivered and the ways we are being delivered. Then rejoice that the same One who has saved us in the past is with us in the present. The exodus may seem to be long ago and far away. It doesn't come up often in our office conversations and is hardly a frequent topic for discussion between frames on bowling league nights. But the reality of God's deliverance from the bondage of sin and our need for His constant nearness in our constant striving against the Adversary is as real as the pedestrian crosswalk light at the next corner. God's deliverance is that real. So is His continual presence. God's deliverance from fear as well as His presence for comfort and strength is always available, always willing, always able. That double awareness of one who saves and also stays should encourage us to stay in touch . . . which we do in prayer.

Pray with Me

Lord, You are a God who can deliver us and a God who desires to dwell with us. I will rest in this thought today. I may be straining beneath the load of this day. I may be wrestling with the problems of this day. I may be bracing myself for the challenges of this day. Yet I may also rest in the great assurance that, "He who can deliver desires to remain."

Deliver me, O God, from the weight of past failures. Dwell with me in the present that I may be free of all that enslaves and defiles.

Deliver me, O God, from seeking to avenge my injuries in order to feed my pride. Dwell with me that I may accept in quiet faith all that comes as part of Your pattern for ultimate good.

Deliver me, O God, from indifference toward the needs of others. Dwell with me that I may have Your spirit of love and care toward those who are hurt and hungry and homeless.

Deliver me, O God, from the encircling fog of doubt. Dwell with me until the light of Your truth and the warmth of Your love dissolve all doubt.

Deliver me, O God, from the torments of fear and the troubled seas of worry. Dwell with me as Lord above all tempests. Your voice can check the fury of the wind and turn wild waves into mirror calm.

Then, being delivered, I shall help to deliver. Knowing Your presence, I shall share with effortless grace the very love and peace of God.

Through Jesus Christ, my Lord, Amen.

MOVING ON IN THE LIFE OF PRAYER

Let us not be delivered *from* something we dread without being committed *to* something (or Someone) we love. Prayer is the channel through which we are repeatedly assured that He has saved us from the past to be of use in the present. Prayer is the way we are assured that the One who is with us in the present will continue to be with us through all our unknown tomorrows until the Land that has been promised is the Land that has been reached. Keep on praying. God will keep on saving . . . and staying.

LOVE ONE ANOTHER

"This is the message . . . we should love one another" (1 John 3:11).

Read: 1 John 3:11-24, 4:7-12; John 13:35.

WHAT IS GOD SAYING?

John, the beloved disciple, remained faithful to the Lord Jesus through years of steadfast witness and a growing love for his Master. There were no recorded ups and downs, no hot then cold, just steady growth, embracing all believers with mature and generous love. As the years passed it seemed to him to be the thing that really and finally counted the most. So, now in advanced years, as he writes this letter to all his children in the faith, he reminds them that we cannot think or say we love God unless we are growing in our love for His other children. It comes so naturally to John, in writing, to use the word *beloved*. It flows from his pen because it was always flowing from his heart. It almost seems as though it was his single great message, the message that included all other messages of value. In the end, he can therefore say, "This is THE message . . . we should love one another." Nothing else counts very much if that is missing. If it is not missing, everything else worthwhile counts even more.

HOW DOES THIS APPLY TO US?

John has a message for us. John was not addressing a certain group of people who had a certain need long years ago and under other circumstances. Love is not outdated and never irrelevant. Love is a universal need and no one in any time or place is spiritually rich or emotionally sound without it. Certainly no one can say that he knows and follows Christ who is not continually motivated by the same thing that brought Christ to this world in the first place. "God so loved the world that he gave . . ." There is nothing that leads us to and keeps us in prayer more effectively than love. *Listen,* for THAT is the message. *Then pray,* for that is one way to say we have heard, that we understand, and that we agree.

Pray with Me

Lord, I get the message.

I get the message in my heart, beyond the whisperings of logic and the subtle suggestions of expediency.

I get the message in my heart, beyond the sounds of inhuman mechanisms and the noise of people who are blinded by hate, living and dying by the law of the jungle.

I get the message in my heart, beyond the restless tides of changing moods and the constant roar of waves as self-concern breaks on the rim of human limitation.

I get the message in Your own self-abandoning love.

I get the message in Your kind and gentle words from the Cross.

I get the message in the living and powerful Lord, written in the Book and lived out in the Son.

I get the message when I am blessed with the touch of someone who has, in turn, been touched by You.

God of all being and Lord of my being, may the message heard become the message embodied until my life flows forth in healing love. Then Your message will become my message and my message will be brought, as Yours has always been, in deeds of kindness, not in words of promise,

Through Jesus Christ, the Lord of Love, Amen.

MOVING ON IN THE LIFE OF PRAYER

As water nourishes a growing plant and as sunlight draws it up to its full and productive stature, so the life of prayer is best prospered and most effectively practiced when love becomes the reason we pray and the reason we keep on praying. It changes prayer from a hollow ritual to a joyful privilege. To love and to pray, to pray because we love and are loved by God, means we have heard John's simple message. Prayer knows no greater incentive and has no greater staying power than love: love from God, love for God, and love for one another. Love must go with us into the closet of prayer and stay with us when we leave.

Day 45

THE EVERLASTING GOD

"*. . . From everlasting to everlasting, thou art God*" (*Psalm 90:2*).

Read: **Psalm 90,** 102:24-28; John 17:3; Hebrews 13:8.

WHAT IS GOD SAYING?

God, the Creator . . . man, the created. God is eternal. Man has a limited number of days. With God a thousand years are but as yesterday when it is past, a watch in the night. With man, his years are soon gone and we fly away. It would seem that man flourishes in the morning and by evening fades and withers. God has a better idea. Our life does not need to end with a sigh and return to the dust from which it came. Jesus, God's loving and inexpressible Gift, came that we might have life and have it more abundantly. John emphasizes that "God gave us eternal life, and this life is in his Son" (1 John 5:11). And there are the matchless words of our Redeemer which move us beyond the concept of life that ends with a sigh and changes like grass into a state of useless nothingness: "I am the resurrection and the life; he who believes in me, THOUGH HE DIE, yet shall he live, and whoever lives and believes in me shall never die" (John 11:25-26).

How Does This Apply to Us?

This passage which stresses the everlastingness of God and the transience of man also emphasizes the importance of our remaining days in this life. Yes, having embraced Jesus Christ in faith as He is freely offered to us in the Gospel, having all eternity to spend with Him, nevertheless, we must make our remaining days count for Him in this life. We cannot count the days that remain, but we can make the days that remain count.

Pray with Me

Help me, O God, to rest in the quiet confidence that my true destiny is an unhurried eternity. Let me relax in the awareness that my true Home is a timeless Heaven.

Then I will be able to bear all injuries as one whose true self is shielded from the poison darts of worry. Then I will be able to bear all losses as one who lives above the flak of wounded pride.

Reconciled to God, my pardon is eternal. Redeemed by God, my salvation is eternal. Kept by God, my security is eternal.

Lord, make *this one day in my life a segment of time in which the sun of Your eternal grace will never once be dimmed by clouds of doubt and fear. Make THIS ONE DAY a day of unshadowed bliss and unbroken fellowship. Make this one day* a day of constant awareness that my God is everlasting.

I cannot count the days that remain, but I can make the days that remain count. Let them count under the light of eternity. Let them count as vessels to be filled with grace and emptied in love. Let them count with things that can never be counted or priced or bought or sold. Let them count in loving surrender, obedient service, and cheerful faith. Let them count for You!

This one day! Others will surely follow . . . until *one day* I am with You . . . never to know the lengthening shadows of the setting sun or the long hours of a starless night. Until then, I would possess by faith the victory of God-given and God-filled everlasting life,

Through Christ my Lord, Amen.

MOVING ON IN THE LIFE OF PRAYER

So we should rise each day with the prayer that for THIS ONE DAY in THIS ONE LIFETIME we will be an instrument God can use, a vessel He can fill, a servant He can send, a window through which the light of His love and truth can shine. That is having a heart of wisdom. That is the way to rejoice and be glad all our earthly days—numbered though they may be. Prayer fills our hearts with God's steadfast love that we may rejoice and be glad all our days until there are no more days. No more days?

"When we've been there ten thousand years,
Bright shining as the sun,
We've NO LESS DAYS to sing God's praise,
Than when we'd first begun!"

Day 46

ARE WE REMEMBERING GOD?

"Desire of [my] soul is . . . to the remembrance of thee" (Isaiah 26:8, KJV).

Read: **Isaiah 26;** Psalm 63:6; Jonah 2:7; Zechariah 10:7.

WHAT IS GOD SAYING?

God wants to be remembered. We need to remember God. In remembering God we go back to our roots. In remembering God, we find perfect peace. In remembering God, we can feel the rock beneath our feet, even though the rushing currents of the world and sometimes the swirling waters of our own mind may almost make us lose our footing. God gives us this promise in this very chapter. "Thou dost keep him in perfect peace, whose mind is stayed on thee [who remembers thee], because he trusts in thee. Trust in the LORD for ever [always remember the Lord], for the LORD GOD is an everlasting rock" (Isaiah 26:3-4).

HOW DOES THIS APPLY TO US?

When are we most likely *not* to remember God? Isn't it when we feel we are making it on our own? When things are going *our* way? When there is plenty of money to buy plenty of goods and have plenty of fun? Yet, putting our whole trust in this kind of material satisfaction is the very thing that leads to spiritual emptiness. Material abundance of itself cannot satisfy the hungers of our soul. What really matters is remembering God. Remembering that God has made us for Himself and there is no rest, as Augustine long ago reminded us, until we rest in Him. Remembering God is the key to real satisfaction. Remembering God is the secret of a holy and wholesome life. Remembering God is the way to forget the gnawing anxieties that nibble away at the happiness which others imagine they ought to have. Remembering God is the real desire of those who seek first the Kingdom of God. Forgetting God is the real mistake of those who sell their souls for a few moments of imagined happiness and a few ounces of fool's gold. Let us remember God and live. In prayer let us remember God and discover more joy and inclination to remember others. Remembering God. There is no better door into the closet of prayer.

Pray with Me

Lord, in You there is the perfect mingling of love and light. All my hope is in Your steadfast love. All my future glows with the light of Your perfect plan.

Yet I often forget. When life is drained of its enthusiasm and joy, it is always because I have forgotten to remember You.

Remembering You is the desire of my soul because it is the only way that life makes sense. Remembering You is the desire of my soul because it is the tide that lifts me from the rocks of despair. Remembering You is the desire of my soul because it is the wind that fills my soul with hope.

At the beginning of this day I desire—I choose—to remember You. When I desire to remember You I am led toward green pastures of pure delight. When I desire to remember You I am led away from the pointless pastimes that mask a vast emptiness and lead to no future but death.

When I desire to remember You, I am lifted above all anxieties and annoyances. I am even lifted above tragic disappointments which can only be seen in true perspective from the silent heights of Your holy will.

When I desire to remember You, I am able to forget all competing desires.

Fill me with Your perfect love and light. Let them also filter down into the sub-conscious part of my life where desires, like hidden seeds, have taken root before they are known for what they are.

Then, eternal Father, I shall find that *all* the desire of my soul is *always* to the remembrance of You. In Christ, Amen.

MOVING ON IN THE LIFE OF PRAYER

Let us come to prayer with this one paramount thought, "The desire of my soul is to the remembrance of God." Let us keep that desire uppermost through every moment of prayer. Let it irradiate our whole being and be the one all-sufficient light in the closet when the door is closed. Then, when the door is open, still remembering God, we will find it easier and more satisfying to go out among men to remember their needs—not only in prayer but with practical help. That is prayer at its best.

Day 47

HOW TO STAY STRONG

"Be strong . . . for the LORD Your God is with you wherever you go" *(Joshua 1:9).*

Read: **Joshua 1;** Genesis 28:15; 1 Corinthians 16:13; Ephesians 6:13; Philippians 4:13.

WHAT IS GOD SAYING?

Upon Joshua's shoulders fell the responsibility of leading the nation of Israel across the Jordan. He was to lead them until they possessed what God had promised. It meant years of constant battle. It was the task of transforming desert-weary pilgrims into battle-ready warriors. They longed for rest after all their hardships but what faced them were more hardships. The Promised Land was bristling with enemies. Strong leadership was required. Even Joshua, a natural born leader, under those circumstances had to draw upon strength beyond himself. It took more than wisdom—something all leaders must have as they stand at the helm and make vital decisions. It also took courage to carry out these decisions against overwhelming odds. To be strong and courageous was the need *and* the command. For courage he could draw upon one single, consistent, and unfailing Source: "For the Lord your God will be with you wherever you go."

HOW DOES THIS APPLY TO US?

Most of us know what it means to face overwhelming responsibilities. Our first reaction might be to turn and run. We look around for the nearest exit. "Let someone else take the heat. Besides, I'm not strong enough and I've had all I can take." All this may be true when we look inwardly at our own resources—or outwardly at own past record. But for the Christian an all-important resource has been added: "I can do all things through Christ who strengthens me" (Philippians 4:13). It is the same Lord. He was with Joshua to make him a leader against deeply entrenched and determined enemies. He IS with us to make us "more than conquerors."

Pray with Me

Loving Father, to "be strong" is the natural condition of the spiritual person. It is not being boastful about one's own attainment in the present. It is not a distant goal to be achieved through tireless effort and determination. "Being strong" is the natural condition of those with whom the Lord dwells.

When You are with me, I am strong to accept the heavy burden and to attempt the impossible task.

When You are with me, I am strong to overcome the great Deceiver and to deny myself such things as might lead others astray. I am strong to remove the seeds of faithless personal license with purity that cares and dares.

When You are with me, I am strong to wage the good fight. I am strong to raise the hand and voice against evil within me and around me. I am strong to love the unlovable. I am strong to help the unthankful. I am strong to be what a citizen of Heaven ought to be.

I rejoice in this strength for it is not something I have achieved or earned. It is always and only Your gift. It is the result of Your life in me.

So I thank You for Your presence, O God. I claim it as my possession and Your glory. Your presence is the treasure in this earthen vessel. The transcendent power belongs to You, not to me.

To the praise of Your strong Son, whose Name is Immortal Love, Amen.

MOVING ON IN THE LIFE OF PRAYER

As we continue in prayer, God may make some unpleasant task or some towering responsibility irrefutably clear. But we need not be terrified. We must not be discouraged. The God who calls is the God who enables. He who is with us in prayer, goes out with us in service. Whenever we pray, He is there. Wherever we go, He is there. Prayer grows strong on the basis of His presence. And we go strong on the basis of His being with us WHEREVER we go.

Day 48

ANYTHING IN GOD'S PLACE?

"Idols . . . which cannot either see or hear or walk" (Revelation 9:20).

Read: **Revelation 9:13-21;** Deuteronomy 11:16; Isaiah 42:8; Jeremiah 10:2-10.

WHAT IS GOD SAYING?

In Revelation 9 God dispenses His wrath in judgment on unrepentant sinners. It is not a pretty picture. For all the agony of these visitations—the sky darkened with smoke from the Abyss; and out of the smoke, locusts, coming like horses prepared for battle and with the sting of scorpions; horses breathing fire, smoke, and sulfur, powerful enough to kill a third of mankind. And still the rest of mankind did not refrain from worshiping their idols. It is incredible that, against the backdrop of such terrible punishment by God, men should cling to their idols instead of returning to God. Such can be the power of anything that takes the place of God!

HOW DOES THIS APPLY TO US?

When God has our first love, idols can exert no authority over us. When God does not have first place, almost anything else *can* take over. That is why the Third Commandment is so important and cannot be ignored without detriment and finally disaster to our souls. Everyone worships something. As we come to prayer let us ask ourselves what is getting more of our devotion, demanding more of our energy, claiming more of our resources than God. That is an idol. Any idol, any thing, any relationship, any love, any ambition and desire, any friendship that comes between us and God is something we must pray about. Because until it is removed and conquered in the grace of God, no prayer can be truly effectual. Let there be nothing left of our idols when we pray. Then see what new blessings God can give us to take their place.

Pray with Me

Dear Lord, there are times when I have been blind to the sure leading of Your truth and deaf to the pure pleadings of Your love. I have squandered time—Your precious gift. I have wandered in paths of my own choosing. I have done this knowing that such paths would lead me away from You and the life You have planned for me.

Help me to call anything that is less than Your best an idol—a pitiful substitute which can neither see my need nor hear my prayer nor talk to me in answering love.

Give me the wisdom to recognize and the courage to deal with any idol that takes Your place on the altar of my heart. Let me be done with unseeing idols that cannot see my hands uplifted in prayer. Let me have no confidence in unhearing idols that cannot listen for the longings of my heart. Let me set aside uncaring idols that cannot walk with me, as You do, in a fellowship of growing light and joy.

Idols can neither see nor hear nor walk. But there is comfort in knowing that You see my heart's need even when it is too complex for me to understand. You hear my prayer even when it is too deep for me to utter. You walk with me even when the last friend on earth may be gone from my side.

Help me to follow Christ in the awareness of Your seeing, in the confidence of Your hearing, and in the fellowship of Your walking. In such a walk there is real fulfillment and endless peace.

In Jesus' Name, Amen.

MOVING ON IN THE LIFE OF PRAYER

Coming to God in prayer is the time and the place to deal with idols. In prayer we recognize all which is not part of His perfect plan for our lives. In prayer, we see truly and hear plainly and "walk in the light as He is in the light." Idols cannot see or hear or walk—or care. In prayer God removes the idols we can't surrender. In prayer we come to One who sees and hears and cares.

Day 49

THE OFFERING THAT PLEASES GOD

"It is a pleasing odor, an offering by fire to the LORD" (Exodus 29:18).

Read: **Exodus 29:1-18,** 30:6-7; Romans 12:1; Philippians 4:18b; Hebrews 13:15-16; 1 Peter 2:5.

WHAT IS GOD SAYING?

Moses has been to Mt. Sinai and has received the Law. We come now to that part of the Exodus where, under God's guidance, specific legislation and organization are needed if the nation of Israel is to survive the long journey to freedom. They were near Mt. Sinai, as far from the Promised Land as they would ever be. Having been delivered from Egypt's bondage and now enduring conditions that would be, for a long time, difficult at best, they must remain close to Jehovah and obedient to His commands. They must know that God is pleased when there is sincerity and loving devotion.

HOW DOES THIS APPLY TO US?

The offering by fire with its pleasing odor has relevance to us. It reminds us that in the life of prayer, as it is joined to the life of service, there should be the offering of our whole selves to God. God must have it all. Nothing less than everything is pleasing to Him. It is symbolic of a past totally surrendered in order that God might make of us and in us a new creation. It means, "Here is my present life which is pliable enough through the fire of fervent love for You, Lord, to make it into a tool You can use." The seal of John Calvin has a pictorial representation of what takes place when we come in this present moment to prayer, bringing an offering by fire with its pleasing odor to the Lord. It is a man's hand holding in the upturned palm a heart engulfed by flame, an offering by fire to the Lord.

Pray with Me

O God, You are pleased with a heart that burns with hatred for sin and glows with desire for righteousness. Let there be in all the offerings I bring to You a burning hatred for what You hate and a fervent love for what You love.

Keep me from just going through empty formalities in worship. Help me to turn from the mere display of religious correctness. May I not fall into the trap of mechanical preciseness in well-grooved ritual, which has neither feeling nor faith.

Help me instead to do the simple thing that helps. I want to perform the kind deed that heals. I want to be ready to speak the compassionate word that may stir long-dead embers of hope in a weary heart.

Help me to remember Him who was always lifting burdens and healing bodies and igniting hope in discouraged hearts. Help me to choose costly involvement to comfortable detachment. Help me to choose fervent faith rather than listless doubt. Help me to choose agonizing prayer rather than neglectful preoccupation. Help me to choose the risk of failure that comes with loving over the guarantee of nothing that comes with indifference.

So I would make an offering by fire to You, O Lord, even the fire of a believing and grateful heart. I want no part of the insipid life that knows only the duty of an offering and misses the beauty of an offering made by love's fire to the loving God of all.

Through Jesus Christ, Amen.

MOVING ON IN THE LIFE OF PRAYER

If we want to be continually blessed in the life of prayer, we must never think of coming to God in these quiet moments merely as in a ritual laid on us as a duty. Ritual has its place in historic Christianity and also as a unifying factor when Christians worship together. But prayer at its best focuses on the beauty of God's love and not on a believer's duty in going through the proper motions. God finds the odor of a heart burning with faith and love far more pleasing. If we pray like that we will see life unfold with meaning ahead of us and all around us.

Day 50

AVOIDING DETOURS
AND DEAD-ENDS

". . . He went on backsliding in the way of his own heart. I have seen his ways, but I will heal him" (Isaiah 57:17, 18).

Read: **Isaiah 57;** Matthew 24:12; Luke 8:13, 11:24-26; Galatians 4:9; Revelation 2:4.

WHAT IS GOD SAYING?

Strong with the passion of a jealous God, Isaiah 57 declares what happens when people turn from God to follow the empty paths of disobedience and sin. "You have made a bargain for yourself with them" (v. 8). In other words, your birthright of freedom, your dignity as a believer, your riches as an heir of salvation have all but gone—and for a bargain price. This is the curse of backsliding. God cannot watch this tragic waste occur without letting us know He still cares. He wants us to regain the stature, the peace, and the riches that belong to those who walk with Him in the paths of righteousness. Therefore, although the "bargain sale" soul is destined with the wicked to become like a restless, tossing sea whose "waters toss up mire and dirt" (v. 20), and for whom "there is no peace" (v. 21), nevertheless God, in His longsuffering love, has seen the places where we have made the wrong turn and chosen the wrong way, and *He will heal us.*

HOW DOES THIS APPLY TO US?

There is no doubt that all of us have sold ourselves for a bargain at some time or other. We may not call it backsliding.

Some ecclesiastical wag has said the "Methodists preach backsliding while Presbyterians practice it." It is certainly true that we cannot backslide out of the Kingdom. Those who are once saved may fall, as on the deck of an ocean liner, and even sustain serious injury. But that is not the same as falling off an ocean liner. Whatever position we hold, we cannot come to prayer without honestly confessing that all our ways have not always been pleasing to God. But once confessed, healing begins and the door to effective prayer swings open.

Pray with Me

Lord, this fits me.

The way of my own heart leads to a dead-end. The way of my own heart leads through detours of vanity and frustration to discouragement and death. When the thoughts of my heart are not under the restraint of Your holy will, lust rides on wild horses toward a goal that, like the desert mirage, always beckons but never satisfies.

Yet, Lord, in Your love and knowledge, You have seen my ways. The most jealously guarded secret in the darkest chamber of my heart is known to You. So I don't need to pretend anymore. I don't need to justify myself. You know the way of my own heart. You are not willing that I should perish in that way.

Thanks be to God who, knowing me best, loves me most. Thanks be to God that beyond the release that comes from knowing I am known, there is the peace of knowing I may be healed.

The ways of my own heart lead to no destination but failure and to no future but death. Yet these ways, even the ways of my own heart, have been healed by the Light whose substance is holiness and whose energy is redeeming love.

Because of this encouragement, I abandon the ways of my heart and choose the ways of Yours.

In the Name of Him who is the true and living Way, Amen.

MOVING ON IN THE LIFE OF PRAYER

The curse of backsliding is emptiness, frustration, and hindered prayers. The cure of backsliding is knowing that God still cares and will heal those who are truly sorry for their sins. Power in prayer returns and continues to be ours when we know that God, having seen our ways, wants to heal us. In love God sees OUR WAYS and heals them. In prayer we see HIS WAYS and choose His way above all others. His ways are ways of health and peace, fulfillment and joy . . . and answered prayer.

Day 51

HEALING FOR ALL

"Is there no balm in Gilead? Is there no physician there?" (Jeremiah 8:22).

Read: **Jeremiah 8:18-9:3,** 30:10-22, 46:11; Matthew 9:12-18.

WHAT IS GOD SAYING?

God yearns for the return of His people. He longs to welcome them into His arms and heal their wounds. "The turtledove, swallow, and crane keep the time of their coming; but my people know not the ordinance of the LORD . . . from prophet to priest every one deals falsely. They have healed the wound of my people lightly, saying 'Peace, peace,' when there is no peace" (Jeremiah 8:7, 10-11). They are putting Band-Aids on a cancer. Find a doctor who knows the real problem and who will treat the sickness. "Is there no balm in Gilead? Is there no physician there?" Such was the lament of Jeremiah.

HOW DOES THIS APPLY TO US?

It is the cry of many sin-sickened souls. Admitting the symptoms of sickness and making the decision to seek a remedy are the first steps in the direction of a cure. We have healing for the soul's most loathsome disease. We have a Physician who cares and cures. He knows and wants us to see that Band-Aids won't do when radical surgery is indicated. Trying to talk ourselves out of sickness into health or thinking better thoughts or turning over a thousand new leaves will not deal with the problem. Jesus took the radical step at Calvary. There He went to the root of the problem: sin, and the death it brings. Hear and trust the great words of Peter: "He himself bore our sins in his body on the tree, that we might die to sin and live to righteousness. By his wounds *you have been healed*" (1 Peter 2:24).

Come to prayer with the assurance that the greatest balm, the love of Jesus, can heal the greatest sickness, sin. That is the foundation of prevailing prayer. No problem too great, no burden too heavy, no situation too hopeless, no loved one too far gone. There IS a Balm in Gilead. There IS a Physician there.

Pray with Me

O God, from many discouraged hearts this cry has risen. In other days, it has risen from mine.

What could possibly reach the depth of my need? It was beyond the reach of human understanding and help. Who could heal my sickness? Who could lay the soothing salve to a troubled mind and a distressed soul?

Yes, Lord, these questions have raced unanswered through my mind. But now You have shown to me that there is a Balm in Gilead and there is a Physician there. There is healing. There is a Healer.

The Cross is healing and Christ is the Healer. There and by Him my soul finds relief. There and by Him hope comes like the dawn of a new day. There and by Him I find strength and direction to walk in a new way.

Stolen pleasures turned to pain have been turned again to the holy pleasure of walking in Your light. Insistence on personal liberties have been turned again to that mature freedom that comes from obeying Christ. Pride turned to humiliation has been turned again to humility that conquers, because its strength is not in self but in the Savior.

So I am delivered from the sickness of disloyalty and pride by the healing and the Healer of Calvary. For this I am thankful today. By this I can face tomorrow. About this my ransomed soul will sing forever.

In the Name of the Healer and by the grace of His healing, Amen.

MOVING ON IN THE LIFE OF PRAYER

Let us come to prayer in the confidence of knowing that the great Physician can put the Balm of His healing love on every wound. Trust in His wisdom and accept His remedy. We will pray with assurance about our own needs *and* the ones we suspect or know in others. Prayer is an avenue of healing. Prayer is the path that leads to the Balm of Gilead and to the great Physician.

Day 52

MATURE THINKING

"*. . . Be babes in evil, but in thinking be mature*" *(1 Corinthians 14:20).*

Read: **1 Corinthians 14:6-20,** 13:11; Ephesians 4:12-15; 1 Peter 2:2.

WHAT IS GOD SAYING?

This portion of God's Word brings us into the center of an old controversy—still a source of division and misunderstanding among Christians. Paul does not deny the gift of speaking in tongues as a valid evidence of the Holy Spirit's presence and power. It is a way of speaking to God and sensing the glow of spiritual well-being as one "utters mysteries" in the Spirit. Other Christians have just as full and rich an experience of Christ and the blessings of His Spirit without ever speaking in tongues. Paul stresses here that their gift of preaching in understandable words and living a life of Christ-inspired love may be a better gift. In 1 Corinthians 12:31 he clearly says, "But earnestly desire the higher gifts. And I will show you a still more excellent way." Then there follows the greatest passage on *agape* love ever written, chapter 13.

Now, in this fourteenth chapter, he stresses again the superior gift of speaking words that make sense to others. Those who are mature in Christ do not attach so much importance to the possession of the spectacular manifestations of the Spirit as they do to building up the Church (v. 12). The apostle calls all this contention about peripheral differences childish (v. 20).

How Does This Apply to Us?

This heated debate in the Corinthian church was centered around the place of tongues in the Christian community. But now Paul writes something that is much more general in its application. As we look to God for guidance through the writings of Paul, we learn that Christians can be childish (not childlike) about many things in which they should be mature. At the same time, they can be mature about some things in which they should still be as children. Evil is one such thing. When it comes to evil we ought to be as babes. This simply means that we are to be more aware of what is good and beautiful and true and give no quarter to what is evil. It is not that, with childlike innocence, we don't know that evil exists or what evil can do. It is just that as childlike innocence does not give any thought or time to what is evil, so when our thinking matures, we give our best energies to what is constructive and none to what is destructive. Mature in thinking, we accentuate the positive commandments of God. We give priority to God's will. We emphasize the purity of God's love, received and shared. We discard the things in life that do not count for God, as a child has no more use for a broken and outgrown toy. Pray for discernment. Pray for the power to discard all evil and grow up to the measure of the stature of the fullness of Christ (Ephesians 4:13).

Pray with Me

Like a Father, with loving firmness, Lord, You intend to bring me to a mature faith. I thank You for Your patience in this long and difficult task.

I especially ask for Your forgiveness as I seem determined to repay evil for evil. In this I am quite mature. I am skillful at vindicating myself. I am quick to repay in kind the slightest injury to pride. I am alert in the defense of my prejudices. I am insensitive to the offenses I give and very keen to feel the offenses I receive.

O Lord of Calvary, may I learn to see and to feel and to react in the spirit that was Yours upon the Cross. There You repaid evil with good, anger with love, injustice with mercy, and offense with forgiveness. Through Your example there and through the grace that always comes from the fountain of Your suffering love, help me to be understanding.

Let this be my constant prayer: "He must increase, I must decrease." Let that really be my prayer. I have often read it. I have often said it. But have I really understood it? Have I really meant it?

When I can say that prayer and mean it, I will no longer be mature in evil and childish in thinking and understanding. Instead, as Your image is formed in me, I shall have the quiet strength and joyful service which belong to those who are mature in thinking and who, in evil, have neither skill nor desire.

In the Name of Him who is all understanding and no malice, Amen.

MOVING ON IN THE LIFE OF PRAYER

Prayer grows in power as we become more mature in Christ. "Speaking the truth in love, we are to grow up in every way into him who is the head, into Christ" (Ephesians 4:15). That is the way to communicate with others. It is also the way to communicate with God. Let Him know that we know the truth about ourselves. Then trust His love to bring us to ever fuller maturity in life and in the life of prayer.

Day 53

GUARDED FROM THE PAST AND IN THE PRESENT

"You shall not do as they do in the land of Egypt, where you dwelt, and you shall not do as they do in the land of Canaan, to which I am bringing you" (Leviticus 18:3).

Read: **Leviticus 18:1-5;** 2 Kings 17:14-15; Psalm 19:11; 2 Peter 3:17-18.

WHAT IS GOD SAYING?

In Leviticus 18 God warns the children of Israel against unlawful sexual relations. Both the country in which Israel had lived and the land toward which they moved through the long years of the Exodus were marked by sexual license. Like fire out of control, there was potential to take something intended for life and good and turn it into a thing of wild and wide-ranging destruction. There must be no compromise. Other nations may be defiled. In their own eyes their detestable attitudes and actions may not seem all that bad. But within these customs are the seeds of their own destruction. God wants to preserve His people from disaster. He lays down rules intrinsic to the well-being of any society. He does so because of His kindness and love, for "in keeping them there is great reward" (Psalm 19:11).

HOW DOES THIS APPLY TO US?

Recognizing how easy it is to succumb to the accepted customs of a godless society, God warns His people against going with the crowd, considering something right because "everyone is doing it." Contrary to the slogan of the Doughboys during World War I, "Fifty million Frenchmen CAN be wrong." It may be right by contemporary standards and still be wrong for the people of God.

This applies to more than sexual license. It has to do with any of God's commandments which become harder and harder to follow when everyone else is marching to a different drumbeat. "For the gate is wide and the way is easy, that leads to destruction, and those who enter by it are many" (Matthew 7:13).

As we come to prayer, let us ask God to guard us from the past and the present. Let us rest in the assurance that He always has the best for us now . . . and on into a future that is bright with His promises and rich with His blessings.

Pray with Me

Dear Lord, Shepherd of my soul, *guard me from the past.*

Let Your forgiveness, like a fortress, hold back the flood of guilt. Let Your grace, like a shield, protect me from the fiery darts of a restless conscience.

I have dwelt in Egypt. I have known the false security of being enslaved to that world. But, redeemed by Your love, I would no longer gear my life to what "they do in the land of Egypt."

O living Lord, *guard me in the present.*

Let my fellowship with You be so real that even as I walk through these present days and in this present place, I may not give in to the evil that is around me. What good is it to be delivered from Egypt only to be enslaved to Canaan? What advantage is there in being freed from the past only to be in bondage to the present? So I would not do as "they do in the land of Canaan."

Since I have discovered Your power that saves from the past, I would also affirm Your power to keep in the present. As I have been delivered, so I am being preserved. As I have left Egypt, so I am kept in Canaan. Deliverance is the gift of Your forgiving grace. Preservation is the blessing of Your living presence.

May I be conformed to the image of Your Son. Then I shall be saved from the past, guarded in the present, and destined for a future more beautiful than words can tell, more wonderful than the mind can understand.

In the power of Your love and by the authority of Your Name, Amen.

MOVING ON IN THE LIFE OF PRAYER

Let God guard us from the past. We accept His forgiveness for mistakes. We pray as if they didn't exist. "I, I am He who blots out your transgressions for my own sake, and I will not remember your sins" (Isaiah 43:25). We find freedom to claim God's blessings not on the basis of our worthiness but on the basis of His grace. We trust God for all our needs in the present. We can be free to move into the future unburdened and unhampered and, walking in the light as He is in the light, we have fellowship with one another and with God in whom there is no darkness at all (see 1 John 1:5-9).

Day 54

SOMETIMES THE LORD SENDS AN ADVERSARY

"And the LORD raised up an adversary against Solomon . . ." (1 Kings 11:14).

Read: **1 Kings 11;** Deuteronomy 28:47-50, 31:15-18; Isaiah 54:11-17.

WHAT IS GOD SAYING?

God gives us a choice. Solomon, wise beyond all of his time, allowed himself to be drawn into folly. He followed the pleadings of his foreign wives and strayed far from God. They made it easy . . . but *he* made the choice. And whenever we make a choice that interrupts our walk with God, He may send an adversary to bring us back.

HOW DOES THIS APPLY TO US?

When we recognize that all of God's providence is filtered through love, we know how to accept and face the adversary which He allows or sends. It would be sometimes unbearable and beyond explanation if we did not know that the hard times and the obstacles thrown up in our path are all because He loves us. God wants us to stay close to Him and true to Him. We should remember that even our adversaries are under the control of God. They can do us no harm. They can only make us pause to think. They can only force us to remember that God has a better plan in which, over all enemies and against all opposition, we will be and even now are "more than conquerors through him who loved us" (Romans 8:37). We are fortified as we pray with the knowledge that "no weapon that is fashioned against [us] shall prosper" (Isaiah 54:17).

Pray with Me

Father, I am glad to own You as the Lord of the way I take. You are also God over all the obstacles that seem to block that way. For my good You can either remove the adversary or raise him up. For Your own good reasons, You can either put him out of the way or in the way.

In love that cares so much and according to wisdom that knows all about me and all that is about me, You can give me freedom or friction, rest or wrestling, leisure or labor.

Help me to trust all the more in Your wise providence because I see it filtered through Your love. When You raise up the adversary, may I recognize and submit to this as all-seeing love and not as blind wrath.

I ask that You will make the rough places smooth and the crooked paths straight. I do not ask for steep and thorny ways. But when in Your wisdom I must be guided back to Your high purpose by pressures I would not gladly accept, may I recognize Your Lordship even over my adversaries. When I find myself in the midst of events I can scarcely understand, may I recognize Your Lordship even over my adversaries. When I am called upon to bear painful crosses I would never have chosen, may I recognize Your Lordship even over my adversaries.

Because I am saved for all eternity and because You have a perfect plan for my life, adversaries can do me no harm. They can only turn me to the higher good that You have ordained. I am a part of Your wholeness in which there can be neither mistake nor imperfection, neither fault nor flaw, neither blame nor blemish.

In the Name of Him who has conquered my greatest adversary through His greatest victory, even Jesus Christ, Amen.

MOVING ON IN THE LIFE OF PRAYER

In prayer God prepares a table for us in the presence of our enemies. They may be meant to bring us back to God but they are powerless to do any harm if our trust is in the wisdom, the providence, and the invincible power of God. He is almighty and all-loving. The power of prayer is to make us calm in the presence of every adversity and confident that all our adversaries are meant to bring us closer to God and to His ideal for our life. Through all circumstances and in spite of all circumstances, prayer gives us quiet assurance that Christ is still on the throne.

Day 55

CARRYING SELF AS A BURDEN

"*. . . A burden to myself . . .*" (Job 7:20, KJV).

Read: **Job 7;** Proverbs 5:22; Romans 7:21-25, 8:12.

WHAT IS GOD SAYING?

There are two readings for Job 7:20. The later translations based upon ancient scribal tradition and the Septuagint give one meaning, while most Masoretic texts give an opposite meaning. The former has Job asking of God, "Why have you made me Your target? Have I become a burden TO YOU?" But the one we are using for this exercise in prayer, says, "Why have You set me as a mark against You, so that I am a burden to myself?"

The segment of the verse we are using does reflect a feeling often found among believers. We do in fact become "a burden to ourselves."

How Does This Apply to Us?

Christians bear many burdens. Some of the burdens are meant to make us stronger in spiritual warfare. Some of the burdens have to do with a desire for the spiritual health and well-being of others. Paul had a burden for the salvation of Israel. He refers to it as "great sorrow and unceasing anguish in my heart . . . for the sake of . . . my kinsmen by race" (Romans 9:2-3). Then Paul instructs us "to bear one another's burdens, and so fulfil the law of Christ" (Galatians 6:2). There is one burden that no Christian should continue to bear: the burden of himself. With Pilgrim in *Pilgrim's Progress* that burden is loosened from our back when we come to the Cross. The great thing about allowing Christ to rid us of our burden of self is that we are then set free to bear the burdens of others. Prayer becomes more and more meaningful as we are more and more relieved of the burden of ourselves.

Pray with Me

Loving Father, through Jesus Christ you have shown Yourself willing to bear all my burdens. Forgive me for the lack of faith that makes myself a burden to me as well as to you.

You have encouraged me in Your Word to cast all my cares upon You. Forgive me that I am so willing to hold back as my own special care the heaviest burden of all, myself.

You have called upon me to be rid of this burden. You have called me to leave the crushing weight of sin at the foot of the Cross. You have called me to leave the dark shadows of disappointment and sorrow at the door of the Empty Tomb. You have called me to leave all physical hungers behind me in the closet of prayer.

You have willed that I should be free. You have broken the captive's chains. You have opened the prison door. You have told me to walk out into the freshness and beauty and joy of a new day, a new life. But in a strangely contrary way, I refuse to leave the cell of self and the chains of my own forging. I insist on taking the burden of myself upon myself.

O Spirit of God, I want to be responsive to Your leading until, in the freedom of faith, I shall become a blessing to others and no longer a burden to myself.

May this day find me closer to Him who said, "He who loses his life for my sake shall find it." Closer to Him, ever closer, until the touch of His love shall bring a flame to my heart that will remove the useless burden of myself. Closer to Him, ever closer, until by the touch of His love, I shall blaze for others a path of hope and good cheer.

In the Name of Him whose love both liberates and lifts and who bore all my burdens on His cross, Amen.

MOVING ON IN THE LIFE OF PRAYER

If we are only concerned about ourselves, we have one burden . . . and it can be a heavy one. If we see beyond ourselves in the life of prayer and begin to be concerned with others, we will have many burdens and they will all seem light. It is good, in prayer, to let Jesus take the burden of ourselves off our shoulders, so we can proceed directly and in love to the many burdens of others.

Day 56

BE SURE TO HONOR GOD

"But the God in whose hand is your breath, . . . you have not honored" *(Daniel 5:23).*

Read: **Daniel 5;** John 5:44; 1 Peter 1:25.

WHAT IS GOD SAYING?

Our passage in Daniel ushers us into a scene of lavish splendor where all the guests were reminded of the greatness of their young and sensual king. That was the real reason for the banquet, and if the king reveled in being admired, who were they to deny him? He was a fool and had not learned from the great humiliation of his unrepentant grandfather, Nebuchadnezzar. Belshazzar was young and vain. Fools rush in! To impress the guests he ordered that the vessels, stolen from "the temple of the house of God" by Nebuchadnezzar, be brought in to adorn the tables. How the gold and silver sparkled! How the guests were impressed! Why not go all out and drink wine to the idols out of these sacred vessels? That would be the crowning touch. He had pushed his peacock strutting over the edge. The crowd was impressed but Belshazzar was sealing his sudden doom with every sip that passed over his drunken lips. Daniel, with characteristic courage, confronts him with the painful, piercing, sobering truth, "But you have lifted up yourself against the Lord of heaven; and the vessels of his house have been brought in before you, and you and your lords, your wives, and your concubines have drunk wine from them; and you have praised the gods of silver and gold, of bronze, iron, wood, and stone, which do not see or hear or know, but God in whose hand is your breath, and whose are all your ways, you have not honored" (Daniel 5:23). Like the fool who kept on multiplying his barns in the New Testament, that very night Belshazzar's soul was required of him. God controlled every breath he took, and still he did not honor Him.

How Does This Apply to Us?

The breath of life is the gift of the Creator-God. Belshazzar had it as a gift and he defied the honor of the One who gave it. But it is not only vain young rulers of long ago in faraway places who must honor God. Every person alive owes his or her next breath to God. God is the Source of life. Let us make Him the end, the reason, the purpose of our living as well. The Shorter Catechism puts it well: "Man's chief end is to glorify God and to enjoy Him forever." That is the foundation of prayer offered and the certainty of prayer answered.

Pray with Me

Lord, my life seems remote from this story of the proud and willful Belshazzar. Yet I must learn *now*, as he had to learn *then*, that every breath I take is in Your hand and living calls for just one thing . . . to honor God.

One word is written across every thought that rises in the interest of self-praise. One word is written across every syllable spoken in wounded self-defense. One word is written across every deed meant to raise the level of self-importance. That word is . . . *tekel:* "You are weighed in the balance and found wanting."

Each breath comes only because Your hand undergirds with power and reaches out in mercy. Let me not play the fool as did the blind and wicked king of old. Let me choose the course of wisdom. Let me put the accent on grateful love and praise. I disavow the error and emptiness of all that does not lead to You. I affirm the beauty and truth of all that comes from You.

You are the Source of Life. You are the Reason for Life. When I make the Source of Life the End of Life, I begin to live. Until then I am only an existence on the way to becoming an encumbrance.

Since my very breath is in Your hand, O living God, let my whole life be to the praise of the glory of Your grace.

Since my breath itself is in Your hand, it shall be used to voice Your praise. A heart that gladly understands now willingly obeys.

For the sake of Jesus Christ, my Lord, Amen.

MOVING ON IN THE LIFE OF PRAYER

We all pray that we may not be weighed in the balance and found wanting. Let us honor God by listening to His Word, by believing His Word, and by being doers of His Word. If we so honor God, our prayers will not be found wanting and our life will be blessed more abundantly than we could ask or think.

Day 57

FAITH IN ACTION

"*. . . That he may teach us his ways and we may walk in his paths*" (*Micah 4:2*).

Read: **Micah 4;** Psalm 25:4-5, 26:1-3, 86:11; 1 John 1:7.

WHAT IS GOD SAYING?

Micah was a prophet who had little to do with the upper echelon of society. He would have been all thumbs if he had prophesied in the royal courts of the land. Still, he had his own brand of courage. He spoke to the common man and to the great number of people who lived close to the land. They had their needs, too, and they were also mired in the social sins of their day. Micah's voice rang out with unflinching directness. He was a contemporary of Isaiah in Jerusalem and Hosea in Israel. As he says in Micah 3:8, his credentials were valid. "I am filled with power, with the Spirit of the LORD, and with justice and might." But Micah keeps his brave and distasteful messages about God's judgment on sin brief. He loves to dwell on and expand the message of hope. And that brings us to Micah 4:2: "Come, let us go up to the mountain of the LORD, to the house of the God of Jacob; that he may teach us his ways and we may walk in his paths."

HOW DOES THIS APPLY TO US?

A fresh message of hope soars from these ancient words. We, too, have constant need of being taught in the ways of God. After being taught (even while being taught), we must convert that knowledge into doing. Being taught in the ways of God is a good first step. But as with all "first steps," they must be followed by other steps—and all in the direction of God's will. That is where prayer comes in as the catalyst which converts faith into action, truth into substance, learning into doing, understanding into realization.

Pray with Me

Yours to teach, Lord. Mine to follow! Let my mind be open to receive Your truth. Let my heart be open to respond to Your love. But let there be more. Give me grace to walk in Your ways.

To know Your ways is good. To go in Your ways is better. I can know the rightness of Your commandments with the mind. I can be impressed with the beauty of Your creation. I can be humbled by mercies that never fail. But until I am willing to walk in Your ways, I cannot know You truly. Faith is not receiving conviction. It is acting on that conviction. Faith is not knowing alone. It is knowing and going.

Give me, Lord, a faith like Abraham's. He knew the futility of trusting in idols. He was told that the living God had better things for him. In his mind he was convinced. Yet more was needed. He must leave his boyhood home and go out, "not knowing whither." He must answer the call of God with his feet. What he knew in his mind could not save him. Knowledge is good but not good enough.

Let my waiting heart be blessed with new understanding of Your perfect ways. Break down all barriers that would keep the clear shining of Your truth from flooding my being. You are the Source of all wisdom. Waiting on You with humility and openness I will be taught by Your promised and always present Holy Spirit.

Then, Lord, I will move out on what I know. I will trust You for all I do not and cannot know. Teach me that my mind may be loosed from ignorance and wasteful fear. Then lead me that I may bring Your love to others and in Your time be brought to Your heavenly Kingdom.

In the fullness of Christ's unfailing love, Amen.

MOVING ON IN THE LIFE OF PRAYER

Since in our span of years we will never take in the full spectrum of knowledge, we must move out on what we know. In prayerful listening and uncompromising response, God can take us where we are and lead us where we ought to be. To KNOW God's ways is good. To GO God's ways is better. That's faith in action. That's love in bloom. That's prayer at its triumphant best.

Day 58

GOD FAITHFULLY LEADS
THOSE WHO FAITHFULLY FOLLOW

"But my servant Caleb, because he has a different spirit and has followed me fully, I will bring into the land" (Numbers 14:24).

Read: **Numbers 13:26-14:25; 1 Corinthians 10:1-11.**

WHAT IS GOD SAYING?

Much of the record of the wilderness wanderings in Numbers indicates that this generation of the Exodus were a rebellious and complaining bunch. Their negative attitudes led to negative actions. God decreed that their many failures, spawned by unbelief, must be punished. There are so many examples in this account of what *not* to do. Caleb and Joshua are outstanding exceptions. Here were two men who, when the tide was running against them, believed God's Word and dared to follow Him fully. Caleb had a different spirit and rose to a different destiny. He and Joshua, following God faithfully, believing God totally, obeying God without excuses, were the only two men of their generation who entered the Promised Land.

HOW DOES THIS APPLY TO US?

In our desire for more effective prayer today, the example of Caleb and Joshua who followed God fully provides strong motivation. Prayer begins with fully hearing God's call. It continues with fully following the Spirit who gives us understanding of God's purpose and strength to carry it to completion despite all opposition. "Giants in the land!" the other spies wailed. "Compared to them we are grasshoppers." Graphic and persuasive comparison, unless we are looking beyond the giants to God over all. Henrietta Mears has a great comparison that provides a sure stepping-stone to success in praying. She compares the ten spies who wouldn't see it God's way and the two who did: "Like the ten, we can be pessimists; or like the two, optimists. Like the ten, we can put difficulties between us and God and say we are not able, or like the two, we can put God between the difficulties and us and say we are able."[1] Having Caleb's different spirit is the way to pray. We need never be

1. Henrietta C. Mears, *What the Bible Is All About,* (Glendale, Calif.: Regal Books, 1966) p. 61.

intimidated by those who say "under the circumstances" when we come to the Lord who is "over the circumstances."

Pray with Me

Great Shepherd of Israel, You faithfully lead those who faithfully follow. Your providence has never failed. Your mercies have never been exhausted.

I will not be afraid to have "a different spirit." The world seeks to press me into its mold. It wants to make me powerless in the paralyzing grip of conformity. The children of Israel wandered in the wilderness. They were pressured by fear . . . stampeded into folly . . . hounded by discouragement. I am also passing through a wilderness. The world is at enmity with God. For all its abundance, it is hollow. For all its panaceas, it is sick. For all its counsel, it is lost. The spirit of evil and fear and compromise may change its pattern but never its purpose.

Give me the courage of Caleb. He knew the same temptations and suffered the same discouragements as others in the wilderness. But he had a "different spirit." He followed You fully. He had no fear except that of doubting or disobeying God. He had the courage to be different.

Lord God of Caleb, let that "different spirit" surround me with insulating grace. Walking in the midst of follies, I will be wise. Walking in the valley of discouragement, I will have hope. Walking through the clouds of doubt, I will have faith.

You are the Source of that "different spirit." Give it to me, Lord, that I may glorify You and escape the peril and misery of conformity to this world,

In the Name of Him whose transforming power can accomplish all my heart desires and more, far more, Amen.

MOVING ON IN THE LIFE OF PRAYER

When prayer fades in its importance in our lives and we enter those dry spells of spiritual lethargy, it is usually because we have allowed ourselves to be conformed to this world. The "different spirit" that brought Caleb triumphantly through all difficulties to the promised end is the same different spirit we need to keep prayer alive and well all the days of our pilgrimage.

Day 59

THE PERSISTENCE OF TEMPTATION

"And when the devil had ended every temptation, he departed from him until an opportune time" (Luke 4:13).

Read: **Luke 4:1-13;** Hebrews 2:14-18, 4:15-16.

WHAT IS GOD SAYING?

Luke, the physician, looked with deep compassion into the physical and spiritual needs of man. It is logical that he should be the one who presents the Son of God as the perfect Man. The God-Man was in every respect tempted as we are, yet without sinning (Hebrews 2:18). Luke knew how humanity could fall prey to the lust of the flesh, to the pride of life, to the demands of immediate satisfaction for physical appetites. He was also aware that man has more than physical hungers. He saw all problems that come to us or that we bring on ourselves with a doctor's compassionate understanding. It is characteristic of the Gospel he wrote. He also knew that, man being what he is, temptations can return. In fact, they can come again and again. Victory over temptation and freedom from temptation are two different things. It was so for Jesus. It will be so for us.

HOW DOES THIS APPLY TO US?

Although we are continually exposed to temptations, we can be continually victorious over them. We can be easily discouraged if a temptation which we thought we had put to rest suddenly stirs to plague us again. But if we know that it *might* come again, that it probably *will* come again, and if we are equally confident that we can meet it in the strength of Jesus when it *does* come again, we will be better able to cope with temptation. Jesus "is able to save those who draw near to God through him, since he always lives to make intercession for them" (Hebrews 7:25).

That is our real strength when it comes to temptation. Our prayer TO Him and His prayer FOR us. That is a winning combination. Temptation will come. Satan plans the attack at a time that is "opportune." But he who saw us through *one* temptation will see us through *all* temptations. We need to pray for the grace of one who was tempted as we are—time and again—to the very end.

Pray with Me

O God, hold this truth before me today: that having *victory over* temptation and having *freedom from* temptation are two different things.

When the great temptation was over, the devil departed from my Lord *only* "until an opportune time." Again and again He heard temptation's voice.

By His obedience and by His life of perfect holiness, Jesus conquered evil and "led captivity captive." He never exposed Himself deliberately to the forces of evil. But He never retreated when a strong stand was required. He who was always free from sin was never free from temptation. He learned obedience by the things that He suffered.

Help me to draw fresh strength from this, dear Lord. Temptation may come as direct pain or subtle pleasure. It may be a swaggering enemy or a seductive friend. It may stir me to angry impatience or lull me to spineless capitulation. However it comes, whenever it comes, help me know that Jesus was tempted . . . to the very end.

You have promised to be with me to the very end. Be near me also in the hour of trial, in every hour of trial, that I may neither be surprised nor discouraged by the persistence of temptation.

In the Name of my ever-blessed Redeemer I offer this prayer.

In the Name of my ever-present Friend I claim this victory, Amen.

MOVING ON IN THE LIFE OF PRAYER

Prayer based on God's Word is our greatest defense against temptation. Jesus answered Satan's every temptation with a quotation from Scripture. This becomes our model for dealing with this ancient enemy. Listen to God's Word, then pray, then conquer. Not just once, but again and again and again. We can have victory over temptation until, when God comes to take us home, we have freedom from temptation. Not until then, but surely then. Thank God.

Day 60

TRUE WEALTH

"He who loves money will not be satisfied with money; nor he who loves wealth, with gain" (Ecclesiastes 5:10).

Read: **Ecclesiastes 5:10-20;** 1 Samuel 8:1-5; Isaiah 56:11; Jeremiah 17:11; 1 Timothy 6:10.

WHAT IS GOD SAYING?

Ecclesiastes follows a style of writing that was popular in its time. It is classified as Wisdom Literature. It seems disjointed to us in this day, with subjects appearing and disappearing suddenly and one could hope to find a better plot in a telephone book. But there are flashes of insight as the sun might catch the window of a passing car and send its quick light in our direction. Ecclesiastes is, of course, inspired, but deals with life "under the sun" as man sees it. It all boils down to this. Life, as man lives it without God, is futile. It is meaningless, pointless, and empty. If life without God is all there is to this brief sojourn on earth, then it's a cruel hoax or a not-so-funny joke. It is vanity, promising a lot and delivering nothing.

However, this book has more than cynicism and despair. Thank God there is more. It states that God can bring joy to life in its many and varied aspects (read 2:24-26; 3:10-15; 5:18-20; 9:7-10). But all this depends on whether we seek our satisfaction in God and in what He gives. This is what Jesus taught in Matthew 6:33.

HOW DOES THIS APPLY TO US?

There is nothing wrong with money or with having money. There is a vast difference between having money and loving money. It is not evil to be financially prudent and thereby to prosper. Where the rubber meets the road is in two questions: "What are we doing with the money we have?" and "What is the money we have doing to us?" There are many instances where rich people are incredibly poor in real wealth and where poor people are truly rich in satisfaction, contentment, joy, and peace. We should pray not for more things but for the wiser use of the things we have. God will give to us all the things we need. That's a promise (Matthew 6:33). The love of money is like water that evaporates in our hands. Being rich in love toward God is like a tree planted by the rivers of water. It prospers. It bears fruit. It gives. It lives. It is rich and enriching. We have to make the choice. No better way, no better time, than in prayer.

Pray with Me

Heavenly Father, direct me in all the things upon which I should set my affection.

I have often loved those things that cannot satisfy. I have sought comforts and advantages that others seem to enjoy. I have coveted fame and talent that others seem to possess. I have wanted wealth and power that others seem to achieve. Envy has made me restless.

May I have Your forgiveness, Lord. But beyond forgiveness give Your always sufficient grace, Your perfect wisdom, and the constant cleansing and filling of Your Holy Spirit. Grant all this that I may know that "he who loves money shall not be satisfied with money."

As silver and gold cannot purchase my redemption, so they cannot purchase my joy.

As increasing riches can mean increasing sorrow, I would be rich toward you in the treasures of faith and hope and love.

As material security rests on rotting pillars, help me to build on the foundation of Your promises and the eternal worth of Jesus Christ.

He who loves money, and all that money represents, shall not be satisfied with money or anything that it represents. But he who loves Christ shall be satisfied with Christ today, tomorrow, and forever.

I affirm this today in a deliberate act of faith.

In the Name of Him who always satisfies the longing soul and fills the hungry soul with His goodness, Amen.

MOVING ON IN THE LIFE OF PRAYER

The more we commit ourselves to God's will by the conscious and willing surrender of self, the richer we become. We become rich in the things that count: love, joy, peace, compassion. Prayer helps us to become rich in freedom from things, rich in faith toward God, rich in love toward others. How rich do we want to be? Love of money leads from riches to rags. Love of God leads from rags to riches. Prayer puts all that in perspective and the view from prayer's mountaintop is glorious.

Day 61

ANTIDOTE FOR THE POISON OF ENVY

"And Haman told them of the glory of his riches . . . 'Yet all this availeth me nothing, so long as I see Mordecai the Jew sitting at the king's gate' " (*Esther 5:11, 13 KJV*).

Read: **Esther 4, 5;** Proverbs 14:30, 23:17; 1 Corinthians 13:4; Galatians 5:26.

WHAT IS GOD SAYING?

During the reign of Ahasuerus (Xerxes), King of Persia, the Jewish nation was perilously close to annihilation. Even to this day the Jews celebrate, with festive joy, their deliverance because of the wisdom of Mordecai and the courage of Queen Esther. Although His name is never mentioned in this book, God was controlling the scene. It is a fascinating story complete with heroes and one arrogant, jealous villain. Mordecai and Esther had become the King's favorites: Mordecai, because he saved the kings's life (6:2) and Esther because of her exceptional beauty (2:7,17). Haman was also a top man on the king's list but he had a deep hatred for the Jews. He bragged about his power. He was puffed up with conceit and to bolster his essential insecurity (people who hate are insecure) he talked freely and often about the honors the king had bestowed on him and "the splendor of his riches."

But there was a restless fear in his heart that would not disappear. As with many people who are poised at the top of the heap, there was irrepressible envy. He couldn't be truly happy with all he had so long as Mordecai was enjoying the king's favor too. "ALL THIS does me NO GOOD so long as I see Mordecai the Jew sitting at the king's gate." His plot to hang Mordecai and get him forever out of his sight boomerangs and in a supreme instance of irony *he* is hanged on the gallows he built, rather than Mordecai, the intended victim.

HOW DOES THIS APPLY TO US?

Pride and envy are dangerous friends to have. The former blows us up with emptiness. The other carries a pin of restless discontent that pricks the balloon and leaves it in tatters. There is no future for envy. Those who envy are their own worst enemies. The backlash is inevitable. The gallows Haman designed for Mordecai turned out to be exactly his size. Prayer is the best defense against the boomerang of envy. Envy is not an innocent toy. It is a poisonous weapon, and prayer is the best antidote for this deadly poison.

Pray with Me

Loving Father, in Christ You have given me all true riches. I don't want my heart to be chilled by the dark clouds of envy. I don't want my spirit to be troubled by a restless discontent. Envy only opens the door to misery. Jealousy sends a deadening blight across life's happiest hours.

To know the real joy of the Lord, I must be both confident and content in the real riches of the Lord. To envy the condition of others is to doubt the wisdom of Your providence. To feel sorry for myself because I seem to lack favor is to question the sufficiency of Your grace.

Help me to learn Paul's secret of joy. Help me to learn it well. Help me to ponder it deeply. Let it become the established rule of my life: "... For I have learned, in whatever state I am, to be content."

Haman knew the favor of the king but was still a miserable man. He could not control his smoldering resentment of another person. Let the folly of his deed and the restless envy that gave it birth be a persuasive example to me today. May I not fail to see the inevitable trap which such passion lays for its own destruction.

I would find my shield against envy in a song of praise and thanksgiving.

I would avoid the fiery darts of jealousy by constant thoughts of Your goodness to me.

Others may seem to want for no material good. By comparison I may seem to be in want. Yet, Lord, keep always before me this thought: being most blessed, I should be least envious, for You have "blessed us with *all* spiritual blessings in heavenly places in Christ."

In Christ, indeed, and for His glory, Amen.

MOVING ON IN THE LIFE OF PRAYER

Paul said "I have learned, in whatever state I am, to be content" (Philippians 4:11). We can safely assume that he learned this through prayer. In prayer, we see the true riches which are ours in Christ. In prayer we are assured of being joint-heirs with Christ. We are rich beyond all reckoning. But, out of practice in praying, we will miss this fact. The best antidote for the worst poison is prayer. Let us lubricate our lives with praise, and envy will keep slipping off. Let us saturate our lives with rejoicing (Philippians 4:4) and we will throw a dead-bolt lock in the door against envy.

Day 62

AGAPE LOVE HAS NO PRICE

"... *A woman came with an alabaster flask of ointment of pure nard, very costly, and she broke the flask and poured it over his head*" (*Mark 14:3*).

Read: **Mark 14:1-11;** Matthew 26:6-16; Deuteronomy 15:11; Jeremiah 31:3; John 16:27; 1 Peter 1:8.

WHAT IS GOD SAYING?

Here we have the striking contrast of God's extravagant love and natural man's narrow greed. They had a name for the senseless thing the woman did: waste. Jesus called her extravagant deed an act of love, a wise and permanent investment. In fact "wherever the gospel is preached in the whole world, what she has done will be told in memory of her." They called it wrong. Jesus called it beautiful. "It is right to care for the poor," He said, "and you can care for them whenever you will, for they are always with you. You don't need to neglect them and you shouldn't." But their sudden interest in the poor, brought on by this display of extravagant love did not ring true. If their love for Jesus had risen from the depths of gratitude, as did hers, they would have seen that helping the poor and honoring the Lord with the best that we have are not incompatible. Their talk about "waste" was really an excuse to mask their own loveless-ness. In a parallel passage in Luke, Jesus says: "He who is forgiven little, loves little." The proud find it hard to be extrava-gant in love because they "waste" so much of it on themselves. There is little left to give to God or others.

HOW DOES THIS APPLY TO US?

We can afford to be extravagant in love because we have received so much, and the source of all love, our Heavenly Father, has so much more to give. Extravagant love is an over-flowing cup, a fountain of blessing fed from an eternal and boundless supply. So let us love extravagantly. There is always enough of God's love. The more we give away, the more we keep. The more we keep, the more we lose. In coming to prayer, the highest priority is to know that which passes knowledge (the love of Christ) and to be filled with that which can never be exhausted, (all the fullness of God). Read Ephesians 3:14-19 again and again with ever deeper appreciation and understand-ing. It is the best threshold on which to stand and enter the treasure house of prayer.

Pray with Me

Lord, in the extravagant love of this woman You have given me a great lesson. She poured out her prized possession. She sacrificed the very best. In doing so she has drawn aside the curtain to show me how You *have* loved me and how I *should* love You.

"God so loved the world that he gave his only . . ." Yours was the alabaster jar of costly ointment. You gave the choicest possession of Your vast riches. The life of Your own beloved Son was broken and poured out.

"Greater love has no man than this . . . " On Calvary there was the apparent triumph of darkness and hate. It was really the victory of light and love. On the Cross I see the self-abandoning love of God.

O God, forgive me that I have not broken the jar of self nor poured out the gift of service in any way that is equal to the debt I owe. Forgive me that I am so willing to lift the cover carefully and measure out the contents drop by drop.

I resolve that my life for you and for others shall not be marked by careful measuring. This is the way of suffocation and bondage. I pray that my life shall be as the gift of this woman: broken and poured out!

Extravagant love does not care for price or pride. Extravagant love is never wasted. Nothing is more permanently or wisely invested.

"Through the whole world . . . *this* . . . (this extravagant act of love) shall be spoken of for a memorial of her."

In the Name of Him whose life was broken and poured out for me, Amen.

MOVING ON IN THE LIFE OF PRAYER

Let our prayer become and remain a continual offering up of ourselves to the love of God and the service of others for His sake. The more we are determined to be extravagant in our love toward others, the more God's extravagant love fills our lives to overflowing. Prayer is the channel for RECEIVING God's blessing and becomes a channel for SHARING his blessing. Prayer becomes a strong and meaningful part of our lives as it helps us who are so greatly blessed to be greatly blessing. Can we afford to be extravagant in sharing God's love? Can we afford not to be?

Day 63

God's Tenacious Love

"How can I give you up, O Ephraim! . . . For I am God and not man . . ." (Hosea 11:8-9).

Read: **Hosea 11;** Deuteronomy 7:7-8; Jeremiah 31:3; Matthew 23:37; John 3:16; Romans 5:8.

What Is God Saying?

In the day of Hosea, the northern kingdom of Israel had gone about as far away from God as they could go. The prophet's message is to a doomed kingdom, yet he kept repeating both the warning of their impending ruin and the truth of God's tenacious love until the end—when Samaria fell to Assyria in 722 B.C. It is hard to imagine how a nation could reject God so completely and plunge itself into the self-destruction and unspeakable degradation of pagan religious practices. It is hard until we reflect upon what is happening in the polluted moral climate of our own day. This is a timely and timeless message. "All have sinned" and all ages, in turning from God, have invited disaster and death. This includes our own age. Hosea speaks from the agony of his own experience. His own wife betrayed him and spurned his covenant love. She left him alone and suffering, as he yearned for a flame to be rekindled in the ashes of their broken relationship. Hosea spoke from the heart, a broken heart. Hosea could understand with painful realism how God must have felt while watching His chosen people turn away from His love. The people God had chosen had not chosen Him. He was rejected. Time and again they gave up the true freedom of being in bondage to God's love and chose the false freedom of being in bondage to evil. And *still* God could not give them up. Oh, the tenacious love of God!

How Does This Apply to Us?

All of us have sinned. All of us have come short of the glory of God. But all of us may and many of us have accepted the love of God in receiving His unspeakable Gift, the Lord Jesus Christ. "How can I give you up, O Ephraim!" The Gospel tells us we may put our name in the place of Ephraim (God's affectionate term for Israel). The Cross is the ultimate proof of God's love. It was God, not man, who suffered there. Only God could save us. The noblest sacrifice of man can point the way (John 15:13), but it was the tenacious love of God that consented to the Cross. Pray in the confidence that God's love will never give us up. The love of God doesn't give us up—it lifts us up!

Pray with Me

Your love, O God, is eternally divine and not capriciously human. You are God and not man. On this is built my confidence. From this flows my joy. Toward this rises my hope.

"How can I give you up, O Ephraim!" These words are so moving. Especially so when I realize that for all practical purposes I have many times given You up. Whenever I live as though You do not exist, I am giving You up. When I turn to lesser comforts and seek to avoid the responsibilities which Your will places in my path, I am giving You up. When cowardly submission to the opinion of human companions takes the cutting edge off Your commandments, I am giving You up.

Yet, because You are God and not man, I may turn to You and find the arms of outreaching and ever-patient Love. "How can I give you up?" Let this unanswered and unanswerable question bring into my heart such peace as the world with all its doubts and fears can never destroy. Let it bring me joy which the world for all its subtle enchantments can never give. Let it make me strong to walk through a civilization of crumbling foundations with neither dread nor despair.

"If God be for us, who can be against us?" If God never gives me up, of whom shall I ever be afraid?

How can I give up You, O God, who has given up all for me in Christ?

In the Name of Him whose sacrifice on Calvary is the proof of Love that never gives up, Amen.

MOVING ON IN THE LIFE OF PRAYER

It helps to pray when we know that God is listening. He has not turned a deaf ear to our cries for help nor to our exclamations of joy. We are moving on in the life of prayer when we pray with this confidence. God has not given us up. That is what strengthens our prayer-life. That is what changes prayer from the emptiness of ritual into the fullness of joyful confidence. Don't give up on prayer. God hasn't given up on us.

Day 64

FAINT, YET PURSUING

"And Gideon came to the Jordan and passed over, he and the three hundred men who were with him, faint yet pursuing" (Judges 8:4).

Read: **Judges 8:1-12;** Job 17:9; Acts 20:20-24; 1 Corinthians 15:58; Galatians 6:9.

WHAT IS GOD SAYING?

Joshua had conquered Canaan. Under remarkable circumstances he had crossed the Jordan. The walls of Jericho fell under the onslaught of faith with weapons no more lethal than the sound of marching feet and the blowing of trumpets. The conquest had been faithfully and bravely begun, but it was not complete. There were pockets of resistance. The Land promised was not yet the Land possessed. It is in this turbulent situation that the Book of Judges is set. Individual tribes were being constantly troubled by hostile neighbors. Terrorism was alive and well. Pestilence stalked in darkness. Homesteading this new land, they were plagued by annoying attacks from those who didn't like what was happening to "their" neighborhood. The "judges" were "liberators," "men (and one woman) of the hour." Notable among these was Gideon. He was called upon to resist the attacks of the barbarous Midianites. They swept across southern Israel, mounted on swift-moving camels. They struck quickly and left great devastation. The problem needed to be faced. Gideon, reluctant at first, became the hero-leader. And the words, "faint, yet pursuing" aptly describe this man of courage, a shining example of faith and obedience in a time of disorder, confusion, and lawlessness.

HOW DOES THIS APPLY TO US?

The same God who gave Gideon courage when he wanted "out" can give us the "will" to go on when everything else says "can't" and when everyone else says "won't." We can be faint when the battle has been long and tiring, and God will give us strength to go on. We can claim Moses' blessing to Asher as our own (Deuteronomy 33:24-25). If God brings us to another day, He will give us the strength to live through that day. "The LORD is the stronghold of my life, of whom shall I be afraid? . . . Wait for the LORD; be strong, and let your heart take courage" (Psalm 27:1, 14).

"So let it be in God's own might
We gird us for the coming fight,

And, strong in him whose cause is ours,
In conflict with unholy powers,
We grasp the weapons he has given:
The Light and Truth, and Love of Heaven."[1]
—John Greenleaf Whittier

We may be faint but God is not. In HIS strength, though ours may be ebbing, we can pursue, we can run the race, we can finish the course.

Pray with Me

Lord, You were the Strength of Gideon. You are the Strength of all who dare to believe and obey. Give me the heart of Gideon that even when I am faint, I will still pursue.

"My strength is made perfect in weakness." This is Your word. Hearing and believing it helps me to move with Gideon's army. One of Gideon's three hundred, I learn that little is much with God. Faintness is not a good reason for turning back.

I thank You for days when victory is mine. I thank you when under kindly skies a glad heart is certain of Heaven's favor. I thank You when my hand is strong and the way is easy.

But, Lord, I pray for the other and greater blessing. When, with Gideon, I am called to do Your will though my body is tired and my heart is heavy, let not faintness of spirit keep me from still pursuing.

Keep this as a banner before my eyes: "Faithful is he who calls you, who will also do it." Leaning on *that* faithfulness, faintness will be changed into strength and fear into courage. Leaning on *that* faithfulness, I shall not be pursued, I shall pursue. Leaning on *that* faithfulness, I shall not turn back. I shall keep on until I see the enemies of Your Kingdom forever and totally conquered. Let this come to pass in Your time, in Your strength, and to Your glory.

"Faint, yet pursuing." So let it be.

In the Name of Him who pursued my redemption even though faint with the burden of Calvary, Amen.

MOVING ON IN THE LIFE OF PRAYER

There is no better cure for a faint spirit than prayer. Prayer is the real meaning of "waiting on the Lord" and waiting on the Lord is the real secret of renewed strength. Prayer is the channel through which strength from above comes into our lives. Strength from above for service below. Faint, yet pursuing. The odds that are AGAINST us are great but the God who is WITH us is greater, infinitely greater.

1. John Greenleaf Whittier, "The Moral Warfare."

Day 65

SHARING THE BLESSINGS

". . . *Indeed they are in debt to them, for if the Gentiles have come to share in their spiritual blessings, they ought also to be of service to them in material blessings*" *(Romans 15:27).*

Read: **Romans 15:25-33;** Romans 11:1-16; 1 Corinthians 13:4-7; Galatians 6:6; 1 John 3:16.

WHAT IS GOD SAYING?

All of the New Testament letters, with their rich treasure of doctrinal facts and spiritual insight, combine their teaching about God and the Gospel with strong practical suggestions about how we are to live in our everyday life. Romans has eleven chapters of strong doctrine. Then, at the beginning of chapter twelve these words appear: "I appeal to you therefore, brethren, by the mercies of God, to present your bodies as a living sacrifice . . ." Our faith is not lived out in ivory towers or in remote monasteries, important as quiet meditation and deep soul-searching may be. That is why Paul reminds his readers that they have received "spiritual blessings" because of Israel: the covenants, the pure teachings of monotheism, and even through "their trespass salvation has come to the Gentiles." Now Jerusalem was hurting. "The poor among the saints" in Jerusalem were in real need. In fact, as Paul concludes this great letter, he was on his way there to bring practical help to them from the Christians of Greece. He who brought them the heavenly Good News was on a mission of down-to-earth helpfulness. And why not? Having shared in spiritual blessings, Gentiles should "be of service" to the poor in Jerusalem with material blessings.

HOW DOES THIS APPLY TO US?

How real is our thankfulness to God for the spiritual riches we have received through His inexhaustible grace? Does our being saved to all eternity make us think of others who are having hard times now? Does our assurance of having peace with God tend to shield us from understanding the great problems people have as victims of injustice? Can we as Christians be accused of having our heads in the clouds without keeping our feet on the ground? If there is even a suggestion of this in our Christian lives, we didn't get it from the Bible. We have received so much that we can spare a little and share a little. Strike that word "little" and make it a "lot." Having received all things IN Christ, let us share all things FOR Christ.

Pray with Me

Father, You have blessed me with all spiritual blessings in Christ Jesus. You have also freely given me everything else that has any value. Let my love and gratitude be so real that I will not even think of separating my richness in spiritual good from my obligations in material sharing.

To hoard Your blessings is an indication of fear. To be miserly or even careful in the sharing of Your blessings is to live as though God does *not* live.

Lord, give me an ever-deepening trust in the steadfastness of Your love. Lead me to the discovery that Your grace is inexhaustible. Living on the banks of a never-failing stream, who needs to hoard water? Assured that I am an heir of God and a joint-heir with Christ, I have no right and no need to keep Your grace to myself.

I would not fail to see the relation between spiritual enrichment and material generosity. How wrong to say we are children of God while holding back material blessings from His other children.

Having shared in spiritual blessings, let me serve with material blessings. Having received all things *in* Christ, let me share all things *for* Christ. Then, and only then, will I deserve the names I wear so lightly and claim so easily; saint, disciple, steward, child of God, joint-heir with Christ.

Through Him who has made the riches of God's grace known and real to me, Amen.

MOVING ON IN THE LIFE OF PRAYER

Prayer should literally unfold our "praying hands" and make them working hands. That is effective prayer. If it falls short of that, it's back to the drawing board. Prayer that doesn't lead to being used of God needs to be re-examined because it borders on the useless. Listen *to* God; then, through prayer be used *by* God.

Day 66

On Being Generous

"And let fall also some of the handfuls of purpose for her" (Ruth 2:16, KJV).

Read: **Ruth 2;** Exodus 36:2-5; Ecclesiastes 11:1; Isaiah 58:7; Acts 4:34-35, 20:35.

What Is God Saying?

The time of the Judges was one of the darkest periods in the history of Israel. The pages were stained with blood. Disorder and chaos were almost perpetual. Fear gripped the hearts of all. The present was hard and the future was bleak. Into all this turmoil God drops one of the loveliest stories of all time. It glows with the warmth of human kindness and love. One can recall paintings by Constable from another century in England that portray peaceful rural scenes. "The plowman homeward plods his weary way." His wife is preparing a simple meal as white smoke curls lazily up from the chimney. Children are playing. Cattle are grazing. The warm slanting rays of the sun illuminate the scene with pervasive peace. And over against it all, an angry, threatening sky. Soon a storm will break, but for now a moment of calm, the blessing of peace. Such is the story of Ruth in the time of the Judges. Boaz has instructed the workers who are gleaning in the fields to "leave a few handfuls of purpose" for Ruth. Generosity and kindness was not the mood of the times, nor through the centuries has it often been so. But God is above the moods of the times and, as in this story, kindness and generosity break through to have their moment.

How Does This Apply to Us?

God shows His generous love through the self-forgetfulness and sacrifice of people whose lives He has touched. It was Boaz then. Who will it be today? The world has need for a respite from war and the selfishness that causes it. Our world, our communities, our families could use large doses of generosity and peace. (They go together!) We have grown weary of distrust and suspicion and strife. We have freely received the blessings of God's peace. Having received tons of God's goodness, we can spare a few handfuls to make life richer and "gooder" for others. (The word is bad but the idea is good). Prayer should help to make the good idea come true.

Pray with Me

Gracious Father, Your hand is open to satisfy the desire of every living creature. Forgive me that my hand is so often closed. Those young men in the past were told by *their* master to be kind and thoughtful. By His words and deeds, *my* Master has given me the same instruction.

You have been purposeful and generous in Your giving.

My life is filled with undeserved blessings like a cup that overflows. How, therefore, can I be anything but purposeful and generous in my sharing?

You have given me many hours to meditate, to dream, to work, to play. Forgive me for begrudging a few moments to the friend or stranger who presumes upon my time. You have given me health and family and friends. Forgive me for failing to bring some evidence of Your love to the least of Your brethren. Forgive me for forgetting those who are forgotten. Forgive me for losing touch with the lost. Forgive me for being impatient with the disagreeable.

I would share all blessings that I have so freely received . . . not with a pinch of kindness here and a few grains of mercy there, but with whole handfuls. Guide me into the kind of life that is known for its purposeful and habitual kindness. Let there be a growing discontent with kindness that is only occasional and sometimes just accidental.

Let me reach purposefully into the storehouse of Your blessings to give out "handfuls of purpose" for others. I cannot be a disciple of my Master in any other way. Has He not given to me many "handfuls" of heavenly bounty by the "purpose" of His patient and self-giving love?

Let this be for His glory, Amen.

MOVING ON IN THE LIFE OF PRAYER

The best way to make room for more blessings from God is to share the ones we have already received. We thank God for what we have. More is coming and will keep on coming, if we give God the room in our hearts to put it. Our lives should stop being self-storage cubicles where goodies are kept under lock and key and start being a transfer point where the good things of God can be freely passed along. If we pray along that line, God will have some surprising handfuls (heartfuls!) of blessings for us to keep on enjoying . . . and all the more because they are shared.

Day 67

TALK AND WALK; ARE THEY ONE?

". . . They said to him [Jehu], 'Is all well? Why did this mad fellow come to you?' And he said to them, 'You know the fellow and his talk' " (2 Kings 9:11).

Read: **2 Kings 9:1-11;** Genesis 19:14; Proverbs 14:23, 18:16; Ecclesiastes 5:3, 10:12-13; Titus 1:10.

WHAT IS GOD SAYING?

Elisha has sent a young prophet to search out Jehu and anoint him king. Ahab and Jezebel were rejected for their crimes but their base activity continued even as an animal, wounded and dying, will continue to have spasmodic jerks. It was God's will that Jehu be anointed king and commissioned to bring down the house of Ahab. The young prophet made his way to Jehu, accomplished his mission and took his leave suddenly. When the guards inquired as to why "the mad fellow" came to Jehu in the first place, Jehu made up an excuse: "You know the fellow and his talk." It was like saying. "You can't believe anything he says. He has the reputation for being crazy." That was easy for the guards to believe, for prophets were known for their ecstatic and uncontrolled behavior. In this instance Jehu tries to throw them off by the remark. They didn't accept his evasiveness and pressed him for the truth. When they learned the truth, they chose to follow him, their new king. Jehu did put an end to the house of Ahab, but his reign eventually collapsed in shame as he fell back into the shameful idolatries begun with Jeroboam.

HOW DOES THIS APPLY TO US?

"You know the fellow and his talk." These words simply underscore the fact that we are known as much (and more) by the life we lead than by the words we say. Remember how Lot's sons-in-law would not believe Lot's warning because he seemed to be only jesting (Genesis 19:14)? His actions and his words were not one. We need to be sure that our walk makes it easy for others to believe our words. A man and his message must be one or there will be those who honestly think we are only jesting when we are trying to be earnest. Our talk and our walk must be one, lest there be those who say of us: "You know the fellow and his talk." In prayer, in the silent words we hear and speak in the Father's presence, let there be the perfect mingling of what we are and what we say. Belonging to Christ, there's no other way to pray. There's no other way to live.

Pray with Me

Lord, I would heed the warning of this verse: a man and his message cannot be separated. The message a person brings is believed or doubted according to the life a person lives. A fool brings falsehoods. A wise man brings truth.

Let me be careful in my walk that others may find it easy to believe in my words. Let the words of my lips and the deeds of my life flow together as two streams whose mingling is never noticed. Let my life give foundation to my message. Let my reputation support my conversation. What comes from my mouth and what shows in my life . . . let them be one.

The weakness of inconsistency sometimes brands me as a fool. Nevertheless, in Your patient love, see me for what I may become. Bring me through all the disciplines and pains of spiritual growth to a measure of the stature of the fullness of Christ. May He be the shining goal of my life. His words and His works were always one. His message and His life were always consistent.

Stir my slumbering conscience. May I not be oblivious to what others must be quick to detect: "the man and the message are one."

When others say, " You know the man and his talk," may I have the joy of knowing that they say it with honor to God and not with scorn. May my life be such that, when others say, "You know the man and his talk," they shall be strengthened in faith and not in doubt.

Let this become a reality, Lord, for the glory of Your name. Let it become a reality for the peace of my own heart. Let it become a reality for the sake of all who are trying to find the Master through the integrity of His disciples.

In the Name of Him whose words and works were always one, Amen.

MOVING ON IN THE LIFE OF PRAYER

We want to pray for consistency in life and prayer. We will say what we mean. We will mean what we say. Some time, sooner or later, let it be said of us, "You know the fellow and his talk," meaning, "You know he has talked with God and from that life of prayer there is coming a life of love and service, a life dedicated to beauty and truth, a life devoted to the service of Christ, a life where God is real, a life that is real for God." Talking to God and walking before men should be one piece of cloth.

Day 68

FAITH, THE GREATEST GIFT

". . .In order that I may gain Christ and be found in him" (Philippians 3:8, 9).

Read: **Philippians 3:4-14.**

WHAT IS GOD SAYING?

Faith is the most precious gift because it opens the door to our most priceless treasure. Through faith we come to think of everything else, however high it may be priced and prized by the world, as worthless rubble. Having Christ is the great and all-sufficient alternative, the Pearl of Great Price. Nothing, literally nothing, compares with being saved and safe in Christ. Paul lists a number of things that he could claim to his credit and about which he might have reason to boast: a good religious track record, a fine lineage, a Hebrew of the Hebrews, even a faultless Pharisee. Nor was he lacking in religious zeal. When he looked at anyone else climbing the mountain slope of religious merit, he had to look a long way down. He had it made. But then Christ came to him. He was blinded on the Road to Damascus and saw for the first time the Road to Heaven. All of those hard-earned religious credentials seemed worthless now. Finding Christ, everything else lost its luster. For all it meant to him now, it could be hauled away with Monday morning's trash.

HOW DOES THIS APPLY TO US?

To gain Christ means simply to receive Christ, and to have the extra satisfaction of knowing how great that really is. It means setting aside all lesser things which we thought so important and valuable. We see them for what they are really worth. Not just worthless but useless. Trash! No longer the way, just in the way! To win Christ means we are not just barely saved but are truly saved—all the way to eternity. Not just saved, but safe. *Found in Him!* Covered by His grace, rejoicing in His pardon, protected from the accusings of conscience, sheltered by His powerful love, at peace with God, and therefore at peace in the world—and in spite of the world. That sets us free from the distractions of worry. We can take our burdens to the Lord and leave them all with Him. It also opens the door in prayer to thoughts of others. Saved, we can pray for their salvation. Safe in Christ, we can reach out in loving concern that others may find security in His sheltering love.

Pray with Me

Father, I thank You for Your gift of faith. Among all Your gifts, that gift is very special. I thank You that You have brought me through the struggle of doubts and fears, until, shining before me in the vast and lonely dark, there is the gift of simple faith.

Faith in Jesus Christ: to receive His righteousness is my only defense; to embrace His victory is my only glory; to accept His death on the Cross is my only hope. This is my victory. This is my eternal security. All other discoveries and all other gifts are insignificant compared to this.

Through faith "to win Christ": through faith to know that I am His and He is mine; through faith to win Him and, in doing so, to win every victory; through faith to possess Him whom to possess is to own every eternal blessing.

"And to be found in Him." Here is my security. Because I am found in Him, I am covered by His grace. I am sheltered from the lashes of my own conscience. I am protected from the wrathful malice of all that is in league with evil. Because I am found in Him, I am no longer lost in the world. Because I am found in Him, my life moves toward fulfillment instead of futility.

Having gained Him, I know I shall always be found in Him.

Thank You, Lord, for the gift of faith by which I embrace forever the gift of Your love,

In Jesus Christ, my Lord, Amen.

MOVING ON IN THE LIFE OF PRAYER

If we have received so much through faith, isn't it time to share it with others? When more and more of our prayer time is spent in thinking of others, we will also find ourselves spending more time just in praising God . . . for the gift of faith, the door to salvation, the light of hope, the shelter of love, the blessing of peace.

Day 69

THE BLESSINGS OF REPENTANCE

"Therefore also now, saith the LORD, turn ye even to me with all your heart . . . then will the LORD be jealous for his land, and pity his people" *(Joel 2:12, 18 KJV).*

Read: **Joel 2:12-32;** Deuteronomy 6:5, 30:1-3; Psalm 119:1-2; Ezekiel 18:31; Acts 3:19.

WHAT IS GOD SAYING?

Man becoming right with God. That is the fundamental and recurring theme of the prophets. The prophets plead with all people, leaders and followers, kings and priests, decision-makers and common workers, that *all* should turn back to God and do it with *all* their hearts. That is all God is waiting for. God determines the outcome of every situation. Again and again His spokesmen repeat: "Don't look for help from even the strongest and most promising of human allies. They are not interested in your welfare. They are always in it for what they can get out of it. But the Lord loves you because He loves you. No hidden motives, no empty promises, no false fronts." God is "jealous for his land, and will pity his people" (2:18). Stay on the Lord's side, the other side can't help you and won't help you.

God hears and God answers. Joel declares that God has allowed locusts to attack the land. The people have been judged for their faithlessness and sin. But given true repentance, a returning to God with all their heart, God will restore the "years which the swarming locusts have eaten." A better day is coming. "God will dwell in Zion . . . Jerusalem shall be holy . . . all the stream beds of Judah shall flow with water" (3:17, 18). That is the future for those who repent. Choose the blessings of repentance. Why delay? God waits.

HOW DOES THIS APPLY TO US?

All that God promised to those who returned to Him in the days of Joel is available to us now. Repentance unlocks the treasures of divine grace. We who have embraced Jesus Christ by faith and entered the family of God are the ones for whom God is jealous. He wants us for His own. He is not an unfeeling, uncaring object set up in a shrine who is satisfied with an occasional bend of the knee and a quick, repetitious prayer. He watches over us with an active, outgoing, jealous love. He has the right to hear and see that we love Him in return. "We love, because he first loved us" (1 John 4:19). Let the Holy Spirit do his work in our hearts. He will not only convict us of sin, He will restore us to life and lead us to the countless blessings of repentance.

Pray with Me

Lord, I thank You for showing me the doorway to Your greatest blessings. Forgive me for allowing myself to think: "a few weak and empty words; a few wistful, vaporish thoughts; a few feeble, formal prayers, and I am safe."

Repentance must be deep to be real. And it must be real to be effective. The ministers of the Lord wept before the altar and cried, "Spare Your people and give not Your heritage to reproach." Let me be moved, in the same way, to deep sorrow for my own sins.

Then I will learn the secret that unlocks the treasures of divine grace. Then I will learn the meaning of God's jealousy for His people. Then I will taste the joys of a fellowship restored. Then I will have the power of a life renewed. *Then!* Not until *then!*

Holy Spirit, do Your work in my heart. Of You it has been said, "When He has come, He will reprove the world of sin." There is something great beyond the pain of reproof and conviction. There are the untold blessings of a God who is jealous for His own. There are the blessings of a God who wants His children to know the fullness of His never-failing love.

How wonderful to be someone for whom God is jealous! I am the object of Your love and pity. Let me never again close my heart to the wonder of Your jealous love. Let me never again imagine that in the loneliest battles of courage and faith, I am ever unpitied.

In repentance I come to You. In faith I would receive from You the blessings of a God who is "jealous" for me and the "pity" of a God who unceasingly cares.

Through Jesus Christ who brought Your love to earth and gave my soul its second birth, Amen.

MOVING ON IN THE LIFE OF PRAYER

We should dwell not so much on our sins as on God's forgiveness. We should come to prayer rejoicing more in God's love than on our failures. We should think more of how greatly we have been blessed and are being blessed than of how sadly we have missed the mark. But . . . if there is an area, even the smallest spot showing on the X-ray of truth and honesty, we should confront it, confess it, and leave it. We should turn with all our hearts to God, turn everything over to God, and then move on to possess and enjoy the blessings of true repentance.

Day 70

THE HOLINESS OF GOD

"Then the men of Bethshemesh said, 'Who is able to stand before the LORD, this holy God?' " (1 Samuel 6:20).

Read: **1 Samuel 6:1-7:1;** Psalm 76:7-9, 99:9; Malachi 3:2; Revelation 1:10-17, 15:4.

WHAT IS GOD SAYING?

The Philistines had captured the Ark of the Covenant, brought it to Ashdod, and set it up beside their god, Dagon. This was going to be a showdown. By morning Dagon had fallen and a plague of tumors spread across the city. "The hand of the LORD was heavy upon the people of Ashdod (1 Samuel 5:6). Perhaps it would fare better in Gath. No relief. They tried Ekron next, but wherever the Ark went trouble was sure to follow. They wanted out. More accurately, they wanted the Ark out. "The cry of the city went up to Heaven" (5:12). Did this plague come upon them because of the Ark or was it just a happenstance? To make sure, they prepared a new cart to be drawn by two milk cows. If the cows left their newborn calves behind to go in the direction of Israel, that would be proof enough to the Philistines that their troubles could be traced to the hand of God upon them.

The cows went straight to Bethshemesh, the nearest point of entry into Israel. Everybody rejoiced in what was happening. The Philistines were glad to have the troublemaking Ark out of their land and off their hands. The people of Bethshemesh greeted its return with elation and joy. But their celebration was to turn to disaster. In their excitement and curiosity some of the celebrants looked into the Ark and paid for it with their lives. This gives rise to the question, "Who is able to stand before the Lord, this holy God?"

HOW DOES THIS APPLY TO US?

God will never be treated as an object of idle curiosity. The Ark was holy. To treat the Ark of His presence with anything but reverence was to presume upon the holiness and majesty of God. Then and now such presumption cannot go on without strong rebuke. Man is the creature. His life is ruled by God. He dares not regard God with easy familiarity. When God becomes a comrade and we come to Him in a spirit of cozy intimacy, we are wide of the mark. He is awesome, totally transcendent, all-powerful, and perfectly holy. Although He is infinitely loving, as we have seen Him to be in Jesus Christ, we must never lose the concept expressed by the hymn writer: "How Great Thou Art!" Not with the fear of those who saw what happened at Beth-shemesh, but with the holy wonder of those who have seen what happened at Calvary. Salvation is free but never cheap.

Pray with Me

Your Name, O God, cannot be spoken lightly. It can only come from a humble heart. It can only be used in prayer and praise. How much less shall any one "stand" before You? Having seen Your glory in nature and Your truth in the living Word, I join those who say, "Who is able to stand before the Lord, this holy God?"

But I thank You, Lord, that I do not need to tremble in the darkness of fear as did the men of Bethshemesh. When I fall before you in worship and cannot even dare to lift my eyes to the glory of Your perfection, I am in the company of John.

Beside the still form of the beloved apostle, the living Christ stood. He spoke with the voice of eternal love and invincible authority: "Fear not . . . I am the living one; I died, and behold I am alive for evermore."

Before You I cannot stand. Before You I do not stand. Yet through faith in Your beloved Son, I dare to rise. Through Him I am clothed in righteousness. Through His death I am reconciled to You. Because He took my sins to the Cross, I am justified in Your sight.

Such love is too wonderful for me. I cannot understand it but I accept it. In myself I have no power and no right to stand before you. "Who shall stand before the Lord, this holy God?" I thank You that in Christ even I may stand. Accept my praise and use my life that others may know the joy of standing forgiven and restored, cleansed and free, before the Lord who is the holy . . . and loving . . . God.

In Christ's own matchless Name, Amen.

MOVING ON IN THE LIFE OF PRAYER

Our prayer is lifted to a holy and loving God. We MAY come to him without fear of rejection. But we MUST come to him with neither pride nor presumption. The strength of prayer is based on the greatness of God. The freedom of prayer is based on the love of God. The result of prayer is based on our faith in the name of Jesus. "Whatever you ask in my name, I will do it" (John 14:13).

Day 71

PERPLEXED?
GOD HAS AN ANSWER

"Now while Peter was inwardly perplexed as to what the vision which he had seen might mean, behold, the men . . . stood before the gate" (Acts 10:17).

Read: **Acts 10:1-17;** Leviticus 11; Romans 11:33-36; Psalm 91:15; Isaiah 55:8-9, 59:1.

WHAT IS GOD SAYING?

There were two men praying. They were praying in different places. They came from different backgrounds. Although they didn't know each other they were praying fervently to the same God. God was about to answer their prayers in ways they never suspected. First, there was Cornelius, a Gentile, searching for the truth. His prayer was answered in an unexpected way. It was a little frightening, of course, but it left no perplexity in his mind. An angel said, "God has heard your prayer and wants you to do as follows: send some of your men to Joppa. Go to the house of Simon the Tanner. Meet a man named Simon Peter, and bring him here." Everything was spelled out in clear detail. It was a strange order to receive, but it was not perplexing.

The other person who was praying was Peter. He *was* perplexed. He became hungry while praying on the rooftop. In a vision, he saw all kinds of animals, including reptiles and birds, being let down from Heaven in something that looked like a sheet. "There you are, Peter, go ahead and eat something. There are lots of choices on this menu." "Not me, Lord, I have never eaten anything unclean." "Peter, if I call it clean you must not find it unclean or common." Peter pushed it all aside three times, growing more and more puzzled. How could God expect a devout Jew to break with tradition so radically?

God was getting Peter ready to share the Good News with Gentiles. And the rendezvous was about to happen. The real hunger was in the heart of Cornelius, a Gentile, and the real satisfaction was to come from Peter in whose heart the barriers were being broken down. He was taken to Cornelius and there he preached the Good News of Jesus.

How Does This Apply to Us?

Peter was perplexed and wrestled with his conscience. God led him through his bewilderment to an answer that was to be a turning point in Peter's life and the life of the Church. If we are in the spirit of prayer and mean what we are praying, God will make His will known. For every human predicament, there is an answer. For all our perplexities, there are divine solutions. When we yield up our prejudices and see things from God's point of view, He not only resolves our dilemmas, He makes us chosen instruments of His blessing to others. The men were at the gate to take Peter where he could be a blessing. Prayer was being answered.

Pray with Me

Lord, sometimes I am perplexed with problems. Sometimes the mysteries of life remain locked against prayer and reason. Nevertheless Your answer is on the way . . . perhaps even here! At the moment Peter was wrestling with the meaning of that vision, men were waiting at the gate. And with them was the answer.

Let me not succumb to problems that will not let me go. There is a solution waiting. A little patience and it is mine. When I look into the heart of a dark enigma, I believe the Light is already shining there. Your love has the ever-present answer.

When each step in the course of duty leads me into deeper night, hold my hand. Lead me through the valley of the shadow. It is enough to know that You are leading. It is enough to know what men of faith are always discovering: If we are in the will of God and in the spirit of prayer, human perplexity and divine solutions are never far apart.

You told Peter to arise and go with these men "without hesitation for You had sent them." So speak to me that without hesitation I may recognize and accept the answer that is always close at hand.

As You are a very present help in trouble, so You have a very present answer in perplexity. When I am on the rooftop of prayer, the answer may even now be waiting at some lowly gate of service.

Through Jesus Christ, Amen.

Moving On in the Life of Prayer

When we pray we must expect the unexpected. God did what Peter had not expected and could hardly accept. But accepting the unexpected made Peter a blessing. We look for new things and good things to happen when we pray. Prayer should melt our prejudices and broaden our horizons and deepen our love. It is the way of blessing for us and for others.

Day 72

THE GLORY OF GOD AND THE SEARCHING MIND

"It is the glory of God to conceal things, but the glory of kings is to search things out" (Proverbs 25:2).

Read: **Proverbs 25:2;** Job 5:8-9, 11:7-9; Ecclesiastes 3:11; Isaiah 40:28; 1 Corinthians 2:9, 10, 16.

WHAT IS GOD SAYING?

Note the contrast between the glory of God and the glory of man. It is the glory of God that He has created a universe which is always beyond the ken of man. It is the glory of man that he is always stretching his mind to the limits of reason. When he reaches the horizon of knowledge, there is still more. That's the glory of God. There is always more than we can grasp. That's to the credit of man. He is always seeking to discover more of the reality which has come from the creative hand of God. The force of this verse is to remind us that God is always beyond and is, therefore, to be worshiped and held in reverence. Man is always on the lookout for more discoveries. He should be grateful that he has been given a seeking mind and that there is so much for him yet to probe. It's an exciting adventure. "The heavens for height, and the earth for depth" (Proverbs 25:3) and it is all ours to probe and to understand, to appreciate and to enjoy.

HOW DOES THIS APPLY TO US?

We believe that our minds are God-given and should be used in the constant search for more knowledge and more understanding. We also believe that God is forever beyond us. "Great is the LORD, and greatly to be praised, and his greatness is unsearchable" (Psalm 145:3). We, therefore, need the Word of God used by the Spirit of God to lead us into all that we *need* to know concerning God for our soul's salvation and peace. Thank God, we can know all we need to know of His love and power and truth. "I am the way, and the truth, and the life; no one comes to the Father, but by me (John 14:6)." Jesus said it. We believe it. We accept it . . . all the way through all of life, for it is all of truth.

Pray with Me

Lord, I am taught by this verse that I should never stop seeking. Beyond all present knowledge and experience, there are new things to be found. I am encouraged to push back the edges of darkness with the hope of finding more light.

"It is the glory of God to conceal things." Sometimes I am bothered by the fact that my heart keeps asking questions that do not seem to be answered or answerable. Then comes a joyful discovery: *because* my questions are not *all* answered and *because* my questings are not *all* satisfied, I have proof of Your glory and greatness. Forgive my lack of trust when answers come that do not agree with logic. Help me to rest in the fact of the great unknowables. Help me to praise Your glory *because* of the great unknowables.

But I thank You, too, for the gift of a searching mind. I thank You that "it is the glory of kings to search things out."

Even as a mountain climber keeps looking up to mountains he may never climb but never stops trying to climb—

Even as an astronomer looks out on a universe with more galaxies than he could ever chart, but never stops studying the many he sees and looking for more—

So let my mind which is God-given be God-directed. Let me not be discouraged by the unanswerable beyond. Let me not be idle in my search for its elusive and beckoning mysteries. I rest in this: All questions have their final answer in Him whose hand formed the highest mountain; all questions are to be finally answered by Him whose hand flung out into space the farthest star; all questions are to be finally answered by Him who for time and eternity is "the Way, the Truth, and the Life."

In this truth my soul will both rest and march, to the glory of God, Amen.

MOVING ON IN THE LIFE OF PRAYER

There is a place for searching in our prayer life. "Ask, and it will be given you; seek, and you will find; knock, and it will be opened to you" (Matthew 7:7). That is the way and the why of prayer in the words of Him who taught his disciples to pray. Let us continue seeking for "it is the glory of kings to search things out" and in Christ it is the privilege of Christians to do the same. But "seeking prayer" at its best is done through the Holy Spirit (1 Corinthians 2:10), for the Spirit searches everything, even the depths of God. Prayer asks in Jesus' Name, and receives for Jesus' sake. In prayer we seek through the Spirit and find all we need to know and all that we can understand of the gifts bestowed on us by God (1 Corinthians 2:12).

Day 73

GOD TAKES US AS WE ARE
TO MAKE US WHAT HE WANTS

"And the LORD took me from following the flock" (Amos 7:15).

Read: **Amos 7:10-17;** Jeremiah 35:15; Ezekiel 33:11; Acts 18:3;
2 Corinthians 5:20; 1 Thessalonians 2:9.

WHAT IS GOD SAYING?

Israel was in an Indian Summer of national well-being.
Jeroboam II was king and the northern kingdom was enjoying a
short upturn in prosperity. But beneath the affluence there was
corruption and a collapsing of moral standards. Jeroboam I had
set up a calf-image as *his* contribution to the welfare of the new
kingdom of the north. It was not an auspicious start. The seeds
of idolatry which he sowed were bound to sprout and yield a
grim harvest. But in the day of Amos, things were going great.
The people were taking their ease. They were settling down to
enjoy the heady pleasures of their false freedom and fleeting
prosperity. They were doing quite well without God. But underneath there was a rottenness that spelled doom and disaster. No
person or nation can go contrary to the laws which God has
built into His universe without facing judgment, defeat, captivity, and death.

Amos was an ordinary man doing an ordinary job, but God
needed someone to warn his people. He didn't need a great
man with exceptional talents. He needed an honest man with
exceptional courage. Amos filled the bill. The king's chaplain
told him to get lost: "Go back to Judah. Maybe you can earn a
living there, but here we don't need your message and we surely
don't need you." Within thirty years, Israel fell to the Assyrians.
Having forsaken God, and having turned a deaf ear to the
warning of Amos, there could be no other outcome. Israel was
ripe for ruin and it came.

HOW DOES THIS APPLY TO US?

In calling Amos God took an ordinary shepherd and an
ordinary farmer to do an extraordinary job. He took him while
he was busy at his job. As we apply this text to our contemporary
situation, we need to remember that the principal ABILITY God
wants is AVAILABILITY. We are well-advised to be faithful in the
humble tasks we have to do: earning an honest living, preparing
a weekly Sunday school lesson, getting a meal on the table,

driving a school bus, working under a car in a garage. Nothing extraordinary. Just the faithful performance of common duty. It is from this source that God draws His best material. That is His way of recruiting. If we doubt that, we need to read again 2 Corinthians 4:7. We are instruments of His blessing. We need only to be vessels that are clean enough to be used, empty enough to be filled, and never fancy enough to be admired.

Pray with Me

Lord, you took Amos while he was busy doing his plain and everyday duty. Let the power also come upon me while I am doing the ordinary and necessary things.

May I not disdain the humble task while searching for You in the heights. May I never grow restless because such labor sometimes goes unnoticed and unpraised. May I see Your glory in the commonplace. May I find Your blessing in the routine.

If I ever do some brave and noble thing, let it not be something that I shall seek. Let it not be the fruit of selfish ambition nor the pressures of human pride. Rather let it just be Your choosing, Your using of a plain, available, and clean earthen vessel.

"Take me" as I follow the ordinary schedule of this ordinary day. "Take me" into Your plan that I may know my life is not in vain and is a useful part of Your perfect design. "Take me" into Your sheltering love that my soul may find relief from the burning blasts of evil.

Then, rested and restored, I will share the healing of Your grace with others. "Take me" for I am powerless to take myself one step along the path that leads to Your glory. Only as You "take me" can my soul be kept from being taken. For other powers seek to destroy our fellowship. Other powers put me out of step with Your purpose.

"Take me," Lord! In the wonderful, lifting, liberating power of Calvary, "take me"! "Take me" while following the flock. "Take me" while following the plain duties of life. Above all, "take me" from following and conforming to the herd. Then I will follow and be conformed to Christ. My life will then become convincing evidence of Your redeeming power.

In the ever-blessed Name of Christ, Amen.

MOVING ON IN THE LIFE OF PRAYER

Let us become increasingly ready to have God use us in ordinary ways and doing ordinary tasks. He should have the glory. In prayer we simply ask that He will "take" us where we are, "take" us where we can be used of Him, "take" to Himself the glory, and then "take" us by His grace to a reward that is better than we could ever imagine and more than we could ever deserve.

Day 74

CALLED AND KEPT

". . . *Preserved in Jesus Christ and called*" (*Jude 1b, KJV*).

Read: **Jude 1-24;** Psalm 37:28; 1 Corinthians 1:26-31; Ephesians 4:1-4; 2 Thessalonians 4:18; 2 Timothy 1:9.

WHAT IS GOD SAYING?

The purpose of Jude's short and urgent letter was to counter a bold and destructive school of false teaching. Its growth in popularity was alarming. To sense the alarm that true Christians felt concerning this, read also 2 Peter 2, for that is dealing with the same situation. These enemies of the faith had slipped in and were creating divisions. They were anti-authority. They arrogantly proclaimed that it is all right to kick over the traces of outmoded morality. Self-indulgence was the name of the game. "If it feels good, do it." They probably had bumper stickers on their chariots saying, "Question authority." They were advocates of a sexual revolution. Posing as intellectual superiors, they were gathering to themselves an increasing number of followers who were hearing what they wanted to hear: "You can have your cake and eat it too." Jude wrote to encourage Christians not to swallow their pleasant tasting poison. See the enemy for what it is, false to the core. This is not living. It is dying.

HOW DOES THIS APPLY TO US?

We need to hear the words of Jude again and again. As we are "built up in the faith," as we "wait for the mercy of our Lord Jesus Christ," we who are called will be kept for Jesus Christ. That is our only safeguard against the ungodly passions of the days in which we live.

Pray with Me

Lord, you have "called" Your own to reach that which is always beyond them. Drawing on Your strength, Your chosen ones can do and be the impossible. You have "called" Your disciples to a life of daring faith and unspotted wholeness. You have "called" Your own to pass through this world with words of peace and good will on their lips and with compassionate love in their hearts.

Thank you, Lord, for today's wonderful discovery: The One who calls is the One who keeps. I know I am called from a life of ease to a journey of faith. Yet may I never forget that behind the Wisdom that prods there is the Power that preserves.

Keep me from being so engrossed with being kept by Christ that I forget I am also called to adventure with Him.

"Called and kept!" All through the unknown ways of my pilgrimage . . . long or short, pleasant or lonely, easy or hard . . . only let me know that I am called *and* kept. Then I will not yield to the temptation of idleness since I am also called to the adventure of faith. I will not become discouraged by unrewarded labor and lonely duty, since I am confident of Your keeping power all through this journey of faith. "Called and kept!" . . . from the first eager stride to the last weary step.

Unto Him who not only calls but is also able to keep, unto Him who is not only able to keep but also calls, unto Him be glory and majesty, dominion and power . . . and the grateful praise of my believing heart, now and forever.

In Jesus' Name, Amen.

MOVING ON IN THE LIFE OF PRAYER

To find the true riches of prayer we must begin by accepting authority, the authority of Jesus. That is why our prayers end, "in the name of Jesus," or by His authority and with the seal of His authority. Jude's brief letter comes to its climax with the words of that beautiful and familiar benediction. The benediction, in turn, ends on the note of the authority of Jesus. "To the only God, our Savior through Jesus Christ our Lord, be glory, majesty, dominion, and AUTHORITY, before all time and now and for ever," We pray by the authority of Jesus and for His glory. It is by His authority and for *His* glory that we are called and kept.

Day 75

WAITING ON THE LORD

"Therefore wait ye upon me, saith the LORD, until the day that I rise up to the prey" (Zephaniah 3:8, KJV).

Read: **Zephaniah 3;** Psalm 25:5, 62:5, 123:2; Proverbs 20:22; Hosea 12:6; Galatians 5:5.

WHAT IS GOD SAYING?

Zephaniah is a contemporary of Jeremiah and prophesied in the early days of King Josiah's reign. Josiah brought good reforms but from the strong words of Zephaniah, ("shameless nation, rebellious and defiled, the oppressing city, she listens to no voice, she accepts no correction") it would appear that he was prophesying before these reforms took place, or early in Josiah's reign. Zephaniah doesn't pull any punches. He speaks of a day of terror about to break on Judah and surrounding nations. He describes this "day of the Lord" in language unparalleled in Scripture for sheer distress and anguish. Zephaniah also points to the final victory of God's redeeming love. "The Lord your God is in your midst, a warrior who gives victory; he will rejoice over you with gladness, he will renew you in his love" (Zephaniah 3:17).

Chapter 3 verse 8 speaks of the importance of waiting on God, trusting in God, and believing that He "will rise to the prey." God, in His time and for His glory, will subdue all His enemies—and ours. Zephaniah grimly warns those who do wrong. He also strongly encourages those who wait upon the Lord, doing His will, biding His time, and trusting His Word.

HOW DOES THIS APPLY TO US?

The more sensitive we are to the leading of God's Spirit and the pure grace of God's holiness and love, the more sensitive we should become to "the prey." What is "preying" on us just now? What is gnawing away at the integrity of our relationship with God? What is making it easy for us to compromise? When we want old temptations to get lost but they keep coming back like bad pennies, we need to wait on the Lord. We must believe that He will rise to the prey. We are not in this battle alone. Our one great need is to wait on the Lord, to pray, to believe, and to trust.

Pray with Me

O God of eternity, with You there is neither hasting nor wasting. Your purpose is never restricted by the measurements of time and space that irk our impatient spirits. I want to learn to wait upon You . . . until my strength is renewed . . . until You "rise up to the prey" in Your perfect time and in Your perfect way.

I am impatient to see sudden justice. If the righteous suffer, my heart wonders why the God whom I love can remain indifferent to pain and aloof toward injustice. May I learn to "wait upon You" *until* the day that You "will rise up to the prey."

I am sometimes discouraged when opposition falls across my path. Teach me to "wait upon You until the day that you will rise up to the prey." When a word of unjust criticism deals a smarting blow, teach me to wait upon You. When other people are slow to respond to things that I find so obvious, teach me to wait upon You. Teach me to wait upon You if, when lifting up my Lord with loving zeal, I feel alone and misunderstood.

Yet I also believe, Lord, that I need not wait for You to "rise up to the prey" that lurks in the shadows of my own heart. Come quickly, Lord. Come quickly to subdue my wandering affections. Come quickly to reign in my heart without rival and without reservations. I *need not* wait and I have faith that You *will not* wait.

When the penitent heart is not ashamed to own its shame, then, O God, You will rise up to the prey. When the humble heart is not too proud to confess its pride, then, O God, You will rise up to the prey. When the believing heart has no doubt that doubt is a vulnerable enemy and a needless obsession, then, O God, You will rise up to the prey.

I claim this victory now.

In Jesus' Name, Amen.

MOVING ON IN THE LIFE OF PRAYER

All of us have things that keep preying on us. All the more reason to keep praying to Him. We should not be surprised at the enemy's constant attacks. We should know that he waits in ambush to strike us at our weakest point and in our weakest moments. That is why we need to pray without ceasing. No evil can prey on us when we pray to God. We can claim the victory always, because it is HIS.

Day 76

GOD IN MERCY NEVER FORSAKES

"Even when they had made for themselves a molten calf . . . Thou in Thy great mercies did not forsake them" (Nehemiah 9:18, 19).

Read: **Nehemiah 9:1-25;** Hebrews 9:16-21; Exodus 32:4; Deuteronomy 9:16-21; Acts 7:39-41.

WHAT IS GOD SAYING?

The principal god of Egypt was the Bull. As the Israelites wandered through the wilderness, they grew physically tired, emotionally drained . . . and thoroughly discouraged. Even their leader had left them for a long absence on Mt. Sinai. What could they pin their hopes on? When could they look for relief and release? Who would understand their problem? Maybe the Golden Calf whom they saw worshiped in Egypt would make himself more readily available than Jehovah seemed to be doing. This is the rationale for what they did. God was angry. Moses, as his instrument, "took the sinful thing, the calf which [they] had made, and burned it with fire and crushed it, grinding it very small, until it was as fine as dust; and . . . threw the dust of it into the brook that descended out of the mountain" (Deuteronomy 9:21). And God still guided them as they continued the impossible wilderness journey.

As we read these accounts of Israel's stubbornness and God's mercies, we need to recall that the Israelites were always worshiping the idols of the peoples around them in spite of the warning and the pleadings of the prophets. It wasn't until their captivity in Babylon that they were cured of these dangerous liaisons with "other gods." From the days of their captivity until now—two-and-a-half millennia—the Jews have never again been guilty of this sin. But in many places in Scripture, the Holy Spirit takes up the refrain to make sure the people of God would never slip back. Our passage in Nehemiah is not only a reminder of how Israel in rebellion behaved toward God, but also of how God, in His great mercy and patience, behaved toward them.

HOW DOES THIS APPLY TO US?

God is still dealing mercifully with those who wander away in rebellion and pride, but return in humility and faith. We have our Golden Calves, our substitutes for the living God. We have things in our lives that seem more important because they promise more immediate gratification. We, too, grow discouraged in a wilderness—a treadmill of monotonous busyness without tangible or meaningful results. To banish our sense of emptiness and lostness in this secular world, we may have looked for satisfaction in lesser gods, although we would *never* call them Golden Calves. Even so, God is patiently waiting for us to forsake these idols. He may discipline us, but in His mercy, He will never forsake us.

Pray with Me

God of all mercy, Your goodness never wavers. My heart is sometimes chilled with pride. It is sometimes hardened by selfish interests. I have made for myself many a molten calf. But now my heart is warmed and softened because I have seen again the great mercies of my unforsaking God.

When I have experienced even slight discouragement, my eyes have turned from the throne of grace.

When pride has lifted me up, I have forgotten that God is my constant need.

When comforts have lulled me into perilous slumber, I have forgotten that my only hope is Your moment by moment grace.

When temptation has beckoned me into the quicksands of a moral short-cut, I have dared to leave Your presence. I have dared to shut You out. I have dared to believe that the One who is always kind is the One who never minds.

In moods of discouragement, I have said, "God may care, but He is not there." In moments of temptation, I have said, "God may be there, but He does not care." So in the middle of a wilderness, I have in effect made a molten calf. I have fashioned an unhearing, unspeaking, and uncaring substitute for You.

My only hope is that You will not leave me with my lifeless toys. My only hope is that You will not leave me with my helpless idols in the wilderness of an impoverished and pointless existence.

Create in me a deeper gratitude for Your unforsaking mercies. Give me a stronger determination never to forsake You.

In the Name of Him who said, and ceaselessly proves, "I will never leave you nor forsake you." Amen.

MOVING ON IN THE LIFE OF PRAYER

Let prayer be a time of consciously tearing down the idols that have assumed a higher priority than God has in our life. Let prayer also be a time of gratitude for Him who said, "I will never leave you nor forsake you." Are we willing to forsake all those things that are bound to forsake us and choose to follow the one God, who will never forsake us? Grow in prayer by forsaking the trivial even though it may not be all bad and embracing the best which is all good: the love and truth of Jesus Christ.

Day 77

Strong Faith and Glory to God

"Strong in faith, giving glory to God" (Romans 4:20, KJV).

Read: **Romans 4;** Genesis 15:6; 1 Chronicles 29:11; 2 Chronicles 20:20; Matthew 17:20; John 6:28-29.

What Is God Saying?

To say *faith* is the single greatest theme in the Bible would not be far off target. And the greatest person associated with this greatest theme is Abraham. In his letter to the Romans, Paul builds the case for faith as the basis of salvation. Nothing else, nothing more, nothing less. He is aware of the fact that Jews in Rome—and everywhere else—were steeped in the laws and traditions of Judaism. Salvation to them was a matter of keeping the laws and leading a flawless moral life. Of course they, as we, must fail if that is the only way. Good works is a ladder that is neither long enough nor strong enough to get us into Heaven. "There is no distinction; since *all* have sinned and fall short of the glory of God" (Romans 3:22-23). Abraham was the father of the Jewish nation and a classic example of one who was morally upright. If Paul could show that Abraham was accepted because of his faith, he would have a powerful argument in support of his thesis.

In Romans 4:20-23, Paul shows that the promise was given on the basis of Abraham's faith while he was still uncircumcised. It was not a Jewish rite but *faith* that counted. The great thing about Abraham was his faith, not his Jewish identity. In the passage before us Paul shows the strength of Abraham's faith against all obstacles. The patriarch's faith in the promises of God gave glory to God. Our strong faith and God's great glory go together.

How Does This Apply to Us?

Above all else, God wants us to be strong in faith. When we have faith, God can do the impossible. When we do not have faith, even His hands are tied (see Matthew 13:58). The promises of God are at the very heart of all praying. They are the substance of prayer, the goal of prayer, the basis of prayer. As Abraham would allow no distrust to make him waver concerning the promises of God, so we need to begin, continue, and end our prayers in the full assurance that *"God is able to do what he has promised."*

Pray with Me

Lord, You are my strength and my salvation. Teach me how to be strong and where to be strong and why to be strong.

Help me to know that when faith has opened the door, strength surges into the soul. Not in feverish labor, not in self-punishing discipline, but in "quietness and confidence shall be my strength."

Let my strength be the supple and vital strength of faith and not the brittle, death-bound strength of pride.

Let my strength be the clear and confident strength of faith and not the vague and fear-laden strength of doubt.

Others may boast of knowledge and pride themselves on knowing their way around. Others may find comfort on the "easy" path of cynical disbelief and stoic indifference. But my strength and my pride and my comfort shall be in a faith that rests in nothing but the promises of God.

"Strong faith and glory to God." They go together. More than that, they hold *me* together. I cannot go to pieces in discouragement. I will not break off into icy segments of pride so long as my faith is strong and God gets the glory.

The strength of faith will be mine. It will not enhance my prestige nor cater in any way to pride. It will only "give glory to God." My sole purpose for living is to glorify You. Any strength of mine received and expressed through faith shall be only and always for Your glory.

I am grateful for the glory I have seen in the face of Jesus Christ. I offer this prayer in His Name and the strength of my faith in His service, Amen.

MOVING ON IN THE LIFE OF PRAYER

Strong faith leads to the glory of God. It believes God can do what He has promised. If we keep on believing as we keep on praying we will keep on seeing the glory of God in answered prayer.

Day 78

GOD IS NEAR IN TROUBLE

"His way is in whirlwind and storm, and the clouds are the dust of his feet" (Nahum 1:3b).

Read: **Nahum 1**; Exodus 34:1-14; Jeremiah 25:32, 30:23.

WHAT IS GOD SAYING?

Nineveh, the proud, cruel capital of Assyria is the focal point of two Old Testament books: Jonah and Nahum. A century and a half before Nahum, God sent Jonah to Nineveh with a message of mercy: If they would repent, God would spare them. They did repent—for a while. But as the city continued its downward drift God sent Nahum to tell them He could no longer tolerate their evil. He would not ignore the pain and suffering Assyria had inflicted on Israel. They would even be punished for plundering the wealth of Thebes, treasures which had been accumulated through centuries, and torn away in a moment. Nahum 2:11-13 describes Nineveh as a den of ravaging lions feeding on other nations. They were the most brazen pirates of the years before Christ.

But justice would have its day. Nineveh was heading for total destruction. Jonah's prophecy refers twice to Assyria's capital as, "Nineveh, *that great city.*" Now, all that is left of *that great city* is a mound of earth known as Tell Kuyunjik, "the mound of many sheep."

HOW DOES THIS APPLY TO US?

God *does* have His way in the whirlwind and storm. Clouds *do* at times furnish the proof of His presence. They are like the dust of His feet. Nahum's original intent of picturing the destructive force of God's vengeance was to show that, "No nation can get away with murder forever." But we turn our attention now to his graphic description of God's presence in whirlwind, storm, and clouds. It is proof that no storm sweeps across our lives without his permissive will. When we are surrounded by clouds, it may be only proof that He is near, not always in judgment but sometimes in mercy. God appeared to Moses and the people of Israel many times in a cloud. He led them through the wilderness with a pillar of *cloud* by day and a pillar of fire by night. The glory of the Lord appeared in the *cloud* (Exodus 16:10). On the Mount of Transfiguration, it was out of a bright *cloud* that God spoke. "The clouds are the dust of his feet," the proof that He is there.

Pray with Me

When, in the history of the world or in the pilgrimage of my own soul, O Lord, Your way leads through whirlwind and storm, teach my heart to trust that the very clouds are the dust of Your feet.

Give me wisdom to choose the way of quiet trust. I am prone to panic. When my way is difficult and my path dark, I surrender to doubt and yield to fear.

Instead of waiting upon God, I worry about God. Instead of depending on Your providence, I debate about Your providence. Instead of letting go of tensions and holding on to God, I hold my tensions and let go of God.

I pray for grace to abandon all this. To leave it behind me in the rubbish of forgotten things.

I boldly affirm that hardships *can* teach me more of Your love and power than I would ever learn in ways of ease and pleasure. When Your wisdom places me beneath clear, warm, cloudless skies, I will recognize Your nearness and praise You for Your love. But I also confidently declare that should the sun be covered and the clouds appear, I will never deny Your nearness nor be ungrateful for mysterious providence.

Have Your way . . . have Your way in any whirlwind and in every storm. But let my love be so deep and my trust so real that, far from dislodging my confidence, the clouds and tempests shall be the proof that You are near.

In the face of all trial, teach my trusting heart to sing: "The Lord God omnipotent reigns . . . the Lord sits upon the flood . . . the clouds are the dust of his feet."

In the Name of Jesus Christ whose undying and radiant love has subdued the storms of sin and will outshine the last cloud of death, Amen.

MOVING ON IN THE LIFE OF PRAYER

How are we handling the whirlwinds, the storms, and the clouds in our lives? Do they just get us *down*? Or do they get us *down on our knees*? Let us be only the more willing to pray when things are hard. God may be melting us to mold us. He may be getting ready to fill us and use us. Pray without ceasing. Pray with deep trust and gratitude through every storm. "The clouds are the dust of His feet." Thank you, Nahum for reminding us that "the Lord is good, a stronghold in the day of trouble; he knows those who take refuge in him" (Nahum 1:7).

Day 79

AS THE LORD COMMANDS

"*As the* LORD *had commanded Moses . . .*" *(Exodus 39:1).*

Read: **Exodus 39.**

WHAT IS GOD SAYING?

After God had delivered Israel from their bondage in Egypt, they encountered the lonely and hostile wilderness. God planned that they should have a visible sign of His presence. They had *their* tents. Now God was to have *His,* a meeting place, a tabernacle. They would see the tabernacle and say: "We are not alone, we have not been deserted, God is with us. His holy place is there." This tent would contain the Ark of the Covenant, the very symbol of His presence. This was so important to God that He gave to the people through Moses the precise specifications contained in Exodus 25-31. Later, in chapters 35-40, these commands were carried out to the letter. Over and over again the words appeared, "As the Lord commanded." The craftsmen built what the Lord *commanded.* The Ark with all its fittings, the vessels used for worship in the tabernacle, the robes worn by the priests, every detail was carefully observed "as the Lord *commanded.*" Nothing was left to chance. It was a divine blueprint carried out with scrupulous attention to detail.

HOW DOES THIS APPLY TO US?

The meaningful symbolism of the tabernacle as it points the way to Christ and His atoning death on Calvary, is worthy of study. Today we apply the often repeated phrase, "As the Lord commanded" to the rule of God's Spirit in our hearts. As the tabernacle's construction with all of its adornments was made to conform to God's design, so we should be willing to see that what God has put on the drafting board for our lives becomes a reality down to the smallest detail. This is not to curtail or stifle our growth. God is not hindering us according to capricious whims. He is rather helping us to come to true maturity. The fulfillment of life at its best. We are trusting that God knows the best and wants the best and, to make it happen, we want to know what He wants.

Pray with Me

Let Your Holy Spirit, Lord, rule in my heart. I would not have Him as a sometime Visitor or casual Acquaintance. I invite Him to take up His permanent dwelling in my heart. But I need

Him for more than that. It may be that I will not always *want* Him to rule, but it is always true that I *need* Him to rule.

So, Lord, let Your Holy Spirit rule in my heart. In the smallest detail of life, let there be a quiet listening, a quick understanding, and a total obedience—as the Lord commands.

May this wilderness journey find me making every decision, building every dream, and pursuing every goal—as the Lord commands.

Let all soul-destroying sin, all that corrupts and beguiles and enslaves be conquered and removed in the atonement of Jesus—as the Lord commands.

Let the most inexpressible desire and unacknowledged passion seeking to hold me in its sway for good or evil, be encouraged or conquered—as the Lord commands.

Give me to see that—as the Lord commands—the Promised Land holds for me an overruling and an ever-ruling Peace. I have an incorruptible inheritance that will not fade away for all eternity.

Then, even more than now, I shall praise You for the grace that led my heart to think, to feel, and to do—as the Lord commands.

In Jesus' Name, Amen.

MOVING ON IN THE LIFE OF PRAYER

The Holy of Holies had three altars of great significance. First, the altar of burnt-offering (Exodus 27:1-8) for the sacrifice of self, the surrender of our best to receive His best. Then, the altar of incense (Exodus 30:1-6), the symbol of prayer. Third, the mercy seat (Exodus 25:17), where the blood of sacrifice was finally sprinkled. Along with the priceless symbols of Christ's sacrifice for us and the surrendering of ourselves to God's perfect will, prayer has its place, according to "the commands of God." Let us obey the command to pray and stay with it until the command to pray becomes the privilege of praying, sharing our best joys and our honest concerns in fellowship with God at the deepest levels.

Day 80

MORE THAN A HAND-OUT

"But Peter said, 'I have no silver and gold but I give you what I have; in the name of Jesus Christ of Nazareth, walk' " (Acts 3:6).

Read: **Acts 3:1-16.**

WHAT IS GOD SAYING?

For Peter and John it was the ninth hour, time for the afternoon prayer meeting. For the man lame from birth, the day dawned and moved through noon with the same dull and pointless routine that characterized every other day. He was carried to a place where he could beg. He hoped those on the way to pray would toss him a coin. But people seldom even looked at him, let alone dug down in their purses to give him something. A not so beautiful life beside a gate called Beautiful. For Peter and John it was the time to pray—and probably to give thanks for the way Peter's faithful testimony was used and blessed at Pentecost. They were witnesses of the Resurrection. They were bold. Exultant. Overflowing vessels. They had something far more than money could buy: the very power of God flowing from their lives. They saw something the others missed on the way to prayer meeting. A person in need, a man they could help, a problem for which they had a solution. God brought healing. The lame man would never be the same man.

HOW DOES THIS APPLY TO US?

Shall we put ourselves in the place of the lame man? We may not be physically handicapped, but we may be living *outside* the Gate that leads to a Beautiful life. Being able to walk, we are not walking as we should or as we could. We need to receive the grace of healing for our crippled spirits. On examination, we may find that too much of our lives is pointless and powerless. Too much of our lives is spent along the wayside. Christ wants us to walk, not limp. He wants us to *leap up* with joy and enthusiasm, not drowse with boredom and lack of purpose. The Lord is still reaching down and lifting up. Many of us have found that there is a better life than begging for an occasional handout. There is a way through the Beautiful Gate of faith to a Beautiful Life of service. Let Jesus touch our lives today at our point of need, for the sake of His glory.

Pray with Me

O Jesus of Nazareth, in Your Name I pray. In Your Name I am healed, forgiven, and cleansed. In Your Name, therefore, I would walk.

The dejected beggar looked for a few coins, a small handout, a little assist that would help him get on with a life that was going nowhere.

But instead of a handout he received a hand outstretched in compassionate, healing love. Instead of being supplied for another twenty-four hours of humiliating existence, he was given a lifetime of deliverance. In the name of Jesus Christ of Nazareth, he walked!

Lord, by Your grace and in the healing, lifting power of Your Name, I too, have been raised from a pointless and parasitical existence by the wayside of life. No longer needing to envy those who are well, no longer needing to sit by the Beautiful Gate with my not-so-beautiful thoughts, no longer needing to dwell on the emptiness of a life going nowhere, You have enabled me to walk.

Now with all my heart I want to use the God-given grace of walking to go on errands of love. I want to be the incarnation of Your grace to others. I want to move in the paths of righteousness for Your Name's sake and to hasten to others in need for Your love's sake. I want to walk wide around every tempting trap set by the Enemy of my soul.

As in Your Name I have the power to walk, so in Your name I would be shown the way to walk. My prayer, my desire, my very life is in the name of Him who makes walking not only possible . . . but beautiful.

It is in His Name I pray, Amen.

MOVING ON IN THE LIFE OF PRAYER

In prayer we can speak honestly with the One who cares greatly. We don't have to be spiritually lame when He can make us whole. The beggar sat along the way that led to prayer. We don't have to beg, for He has allowed us to boldly *claim* the blessings of our living Lord.

Day 81

THE LOVE OF GOD AWAKENS LIFE

"My beloved speaks and says to me: Arise, my love, my fair one, and come away; for lo, the winter is past, the rain is over and gone. The flowers appear on the earth . . ." (Song of Solomon 2:10-12).

Read: **Song of Solomon 2;** 1 Kings 4:33.

WHAT IS GOD SAYING?

The Song of Solomon defies analysis. For that reason, it has been subjected to many allegorical interpretations. The Jews see how it points to the love of God for Israel. Christians perceive Christ's love for His bride, the Church. Yet on the surface, Solomon's tender verse celebrates the gift of human love. God clearly intends human beings to enjoy physical love within boundaries ordained for our good.

Today's reading takes place in the fragrant blossoming of springtime. Solomon wrote 1,005 songs (1 Kings 4:32), and it is possible that this was his favorite . . . "the Song of Songs."

HOW DOES THIS APPLY TO US?

Looking beyond other possible interpretations of these verses, let us consider how the love of God awakens us from the winter of indifference to a spring of life and faith and joy. As the seasons go through their cycles, so God is continually bringing new springtimes into our lives. While Christians are not shielded from winter's chill, they can always be confident of spring's return. Eventually we come to realize that we can live through every winter because the hope of spring and the power of the risen Christ is always in our hearts.

Pray with Me

Your call, dear Lord, is a call to beauty and joy.

It was Love that awakened me from the deadness of winter. It was Love that brought me out of sin's hibernation. It was Love that stirred me from slumbering half-content.

I did not and could not realize in such a state that heavenly springtime had already come to this earth. I was not aware that flower-form and bird-song had blessed the land. I could not see that life was bursting with beauty. I did not know that God had called and, from the deepest springs of all being, resurgent power was answering. I did not and could not realize that all this was mine for the waking and for the taking. But O beloved Christ, Your Voice came in kindness to stir me from the stupor of an existence that was all rigid with pride. When Your touch came, I even resented being aroused. The dreams of little things can be so beguiling.

Yet in patient love, Your voice insisted. In longsuffering grace, Your hand kept shaking. Now I rise in gladness to a life all-glorious with forgotten fragrance and splendor. I rise to a life that need not know again the deadening chill of winter. I walk forever in the presence of the Lord, the Beloved One, who burst through the sealed tomb of death to bring eternal springtime to mankind.

Your touch has awakened me and I am glad. Your voice has called, "Rise up, My love," and I obey. Love can make us rise and leave the past. But greater, far greater, is my joy in knowing the eternal love that leads in the way everlasting to life everlasting . . . where winter is forever past and birds forever sing and the year is forever spring.

In the Name of Him who through conquering winter's death has given eternal spring, Amen.

MOVING ON IN THE LIFE OF PRAYER

Let us be confident that Christ will bring the freshness and fragrance of spring into our lives. It may be winter all around us. The earth may be frozen and hard. Yet prayer can bring springtime to our souls, because it is centered on the living Christ and based on the power of His resurrection.

Day 82

THE UNITY OF BELIEVERS

"Now the company of those who believed were of one heart and soul" (*Acts 4:32*).

Read: **Acts 4;** Isaiah 52:8; John 17:22-23; Romans 12:5; Ephesians 4:13.

WHAT IS GOD SAYING?

The healing of the incurably lame man continued to draw attention to Peter and John. So much so, that the rulers and elders who wanted the two apostles off the streets and out of their way didn't dare do more than slap their wrists. The boldness of the ex-fishermen annoyed the leaders, but their fear of a backlash from the people dictated something other than imprisonment. The preaching went on bolder than ever. But an even greater power was being generated. "And when they had *prayed,* the place in which they were gathered together was shaken; and they were all filled with the Holy Spirit" (Acts

4:31). Result: continued boldness in preaching and a strong sense of unity. This unity was deep and real. Those who believed were of *one heart and soul* (Acts 4:32).

Their new sense of unity manifested itself in practical ways. The believers sacrificed for one another, selling their property and distributing the proceeds to those in need. In that glorious moment of the early church, the need of others was given priority. It was important that none should have need. It was unthinkable that any should have greed. It was a foretaste of Heaven. Great prayer and faithful preaching brought unity, and unity brought a desire to care with a willingness to share.

How Does This Apply to Us?

This was a unity of *believers*. There was a reason behind their sacrifice and sharing. It was the fact and the power of the resurrection: "And with great power the apostles gave their testimony to the resurrection of the Lord Jesus, and great grace was upon them all" (Acts 4:33). Belief leads to unity and sharing when it does not come out of a book but out of the shining radiance of an empty tomb. Academic belief is sterile. It cannot reproduce itself. Faith founded on the reality of a living Christ is powerful enough to bring unity in prayer, boldness in preaching, and the kind of caring that is not at rest when others are in need.

Pray with Me

O Lord, in whom is all our hope and our only hope for unity, give to me this day a deep desire to be of one heart and soul with all believers.

Help me to be "one" with all who call upon Your name. Help me to understand the unspoken needs of other believers—and how I may demonstrate the love of Christ in meeting those needs. Help me to be "one" with all who call upon Your name by not always insisting that things be done in my way, to suit my convenience, or to feed my pride.

Help me to be "one" with all who call upon Your name, but never to purchase a cheap and shallow peace through compromise. Help me to hold my ground when Your Spirit clearly directs me to do so. May I even be willing to be thought difficult and unreasonable if the end is for Your glory and the final unity of all believers.

Help me to be "one" with all who call upon Your name in counting false and harmful every dream, desire, plan, or ambition that does not find its origin in love and its end in the purposes of God.

Help me to be "one" with all who call upon Your name in looking with eagerness of spirit and hunger of heart for that blessed hope, the glorious appearing of Jesus Christ.

Send this kind of living unity upon Your Church and deliver us from all deadening uniformity. Let each of us bring our gifts, as varied and as beautiful as the colors of a rainbow. Then let the rainbow arch of Your blessing bind us all together until in deed and in truth we are one in the Spirit and one in the Lord.

In the Name of Him who makes and keeps us one in the hope of our calling and in the strength of His love, Amen.

MOVING ON IN THE LIFE OF PRAYER

The prayer of believers should touch upon the unspoken needs of other believers. The prayer of believers should concentrate on the greatest need of unbelievers: that they may come to know Christ. The prayer of believers does not seek compromise that leads to shallow peace but does seek understanding that leads to accepting believers who are "different." The prayer of believers brings "great grace upon all," those who pray and those for whom they pray. This kind of praying makes sense. It also makes saints.

Day 83

RESTORING PRIORITIES

"Consider how you have fared. You have sown much, and harvested little; you eat, but you never have enough . . ." (Haggai 1:5-6).

Read: **Haggai 1, 2:10-19;** Ecclesiastes 2:11, 6:7; Isaiah 55:2; John 6:27; Ephesians 4:17.

WHAT IS GOD SAYING?

The last three books of the Old Testament concern themselves with the problems Israel faced upon its return from exile. The first wave of returning exiles fell to the task of rebuilding the Temple with fresh enthusiasm. Home again! The Temple had been demolished by the Babylonians in 587 B.C. And the priority that lay on all their hearts was to build the most important thing in the land. The Temple: a place to unite their voices in praise, a place to pray, a place to show their thankfulness for deliverance from the humiliation and shame of the Babylonian captivity.

One would think that this glorious task, this highest of priorities, would proceed without a hitch. But time and diverse loyalties and human apathy have a way of dulling the keen edge of national goals. The work slowly ground to a halt. For years trivial pursuits claimed priority. The zeal faded. Work on the Temple was neglected and eventually abandoned. But Haggai's message should be remembered as much for re-establishing priorities as for its appeal to get busy on the Temple. Read also Haggai 2:10-19. On the day the people stopped being wrapped up in themselves, their own comforts, their own ambitions, their own welfare, their own security, from that day on God would begin to bless. Put first things first and God will bless every aspect of life.

How Does This Apply to Us?

Consider the things of lesser importance that have "taken over" in our lives. It is not the rebuilding of a Temple that has suffered by our neglect. But it may well be the de-emphasizing of worship, the absence of prayer, the lack of involvement in the needs of others, too much reticence in the sharing of our faith, and on and on. Priorities! We need to make conscious, daily decisions that His ways will be our ways, His thoughts our thoughts, His love our love, His work our work. Then for our labor there *will* be results and in receiving nourishment we will find satisfaction. In coming to prayer always search out priorities.

Pray with Me

Lord, Your way alone brings enduring peace. Your way alone brings satisfying abundance. Give me wisdom now, as I consider my own ways.

Am I directing my feet into the path of Your will? Is there a shred of self-defense or an ounce of pride that would resist my heart's desire to walk in fellowship with You? Yes, Lord, there is. Only honest answers will do.

Remove these inner frictions. Bring an end to my heart's civil war. Convict me and cleanse me, Spirit of the living God. Do not let me accept anything less, until Your will is my will. Until I go beyond considering my ways to deliberately choosing Yours.

When wayward affections lead me away from You, I have known the futility of unfruitful labor. Apart from you "sowing much" can bring in "little harvest." Apart from you "eating" to the full can leave one hungry. Have I not known enough of this barren existence? Has it not shown itself to be all the emptiness that You declare it to be?

In Your untiring grace strive with me until I choose the better part. Leave me not to the tyranny of self-will. In the light of Your perfect knowledge and patient love, I would consider and reconsider my ways until each new day finds me deliberately and gladly making Your way my way.

I believe that if I spend my life in this way, my sowing will yield fruit to all eternity. I believe that feeding on Your truth will satisfy the hunger of my heart—fully—and forever.

In the Name of Him whose love forever satisfies and whose blessing forever endures, Amen.

MOVING ON IN THE LIFE OF PRAYER

Prayer is the time to search out and hold on to *God's* priorities. In the stillness of prayer, God has a chance to spotlight the places we ought to go, the things we ought to do, the people we ought to care for and love in special ways, the letters we ought to write, the relationship we should restore or abandon, the forgiveness we ought to give or to seek, the little ambitions we ought to give up, the little acts of kindness that mean so much and go so far. Prayer is the time for prioritizing.

Day 84

NOURISHED BY THE WORD OF GOD

". . . Nourished on the words of the faith . . ." (1 Timothy 4:6).

Read: **1 Timothy 4;** Deuteronomy 8:3; Psalm 119:103; Jeremiah 15:16; 1 Peter 2:2.

WHAT IS GOD SAYING?

First Timothy is a letter of encouragement and warning based on a father's love for his son. "To Timothy, my true child in the faith" (1:2). It has become a guide to all ministers, especially younger ones. It must have proven effective then. Without benefit of seminaries, the work of preaching, teaching, evangelizing, and organizing went on more rapidly than at any time since. Could it be that this happened because the ministers of the early Church kept their minds on the essentials and were not burdened with time-consuming and superficial extras? In his advice to young ministers in chapter 4, Paul speaks of four of these essentials. You will be a good minister if: (1) you are nourished on the words of faith (4:6); (2) if you get into a spiritual fitness program (4:7); (3) if you watch what you *are* (4:16); and (4) if you watch what you *say* (4:16). It is the first of these "essentials" that has our attention today.

How Does This Apply to Us?

There were many false teachings in Timothy's time. We have more than our share today. The fact is, we have more than we can handle unless we "are nourished on the words of faith." "Isms" have risen in all centuries. In our time, Satan may be redoubling his efforts. But nothing can stand as a bulwark against false teaching so much as true nourishment in the words of faith. We are to seek and to find spiritual strength from the Word of God. We are not to read it with casual interest. People are not fed by dawdling over their food. (A little here, a little there, and then who cares?) We are not to argue about the Word. We are not to use it as a decorative piece in the living room. We are not to enshrine it as a sacred relic, perhaps the legacy of devout parents. We are not to sit in judgment of it. We are *to be nourished by it.*

Pray with Me

Help me, Lord, to take the nourishment which is promised in Your Word. Keep me from merely admiring it. Don't let me linger on that dangerous periphery where men argue about it and analyze it and sit in judgment of it. I don't want to hold it in such distant awe that I fail to see it as my daily food. Guard me from attaching to Your Word such mysterious wonder that I fail to see its very available strength.

As food strengthens my body and is daily eaten for physical health, so let Your Word strengthen my soul and be daily received for spiritual health.

As the best food is eaten because of its health-giving value and not mainly because of its pleasing taste, so let me accept— no, let me long for—the spiritual food I need. Not what I *think* I want or what gives immediate and passing pleasure.

Help me not to labor for the "food which perishes." Let my desire be set on food that endures . . . and helps me to endure . . . to everlasting life.

Give this food to me, for then I will leave behind the misery of a weak and listless soul, continually infected by sin. Nourish me with a vision of Yourself, O living Word, for this is the nourishment that conquers the anemia of a vacillating faith. This is the nourishment that raises the soul's resistance to infectious sin.

In fellowship with You, I will have the glow of spiritual well-being, and Your name will forever have the praise of a well-nourished heart.

Through Jesus Christ, the true Bread of Heaven, Amen.

Moving On in the Life of Prayer

Prayer leads us to the Word. Prayer flows out from the Word. "Nourished on the *words* of faith," we are more ready to offer the *prayer* of faith. To go on in prayer and to grow in prayer, nothing is more important than giving our souls regular, repeated, and adequate nourishment from the Word. Sit at God's training table. Don't skimp. There's more in the Kitchen.

Day 85

Life Is More than Existing

"He brought me forth into a broad place" (2 Samuel 22:20).

Read: **2 Samuel 22;** Psalm 3:7-8, 118:5-6; 1 Chronicles 4:10; John 10:9-10; 2 Corinthians 9:8; 2 Peter 1:11.

What Is God Saying?

Even after David reached the zenith of his popular reign, his troubles were far from over. The heaviest burdens he would ever face were gathering like ominous clouds on the horizon. Chapters 13-21 of 2 Samuel tell of the things that broke his heart again and again: Absalom's attempt to steal the throne and his subsequent death, the defection of David's trusted advisers, still other attempts to undermine his reign from within, and a resurgence of his old enemies, the Philistines. The depth of his trial in those years can be sensed but not fully comprehended.

But for all his sin and for all the waywardness of his family, David was still "the man after God's own heart" (1 Samuel 13:14). He emerged from the trials with the royal dignity of the king he was intended to be. He trusted God who had never failed him. He lived to write a great and final psalm of victory and praise to the Almighty, "This God—His way is perfect; the promise of the LORD proves true" (2 Samuel 22:31). The enemy came on in waves, too mighty for a man, even David, to handle in his own strength. But "the LORD was my stay," sang David, "he brought me forth into a broad place."

How Does This Apply to Us?

Are we thankful for the broad places in our lives? Are we even aware of them? There are times when we do realize the expansiveness of God's love and protection, the abundance of His blessing. As we come to prayer, we may have the same joy as David had. No more shadowy images appearing at the narrow passes to attack us while they wait in ambush. No more depression of mind and spirit, no more discouragement, no more feeling useless, weak, and outnumbered. We are praying to a God of omnipotent power and abundant blessing. "His way is perfect; the promise of the Lord proves true" (22:31). Let that thought be filtered through our prayers, let our hearts be saturated with that kind of confidence. It's the way we *come* to a broad place. It's the way we *stay* there, too.

Pray with Me

O Christ, my strong Deliverer, on the Cross and through the Cross You have brought me forth into a broad place.

Out of the narrowness of an existence in bondage to sin; into the largeness of a life in obedience to truth.

Out of the darkness of an existence haunted by fear; into the light of a life strengthened by hope.

Out of the prison of an existence devoted to self; into the liberty of a life devoted to You and to others.

From the little pains that seemed so big, from the little complaints that seemed so important, from the little excuses that seemed so valid, from the little victories that seemed so great, from the little plans that seemed so bold, from the little self-denials that seemed so commendable, You have brought me forth into a broad place where I can see that nothing is big or important unless it is done in Your Spirit and for Your glory.

As Your living presence continues to bring strength to my hand and courage to my heart, I am growing to a measure of the stature of the fullness of Christ. It is wonderful to live in the broad places of Your love! As You love the whole world and send Your rain to fall on the just and the unjust, so let my life be a continual blessing to others.

You have brought me forth into spacious regions that I may serve as one who has unlimited freedom. You have brought me forth into a broad place that I may share as one who has inexhaustible blessings.

Forgive me and deliver me whenever this hard-dying self tries to hold Your blessings in and Your other children out. As You have brought me forth, so keep me in the broad place of Your usefulness, Your blessing, and Your love.

For Jesus' sake, Amen.

MOVING ON IN THE LIFE OF PRAYER

The burden of our praying should be that of claiming God's abundant blessings moment by moment. We are not beggars asking for a handout. We are sons, joint-heirs with Christ, claiming the family riches. When prayer takes on this dimension and proceeds on the basis of this spiritual fact, we are delivered from a cramped, narrow existence that frustrates and hampers on every side. We discover what we can never explain, the freedom and joy of abundant life in a "broad place."

PERFECT IN JESUS CHRIST

". . . Perfect in Christ Jesus . . ." (Colossians 1:28, KJV).

Read: **Colossians 1;** Matthew 5:48; Ephesians 4:13; Philippians 3:12-14; Deuteronomy 18:13; 1 Kings 8:54-61.

WHAT IS GOD SAYING?

Anyone who wants to point a non-believer to the full majesty and perfection of Jesus Christ should make use of Colossians. It illuminates His deity. It gives a definitive answer to those who question the foundational truth of Christianity: that Jesus *is* God. Read especially Colossians 1:15-19. Jesus, perfect Man, is fully God. "In him all the fulness of God was pleased to dwell" (1:19). Then a wonderful thing develops as Paul goes on with this theme. When the perfect Christ is *proclaimed* and *claimed* by believers, THEY become perfect in Him. Through faith, not works, the perfection that is Christ is given to and shared by the Christian. Christ in us is our hope of glory (Colossians 1:27).

The meaning of the phrase "perfect in Christ" is better understood by the words "mature in Christ," and so it is translated in later versions. In any case, it is *His* perfection that is intended and it is *His* perfection we may have. This is not to get a passing grade on the heavenly finals, but to be like Christ *now*.

HOW DOES THIS APPLY TO US?

We don't feel very perfect very often. But it isn't our feelings that count! To avoid the accusings of a failure-marked past and to move on with confidence into an uncertain future, we have to use the whole phrase of today's key verse: "perfect in Christ Jesus." We don't have to struggle to make it because we are already accepted. We do need to look unto Jesus as we run the race that is set before us (Hebrews 12:1-2). Our hope lies in *His* perfection. We need to reflect *His* perfect truth. We need to share *His* perfect love. We don't need to search for perfection. We don't have to earn it like a merit badge and we must not display it as a merit badge. It's just the way we live because He lives . . . and because He lives in us.

Pray with Me

Father, surrounded by Your love and encouraged by Your grace, I dare to open my whole being before Your perfect holiness.

Looking inward, I see cracks and blemishes. Looking inward, I see scars and stains. I know what Isaiah was going through when he said, "I am undone, a man of unclean lips, dwelling in the midst of a people of unclean lips."

But, Lord, with each new dawn and even in the weariness that comes at the end of the day, I may look away from my incompleteness and rest in the certainty of Your perfection.

I thank You for this truth . . . that I am perfect in Christ Jesus. With His righteousness freely given and received by faith, I am perfect now. I do not need to wait and worry and wonder. It is mine because He is mine.

I, who could never be perfect in myself, have been made perfect in Christ Jesus. It is not the reward at the end of a long struggle. It is not the prize at the end of a long race. The very perfection of Christ Jesus is mine right now because He is mine right now.

So let the perfection that is Christ Jesus become the me that is truly me. I leave behind in the ocean of God's forgetfulness the imperfection that was me before I became the possession of Jesus Christ.

Thank You, Lord, for this discovery. I have known it with my mind. Now I claim it with my heart. He who is imperfect in self may become perfect in Christ . . . through faith.

In the perfect holiness of His love, my prayer is offered and my heart finds its rest, Amen.

MOVING ON IN THE LIFE OF PRAYER

It helps to pray when we know we are drawing upon unlimited resources. Prayer is a powerful weapon, an effective tool, and a joyful exercise. We may ask for and expect to receive the touch of Christ's perfect love and healing compassion. This is a blessing we may ask for ourselves and for all whom we love. We pray because He is perfect. And we pray to become more perfect in Him: more loving in spirit, more peaceful in turbulent times, more committed to the work of His kingdom, more confident of victory, and more faithful in service.

WHAT WE SOW, WE REAP

". . . As you have done, it shall be done to you . . ." (Obadiah 15).

Read: **Obadiah;** Deuteronomy 7:9-10; 2 Samuel 12:1-15; Esther 7:10; Proverbs 22:28; Matthew 7:12; Galatians 6:7-8.

WHAT IS GOD SAYING?

Obadiah's prophecy is against Edom. The Edomites descended from Isaac through Esau, while the Israelites descended from Isaac through Jacob. There never was any love lost between these cousins, but the Edomites proved to be especially vindictive and treacherous. They carried on an ancient grudge and they carried it well. Their main city, Sela, was on a plateau at the top of a rocky cliff. The only access to it was through a narrow gorge. They were virtually unassailable. They would make quick sorties to invade Judah. Having done their damage, they would hurry home and take pride not only in the harm they inflicted but also in the invincible nature of their home territory. The unkindest cut of all came when Jerusalem was being sacked by the Babylonians in 587 B.C. The Edomites took this occasion to plunder Judah while their attention was focused on another and far greater enemy. Obadiah denounces Edom for its pride. Destruction did, in fact, come to their invincible strongholds, first by the Arabs and then by the Nabateans who built the rock-city of Petra.

Obadiah is saying here "you have been priding yourself on bullying others when they are down, but for all your defenses, your time is coming." And it did.

HOW DOES THIS APPLY TO US?

The truth expressed in Obadiah 15 is similar to Paul's word in Galatians 6:7: "God is not mocked, for whatever a man sows, that he will also reap." As with so many other biblical injunctions, the truth is best expressed by Jesus: "So whatever you wish that men would do to you, do so to them" (Matthew 7:12). It is one coin with two sides. On one side a warning: "You can't get away with it. The evil you bring or allow to come into the life of another will return to haunt you." On the other side, an encouragement: "You can't bring good into the life of another without being blessed."

Pray with Me

In these words, O Lord, I hear the sound of distant trumpets. I am nearer to Your words. They gleam like gold in the grayness of a world so lacking love. But these words of Obadiah, like the later and greater words ("as you wish that men would do to you, do so to them"), have stopped me in my tracks.

Those who show mercy will obtain mercy. Those who will not let passion's flames become quenched by Heaven's purity will be consumed. Those who give themselves to pride and envy will find only rusty doors and stony paths and wilted flowers.

Esau stood off and watched foreigners casting lots for Jerusalem. He was sowing the seed of his own destruction. Esau rejoiced over the fall of his brother, but his laughter was to come echoing back in the sound of weeping along empty streets and in the desolate homes of his own land. "As you have done, it shall be done to you."

Lord, help me to remember this warning. Truthful with You and honest with myself and all men, I shall stand above the mists of deceit and be warmed by the sun of Your favor. If I practice deceit, the foundation on which I stand has rotting timbers and the ground on which I walk is sinking sand. If I spend myself for the good of others and seek to bless more than to be blessed, to serve more than to be served, I shall learn the mystery You have tried so patiently to reveal: "Give and it will be given to you: good measure, pressed down, shaken together, running over . . ."

Let this bright glimpse of Your way increase in me until it shall be the light that shines across my whole horizon. Let flickering insight become steady habit. Let struggling faith become triumphant assurance. Let every thought and desire be controlled by Your own changeless decree: "As you have done, it shall be done to you."

In the Name of Him who was crowned with glory, when He endured the shame of the Cross, Amen.

MOVING ON IN THE LIFE OF PRAYER

As we pray for the welfare of others, we are opening the door through which the Lord can come into our lives laden with blessings. "Give and it will be given to you." Pray for others and see how God sends the same or greater blessing on us. Prayer taps a vast reservoir of grace. We can't open the flood-gates of God's mercy on behalf of another without getting splashed or drenched ourselves.

Day 88

FRIENDS OF PAUL: DO WE QUALIFY?

"Paul . . . to Philemon our beloved fellow-worker . . . and Archippus our fellow soldier . . . [and] Epaphras, my fellow prisoner in Christ Jesus" (Philemon 1, 2, and 23).

Read: **Philemon**; Acts 13:2.

WHAT IS GOD SAYING?

Diamonds are small but very valuable. So it is with Paul's letter to Philemon. It is a small gem. Philemon was a well-to-do convert of Paul's in Colossae. Onesimus, his slave, was probably a bright and talented young man sold to Philemon by the Roman army. Onesimus stole money from his master and ran away to Rome. There, with the stolen money probably all spent, he remembered Paul and managed to find him. He also found the Lord, repented, and made himself useful to Paul. The burden of this letter is to persuade Philemon to take him back, forgiving him, and accepting him, not as a slave, but as a "beloved brother."

It tugs at Paul's heart to do so because of a beautiful close relationship that had developed between them. It was friend with friend in the bonds of Christ. Slavery was out of the question. What a difference the love of Christ makes! It was the same compulsion that caused Paul to give him up and send him back. It is a beautiful and tender story. It shows a better way than slavery (vs. 16) at a time when the majority of people in the Empire were slaves. Paul asks Philemon to reinstate Onesimus, not as a "profitable" (that is the meaning of the name Onesimus) tool at his disposal, but as a brother in the Lord. "Receive him as you would receive me" (v. 17).

HOW DOES THIS APPLY TO US?

Our focus in this brief letter, however, is not a runaway slave who found new life in Christ. We are looking at three names and three vocations. Philemon . . . *fellow worker;* Archippus . . . *fellow soldier;* Epaphras . . . *fellow prisoner.* They were all friends of Paul. On the basis of their personal relationships with Paul, would we qualify? Would we be fellow workers, fellow soldiers, fellow prisoners of Paul? Is our love for Jesus and our devotion to the Gospel such that we would merit these names? As fellow workers with Paul in the service of Christ, we may be truly at rest. As fellow soldiers in the battle for righteousness, we may be truly at peace. As fellow prisoners for the Gospel, we may discover what it means to be perfectly free.

Pray with Me

Lord, with Philemon I want to be a "fellow worker" with Paul. I would neither shirk the duty nor shun the discipline which come to those who want to be fellow workers. There is a place for work in Your kingdom. I thank You that I can work for You: beat the strain, spend and be spent, submit to discipline, and do things I would not ask to do and often do not feel able to do. I thank You that I may do all this not to receive praise or to earn salvation but simply for the joy of being near You and with You.

With Archippus, I want to be a "fellow soldier" with Paul. I would not sleep through the call to battle. I would not be afraid to rise against the enemy when the summons comes. The same war is on. The same enemy is to be met by those who fight the good fight of faith today. Christ has won the victory on Calvary. He removed the sting of death. But evil still seethes around us. Under the standard of the Cross, I enlist to serve. Under that symbol of darkest shame and brightest glory, I would have the courage to fight and the confidence to win.

With Epaphras, I would count it glory to be with Paul as a "fellow prisoner." Let me not waver under trial when to deny Jesus would mean my release. There is a glory along the path of patient and passive suffering as well as in working and fighting. If being restrained by circumstances not of my making, if being required to endure idleness, and if laboring through the tasteless chores of a captive existence be a part of Your perfect plan, let me accept it in faith and endure it with courage. Only let there come out of such bondage, testimony to the living God in whose presence is the only liberty which is worthy of the name.

By Your grace, make me worthy of being a fellow worker, a fellow soldier, and a fellow prisoner with Paul.

In the Name of Him who did the greatest work and fought the greatest battle to give the greatest freedom, Amen.

MOVING ON IN THE LIFE OF PRAYER

When we enter the closet of prayer, it is to find the strength and to review the goals of all our work. Our real Master is the Lord. Our work is wasted if it is not centered on the goals of His kingdom. Our work is futile if it does not serve the purposes of His love. In prayer as soldiers, we receive instructions from our Commander-in-Chief, for there is a battle, perhaps many this very day. We must remember that the value of a soldier is determined by how he accepts discipline and how he obeys orders. In prayer we come to see that being imprisoned for Christ is to be set free in the Spirit. We make the choice in prayer.

Day 89

SIN: WHEN THE RULERS BECOME THE RULED

"The crown has fallen from our head; woe to us, for we have sinned!" *(Lamentations 5:16).*

Read: **Lamentations 5;** Proverbs 13:15; Romans 3:16; 2 Timothy 4:8; 1 Peter 1:17-18, 3:18.

WHAT IS GOD SAYING?

Lamentations gives vent to the deep anguish of God's people. The book consists of five distinct poems. It is not all sorrow. See how the sun breaks through in 3:22-27. But mainly Lamentations focuses on the suffering that sin inevitably brings. God had rejected Israel because of her sin. Jerusalem lay in rubble. The Temple had been violated. A whole nation had lost its freedom. Poverty, famine, shame, and humiliation blackened the landscape. "Why?" asks the poet-prophet. "Why? Because we have sinned." Lamentations is not pleasant reading. But the harvest of sin can lead to nothing else. After reciting the terrible consequences of sin, the prophet, in the final words of the book, points to the restoring power of God. God is still in control (v. 21).

HOW DOES THIS APPLY TO US?

As God can and will restore His people, so Christ can put back on our heads the crown—*His* crown of righteousness as promised in 2 Timothy 4:8. We don't have to be ruled by sin nor consigned to its fatal destiny. Through repentance and faith "the crown that has fallen from our head" can, in the strong hands of Jesus, be replaced. We can rule and not be ruled. We should pray for a deeper and more constant realization that we have been "delivered . . . from the dominion of darkness and transferred to the kingdom of (God's) beloved Son" (Colossians 1:13).

Pray with Me

Lord, because Your conquest of sin is absolute, You have been given a name that is above every name, You have been exalted to an eternal throne, and You have a crown that shall never fall. Let me see You in Your risen and reigning glory.

Oh, that I might govern all desire as if the power of my reigning Lord had its unquestioned sway in every corner of my life. This is the prize of the high calling of God. This is the joy unspeakable—but not unreachable. Toward this goal I will press in full confidence of Your ever-sufficient grace.

In sorrow I must confess that through pride and indifference, the crown has fallen from my head at times. Sin has robbed me of my regal status in Christ.

Instead of reigning in freedom, I have served in bondage. Instead of ruling, I have been ruled. Instead of giving orders to the legions of darkness, I have taken them.

No man can serve two masters. No man can hold a scepter in his hand and sin in his heart. No man can be crowned with Your blessings while compromising with Your enemies.

Therefore, dear Lord, to the throne of my heart return and reign, for in Your reigning, I reign, and in Your mastery, I am free. In the strong Name of Your longsuffering yet ever-sovereign love, Amen.

MOVING ON IN THE LIFE OF PRAYER

Lamentations ends in hope. The sun still shines to show that God is still there and still cares. We have been "ransomed from the futile ways . . . with the precious blood of Christ, like that of a lamb without blemish or spot" (1 Peter 1:18-19). Now we can subdue our enemies in the strength of Christ. We can rule and not be ruled by tapping into His strength, by believing His promises, and by keeping on the beam of His perfect plan for our lives. And all this comes through prayer. "They who wait for the LORD, shall renew their strength" (Isaiah 40:31).

PAST FORGIVEN; FUTURE GLORIOUS

"So Christ, having been offered once to bear the sins of many, will appear a second time, not to deal with sin but to save those who are eagerly waiting for him" (Hebrews 9:28).

Read: **Hebrews 9;** Isaiah 53:12; 1 Peter 2:24; 1 John 3:5; Titus 2:11-13.

WHAT IS GOD SAYING?

Hebrews 9 stresses three appearances of Christ. He who promised to be with us always meets our need, not only in every situation but also in every tense: past, present, and future. Ponder Hebrews 9:26: "He has appeared once for all at the end of the age to put away sin by the sacrifice of himself." That takes care of the *PAST*. Now read Hebrews 9:24: "For Christ *has* entered . . . into heaven itself, *now* to appear in the presence of God on our behalf." He is there to meet every need in the *PRESENT*. Finally read Hebrews 9:28: "So Christ . . . *will* appear a second time not to deal with sin but to save those who are eagerly waiting for him." Such is our *FUTURE*.

HOW DOES THIS APPLY TO US?

Isaiah said it would happen: "He bore the sin of many, and made intercession for the transgressors" (Isaiah 53:12). And it did. "[Christ] bore our sins in his body on the tree" (1 Peter 2:24). We have been forgiven. God has forgotten. The past has been put to rest. All because of Christ's atoning death. Now our concerns are only with the present. Not even the future should worry us. If we walk with Jesus *now,* God will take care of the future. We trust Him for that. Our greatest need is to show our gratitude *now,* to discover and do His will *now,* and to exercise the God-given grace of prayer *now.* In that spirit we "eagerly wait for his appearing the second time," when every wrong will be righted, every heart will be clean, every joy will be pure, and every mystery of Providence will be understood.

Pray with Me

O the joy, dear Lord, of knowing that because of Your first coming, when You were once offered to bear the sins of many, my heart can be filled with eagerness as I wait for Your coming again.

Having dealt with the guilt of the past, You will lead the redeemed into the glory of the future.

Having canceled our debt, You make us joint-heirs with Yourself to riches untold and to joy that will never diminish.

Having taken our place upon the Cross, You will give us a place near Your side in the glories of Heaven.

In waiting for this full redemption, let me be as one whose forehead reflects the growing light of dawn, for more certain than the morning is Your coming.

In waiting for this full redemption, let me be as one whose eyes sparkle because they have seen a great vision of things that are to be . . . more beautiful than eye has ever seen, more comforting than ear has ever heard, more wonderful than the heart has ever imagined.

In waiting for this full redemption, let me be as one whose face shines with a quiet strength as if it were the visible screen upon which the heart projects its confident dreams.

With a heart set free from the burden of all guilt, with a heart that is being cleansed from all unrighteousness according to Your promise, with a heart that is filled to overflowing with the love of Your name and with the hope of my calling, I will be among those who eagerly wait for Your coming.

With all this glory coming to me because You are coming for me, I have good reason to do more than "eagerly" wait. I have every reason to "willingly" work. And whether waiting or working, I would do all for Your glory.

Through Christ whose coming in grace the first time has removed the dread of His coming again, Amen.

MOVING ON IN THE LIFE OF PRAYER

"Eagerly waiting" may seem to be a difficult concept to handle. But it is the hallmark of real prayer. We have a blessed hope. We have everything to win and nothing of any value to lose. We are on the winning side. Have we come to regard prayer as "listless routine?" It ought to be "eager waiting." It *can* be so when we know whose side we are on and how wonderful is the One for whom we are waiting. Let all our praying be a blend of eagerness and waiting. God will honor that.

WHERE HE LEADS ME

"And Deborah said to Barak, 'Up! . . . *Does not the LORD go out before you?'"* *(Judges 4:14)*.

Read: **Judges 4:1-16;** Numbers 14:7-9; Exodus 33:14; Psalm 20:6-8; Deuteronomy 20:1; Romans 8:37; 2 Corinthians 12:9.

WHAT IS GOD SAYING?

Joshua had died, his task bravely begun but not finished. The leaderless people were in for turbulent times. The pendulum swung between abject failures and brief periods of success under judges with varying degrees of strength. On the one hand, the people were disheartened and afraid. It was easier to just give in to the pressures of their environment (Judges 2:12-13). They fought, but zest for victory was gone. "They could no longer withstand their enemies" (2:14) for they had become too much like them. God was distant and unreal. In time they followed their neighbors' practices, worshiped at their shrines, and forsook the Lord.

Then, in His mercy, God raised up judges to call the people back and to lead them out against the enemy . . . the enemy who in *taking them in* had nearly *done them in*. Is God's steadfast love patient? Seven times in two-and-a-half centuries they left Him and seven times He sent a leader to bring them back. One such leader was Deborah, a woman of strong character and good judgment. She gave moral leadership to Israel and was an honored judge. Barak was the military leader but Deborah provided the inspiration and real leadership—a woman of the hour! Sisera with nine hundred chariots of iron? What is that compared to the power of God? "Up, Barak! Now the time is right. This is the day in which the Lord has given Sisera into your hand. Does not the Lord go before you? Sisera is no match for Him!"

HOW DOES THIS APPLY TO US?

God goes before us whatever enemy crosses our path. God knows us and God knows the enemy. He knows how in our own strength we may be afraid to be up and doing: Our fear of the unknown, our feelings of inadequacy, failures from the past that haunt us and make us hesitant to try again. God also knows the enemy: his subtle ways, his deceit, his appeal to our weakness, his determination to bring us under his control. In spite of the enemy's strength and our weakness (more imagined than real!), "we are more than conquerors through him that loved us" (Romans 8:37).

Pray with Me

Lord, You have gone out before me and I would rise to follow. You have gone out before me into every problem this day can hold. You have gone out before me with a pattern of holy love for all mankind. You have gone out before me into the darkness and I may walk without fear along all the paths where Your love and the voice of duty shall call this day.

In Your grace, let me both hear and heed the command to arise, "Up!" Help me to see how real are those enemies whose company I have not come to despise enough, the enemies of a Slumbering Will and a Listless Spirit. In Your kindness shake me until these self-forged chains shall fall away. Strike all fatal drowsiness of spirit. Scatter all false dreams of security. Help me to rise in response to Your call and to recognize in Your awakening a call to great adventure and real life.

Up—above the level of self-satisfaction, beyond the small goals of pride, through the mists of doubt.

Up—O Christ, where You have gone, on a road of selfless love and sacrifice. Up, O Christ, for taking up the cross is no task for a sleeping disciple. Up, O Christ, for walking the low road of service can never mean lying in a soft bed of ease.

You have spoken in these words. "Up . . . does not the Lord go out before you?" But now I pray for the greater secret of prevailing strength: not only, "Does not the Lord go before you?" but above all and through all and until the end of all: "Lo, I am with you always."

This be my reason for rising, my strength in going, and my joy in arriving: "Up . . . does not the Lord go out before you?" AND "Is not the Lord ever beside you?"

In Jesus' Name, Amen.

MOVING ON IN THE LIFE OF PRAYER

In prayer we are assured of God's presence. He does not go before us and leave us behind alone and forsaken. He is with us *now*. We are given wisdom for the decisions we need to make *now*. We can go out to meet and defeat the enemy, not only because the Lord has gone *before* us but also and supremely because He is always *with* us. "Lo, I am with you always, to the close of the age" (Matthew 28:20).

Day 92

CHRIST IS THE DIFFERENCE

"Once you were no people but now you are God's people; once you had not received mercy but now you have received mercy" (1 Peter 2:10).

Read: **1 Peter 2;** Deuteronomy 14:2; John 1:12; Galatians 4:5-6; Ephesians 5:8; Colossians 1:12-14.

WHAT IS GOD SAYING?

Peter was always out in front. John and Peter were the first to hear that Jesus was not dead. They both ran to see if the tomb had surrendered its victim. John was younger and outran Peter. But it was Peter who went in first and saw the evidence that was to change the world. Peter was also the one who folded in the time of crisis, denying he even knew Jesus. In His great compassion our Lord chose to go to Peter first in His post-resurrection appearances. He knew he must be suffering because of his denial. Restored to his Lord, Peter was the first to preach the Gospel (Acts 2), and never wavered again, preaching and teaching the Good News to Jews and Gentiles. During the terrible persecutions of the Emperor Nero, he was crucified. Peter was living proof of the power of the Resurrection for he was a *totally changed* person. He preached what he knew. His conviction came out of the fires of testing and the lessons of experience. He was not passing along something he read in a book. He was living out the life and the love that he saw in Christ.

HOW DOES THIS APPLY TO US?

What better person could there be to counsel Christians about the inevitable suffering they would have to endure while being faithful to the Lord in a hostile and pagan world? Peter knew it firsthand. What better person to tell about the difference the living Christ can make in any person's life? From boasting to shameful failure in the space of a few nighttime hours. Then, from cowardly denial to courageous preaching when he saw the evidence and felt the power of the Resurrection.

Peter was a changed man. He could speak with the authority of personal experience about the difference Christ makes. His own life was the evidence. First, he knew the reality of God's *"but now"* Gospel. That is why he could speak to others so convincingly about the *"but now"* that can come by faith into every life. All our prayer is based on the confidence we *now* have in the mercy of God, the mercy we know we will have forever because we are in Christ.

Pray with Me

Dear Lord, the words *but now* are filled with meaning for me.

Before, I knew only the assaults of conscience, *but now* there is the mercy of a forgiving God.

Before, I walked in loneliness, *but now* I walk with the living Christ.

Before, I was "dead in trespasses and sin," *but now* I have been "born again."

Before, I groped in the darkness of fear, *but now* I walk in the light of faith.

Before, I had nothing except the death that my sin had earned, *but now* I have everything in the life that God has given.

Let these words, "but now," stand as a wall against the arrows of self-accusation. Let them be as a door sealed against doubt. Let them be as a shaft of light to drive back the shadows. Let me live in the joy and freedom of Your own Word: "But now . . . you have received mercy."

Father, I know now that I grieved you while I lingered in the "far country," *but now* I would serve you in willing surrender.

I wandered in sin, *but now* I would walk in righteousness.

I gave no heed to Your pleading, *but now* I love Your Word.

I lived as though my life had no need of Your sustaining mercies, *but now* in Christ I see how much You loved me all the time.

I thank You for the "but now" that is right now. I thank You for that which gives me confidence as I live in the presence of heavenly love and in the promise of eternal hope.

Through Jesus Christ my Lord, Amen.

MOVING ON IN THE LIFE OF PRAYER

In prayer we look at ourselves as God sees us. If we go anywhere else for an understanding of our "selves," we will dredge up the past, we will focus on failure, we will be where we used to be. And that is not a pretty picture. Coming to God in prayer we see ourselves as ones in whom God has brought about a merciful change. We live on the "sunny side" of *"but now."* That makes a powerful difference when we pray. It is praying from a position of strength. It is putting the accent on hope. It is drawing on the inexhaustible riches of Christ. It is claiming the blessings of redemption and forgetting the frustrations, the emptiness, and the poverty of life and spirit that we knew on the other side, the shady side, of *"but now."*

PRAYER BEFORE GOD; CONFIDENCE BEFORE OTHERS

"So I prayed to the God of Heaven. And I said to the king . . ." (Nehemiah 2:4, 5).

Read: **Nehemiah 2;** Numbers 14:8-9; Psalm 3:5-6, 27:1-3, 119:147; Acts 4:18-19, 29.

WHAT IS GOD SAYING?

Nehemiah, the king's cup-bearer, had an important position in the Persian court. In Nehemiah's day those who were in the public eye had to guard against poisoning. That was the responsibility of the cup-bearer. It was a dangerous position, but carried with it great honor. It meant tasting the wine before the king drank it; not to *approve* its taste but to *prove* it was safe. The man who held that position had to be trusted by the king and would for obvious reasons have quick and easy access to him. Nevertheless, it took courage for Nehemiah to speak to the king, especially when he was making a big, even kingdom-shaking, request. But after praying to God, Nehemiah was ready to talk to the king.

HOW DOES THIS APPLY TO US?

If we draw strength from the vertical, we will have more than enough power to deal with the horizontal. When we have the assurance that God is for us, we won't fear what man can do to us. We won't crumble before man's criticism if we have God's approval. Too often we go to others unprepared, afraid of sounding weak or foolish. We are afraid we will say the wrong things to people who won't understand. This is removed when we first go to God in humility and faith. We won't say the foolish thing when we have heard the wise thing from God. We won't say the false thing when we have been exposed to the truth. We won't yield in the weakness of compromise when we are supported by the strength of commitment to God. We can speak the truth in love to anyone when we know we are loved by God.

Pray with Me

Give me the confidence of Nehemiah, Lord, as he prayed to God and spoke to kings. With authority and grace from above, I don't have to be afraid of the arrogance of human pride or the malice of human ambition. Having unbroken union with the vertical, I have unfailing strength on the horizontal. Having bowed before you, I need never bow before men.

Now I see that when my relationships break down with others it is because they have first broken down with You. To God in prayer; to men with power. To God in humility; to men with composure. To God in the brokenness of a contrite heart; to men with the soundness and strength of those who say, "If God be for us, who can be against us?"

Let this rhythm never be interrupted: To God in prayer—to men with power—and back again to God in prayer. As night with its rest follows day with its labor, as food replenishes bodies, as water quenches thirst, so I come to You. I come from the demands of my daily life among people that I may find greater strength and calmer wisdom. From you, armed with Your truth and upheld by Your love, I can go again to the world.

When I come to You in prayer, let my heart be filled with a small but real portion of Your limitless love as my lungs are filled each moment with a small but real portion of the limitless air. Then I shall go before men—not in pride and judgment—but with the desire to love and to serve in the Spirit of my Master, who came from Heaven, the very God of Heaven, to save all kings and all subjects, all princes and all paupers, all men and all women for all time.

In His own wonderful Name, Amen.

MOVING ON IN THE LIFE OF PRAYER

So much of our prayer life has to do with our relationship to others. How do we react to others' failures? What do we say when we have been betrayed or mistreated? Where do we find the courage to give a needed warning to someone who has chosen the wrong way? Where do we find the courage to ask forgiveness of someone we have wronged? Time and again what happens in the silence of the prayer closet will result in words that must be spoken to others. When we *first* pray to the God of Heaven, we can *then* speak to people we need to love on earth. Pray to God, speak to others. In to God, out to others. Take God's hand and start walking. Hear God's Word and start talking. Inhale, exhale. That's it. That's prayer. That's life.

Day 94

DOES OUR LIFE PROCLAIM CHRIST?

"Philip went down to a city of Samaria, and proclaimed to them the Christ" (Acts 8:5).

Read: **Acts 8,** 10:36; 2 Corinthians 4:5.

WHAT IS GOD SAYING?

Saul, the zealous defender of the Jewish religion, began to lay waste the church. It was serious business to him. He entered house after house and dragged believers off to prison (Acts 8:3). God's plan in the Diaspora (scattering because of persecution) was under way. As burning embers are scattered from a fire that has been trampled on to put it out, the fire spread far and wide. Among those who were scattered, God sent preachers. Philip the evangelist was one of those who used the trial of persecution as the impetus for proclaiming Christ. Philip was a Hellenist, a Greek-speaking Jew, and someone who really cared about people, all people. He would be God's messenger to the Samaritans.

Wherever Philip went, he preached. He became a part of the "second stage rocket booster" in the launching of the Gospel. First Jerusalem (Acts 1:8). The power Jesus promised would then carry the Gospel into Judea and Samaria, and finally into "orbit" around the world. The people of Samaria, plagued so long with the hostile attitudes of the Jews, responded to Philip's preaching and the Holy Spirit's miracles with great joy (Acts 8:8). But Philip kept on proclaiming Christ. In the midst of success in Samaria, he was called to proclaim Christ to an Ethiopian official of some importance who was leaving Jerusalem. After worshiping in that city, the official was on the road back home to resume his position as Queen Candace's treasurer. He was converted, and may have been the channel by which the Gospel entered Africa. Philip kept on preaching. He was found (and heard) at Azotus. Then through all the towns till he came to Caesarea. There he settled down. But his preaching went on. He raised an exemplary family and Paul found him faithfully at work in Caesarea on his last journey back to Jerusalem.

HOW DOES THIS APPLY TO US?

The lesson we learn from this early and faithful itinerant evangelist is that wherever he went, he proclaimed Christ. Some of his assignments were not too popular: Samaria, of all places;

then hitching a ride with an Ethiopian; then Azotus; then all the towns leading to Caesarea. His primary task was to preach Christ. He did it faithfully. He was sensitive to the Spirit's call. His life and message and compassion were all of one piece. Whatever he did, wherever he went, whoever was listening, Philip proclaimed Christ. Can this be said of us? Our words, our lives, our concern for others? Do they *all* proclaim Christ?

Pray with Me

Lord, I will go anywhere *for* You because I know I can go anywhere *with* You. Philip possessed in his heart the Christ that he proclaimed in Samaria. So let it be in my life. Let me not choose the circumstances. Let me not choose the time. Let me not choose the place.

I would proclaim the Christ in life. I would surrender the control of my life—not as a puppet doing his mindless dance at the end of a maze of strings but as a glove responding to a hand within. As a glove I would surrender to the hand, Your Hand inside and in control. So I would proclaim the Christ.

I would reflect the radiance of one whose heart is at peace. It has already surrendered to God whose victory in the love of Calvary and in the glory of the Resurrection is both certain and final. By the peace of this surrendered heart, I would proclaim the Christ.

I would move with the joy of one who has seen the unlocked door of a prison. I would live as one who has in his hand the full pardon from all offenses. I would rejoice as one who has before him a life, whether it be long or short, that cannot lead to emptiness or to the bitterness of frustration or to the misery of defeat. So I would proclaim the Christ.

I would proclaim the Christ in word. I would not suppose that it all depends on my eloquence. I would not imagine that people will respond because I say something clever. I will not fear that they will be turned aside because I cannot think of anything clever. Such wonderful facts to tell, such a wonderful deliverance to report, such wonderful love to share. Let me do it in words that are simple and loving and true. So let me proclaim the Christ: in the energy of an active life, in the peace of a calm assurance, in the joy of a liberated spirit, and in words of simple truth. So I would proclaim the Christ.

For His glory, His glory alone, Amen.

MOVING ON IN THE LIFE OF PRAYER

We have the great Good News. The world may reject it. Not surprising when the Lord said it would. People may hide from us their real hungers. They may seem to put up a strong defense against anything that disturbs their prejudices or penetrates their shells of pride. They may be telling us to get lost. But deep down, they really want to be found. People are searching for meaning in a world that makes less and less sense. We must keep others on our hearts for the good of their souls and we must pray that our lives in word and deed will keep on proclaiming Christ.

Day 95

In Christ There Is No "If Not"

"... *Our God whom we serve is able to deliver us* .... *But if not, we will not serve your gods*" (Daniel 3:17-18).

Read: **Daniel 3;** 1 Kings 13:4-10; Job 17:9; 1 Corinthians 15:58; 2 Corinthians 1:10, James 1:12.

What Is God Saying?

Daniel contains an account of some remarkable people whom God had raised up as witnesses to His power and glory— in places where such witnessing was hard and dangerous. Daniel was a young man of a noble, perhaps royal, family in Judea. He was only a boy but God gave him a rare kind of courage and the power to live a disciplined life. He was one of four young men described as "youths without blemish, handsome and skillful in all wisdom, endowed with knowledge, understanding learning, and competent to serve in the king's palace" (1:4). They would not defile themselves with the king's rich food and drink (1:8). They became vegetarians. In their depth of insight and understanding, unclouded by the indulgence of appetite, they were able to tell the king the meaning of his dreams—ten times better than the best astrologers of the land (1:20). However, these young men incurred the wrath of the king, who was rapidly approaching the brink of insanity, when they refused to bow down before the image of gold on the plain of Dura. They couldn't have touched a quicker nerve. In his "furious rage" the king ordered them to be cast into a burning, fiery furnace, heated seven times beyond the usual temperature. Their answer showing courage, born of faith and prayer to the true, living God, was classic: "Our God whom we serve is able to deliver us, but if not, we will not serve your gods."

How Does This Apply to Us?

We all have our fires of testing. There is always the temptation to compromise. We know God's way is right. We know His
purpose for our life is spelled out with unmistakable clarity in
His Word, in the majestic teaching of Jesus and in His own
flawless life. But sometimes through lack of discipline, through
careless neglect of devotional exercise, through preoccupation
with the pressing demands of life around us, through the fear
that others might think us strange, we lose sight of God's perfect
plan for us and we fail to give the strong, clear answer of
courage and faith. We need to trust God when the tide of the
world's tarnished morality and mounting corruption is running
against us. We will dig in our heels. We will face upstream. We
will say: "God can keep us from going downstream to destruction, but if not, at least we are headed in the right direction."

Pray with Me

Lord, give me confidence in Your saving power and purpose. Even when others feel that I am deserted, may I know I am
not. I will not judge Your blessings by outward circumstances
which impress men as favorable, but rather by inner assurance,
knowing Your love never fails and Your purpose is never
defeated.

Help me to say in the face of any trial: "My God is able to
deliver . . . but if not . . ."

"If not," I will never distrust Your ultimate purpose in the
disappointment of present events.

"If not," I will not let Your enemies, either fears within or
foes without, get the upper hand and rule my spirit.

"If not," I will look for the breakdown in my own relationship with You. I will find the place of my own lack of obedience.
I will own up to my lack of trust. I will blame my own lack of
discipline. I will continue to believe that You are my willing and
able God. I will continue to say that the "name of the Lord is a
strong tower; the righteous runs into it and is safe."

"If not," I will never serve those gods or become enslaved
to those forces which are set against You.

"If not?" O, I thank You, Lord, that this will never be my
choice to make. For in Jesus Christ You have delivered my soul
already. In Jesus Christ "if not" can never be! My heart is glad
and my spirit rejoices.

Through Him who, in praying for deliverance, said "If
not . . ." and then endured the Cross that He might bring
Heaven to God's children and God's children to Heaven,
Amen.

Moving On in the Life of Prayer

We all need courage. Courage is born of faith and faith is the essence of prayer. Faith brings us to prayer. Faith keeps us in prayer. Faith sends us away from prayer with the assurance that God is right, that God is in control, that God can do the impossible. And even if things *don't* seem to be going our way, at least we will know and those who know us will know, that we are on God's side in the battle.

Day 96

TRUTH AND LOVE

"And this is love, that we follow his commandments" (2 John 6).

Read: **2 John;** Deuteronomy 26:16; John 13:34-35, 15:5-10.

What Is God Saying?

At the time of this letter, John was advanced in years. He was the last surviving companion of Jesus. The firmness and tenderness of long years of experience characterize all of his letters. He defends the truth with the kind of settled conviction that is found in those who have walked long in the way of truth and have seen the dangers, the subtle deceits and the emptiness of false doctrine. Truth was always on his mind. To hold on to that truth and to be held by that truth was the only defense against satanic lies that came like wolves in sheep's clothing. At the same time, the years he has spent obeying Christ's great commandment to love gave him a mellowness of spirit that filtered its way through everything he said. *Truth* appears five times in this short letter. But *love* also appears five times. Truth and love. They must go together.

How Does This Apply to Us?

Second John is a little gem with two shining facets: truth and love. As the light of inspiration plays on these two concepts, they not only flash independently, but they also blend into a single light of beauty, a single recipe for living. Live *by* the truth of God, then live *out* the love of God. Truth and love are never out of style. The best thing that can be said about a Christian is that he or she LOVES THE TRUTH and also LOVES IN TRUTH.

Pray with Me

O Lord, how easily do I say it. How hardly do I do it.

Love is obedience. Love is the response of a life. Yet often I think of it merely as the indulgence of a benevolent feeling. My love has sometimes consisted of words rather than works, sentiment rather than service, enjoyment rather than enlistment.

I have praised You for Your seeking love and I have pledged to You my answering love. Yet to my shame I have failed to answer Your seeking love with a performing love.

A lifetime, an eternity, of loving service could not repay the debt I owe. I would give up the subtle notion that "following Your commandments" might earn the salvation which grace has given. Yet, Lord, I would give up with equal haste the thought that love can be an idle sentiment.

Let my love take to the road and lift the load. Let my love speak the difficult word and forgive the impossible wrong. Let my love sweep as a purifying flame through the rubble and ruin of a slumbering morality. Let my love give at least the same mercy it has obtained and let it pass along at least the same blessings it has received. Let my love *walk*. Let it not sit and stare. Let it not hesitate and debate. Let my love walk after Your commandments.

Let such love show the way to me. Let such love go on the way with me. Let such love be the distinguishing quality of a life which today is newly surrendered to Him whose love constrained Him to become obedient to death, even death on the Cross.

For the sake of His glory, Amen.

MOVING ON IN THE LIFE OF PRAYER

When Jesus washed His disciples' feet, He showed that love is something you do! To meditate in prayer on the *truth* of Christ is a good first step. But prayer must also include the making of plans to live out the *love* of Christ. When we have the truth of Christ that informs and the love of Christ that inspires, we have the building blocks of real prayer.

Day 97

CHRIST CAME DOWN TO LIFT US UP

"I went down to the land whose bars closed upon me for ever; yet thou didst bring up my life from the Pit, O LORD my God" (Jonah 2:6).

Read: **Jonah 2;** Psalm 123; Proverbs 5:22; Luke 4:18; Romans 6:16, 7:23; Galatians 6:1.

WHAT IS GOD SAYING?

Jonah ran away from the "presence of the Lord." He ran away from his responsibility in an unpleasant assignment. He couldn't live with the idea that God's love and mercy reached beyond Israel. To be an instrument in God's hand to save Nineveh was unthinkable. How and why should the God of Israel do such a thing to people who were totally ignorant of God and His laws? That was more than Jonah could handle, so he ran away as far and as fast as he could. And it was all downhill. That is the direction and destiny of all disobedience to God.

It took courage for Jonah to admit that the raging sea that "threatened to break up the ship" might be traced to God's displeasure with *him*. "I know it is because of me . . . throw me into the sea" (1:12). To their credit the sailors tried hard to bring the ship back to land. But the seas grew only more tempestuous. Jonah went overboard. The Lord had a great fish handy to take him on the next leg of his reluctant journey, back to his senses and back to his God-assigned task. But to Jonah this was the ultimate horror. Running away from God always ends in a cul-de-sac. For Jonah it was the "belly of Sheol" (2:2). He had come to the end of himself. No running now. Just captivity and darkness and bars closing in. Then when his soul fainted within him, he remembered the Lord (2:7). He couldn't forget God and God wouldn't forget him.

HOW DOES THIS APPLY TO US?

Whatever may be our form of disobedience, whatever may have made us want to run away from God's best for our life, whatever unpleasant task we may have shirked supposing there was another or an easier way out, the direction of not choosing God's way leads at last to what is called "the belly of Sheol . . . a land (call it what we will) whose bars close in upon me for ever." Yes, forever, unless we turn to God and let him bring up our lives "from the Pit" (2:6). That is what Jesus came to do. That is what He wants to do. As helpless as Jonah lodged in the great fish's interior, so is the one who has run away from God and into the lethal embrace of sin. We can run away from God but it's downhill all the way until Jesus, our Savior, breaks the bars and lifts us up—up into His presence where there is fullness of joy and to His right hand where there are pleasures forever more.

Pray with Me

Lord, I went down but You brought me up.

The whole course of life without the lifting power of Your love is down to "the land where the bars close in for ever." From the darkness and captivity of sin, from the bondage of evil and the burden of guilt, I have cried and not in vain. Yes, even from the depths You heard my voice.

Through power that brooks no resistance even in the land of sin's imprisonment You lift and rescue and redeem.

You have given me a song of jubilant victory instead of a cry of mournful defeat. Mine is now a living hope instead of a dying despair. My path leads now to the sunrise of liberty and life and not toward the darkening sky of bondage and death.

I went down but You brought me up. I went down in humility and You brought me up in the glory of the Resurrection. I went down in penitence and You brought me up in pardon. I went down into the gates of death and You brought me up into the way everlasting.

In Christ, the God of Heaven came down to the "land whose bars had closed in" on sinning and suffering humanity. Now in the magnetism of Your ascended glory and by the authority of Your love, lift me into Your holy presence, where I shall be cleansed in heart and renewed in spirit. There I shall walk in blessed fellowship with You.

Bring me up from the murky depths of conflicting loyalties and torturing doubts. Bring me up into the clear heights of a new consecration and a trusting faith.

To the eternal praise and glory of Him who came down to earth that He might by the power of His love lift our souls to Heaven, Amen.

MOVING ON IN THE LIFE OF PRAYER

We can "run away" from God. It is an option that many have taken to their sorrow and regret. The other option is to "wait upon God" in prayer. In the first option we go downhill to a land where the bars close in upon us. In the second choice our strength is renewed and we mount up with wings as eagles (Isaiah 40:31). Jesus brings up our life from the pit. "Love lifted me" is more than an old hymn. It is a precious and present fact. Through prayer, we experience its reality.

GOD IN THE CENTER OF LIFE

"The people of Israel . . . shall encamp facing the tent of meeting on every side" (Numbers 2:2).

Read: **Numbers 2;** Psalm 37:5, 95:10-11; James 4:1-4.

WHAT IS GOD SAYING?

All the tribes of Israel, each in its own place and each with its own standard camped around "the tent of meeting," facing the dwelling place of the Lord. The tent of the Lord's presence was the focal point. The magnet in the middle. It kept them *for* each other, *with* each other. It gave them a sense of community, kept them mindful that they faced a common enemy—which was not each other. They belonged to God and so they belonged to each other. No, it did not work perfectly, but that it worked at all in that vast, frequently faithless multitude was a miracle.

HOW DOES THIS APPLY TO US?

You and I are moving through a world which, for all its potential beauty and abundance, is really a barren and hostile wilderness. Secularism sprouts poisonous weeds of greed and unrest, hatred and war. Our enemies are determined and numerous. We are passing through a world at enmity with God. James reminds us that "whoever wishes to be a friend of the world makes himself an enemy of God" (James 4:4). Like the people of ancient Israel, we need to keep God as the focus, the center, the heart of all we do. By doing so, we find our unity and our united front against all the enemies of faith and righteousness. Facing the "tent of meeting," we know God is with us, with all of us, through the wilderness . . . until we all come to the place prepared for us by our loving Savior.

Pray with Me

O Lord, You are the cause of all being. You are the center of my being.

With the people of Israel I am moving through a wilderness and toward a Promised Land. Yet even that wilderness can be a paradise when I am aware of Your presence. I will not be lonely or disheartened when I am listening for Your voice. I will not be bewildered and wandering when I am obedient to Your will. I will not be weary when I am sustained by a living hope. I will not grow faint when I am nourished by the truth of Your all-conquering love.

Give me grace, Lord, never to settle down in any attitude or relationship that will keep me from facing "the tent of meeting." As the Israelites set up their camp in a way that kept the symbol of Your presence always before them, so let there be no side of my being that remains turned away from that which, for my welfare and peace, must always remain central.

Then I shall leave the past without the regret of remembered failures or the burden of unrelinquished guilt. Then I shall live in the presence of a transforming yet affirming friendship. Then I shall move into the unknown with quiet confidence and even with the excitement of a new adventure.

Yes, the brighter, better tomorrow, the land that flows with milk and honey, the peace that guards all the borders of a wonderful life, will never be an empty dream, so long as I determine that on every side, with every part of my being, in every day and every hour of my life, I shall camp facing the tent of meeting . . . the place of Your presence, and the smile of Your favor.

Through Jesus Christ by whose love I am faced on every side. Amen.

MOVING ON IN THE LIFE OF PRAYER

Prayer is the way Christians keep facing the "tent of meeting." When Christians are all in one accord in one place, things always happen (Acts 1:14, 2:1, 2:46, 4:24, etc.). It brings unity and strength to Christians when they are together. Having faced the "tent of meeting" in prayer, we can then face the wilderness, the world, the enemy, and be more than conquerors through Him who loves us.

Day 99

SHARING OURSELVES
WITH THE GOSPEL

" . . . We were ready to share with you not only the gospel of God but also our own selves" (1 Thessalonians 2:8).

Read: **1 Thessalonians 2;** Acts 21:24; 1 Corinthians 9:22-23; 1 Corinthians 10:24, 33; 1 Peter 1:22.

WHAT IS GOD SAYING?

The letters to the Thessalonians were written early in Paul's ministry. He never lost his enthusiasm and total commitment to the Gospel. As the years went by, he became more and more convinced that it was the single greatest thing in his ministry. It was, in fact, the single greatest thing that happened in the world and for the world. That is why, in the opening sentences of his greatest letter, he writes, "I am not ashamed of the Gospel: it is the power of God for salvation to every one who has faith" (Romans 1:16). But there is a freshness about this earliest letter that is like the bracing lift we feel in the air when the day is newborn. Simple, uncomplicated, and right to the point. "Because we loved you we gave you the Gospel. But we loved you so much we gave you our own selves as well. You were dear to us." The message of Paul and his companion was not to please men (2:6), it was not used as a cloak for greed (2:5), it was not to take any glory to themselves (2:6), it was not given for personal gain (2:6). They worked night and day to support themselves in order *not* to be a burden to the Christian community (2:9). So, in every way, they shared themselves with their Gospel.

How Does This Apply to Us?

Most of us want to share the Gospel with others. Many of us are ready to share the Gospel. Not quite so many of us are willing to share the Gospel if it involves too much of our time, our energy, our resources, ourselves. To share the Good News calls for genuine love that may well lay on us unwanted disciplines. To give *out* the Gospel may require giving *up* something of ourselves. Some of us may remember the day of "Gospel Bombs." Was it during the war years? Some well-meaning Christians would wrap Gospel tracts in plastic containers and toss them by the thousands like innocuous bombs from an airplane or a speeding car. In so doing they weren't really winning many of the environmentalists, but they thought they were in business as evangelists. This is a country mile from Paul's sharing of himself with the Gospel. Evangelism "at arm's length" will never make it. It does little good and may do much harm.

Pray with Me

O God, Your Son is perfect love and Your Gospel is redeeming grace. Eternity will not be long enough for my grateful heart to sing Your praise.

The chains of guilt have been broken. The burden of sin has been lifted. The meaningless existence of living for self has been transformed into the purposeful adventure of living for You. Heaven is on my horizon. Eternal life is mine. I live in the joy of life that is unperturbed by death. This is the Gospel of God. This is the Good News that lifts me up and carries me on. From a heart brimming with unmerited blessings I thank You.

But there is something else, something more, I must hear today. It is not new, for I have known the cost of sharing myself with Your Good News. It drains the energy and it tests the mettle. I cannot be impatient with others nor indulgent with my own weaknesses. The sharing life is the disciplined life. But let me see You, risen Lord, through the mists of rising doubt and through the haze of passing time. Let me see You clearly. And by the marks of Your suffering love let me never draw back from the costs of sharing myself with Your Gospel.

Give me to see that I, even I and even now, can make the Gospel a thing to be esteemed, sought, and welcomed. I can also make it something to be ignored, neglected, and despised. And this all depends on whether I am willing to give myself when I give the Good News.

I do not understand how I could ever be counted worthy to be a trustee of such a message. But I pray that Your patient grace will fashion me until I am a fit vessel. I pray that Your Holy Spirit will cleanse me until I am an open channel. Let there be no bewildering and faith-weakening discrepancy between the Gospel I speak with my lips and the Gospel I show with my life.

In the Name of Him whose once giving of Himself is the everlasting gospel, Amen.

MOVING ON IN THE LIFE OF PRAYER

In prayer we acknowledge that Paul's way is the best way. In prayer, we can move mountains and open doors. We must pray for ways to share ourselves *with* the Gospel of God. Then prayer will cease to be a treadmill—praying hard and getting nowhere. It becomes instead a joyful exercise in purposeful living. What is the Gospel according to *me?*

Day 100

GOD CARES

"And God heard . . . God remembered . . . God looked . . ." (Exodus 2:24-25, KJV).

Read: **Exodus 2:11-25;** Deuteronomy 7:9; 1 Kings 8:56; Psalm 55:1-2, 142:1-3; Romans 6:16-19; Hebrews 10:23.

WHAT IS GOD SAYING?

The people of Israel have always longed to be free. Their perseverance and preservation as a united and freedom-loving people is one of the great footnotes of history. These people are the tangible evidence that God is able to carry out His purpose with invincible power and authority.

We see them in this portion of Exodus laboring under the intolerable burdens of slavery, yet remembering the promises God gave to Abraham and his offspring. The people of Israel have always cherished their traditions. They have always guarded their memories. The memory of the destiny God had planned for them and promised to them must have been kept alive during the long and oppressive years under the pharaohs after Joseph. They were regarded with suspicion by the Egyptians, and why not? They had grown from seventy Hebrews who went to Egypt at the time of the famine to a nation of three million. It served the best interests of the Egyptians to keep them in perpetual bondage.

But God was in control. When "their cry under bondage came up to God. And God *heard* their groaning, and God *remembered* his covenant with Abraham, with Isaac, and with Jacob. And God *saw* the people of Israel, and God knew their condition" (2:23-25). First they cried for help and then God, who was their "help in ages past and their hope for years to come," set in motion the long and painful process of deliverance in which he would be "their shelter from the stormy blast and their eternal home."

How Does This Apply to Us?

God is still in control. God still *hears* our prayer. God still *remembers* His own. God still *looks* upon those who suffer with compassion and redeeming love.

God *hears* our prayer to be released from the bondage of sin. God *remembers* that Jesus died in our place on the Cross to set us free from the slavery of sin—its penalty, its guilt. God still *sees* us as we are and even more for what we may become. All our praying should be in the confidence that God who hears and remembers and sees—and above all, cares—is able to do what He has promised.

Pray with Me

Out of the depths have I cried unto you, O Lord.

In bondage, Your children groaned. Under the whip, they cried. Everyone has been—or is—in bondage to sin. The problem is universal and Egypt is everywhere. "So I find it to be a law," said Your apostle, "that when I want to do right, evil lies close at hand." Out of the depths of such bondage, out of total helplessness, I have cried and You have *heard*.

Yet, Lord, I pray for more. As You *remembered* Your covenant with the children of Israel, remember me.

In Your kindness, do not remember my sin and my pride.

In Your patience, do not remember the times I turned away from Your life *for* me and ignored Your life *in* me and hindered Your life *through* me.

In Your steadfast love, do not remember my big boasts and little deeds. Remember only, Lord, Your covenant and *look* on me as one who needs and pleads the righteousness of Jesus Christ.

I glory in nothing but the Cross. Your suffering there turned the shame of sin into the glory of redemption. In dying there You have transformed the shadow of death into the light of life.

For His sake and by the merit of His love, hear, remember, and look on me: the prodigal son returned, the wandering sheep reclaimed, and the penitent sinner redeemed. It is all to the praise of the glory of Your grace.

Through Jesus Christ, Amen.

Moving On in the Life of Prayer

Prayer becomes a wonderful and joyful exercise when we realize we are not poring over a book with printed words but are pouring out the needs of our hearts to One who hears. We are not talking to a figure in a shrine or a picture on the wall, but to a living God who remembers and sees and cares. God remembers His covenant and His promises. He remembers them and makes them good. When we remember *that*, prayer will change from an empty ritual to a fulfilling joy.

Day 101

God Alone Is God

"Arise, O Lord! . . . Let the nations know that they are but men!" (Psalm 9:19-20).

Read: **Psalms 9 and 10,** 33:13-22; Isaiah 8:9-15; Hebrews 12:23.

What Is God Saying?

The Psalms are rich in meaning and varied in content. There is praise and there is penitence. There is the joy of victory and the anguish of defeat. There are songs of encouragement and sighs of despair. There are songs to lift us to the mountain-top and songs to accompany us in the valley of the shadow of death. There are songs that comfort and songs that challenge. They cover the whole spectrum of life and many of them point to Christ who said Himself that all of Scripture—Moses, the prophets, *and* the Psalms—was fulfilled in Him (Luke 24:44).

Psalm 9 declares the victory of God over all enemies, His and ours, great and small, national or personal. This is a reality which believers *always* need to keep before them. It should never be forgotten, ignored, or neglected. It is the secret of our joy, the reason for our praise, the inner resource of our strength, and the confidence that keeps us moving on. Could that be the reason that these two psalms (9 and 10) are written in the form of an acrostic, where the first letter of successive verses follows the Hebrew alphabet? That makes it easier to repeat and to remember. We need to repeat and to remember the truth of this entire psalm but especially verse 10.

How Does This Apply to Us?

The message of the psalm must be applied as well as remembered. The God of David is still ruling over all. He "sits enthroned for ever" (9:7). The nations of men who depart from the ways of the Lord "have sunk in the pit which they made; in the net which they hid has their own foot been caught" (9:15).

God can be trusted. On the other hand, nations, for all their vaunted power, are only men (Psalm 33:16-17). God alone is God. His way is always right. His love is a better way than hate. His power conquers *all* enemies. His glory He will not give to another. As we ask God to "arise," it is important that we look to Him and believe that when He is lifted up in the power of deathless love He "will draw all men to [himself]" (John 12:32).

Pray with Me

Eternal and loving God, Your ways are always right. Your plan is always perfect. Your purpose can never be defeated. "Arise! O Lord, arise!"

Arise in Your power to defeat the enemies of righteousness in all the nations of men . . . and in me.

Arise in Your love to show there is a better way than hate and a better solution than greed in all the nations of men . . . and in me.

Arise in Your glory to turn our erring humanity from its selfish, little concerns and its earthbound ambitions.

As You "arise" to the place of highest praise, as we begin to see You in that place which You alone deserve and as we begin to see that Your all-conquering love is as great as Your invincible power, only then shall we come to see that the *power of love* is the only remedy for the *love of power*.

Let the nations know that they are but men, limited in vision, lacking in wisdom, and lost in sin. Let them know this not to engender a sense of worthlessness, nor to cultivate self-loathing, nor to compound feelings of inferiority, but to help them see that You have made man "little less than God, and dost crown him with glory and honor" . . . a little less, but surely less.

Arise, O Lord! And, in rising, lift us closer to Your perfection.

Arise, O Lord! And, in rising, show us who You are and what, in You, we may become.

Arise, O Lord! And, in rising, draw us with the very power of Your resurrection into a life of more constant victory.

Let the nations know not only that they are men but that You alone are God. Until then we shall keep going on to our destruction in the love of power and miss the salvation that awaits and accompanies the power of love.

In the Name of Him who redeemed us from the power of all evil through the power of His love. Amen.

Moving On in the Life of Prayer

In prayer we turn our thoughts toward God. He is our help. He is our hope. Prayer is a time when we look away from people however much they try or however good may be their intentions. Prayer is a time to concentrate on the power, the love, and the glory of God. We follow the lead of the psalmist who wrote: "Our soul waits for the LORD; he is our help and shield" (Psalm 33:20). Then, having looked away from others to find our true help in God, we are prepared to come back to others: to respect their desire to help and, now strong in the Lord, to be of help to them.

But whether we give help to others or receive help from others, there is a right time and a right way. Prayer helps us with that, too. It is looking to God for help and looking to others to be of help.

Day 102

Blessed Are the Pure in Heart

"To the pure all things are pure" (Titus 1:15).

Read: **Titus 1;** Psalm 24:3-4; Habakkuk 1:13; Luke 1:44-45; Philippians 4:8; 1 Peter 1:16; 1 John 1:7.

What Is God Saying?

This is another personal letter from Paul to a younger minister, although it was intended to be read to the churches as well. Titus was left in Crete—the seat of the Minoan civilization, older than that of Greece—to administer the Lord's work there. Titus had a great responsibility under difficult circumstances. He had served well in the ferment of crisscrossing cultures in Corinth. Yet Paul wanted to encourage him and to give him the benefit of his mature reflections on how to live the Christian life in a pagan culture. His goal was to "further . . . their knowledge of the truth which accords with godliness" (Titus 1:1). This thought is repeated in verse 8 where, among other qualities, the elders or bishops are instructed to be "lovers of goodness."

The background of native Cretans did not favor pure living. One of their own prophets wrote (and we quote Paul quoting him), "Cretans are always liars, evil beasts, lazy gluttons. This testimony," adds Paul, "is true." Strong words, but they state the case. Purity did not come naturally to the people of Crete, nor does it come naturally to unregenerate people anywhere in any time. "To the pure all things are pure, but to the corrupt and unbelieving nothing is pure . . . They profess to know God, but they deny him by their deeds" (Titus 1:15-16).

How Does This Apply to Us?

Those who *know* God must *show* purity: purity of speech, purity of thought, purity of motive, purity of life. Nothing less honors God.

If we say we know God and our deeds are corrupt, we are not different from the Cretans; a little more refined, perhaps, but still "liars." Think pure thoughts and see beauty everywhere. Is that not a part of the "blessedness" in the Beatitude? "Blessed are the pure in heart, for they shall see God" (Matthew 5:8). God is everywhere to be seen but is often missed. It is the pure in heart who see God: in the laughter of children, in the joys of marriage, in the sacrificial life of Christians, in a "rosy-fingered dawn," in the rain-washed fragrance of a garden, in the reverent hush of a starlit night—everywhere, all the time, "to the pure all things are pure."

Pray with Me

O Lord, You are of purer eyes than to behold iniquity. Although I am very human and troubled with errant desires, help me through the patient grace of the Holy Spirit to grow into Your likeness. As You are of purer eyes than to behold iniquity, so let my eyes be constantly seeking what is good and true and beautiful.

Let these eyes be so filled with Your glory and so satisfied with Your truth that there shall be no time to waste on what is impure. Too often in weakness I have excused myself. I have known the futility of arguing my own defenseless case. I now affirm that had my vision been filled with Your beauty as it may be seen in Jesus Christ, my eyes would have seen only that which is pure.

Help me so to walk in Your fellowship and so to see with Your vision that all things shall be pure. Pure in the letters I write, the words I speak, and the things I do. Set me free from any scheming for advantage. Help me to see the good that is striving to be born in others. Help me to believe in and to encourage purity in myself until my heart refuses to be subdued by lust or suffocated by cheap and quick substitutes for joy.

"To the pure all things are pure." I look for beauty and I find the earth at my feet alive with fragrance and color. I listen for the song of the birds, and the air is filled with music. I turn in reverent wonder to the stars, and the heavens are aglow with the watch fires of the Eternal.

O, I thank You, God, that the blessings of pure thought and pure desire are as inexhaustible as eternity itself.

In the Spirit of Jesus Christ, who could see and help all who hungered for purity, I would learn the exquisite secret that all things can be pure. And, to the pure, they are.

Amen.

MOVING ON IN THE LIFE OF PRAYER

Prayer finds its most fertile setting when, above all, our hearts are centered on that which is pure. Prayer guards our hearts from impurity. Prayer nurtures pure thoughts. When we keep on praying with thoughts focused on the holiness of God, He brings into our silent hearts His soul-refreshing grace. He is pure love. Loving Him purely, we come to love all things that are pure. Loving Him purely, we come to think about all things purely. Loving Him purely, we are not trapped in the complexities of mixed loyalties. "To the pure all things are pure."

Day 103

THE LORD: FINAL CONQUEROR, PERFECT COMFORTER

"The Lord Jesus will slay him [the lawless one] with the breath of his mouth. . . . Now may our Lord Jesus Christ . . . comfort your hearts and establish them in every good work and word" (2 Thessalonians 2:8, 16, 17).

Read: **2 Thessalonians 2;** John 16:33; 1 John 2:18-25.

WHAT IS GOD SAYING?

Notice in this passage the certainty of a great conflict between evil and good. See also that ultimate triumph belongs to God and to those whom He has "called by our gospel, to the obtaining of the glory of our Lord Jesus Christ" (2:14, KJV). The chapter has a break that can be compared to a fire wall. From verse 8 to verse 13, there is "the coming of the lawless one by the activity of Satan . . . with all power and with pretended signs and wonders" (v. 9). His great weapon will be deception (v. 10). Part of the delusion will be enjoying what is wrong and finding pleasure in what is evil.

Up to this point, Satan is in control. But then comes the fire wall. As promised in verse 8, "the Lord . . . shall destroy [him] with the brightness of his coming" (KJV). We are called by the gospel. We are saved through the sanctification of the Spirit and belief of the truth (vv. 13-14) and we are given everlasting comfort and good hope through grace (v. 16). Satan and evil are strong but God and good are stronger and in this our hearts find comfort (v. 17). Jesus is the final Conqueror and the perfect Comforter.

HOW DOES THIS APPLY TO US?

This conflict is carried on every day and in nearly every place. We can't avoid it. We don't have to look for it. It comes to *us.* It is blasted from the media and blazoned in the headlines. It is found in the small print on the back page. It glares at us from the newsstands. It infiltrates our subconscious in subtle ways when our guard is down. There is no escaping. It is the way of the world. It is Satan saying and getting others to say: "Evil be thou my good."

But, being *in* the world we can choose to be not *of* the world. With the Thessalonians we can face a defeated enemy in the power of Christ's love and in the confidence of His final victory. And in this we, too, may be comforted (or strengthened) by "good hope through grace" (2:16).

Two verses now speak directly to our need as we wage our continual warfare: "But the Lord is faithful; he will strengthen you and guard you from evil" (3:3), and "May the Lord direct your hearts to the love of God and to the steadfastness of Christ" (3:5). On the basis of that, in the heat of the conflict, our prayers will go from asking to praise and thanksgiving. The Lord *is* the final Conqueror and the perfect Comforter.

Pray with Me

Lord, we live in a world that seems to be controlled by the Lawless One. Thank You for the strengthening grace of Your Word which assures me that the Lord Jesus is both the final Conqueror and the perfect Comforter.

He who is the Prince of this world will be conquered. They who are the pilgrims of this world will be comforted.

It is easy to lose heart when wickedness runs on unhindered. It is easy to run for cover when nothing seems able to resist the downward drag of evil. It is easy to be discouraged when one sees how lawlessness even seems to stain the hearts of those who follow the Stainless One. Yet I claim the promised victory now. I accept it by faith. My heart is comforted now.

I expect the answer, for You have given it. I live by this promise because its source is the eternal God. To have less boldness would be to question the power of the invincible Christ. To have less assurance would be to doubt the validity of Your perfect Word which will never pass away.

As You conquer the evil that controls and afflicts Your people, so comfort all who hunger and thirst after Your righteousness. Christ is the final Victor. This I affirm. By this I live. Toward this I look. Beyond this I know there will be eternal life, unshadowed by any dread of the Lawless One.

Until that time, let my life show the calm trust and the quiet strength of those who know that the future as well as the present is in the hands of our all-conquering and all-comforting Christ.

In His ever-conquering and ever-comforting Name, Amen.

MOVING ON IN THE LIFE OF PRAYER

"In the world you *have* tribulation" (John 16:33). In the world there are restless seas driven and tossed by evil. In the world there is the unrest of envy, pride, vengeance, and lust. But in prayer we have a refuge, a great seawall that tames the angry swells and negates the subtle undertow of evil called good. Here we are quiet. Here we can listen. Here we are heard. Here, also, we see the glory of Him who *is* the final Conqueror and here we rejoice in the good hope that is promised by One who *is* the perfect Comforter.

Day 104

STRONGER AND STRONGER IN CHRIST

" . . . *And David grew stronger and stronger, while the house of Saul became weaker and weaker*" *(2 Samuel 3:1b)*.

Read: **2 Samuel 3:1**; Exodus 14:30-15:2; Isaiah 40:31; 2 Corinthians 12:9-10; Ephesians 3:16.

WHAT IS GOD SAYING?

First Samuel is a record of failure. Saul is in the spotlight. He was the people's choice for a king and, although he showed great promise, he proved to be a disappointment.

Second Samuel is the record of *God's* choice for a king. David had many faults but he always gave glory to God. God could use him. When he destroyed Goliath, armed with a slingshot and five smooth stones, he cried out, "That all the earth may know that there is a God in Israel." His exploits of courage and singleness of heart toward God go on until he becomes the king of all Israel.

Second Samuel is David in his ascendancy. Here is David at his best. But for all his signal honors and brave accomplishments, David proved to be human. At the height of his success, he fell. Through sincere repentance, he was restored and ended his days on top. Although he endured compounded sorrows in his later years, he was to the end a "man after God's own heart."

As we look in on him here we see that David's house or dynasty is getting stronger and stronger. The struggle for power went on between Saul's house and David's, urged on by Abner, for seven and a half years. Saul's house did not die easily, but its cause was a lost one. It grew weaker and weaker. The reason: God was against it.

HOW DOES THIS APPLY TO US?

Our strength or lack of it depends on our relationship to God. If we love Him, obey Him, and seek His glory in all that we do, we grow stronger. If we live as though He were not important and if we regard His Word with only casual interest—if at all—then we grow weaker. Strength that does not have its origin in God is really weakness. Weakness that makes itself available to God is really strength. Paul said, "I will all the more gladly boast of my weaknesses, that the power of Christ may rest upon me. . . . When I am weak, then I am strong" (2 Corinthians 12:9-10).

To be in Christ is to have more and more of Christ. Simply being in Christ means more Christ. Saul was a man after Saul's own heart and his house grew weaker. David was a man after God's own heart and his house grew stronger. "I Did It My Way" is the vacuous sentiment of an old song and it ends in a cul-de-sac. "I did it God's way" is the sure promise of a life that counts for something and its destiny is Heaven.

Pray with Me

Lord, by deliberate choice, I make You my Refuge. I seek no other help. I need no other hope. My grateful heart sings with joy: "Your grace is sufficient for me and Your power is made perfect in weakness." I am in constant touch with the almightiness of God.

Help me to understand that so long as I remain in the fellowship of Your love, and so long as I walk in the light of Your truth, and so long as I abide in the life of Your Son, I will, like David, grow stronger and stronger. "To him who has will more be given." To have Christ is to have more Christ. To be like Christ is to be more like Christ. To be strong in the Lord is to be stronger in the Lord. The life of faith is a life of increasing joy and growing strength and greater victories.

May I give all diligence to remain in this relationship with You. May I remember that "from him who has not, even what he has will be taken away." The house of Saul became weaker and weaker because Saul had broken away from a life of obedience. Deliver me from such a foolish decision. The choice is so near at hand, so easy and so tempting. I cannot relax my guard.

The Lord sought out David, a man after His own heart, and he grew stronger. The Lord turned from Saul who was a man after Saul's own heart and his house grew weaker and weaker.

Give me the grace and wisdom to abide in You, to set my affection and to place my confidence in nothing less than You, and to value Your presence more than the companionship of men or the love of friends. Let me, like David, be a man after Your own heart. Then, by a law that is indelibly written and by a grace that is inexhaustibly available, I shall grow stronger and stronger.

To the glory of the Lord who is both my Strength and my Redeemer, Amen.

MOVING ON IN THE LIFE OF PRAYER

The *purpose* of prayer is to determine God's will. The *blessing* of prayer is to receive God's strength. Through prayer, we grow stronger and stronger in the things that count. Stronger in courage, stronger in love, stronger in faith, stronger in virtue, stronger in character.

Stronger or weaker? Prayer makes the difference. Sometimes *all* the difference.

Day 105

FROM OUR FATHER WITH LOVE

"The LORD lift up his countenance upon you, and give you peace" *(Numbers 6:26).*

Read: **Numbers 6:22-27;** 2 Samuel 7:27-29; Psalm 4:6, 67:1; Proverbs 10:22; Romans 4:7-8; Ephesians 1:3.

WHAT IS GOD SAYING?

Numbers 6:27 concludes the three-part benediction known as the Priestly Blessing. No blessing is older or more widely known or more greatly appreciated. It is all sunshine and joy. It stresses the beautiful relationship of almighty God with His children.

The words repeatedly emphasized are "the LORD" and "you." Each of the three sections begins with "the LORD" and each section contains the word "you" twice. There is no evidence that this "three-in-one" formula has any bearing upon the Trinity. But there is nothing to prevent Christians from being helped by repeating this prayer with the Trinity in mind. Prayer and its blessings are as often based on heart knowledge as they are on head knowledge.

The blessing invoked by this timeless benediction extends to far more than material benefits. The words "keep you," "be gracious to you," and "give you peace" transcend all material considerations. They are blessings of the Spirit. They do not come and go with the pendulum swing of fortune and prosperity. *Keeping* us from evil and *keeping* us close to Himself is the graciousness of God and the basis of peace.

HOW DOES THIS APPLY TO US?

In our world the pure waters of refreshing *grace* are often polluted by self-serving ambition and by a careless disregard for God's rules for the game. The still waters of *peace* are troubled by willful disobedience, lawlessness, and pride. For this kind of world and for the living of these days, this benediction is timely. We need it now and we are blessed when we share it now.

It is also timeless. It is the most ancient of benedictions. It has been a source of strength and encouragement across the centuries and will be around tomorrow. Count on that. The Lord who has blessed is the Lord who is blessing and will be blessing to the end of time and forever. Our great need is to look in His direction. Then we will see His face is shining upon us with grace and His countenance lifted upon us with peace.

Pray with Me

Help me, Lord, to be in the place that You can bless. Help me to be in the spirit that You can bless.

When I hide from You in the fear that sin always creates, I cannot expect to know the "lifting up" of Your countenance. When I walk in paths that are not of Your choosing, I cannot expect to know the gift of Your peace. When I turn toward the darkness and the bondage of self-styled liberties, I cannot expect to know the joyful freedom that Your blessing always gives. I must be willing to be where Your countenance is not obstructed and where Your approval is not withheld.

Yet the lifting up of Your countenance, Your power to see me as I am and for what I may become, is all of Your goodness and mercy.

Lift up Your countenance upon my need and supply me with the riches of Your mercy. Lift up Your countenance upon my many failures and give me grace to try again, this time resting on the promises of Christ who has already torn the scepter from the hand of evil, and, having tasted the worst defeat, has turned it into the greatest victory. Lift up Your countenance upon my willfulness and in the power of Your infinite grace change it into willingness. Lift up Your countenance upon what might have been and let me see what it still may be.

Because You lift up Your countenance upon the weak and the wandering as well as on the strong and the stable, because You lift up Your countenance upon the potential as well as the actual, because You lift up Your countenance upon the unlikely as well as the promising, the losers as well as the winners, the broken as well as the whole, there is this assurance (and O! may I live and triumph and persevere to the end with this wonderful promise always before me and within) that You give peace.

In the Name of the uplifted Savior who gives us peace when our countenances are lifted up to Him, Amen.

MOVING ON IN THE LIFE OF PRAYER

In prayer, we are still. In being still, we know that God is God. In knowing God is God, this ancient benediction comes alive: we *are* kept from evil and close to Him, He *is* being gracious to us, and we have peace, peace that passes all understanding.

Day 106

THE MOUNTAINS OF GOD

"Thy righteousness is like the mountains of God. . . ." (Psalm 36:6).

Read: **Psalm 36,** 121:1, 125:2.

WHAT IS GOD SAYING?

This is a song in praise of God's unfailing love. It stands like a mountain range from whose presence we derive strength (read Psalm 121:1) and protection (read Psalm 125:2). It is a song that carries us beyond. It opens with the sad state of anyone who is wrapped up in himself, dedicated to his own evil ways and to transient and trivial satisfactions (36:1-4).

The song changes suddenly to show the contrast between self-deception and the majestic faithfulness of God in His steadfast love. There they are, the "mountains of God" (v. 6), towering over a man who "plots mischief while on his bed" (v. 4) and "flatters himself . . . that his iniquity cannot be found out and hated" (v. 2). So it is that both Psalm 36 and 37 are meant to lead us beyond all fretfulness, anxiety, and worry; beyond the wickedness of godless men; and beyond the limitations of our own strength and virtue, until we come to trust in the mercy and faithfulness of God.

HOW DOES THIS APPLY TO US?

Let these great psalms move our hearts to a deeper trust in God's faithfulness and steadfast love. Let us lift up our eyes to the hills and put our trust in the mountains of God. Let us get past the underbrush of little cares, let us see beyond the foothills of entrenched wrongs that seem so great and so insurmountable, let us look above the clouds of doubt that hang low over the valleys of discouragement. Just over yonder are the mountains of God.

Plagued by the changefulness of human nature, our own as well as others', we look to the changeless mountains of God's steadfast love. Lost in the lowlands of conflicting ideas and stumbling through the wilderness of human opinions, we get our direction by looking to the mountains of God's wisdom. So we are directed into the way of everlasting truth. So we lay hold on the truth of the everlasting way.

Pray with Me

Like the mountains which You have created, O God, so is Your righteousness: changeless and everlasting, strong and majestic. The ideas of men are like passing clouds. The ideals toward which we strive are fleeting and illusive. They are no sooner born than abandoned. But Your truth, even as Your Son whom we love and worship, is "the same yesterday and today and for ever."

It is encouraging, Lord, to look up to the changeless mountains and receive from the sight of their silent grandeur the strength of quiet confidence. Whatever burdens are wearing me out, whatever temptations are grinding me down, I have something to which I can turn that never changes and never fails: Your mountains and Your righteousness! They are still there, silent and eloquent evidence that *You* are still there.

I have known mountainous fears and mountainous resistance and mountainous anxieties but they all melt before my eyes when I see the mountains of Your righteousness and the fullness of Your vindicating love. Great ills become tiny hills when seen beside the mountains of God.

Let Your righteousness as a mountain inspire and direct me. As the great mountains give a lift to weary hearts, so they give unfailing guidance to wandering feet. As they inspire, so they direct. As they direct, so they challenge.

Let Your righteousness be to me as the mountains of God that I may be inspired and directed and challenged into the way of everlasting truth and into the truth of the everlasting Way.

In His Name whose righteousness is my everlasting and solitary hope, Amen.

MOVING ON IN THE LIFE OF PRAYER

Something must have moved the psalmist to say and to pray: "I lift up my eyes to the hills." Did he not see in them the quiet strength of God? When we pray, we turn to One who is greater than the mountains (He made them); but in their changeless strength and soaring majesty they are reminders that God is always there, always above, always waiting to bless. "Thy righteousness is like the mountains of God." Look to Him. He was there yesterday. He will be there tomorrow. And the unspeakable Gift of His love, our Lord Jesus Christ, is "the same

yesterday and today and for ever.'' Pray in that confidence. Live
by that truth.

SIMPLE TRUST IN THE LIVING GOD

" *'The LORD who delivered me from the paw of the lion and from the paw
of the bear, will deliver me from the hand of this Philistine'* " *(1 Samuel
17:37)*.

Read: **1 Samuel 17;** Psalm 3:1-6, 20:6-8; Isaiah 12:2.

WHAT IS GOD SAYING?

David faced a great challenge. It stood nine feet tall and
was enough to shake a whole army. What little strength was left
in their knees was used to run away. What little breath was left in
their heaving chests was used to say, "Have you *seen* this man?"

Goliath carried 150 pounds of armor and wielded a spear
whose head alone weighed four pounds more than the average
bowling ball. What kind of man would or could go into battle
with that much weight hanging on him? It must have been a
man who was strong enough to carry it, a man who had no
intention of running away. That is what David faced—a giant of
a man, fully armored, whose appearance and big talk had scared
off an army.

But David had a secret weapon against which even the
"incredible hulk" would be powerless. David had trust in the
living God. Goliath could defy the *men* of Israel but he could not
fight the *God* of Israel when that God had a single young man
who trusted Him all the way.

David, trusting God, moved toward his greatest challenge.
The giant looked down and barked: "Am I a dog, that you come
to me with sticks?" David looked up at the giant and said, "You
come to me with a sword and with a spear and with a javelin"—
the wrong weapons— "but I come to you in the name of the
LORD of hosts." In his sight the mighty giant was a helpless
midget. David went to the battle line armed only with a sling
and a stone and faith in God. He who did it before would do it
again.

HOW DOES THIS APPLY TO US?

God who has done it in the past can do it again. That is an
important source of confidence.

When *we* have done something well in the past, do we not
feel a surge of confidence when called upon to do it again? It is

doing something hard for the first time that makes us ill at ease and afraid. It is the feeling a pilot has who is suddenly told by the instructor, "Now it's your turn to go solo." Then he recalls that he has practiced his "touch and go's" many times. He has done it alone even though the teacher was at his side and he can do it again.

But in 1 Samuel 17:37, David is not talking about *his* strength and skill. He is giving glory to God. God gave him deliverance. The God who did it then can do it now. Let that be our very present help and our strength in any challenge of the future.

Pray with Me

Strong Deliverer! God of all grace and power, let the victories You have given in the past bring me encouragement in the present and challenge for the future.

Let me be so sure of Your presence and power that I shall be able to face any enemy without giving up in discouragement or being paralyzed by fear. Then, having known the help that never comes too late, I will rise to meet any opposition. I deliberately choose Your strength, for even in my weakness it is greater than any enemy.

David moved from victory to victory with nothing more than simple trust in the living God. So will I move on to meet the future victoriously with the calmness and strength of deep trust. David knew Your deliverance from the paw of the beast and believed in Your deliverance from the hand of the Philistine. So will I be fortified by the knowledge and experience of the past and by confidence and faith for the future.

David might have rested on his laurels with these two victories. Instead he was on the alert for greater conquests. He knew that to have only what we have experienced is to have less than the best. He knew that his reach should exceed his grasp . . . and You honored his faith. He was not content merely to remember the past. So You gave him the future.

Help me, as You did David, to remember the past only as a foundation for courage—never as an excuse for pride. Greater battles await me than those I have fought with lions and bears. Your strengthening grace always rises with the need until, through Christ, I can be more than conqueror against any giant passion or any swaggering fear.

In His Name whose strength is made perfect in weakness, Amen.

Moving On in the Life of Prayer

We all face battles. Peace does not come in running away *from* the front lines. It comes from trusting God *in* the front lines. When we pray in the name of Jesus, we are praying in the strength of Jesus, for the sake of Jesus, and for the glory of Jesus.

No giant opposition can overcome us because we are "more than conquerors through him who loved us." He has done it before. He is doing it now. He will do it for us and with us again—and again.

Day 108

Dying to Live

"The saying is sure: If we have died with him, we shall also live with him" (2 Timothy 2:11).

Read: **2 Timothy 2;** Romans 6:5-11; Galatians 2:20, 5:16-26; Colossians 3:1-4.

What Is God Saying?

Second Timothy is the last of Paul's letters; he is coming to the end of his life. So what might we expect? Mournful dirge? Whimper of defeat? No way! It is praise and hope and victory. Above all it looks ahead with nobility of spirit and the confidence of faith.

The days were dark for Christians. Persecution was everywhere and apostasy was infiltrating the Church, but, for Paul, God was still in control. Christ was alive. His Kingdom would prevail.

Paul knew the truth about the great fire in Rome and so knew Christians had been unjustly blamed for starting it. As a proudly ambitious builder, Nero had a lot of "good" ideas, none of which bore any resemblance to "goodness." He decided to launch an "urban redevelopment program" for Rome and started by setting fire to the city. That is why he watched with delight as the flames danced from building to building. Christians were blamed in order to divert suspicion from Nero, the real villain. It was the worst of times.

But 2 Timothy is not a litany of defeat and despair. It is a letter of hope and victory. Death was near. Paul sensed it. His friends, except for Luke, were far away—but the Lord was near. This letter is based on the confidence that life in Christ reaches beyond the terminus of this life. Listen to the final words of his final letter: "The Lord will rescue me from every evil and save me for his heavenly kingdom. To him be the glory for ever and ever. Amen" (2 Timothy 4:18). That is the deep meaning of Paul's words: dying *with* Christ, yes, dying *for* Christ; but that is only the beginning. We *shall* live with Him . . . forever.

How Does This Apply to Us?

As we go through the normal routine of life we are absorbed with its necessities and its pleasures, its duties and its goals. Somewhere down the line there is the Great Intruder who will stand across our path and make a shambles of our ambitious schemes and pleasant dreams. The castles of sand we so feverishly build along the shorelines of life will melt under the incoming tide with its cold waves. They are no respecter of persons—or castles. Life is real and death is distant.

Paul was speaking of life in the presence of death. They were both near and they were both real. But the life of which he spoke and on which he built his hope was life that could never be vanquished by death. So he looks at death and beyond it to Life. In fact, to live with Christ is to live both now and forever. Hear Jesus' own words: "Whoever lives and believes in me shall never die" (John 11:26). There, in one sentence, is life and death. Through faith, death is subdued and life goes on. But there is more good news . . . to live *for* Christ now is the best life. To live *with* Christ is our destiny. Isn't that the best of both worlds?

Pray with Me

Lord Jesus, I come to You in the quietness of this early hour. The air is clear and clean. It is not filled with the dust of fretful care. The stream of thought has not been soiled by contact with anything less than the beauty of Your holiness. In this hour of deep and unhindered grace, I see that if I am ever to *live* with You, I must be willing to *die* with You.

I have thought that I might have some of You and some of self. I have deceived myself into believing that I might receive the blessing of Your company while keeping company with things You have never blessed. I have supposed that I might own Your lordship in some areas of life while holding back other places where I still want to be the master.

To live with You is to live both now and forever. To live with You is to be under bondage to the best and at liberty from the worst. To live with You is to possess riches that can never perish. To live with You is to be set free from total dependence on material things, the abundance or the lack of which can bring care or misery. To live with You is to love mercy and truth, the root of all good. To live with You is to be at liberty from earthly treasures, the love of which is the root of all kinds of evil.

I do not hesitate any longer to take the step of faith. Pausing at the brink is only misery prolonged. A double-minded man is both unhappy and unstable. A two-mastered man is both miserable and ineffective.

Whatever "dying with You" may mean, bring it to pass. I accept this truth today: Dying with You is surely the bright door of hope, the open door of grace, and the only door to life.

Let me die with You, for then and only then shall I live with You.

In Your life-giving Name, Amen.

MOVING ON IN THE LIFE OF PRAYER

In every prayer we should ask God to make clear those things that ought to be buried and forgotten because *they* died with us when we died with Him. It is equally important to identify and encourage those things which ought to be kept and nurtured because they are a part of the life we now live and shall forever live with Him. For help in identifying both, read Galatians 5:16-26.

Day 109

THE PRESENCE OF GOD

"And when the cloud was taken up from over the tabernacle, the children of Israel went onward in all their journeys" (Exodus 40:36, KJV).

Read: **Exodus 40:34-38;** Numbers 9:15-23; Nehemiah 9:12; Psalm 23:2-4; Habbakuk 2:4-9; Matthew 17:5, 28:20.

WHAT IS GOD SAYING?

The Israelites, led by Moses, were making their way through the perilous land to the Promised Land. The way was long and difficult. Because His love never fails and because He had destined Israel to fulfill His holy purposes for the world, God stayed with them and went before them. Without His presence those who were almost lost would have become totally lost and the Exodus would have ended in failure, nobly conceived but pathetically aborted. All the difference would lie in God's presence.

For that reason God gave the cloud as a symbol of His presence. When it rested on the Tabernacle, the people rested. When it moved on, the people followed. The Shekinah glory became an integral part of Israel's heritage. The cloud as an expedient but temporary manifestation of God's presence in the wilderness became an abiding presence in the Temple of Solomon and finally in the Word that became flesh and dwelt among men. In Haggai 2:9 we read, "The latter splendor of this house shall be greater than the former, says the LORD of hosts." God made it come true in the Person of Jesus Christ.

How Does This Apply to Us?

It gives a far greater meaning to that ancient cloud of the Exodus, when we trace it from the wilderness Tabernacle to the great Temple and finally to the visible presence of Jesus, the Word become flesh, full of grace and truth. The presence of God in the life and teachings of Jesus Christ is still for us a call to advance through this wilderness world or to rest and refresh our spirits. Israel needed the cloud by day and the fire by night. It told them whether to move on or to stay in their tents. The cloud was the ancient token of God's presence. Now the words, life, death, and resurrection of our Lord and, not least, the promised presence of the Holy Spirit, are the "clouds" God uses to lead us on or to call us to rest, as He knows best.

Pray with Me

Lord, You are the God of my going out and my coming in. The Israelites were led by Your saving presence and fed by the miracle of Your provident grace. Unwanted by others, they were undaunted in You. They wandered in a barren land, but the glory of Your presence was never withdrawn. They saw Your presence in the cloud over the Tabernacle when they rested. They saw Your presence in the cloud over the path when they needed to move on.

So Your glory has filled my heart in those quiet moments of vision and rest. Give me also the wisdom to rise and go onward when "the cloud [is] taken up from over the tabernacle."

Help me to see that the cloud lifting is the cloud leading. Help me to see that the glory receding is the glory beckoning. Help me to see that the presence withdrawing is the presence drawing.

Lift me away from satisfaction with victories past. Beckon me away from contentment in the easy present. Draw me through Your wise and loving discipline into the fully committed way that leads through tomorrow to Heaven, through darkness to light, and through the desert to the land of promise.

Then, feeding not on the husks of glory past, nor striving with anxious fears to hold the glory present, I will know the freedom and joy of being led from "glory unto glory."

Through Jesus Christ, my Lord, Amen.

MOVING ON IN THE LIFE OF PRAYER

We lean hard on the promises of Jesus. We must completely trust that He has given us, as He promised, "another Counselor, to be *with you for ever*" (John 14:16, emphasis added). Believing this we pray in the Spirit. The "greening" of our prayer life comes when we know God is *with* us and not far off, *with* us and not opposed to us. We don't have to overcome the reluctance of God if we are praying in the Spirit of God. For then we ask for all the right things and receive all the best things.

Day 110

WHERE TO GO WHEN TROUBLE COMES

"Out of the depths I cry to thee, O LORD" (Psalm 130:1).

Read: **Psalm 130,** 42; James 1:5-8; 4:2-3.

WHAT IS GOD SAYING?

The importance of "listening" to God has been the thrust of much of our prayer studies and examples so far. We should hear *Him*! We should learn who He is and what He wants as He speaks to us in the Word. That is prayer's highest priority—and often its most common missing ingredient. But it is not prayer's only agenda. There is much more.

For example, in this psalm and in the example of saints and servants of God across the years, there is a time and a place for us to ask God to hear *us*. "Lord, hear my voice! Let thy ears be attentive to the voice of my supplications!"

Is that just a rhetorical device or something to fill out a poetic form? Or is there a time when we feel something so deeply we find ourselves desperately concerned to know that *God* is listening to us? Such a feeling is not wrong. Such a request is not presumptuous. We don't have to overcome God's reluctance or get His attention because He may be busy at the moment with someone else's "really big and important" problems. This is the psalmist crying out of the depths of his need with deep sincerity and heartfelt longing. It is the kind of feeling we have when we say to a friend or loved one, "I need you. I *really* need you."

How Does This Apply to Us?

The Book of Psalms is truly the best book on prayer. It has all the elements: praise for God's goodness, confession of our sin, the vision of God's splendor, joy and wonder over God's creation, thanksgiving for God's re-creation, and the recognition that life is not always rosy and does have ragged edges.

The Psalms plumb the depths of human sin and failure. The Psalms soar to the heights of God's holiness and ultimate triumph. So, if we need to cry out from the depths of disappointment or persistent failure or plaguing weakness, be God's guest—go ahead. Our depths are not beyond His reach. Our needs are not too big for God to handle nor too small for Him to be bothered. Out of the *depths*, we cry. Out of the *heights*, God hears. *Out of* the depths, we cry. *From* the depths, God lifts. That's how it is . . . because that's who He is.

Pray with Me

Most wise and loving Father, I believe that the light of Your knowledge and the patience of Your love can reach the deepest and darkest need of my life. I believe that you can hear the weak and wordless cry that rises from every heart. Feelings of unworthiness and guilt cannot quench that cry. Neither the thunderings of judgment nor the whispers of self-condemnation can keep it from Your hearing. Out of the depths I cry. Out of the heights you hear.

"Out of the depths" of sin I cry, but "there is forgiveness with Thee." Forgiveness is Your gift. Forgiveness is Your grace, Your glory, Your power, Your way, and Your purpose. I cannot doubt it from any depth of sin. I have seen Your suffering love on Calvary.

"Out of the depths" of despair I cry, and I look for the dawn of righteousness "more than they watch for the morning." Turn my eyes from the shadows of failure until I look—not in vain—for the light of Your steadfast love and the glory of Your righteousness.

"Out of the depths" of an unconquerable hope I cry, for I am persuaded that "with You there is plenteous redemption." No failure is so disastrous, no despair so dark, no accusation of conscience so intense that the God-given flame of hope must cease to burn. For with the Lord there is plenteous redemption.

Out of the depths I cry. From the depths You lift.

To the praise of Your glorious grace which You have freely bestowed on us in the Beloved, Amen.

MOVING ON IN THE LIFE OF PRAYER

Prayer is not only praise for God's blessings but expressing our need for God's help. Praise is uppermost because we are always receiving. But "asking" has a place. It is more than a privilege. In the Sermon on the Mount it is a command. Jesus said, "Ask, and it will be given you." James is a good guide for this. Read James 1:5-8 and 4:2-3. Do we really need to be encouraged to ask? For some of us, prayer may seem to have *no other dimension.* The point is we must ask on the basis of heartfelt need and we must ask in faith that God can and will meet that need. That kind of praying is not so common, but it *is* uncommonly rewarding.

Day 111

WORKING FOR NOTHING

"What hath man of all his labor?" (Ecclesiastes 2:22, KJV).
". . . Ye know that your labor is not in vain in the Lord" (1 Corinthians 15:58, KJV).

Read: **Ecclesiastes 2;** Isaiah 55:6; 1 Corinthians 15:58, 3:9; Mark 16:30.

WHAT IS GOD SAYING?

Ecclesiastes offers a running commentary on the futility of working for anything less or other than that which God can approve and bless. Get a fortune and leave it *all* to be enjoyed by someone who didn't lift a finger for it (2:21). "Toil and strain" for selfish ends and have "days full of pain" and a mind that does not rest at night (2:22, 23). The exception to this only proves the rule.

There is a better way. Go to work for the Lord. This is so important that Paul closes the great fifteenth chapter of 1 Corinthians by saying, "always abounding in the work of the Lord, knowing that in the Lord your labor is not in vain" (15:58). Working for the Lord shows our thankfulness for His victory over death. It also delivers us from the string of zeros that wait at the end of life's journey for those who work feverishly to get what they can never fully enjoy here and never, ever, take with them. "This also is vanity."

HOW DOES THIS APPLY TO US?

God gives us the desire to work and the ability to work. Work is good and it can be meaningful. Lack of work is one of society's great problems for it leads step by step through loss of self-esteem, to discontent, to poverty. From there, unemployment leads to anger and unrest, drug-related crimes, and other social evils. Work is a blessing and unemployment is a curse. No doubt about that.

But what really matters is for what are we working, or better, for whom are we working? Paul made tents to make a living. He preached the gospel to put Life in living. Peter fished for a living. Jesus Himself dignified work by being a carpenter. Though it wasn't His important work, He made work an important thing. What *are* we working for? We can work for nothing. But doing things for Christ and for others in His love, we never work for nothing.

Pray with Me

Lord, everywhere men are laboring for security, riches, and comfort. Yet Your Word teaches that all such labor leads only to vexation and vanity. How slowly the lesson is learned! To work for self-glory leads to emptiness. To struggle for this earth's fleeting riches leads but to misery. "To a man that hath not labored therein shall he leave it." This is a changeless verdict, an inescapable destiny, a certain harvest. The truth is written deep and in letters large and clear: "What hath man of all his labor?"—vexation and vanity; worry and fear; existence that is stifling, narrow, and small.

But, Lord, you have a blessing and a purpose for labor. There is a way to keep it from being in vain. "Ye know that your labor is not in vain *in the Lord.*" Teach me the secret of possessing this joy. Help me to surrender to You all wealth and the strength to get it, all success and the talents to win it. Only labor that is spent for You can be stamped with eternal value and escape the curse of vanity. "The world passes away, and the lust of it; but he who does the will of God abides for ever."

"In the Lord"—in the spirit of compassion, in the energy of love, and in the deep desire to see wrong righted and evil subdued—I would labor.

To labor for self is always vain. To labor for You is never vain. Here is a choice I need to make. By Your grace help me to make the wise decision. May I choose the path that leads through labor to endless good and avoid the path that leads through endless labor to vanity.

In His Name who came to give meaning to labor and abundance to life, Amen.

Moving On in the Life of Prayer

God has a blessing and a purpose for us in labor. Let us pray until we know that our ideas, our energies, our time (it is strictly limited), and our skills (not so limited as we think) are being channeled into things God can bless and use. Let us pray to be on our guard against pointless activity in pursuit of non-goals and headed for the harvest of the empty heart. In the end, what *has* man for his labor? It can be nothing or everything. Pray to know the difference.

Day 112

Back to Our First Love

"And he journeyed on from the Negeb as far as Bethel, to the place where his tent had been at the beginning, between Bethel and Ai, to the place where he had made an altar at the first; and there Abram called on the name of the Lord" (Genesis 13:3-4).

Read: **Genesis 12, 13;** Jeremiah 2:2; Matthew 24:12-13; Revelation 2:3-5.

What Is God Saying?

At Shechem and then at Bethel, God told Abraham he had arrived. His journey of faith was not ending; there was still much to do and many further testings of faith. But he *had* come to the place God had in mind. Typically, he built an altar to the Lord (12:8). It was a symbol of faith, blending with joy, enthusiasm, and total commitment. It was Abraham saying: "This is it. This calls for celebration. God was true to His word. I will be true to mine. This is holy ground. To God be the glory." And he said it with an altar. Every stone was laid with the inexpressible glow that comes upon anyone who is prompted by his or her "first love."

Then the scene shifts. Because of a famine, Abraham went down to Egypt. He got rich. He acquired cattle and gold and silver; all the things the world associates with a clever and lucky person. But it was not without compromising moral integrity and basic honesty (read 12:10-20). By the mercy of God he came through the crisis and knew where to go to express his thankfulness. God was with him in the "far country" of cowardice and compromise. God would meet him and bless him again if he came back to his first altar at Bethel and there renewed his first love. God would. God did.

How Does This Apply to Us?

God does the same thing with us! We have all had our "Egypts" of compromise. We have known conditions, even as Christians, when luck and cleverness have brought a season of affluence and success. But in our hearts we have known that our true riches lay in another direction. We have known that God has a better life for us, more fulfilling, more productive, more meaningful. Material well-being, dependent on the bouncing ball of luck, is not the way to go. Affluence that can be lessened or removed by the whims and wishes of someone else (maybe a large corporation) is hardly a good foundation.

God has a better way. To discover it we need to go back to our "first love," to the God who loved us then, to the God who loves us now, to the God who will love us forever, to the God of our early and uncomplicated faith, to the God of Bethel.

Pray with Me

Loving Father, Your arms are always open to receive the returning prodigal. Your love never changes. It is like the ocean's fullness without the ocean's tide. Forgive me that my love toward You is so changeful: now strong, then weak; now gladly free, then miserably enslaved; now pure as that of children, then mingled as old men barter.

My first love was without compromise. You had my heart, my whole heart. There were no rivals. My first faith was without doubt or fear. You had my unquestioning obedience. Where Your Spirit led, I followed. What Your Word said, I did. My first altar was a place of beautiful worship. It was a single doorway to blessings untold. There were no other gods before You, indeed, there were no other gods. That is the way it was . . . at first.

But then I looked toward Egypt. I began to wonder and then I began to wander. Through cowardice I turned elsewhere for strength. Through fear I wanted to be bolstered by others whose resources were weaker than mine. Through carelessness I allowed other altars to be crowded into my heart.

Now, gracious and loving Lord, bring me back from the Egypt of cowardly compromise to the Bethel of my first love, my first faith, my first altar.

Then I will praise You as I ought to praise You. Then I will love You as I ought to love You. For I will see You—again—as I ought to see You: almighty yet all-loving, all- holy yet all-forgiving. How wonderful it is to know that my love, which is all I can bring, is really all that You ask.

Through Jesus Christ my Lord, Amen.

Moving On in the Life of Prayer

In a sense, every time we pray it is a return to Bethel. In prayer, the fog of compromise is lifted. The pollution of mixed motives is washed away. The web of entangling loyalties is cut cleanly through. We are free to listen, free to speak, free to start all over again, free to become what God wanted us to be when we met Him in that moment of "first love." Prayer is saying, "I can be reached at Bethel. This is my real address. This is where I belong."

Day 113

Faith and Patience

" . . . *Followers of them who through faith and patience inherit the promises*" *(Hebrews 6:12, KJV).*

Read: **Hebrews 6,** 12:2; 1 Peter 2:21; Ecclesiastes 7:8; James 1:4, 2:5.

What Is God Saying?

This passage contains stern warning and strong encouragement. Apostasy or falling away is serious business. It can have irreversible consequences. The passage does not deal with Christians who, through weakness or discouragement, may stumble and hurt themselves and/or others. Given repentance and, where indicated, restitution, forgiveness is the sweet gift of God. It brings joy to angels in heaven and peace to men's hearts on earth. Hear Jesus' words to the woman who stumbled: "Neither do I condemn you; go, and do not sin again" (John 8:11).

The fearful warning about apostasy here has to do with a deliberate and final rejection of Christ. It is the same finality that comes to a person who rejects rescue efforts by cutting the rope that is thrown to him.

To counter this mood of apostasy with its dire consequences, the writer to the Hebrews moves the spotlight from a scenario of doubt and defiance to one of faith and patience. Don't give up! Don't give in! Follow those who have blazed the path! They did it through faith *and* patience. The dark background painted in Hebrews 6:1-8 is relieved and superseded by the "better things" of verses 9-20. Unless a person is contemplating total and final rejection of Jesus Christ, his attention is "better" drawn to faith and patience and God's great faithfulness. Keep "the full assurance of hope until the end" (6:11).

HOW DOES THIS APPLY TO US?

We all follow something or someone. Even the rugged individualist who consciously rejects the herd instinct has a role model somewhere along the line. He may be following another "independent thinker," but he is following. He is using an example.

Our choice is to follow the example of those who have kept the faith to the end. Jesus is our supreme Example. Following Him we will not wind up in a swamp of blasted hopes and vanished dreams. Following Him we are led by the "true Light" through the perplexities of life to the glory of Heaven. Abraham's faith is another example to follow. And there are those whose names are written not in the Bible but on our hearts. Since we all follow something or someone, let us follow those who "through faith and patience" do "inherit the promises." If we choose to follow a winner, we will be near the victor's circle. If we choose to follow Christ we will be *in* the victor's circle.

Pray with Me

O loving Redeemer, you saw beyond the Cross eternal victory. You endured the shame because You knew it was the Father's will and our only way to heaven.

Through faith and patience, in the face of the worst You believed in the best. Through faith and patience You inherited the promise. Through faith and patience You accepted humiliation in order to be exalted. Through faith and patience You gave Your life and received a name that is above every name.

Following You, Lord, there are many believers who with the simplicity of faith and with patience which Your grace has always supplied have served You in their hour of opportunity.

I would follow You and I would follow them. I am not ashamed to be a follower, for to follow You and to follow those who follow You is to find the way that leads to everlasting life. It is not a token of ignorance or servility. It is the wisest decision anyone can ever make.

I thank You, Lord, for this discovery: to inherit the promises I must have faith and patience. Believing is easy, but waiting is hard. Hoping is natural, but enduring is a discipline. Looking up is pleasant, but walking on is painful. Help me to believe that over the steepest hill and after the most disciplined duty and at the end of the longest journey, there is the fulfillment of all Your promises.

Lord, I ask for more of Your patience. I do not have it naturally. It can only come as Your gift. In faith I pray for patience. In patience I would show my faith.

These are the gifts I need and want and claim: Faith to accept and patience to endure until the real promises of Your love become the real blessings of my life.

Through Jesus Christ, whose own faith and patience are my heart's most shining goal, Amen.

MOVING ON IN THE LIFE OF PRAYER

Prayer is the place where choices are made. Talking with God we can choose whom to follow. Prayer is the place where tarnish is removed from our shining goals and God's promises are seen in their true light. Prayer is the place and the time when the seed of "faith" grows into the plant of "patience" and both come to bear the fruit of "inherited promises."

Day 114

GOD IS BLIND TO SIN BUT KIND TO THE SINNERS

"Thou who art of purer eyes than to behold evil and canst not look on wrong . . ." (Habakkuk 1:13).

Read: **Habakkuk 1:1-2:1;** Romans 5:1; 1 John 1:7-9.

WHAT IS GOD SAYING?

It is hard for the spirit to soar when the mind plods along on leaden feet. Habakkuk saw his nation falling apart. Defeat was almost certain. Israel had succumbed and Judah was ripe for the plucking by "the Chaldeans, that bitter and hasty nation." It was just a matter of time. Why didn't God do something to stop this outrage?

Judah *was* wicked. As a king, Jehoiachin rivaled the worst. The sins of Judah deserved God's punishment. But why should Judah become the target of a nation whose wickedness was incomparably worse? It didn't make sense, Habakkuk complained. But he discovered that God was "rousing" the Chaldeans for a purpose. "I am doing a work in your days that you would not believe if told" (1:5). God was saying, "I will *use* them but I will not *lose* to them."

When Habakkuk saw things in this perspective he understood that God had "established them for chastisement." The prophet did not lose his trust that God is "of purer eyes than to behold evil and canst not look on [or tolerate] wrong" (1:13). God *will* triumph. "The earth will be filled with the knowledge of the glory of LORD, as the waters cover the sea" (2:14). The God of all purity, who cannot look on sin, can look on the sinner. According to Habakkuk's great prayer of chapter 3, "in wrath [God will] remember mercy." God's people will *yet* rejoice in the LORD as their strength (3:18, 19), their true strength and their true joy.

How Does This Apply to Us?

As God is God, so evil is evil. Anyone who has light thoughts about sin cannot have great thoughts about God. But because we are forgiven in God's mercy, He does not and cannot see the sins and the failures that have marred our lives in the past. He sees us in Christ for what we are becoming. Jesus was "put to death for our trespasses and raised for our justification" (Romans 4:25). That is how God sees us. Let us live with that joy and pray with that confidence. The slate is forever clean. We are free to move on in His perfect design for our lives. We are unhampered by the guilt and freed from the burden of sin. Looking at us through Christ, He doesn't even see it.

Pray with Me

O God, Your ways are higher and better than ours. Today I want to know Your will and do it. That is my supreme goal. Today is Your gift. I want to give it back.

Show me through Your Holy Spirit that the eyes of the Lord are absolutely blind to evil. You are too pure to condone one willful step into impurity and sin. Yet You are too faithful and just not to forgive Your children the sins they confess.

You are blind to that evil which ruled my heart before I knelt to receive forgiveness through the mighty love of the Cross. That evil is canceled, removed, buried, and forgotten. While it seems impossible for the human mind to be blind to evil that has been pardoned, I thank You for Your blindness to sins forgiven. All my transgressions are buried in the seas of Your forgetfulness.

Looking on me only through the righteousness of Your Son, O Lord, You are blind to me as a failure. Instead You see me as one who is joyous and liberated, a triumph of Your grace.

You are blind to sin confessed but never blind to sinner confused. For when, in faith and repentance, I turn to You, carrying the burdens of sin, in tender, patient, all-conquering love You look through the sin to the sinner. You are blind to my sin but You are always looking on me that I may find the way home, the way that is higher and better, the way to Christ and life and peace.

Your love is blind to sin but kind to the sinner. I would answer that love by leaving that which You cannot behold and loving that which You can both give and bless.

Through Jesus Christ, my Lord, Amen.

MOVING ON IN THE LIFE OF PRAYER

God cannot look on evil, but evil can look on us. We need daily forgiveness and cleansing. This comes from God and gives meaning and power to our prayers. He looks through the sin confessed and blesses the sinner confessing. The function of prayer is to see that through God's forgiveness, we face each new day with the joy of a friendship renewed, a relationship restored, and the peace of His pardon casting its healing goodness on our hearts.

Day 115

THE BLESSING OF SEEING JESUS

"Your father Abraham rejoiced that he was to see my day; he saw it and was glad" (John 8:56).

Read: **John 8:12-59;** Hebrews 11:8-16.

WHAT IS GOD SAYING?

Jesus often spoke of His deity and it aroused the anger of Jewish leaders. They considered His claims blasphemous. It was urgent to stop His voice and get on with the important business of "religion." The claims of Jesus were sweeping and, to the leaders, brazenly presumptuous. Yet they kept coming.

Consider the many times He said, "I am," followed by expressions that could only be predicated on deity. Jesus touched a tender nerve when he said, "Before Abraham *was,* I *am* (8:58). Today's reading drops us right into the middle of a heated debate. The great calm of Jesus versus the offended prejudice and the self-righteous anger of the Pharisees. By the end of the chapter, their argument was lost, their facade penetrated, their cover blown. What was left? In Palestine there are stones, plenty of them. As television newscasts report Arab-Israeli confrontations today, no one is at a loss for a stone or two. "So they took up stones to throw at him."

Through it all there shines the calm and radiant truth. Christ is God. Not just a good man, not just a penetrating intellect, not just a courageous prophet, but Emmanuel, God with us. It brought rejoicing to Abraham. It brought rejoicing to some of Abraham's descendants. It has brought rejoicing to history's saints and martyrs, and it still brings rejoicing to every heart that invites Him in today.

How Does This Apply to Us?

It *is* a blessing to see Jesus. Abraham saw His day. He trusted God would save His people. It would be a day of salvation and redemption. It was a reason to rejoice.

How much more satisfying it is for us who can look back on Jesus' day. A day when the light truly dawned. A day when the miracle of love began to spread its blessing across a world wrapped in the darkness of hate and anger. In today's world—in the broad expanses across the horizons, and in the smaller, closer world through which we move every day—there is still the curse of hatred, anger, and selfish strife. But we know that Christ is real and His love will rule at last. We need to be sure that He is on the throne of our hearts right now.

Pray with Me

O Lord, You came into the world. You even came by invitation, into my heart. Knowing this is a fact, I can rise up to meet this day.

Abraham was the friend of God. What a title to earn! What a reputation to enjoy! What a treasure to possess! Being a "friend of God" is both a privilege and a responsibility. A friend: doing what friends ought to do and being what friends ought to be. If the blessing of human friendship can mean so much, how much more satisfying it is to be a friend of God. And the greatest blessing You gave to Abraham, as Your friend, was to see the day of Jesus Christ.

So, dear Lord, remove from my heart all the gloom of doubt. Take from my face all shadows of worry. Keep my lips from any complaining sigh. Have I not seen the day of Jesus Christ?

Abraham saw Your coming through the veil of history future. I can see the evidence of Your coming, O Christ, in history past and history present. There is no haze along the distant hills of time to obscure or distort Your perfect reality. There is no mystery to shroud Your beauty. There is no bend in the road, no brow of the hill, no worry, no wishing, no waiting. You have come!

As Abraham rejoiced to see ahead to Your day, so let me rejoice, O Christ, that I have seen Your day. The very feet of God have walked on this earth. The authentic voice of the Eternal has sounded in the ears of men.

Dawn has come to this earth and continually comes to the open and waiting and seeing heart. Turn me, Lord, until I face the Dawn. Turn me until all shadows are at my back. Turn me from all false and failing hopes. Turn me from looking toward and sometimes even choosing the darkness. Turn me toward Your love in Christ, as irresistible, as quiet, and as refreshing as the dawn. Turn me until Christ fills all my vision and with Abraham I can see His day and be glad.

In the Name of Him who came to make every day perpetual dawn and every life perpetual spring, Amen.

MOVING ON IN THE LIFE OF PRAYER

Every day we pray to *see* His day. We pray to make *this* day His day. Seeing that this day can be His day brings the gladness Abraham knew and much more: it brings courage to our convictions, strength to our steps, peace to our minds, joy everywhere we go, and healing love to everyone we meet.

Day 116

TRUE TO THE LORD —ALL THE WAY

"If Balak should give me his house full of silver and gold, I would not be able to go beyond the word of the LORD, to do either good or bad of my own will; what the LORD speaks, that will I speak" (Numbers 24:13).

Read: **Numbers 22, 23:11-24, 24:1-13;** Deuteronomy 23:4-5; Nehemiah 13:2; Micah 6:5; Jude 11.

WHAT IS GOD SAYING?

The record of Balaam is a strange blend of nobility and covetousness. It is perplexing to say the least. He is enlightened: "The oracle of the man whose eye is opened, . . . who hears the words of God, who sees the vision of the Almighty, falling down, but having his eyes uncovered" (Numbers 24:3-4). We also note that it was the Spirit of God that came upon him (24:2) and from his lips flow some of the greatest prophecies in the Bible, for example, Numbers 24:17.

The plot thickens. He is not an Israelite. He lived on the distant Euphrates. His reputation for cursing and blessing (and that was then a profitable business) came to the attention of Balak, king of Moab (22:4-6), and he needed help badly. Israel was crowding him on the western front. Three times Balaam refused the commission to bring a curse upon Israel. He said,

"How can I curse whom God has not cursed?" (23:8). This took some intestinal fortitude.

But it was always hard to disregard the fact that Balaam was doing what he did for money. He turned down the lure of money because he feared what God would do if he didn't. That is why Jude 11 refers to Balaam's error as the lust for gain. Balak dismissed Balaam since, through the latter's determined refusal to do what Balak was wanted, they had reached a stalemate. "All right" said Balak, "if you won't curse them at least don't bless them." They parted. Mission unaccomplished. God had prevailed.

There is a sad ending for this potentially heroic figure. Read Numbers 31:8, 16. By his advice the Israelites were seduced into the worship of Baal with disastrous consequence. Balaam perished miserably. He had caused others to sin.

How Does This Apply to Us?

The old adage comes to mind: "Reputation is won by many deeds and lost by one." God's purpose was clearly revealed. He kept preventing Balaam from yielding to the lure of gold. But there was always that weakness just below the surface. At the end, having faced up to Balak with noble courage (and a large measure of fear) he finally "abandoned himself for the sake of gain." With his shameful end, Israel was drawn into one of the darkest chapters of her history. Balaam is a classic biblical example of *not* going with God—all the way.

Pray with Me

Lord, give me the daring spirit of Balaam. But, even more, I ask that You keep me from the final weakness that marred his witness and spelled his doom. Let the dawn-gladness and the morning-freshness of life devoted to Your Word linger with me through the heat and the trial of the day. When the shadows lengthen let the light of Your Word still shine. When the evening comes, let the truth of Your Word still be faithfully spoken.

From Balaam we learn that even though one has deep convictions about the Word of the Lord, temptations to act against it can be very strong. To join with the enemies of God can be made attractive and easy. Only a constant awareness of my riches in Christ can shield me from looking with covetous eye on "Balak's house, full of silver and gold." Only a deep trust in Your perfect Word can keep me from the rashness of my own will. Only what the Lord speaks shall I speak, for only this brings salvation and blessing and hope.

O God, as You met with Balaam on the bare heights where nothing was seen but Your glory and nothing was heard but

Your voice, so meet with me today. Then, fortified with Your Truth and encouraged by the reality that Yours will be the final victory, let me return to all the "Balaks" I shall ever meet saying, "God is not man, that he should lie. . . . Has he said, and will he not do it? Or has he spoken, and will he not fulfill it?"

Conviction in the Word means no compromise with the world. Your message is unchanging and unchangeable. Your light is unfading, unfailing, and unbending. May it be "a lamp unto my feet and a light unto my path" to the very last step of the very last mile until heaven's morning breaks. Then I shall see and possess the riches of glory, the reward of faith—the face, the smile, the presence of my sovereign Lord.

In His wonderful Name, Amen.

MOVING ON IN THE LIFE OF PRAYER

We need to hear what God says to Balaam. We need Balaam's visions of the holiness and power of God. But we also need to remember that the flaw in his character has a modern ring. We must listen to God and obey His Word. We must stay free of the lure of covetousness. It was Balaam's error and except for God's grace it will draw us under. We should pray in the heights with Balaam that we might see God's glory *and* we should pray to avoid the error of Balaam. "The love of money is the root of all evils." Prayer is for *receiving* the blessing of God and *avoiding* the curse of sin.

Day 117

THE REAL CAUSE OF HEARTBURN

"*. . . There is in my heart as it were a burning fire*" (*Jeremiah 20:9*).

Read: **Jeremiah 20, 1:9, 5:15;** Exodus 4:12; Job 32:8; Psalm 39:3; Luke 24:32.

WHAT IS GOD SAYING?

Jeremiah had "as it were a burning fire" in his heart. But before that he had been taking a beating from the "chief officer in the house of the LORD." Pashhur was a priest who ought to have been dispensing love and understanding. Instead he had it in for prophets who called the bluff of those who were entrenched in religious power and privilege and who didn't take well to being disturbed. Jeremiah was an especially annoying troublemaker. Pashhur had the solution. Beat him up and put him in stocks. Jeremiah had a name for him: "The LORD does not call your name Pashhur, but Terror on every side,"

Jeremiah said. "The terror you create will come home to roost. Judah will be plundered of the wealth you boast and you yourself will go into captivity and die, you and all your friends who have swallowed your lies and are in league with you against the truth" (20:1-6, my paraphrase).

After setting the record straight, Jeremiah turns his anguished heart to God. It not only hurt to be beaten, it hurt to be hated. It hurt to be a laughingstock (20:7-8). Despite it all, he had to speak God's Word. For God had not only put His Word in his mouth (1:9), He had also made the words in his heart a burning fire. His heart was like a heated boiler that must have an escape valve or it will burst. "I am weary with holding it in, and I cannot" (20:9).

How Does This Apply to Us?

The same words of God's *anger against sin* and *love for the sinner* are a burning fire within the hearts of those who have experienced His saving grace. The facts cannot lie as inanimate pieces of stone in a museum or as printed words safely tucked away in an old book on a remote shelf in a library. We who love the Lord cannot keep these things to ourselves. With the disciples on the road to Emmaus, our hearts *do* burn when Jesus shares the truth of His salvation. Anything that is really burning will make itself known. The fact of its burning cannot be hidden forever. Fire will get out! So the love of Christ when received and truly experienced cannot be kept under cover.

Pray with Me

Come, dear Lord, upon my waiting heart. Enter my open heart. Possess and rule my yielded heart until it burns with the love of Your name and a love for the souls You love.

In the quiet retreat of prayer, Your voice is heard without the jamming of sin. Your glory is seen without the misting of doubt. I have shut the door of the closet. I can see the Source of hope. I can sense the reality of inner and invisible resources.

Let redeeming love ignite obedient faith. Let a fire be kindled to purify with all holiness, to enlighten with all truth, and to empower with all strength. This will bring new life in the place of old, true life in the place of false, and abundant life in the place of barren.

Hearts are always burning. They are either burning with lust that yields the ashes of death or they are burning with love that yields the gold of life. Hearts are ignited by temptation and, burning, are consumed or they are ignited by the very love of God, and, burning, begin to live.

Let it be Your love, O God, that burns on the altar of my heart. Let this burning heart be Your burning heart. As You have given the heart, now use for Your own glory the burning of that heart.

In the Name of Him who came to baptize with the Holy Spirit and with fire, Amen.

MOVING ON IN THE LIFE OF PRAYER

Prayer is the time when the love of God is rekindled in our hearts. Prayer is the time when God's Spirit, as fire, purifies our thoughts and cleanses our motives. Prayer is the time when God's Spirit, as fire, can burn away the dross of unworthy desires and leave the gold of God's love and peace. Prayer is the time when God's Spirit, as fire, can ignite our hearts with a love we cannot help sharing. Prayer is the time when we yield our burning hearts to God as light for those who are lost and as warmth for those who have come to feel that, in this cruel and impersonal world, no one really cares.

Day 118

MIND YOUR TONGUE

"A wholesome tongue is a tree of life" (Proverbs 15:4, KJV).

Read: **Proverbs 15:1-4;** Psalm 37:30, 39:1-3; Malachi 2:5-7; James 1:26, 3:1-6; Colossians 4:6; Revelation 14:5.

WHAT IS GOD SAYING?

This brief reference to the "tongue" in Proverbs touches upon a subject that is usually not given enough attention. So many people take up the refrain from James who with good reason refers to the tongue as a small fire that sets a whole forest ablaze (3:5). Or as "an unrighteous world," "set on fire by hell," "staining the whole body" (3:6). He speaks of the tongue as an unruly beast, with potential of great harm, needing to be bridled (1:26). All of this is true. Tragically so.

But we are scripturally on target if we turn our attention to the tongue as an instrument boundlessly capable of doing good. Proverbs starts us off on this tack but we can trace its course through Scripture and through history and very much in our own lives. "A soft answer turns away wrath" (Proverbs 15:1). "A wholesome tongue (or as some versions have it, a "gentle tongue") is a tree of life" (15:4). Either way, it speaks of the tongue's capacity to be a blessing. It *can* and *does* go wrong and lead others into wrong. But it can be a "tree of life" offering shade to the weary and fruit to the hungry.

How Does This Apply to Us?

Are we minding our tongue? Or better, is the Lord in control of it? When others hear our speech do they think of a bush with thorns or a tree with fruit and leaves? Do they think of a tumbleweed that rolls carelessly across the plains or do they see a "tree planted by the rivers of water" drawing life from the love of God and sharing that life in spreading branches and ripening fruit?

Our speech can be a source of blessing. It can turn someone's night into day. It can make somebody's burden seem like a balloon filled with helium. It can put a rainbow across someone's cloud-heavy sky. The tongue can do great harm. It can also do great good. It's up to us. Who's minding our tongues?

Pray with Me

Give me a wholesome tongue, O Lord, like a tree of life that draws its strength from the deep nutrients of a heart that is hid with Christ in God. Rooted and grounded in Your love, trusting in that never-failing supply, I can express Your love to others and for others. I can be a channel of Your blessing. I can relay in spoken words of love what I have experienced in the depths of silent and nourishing communion.

Give me a wholesome tongue, O Lord, like a tree of life that rises tall and stands straight. Let me speak such words as can be depended on. Let me speak words of quiet strength to those who need a place to lean and who, amid all the wavering half-truths of their world, long for a word on which they can depend.

Give me a wholesome tongue, O Lord, like a tree of life that offers the cooling comfort of shade. Help me in my conversation to shelter those who are weary from walking in the wilderness and who need relief from its relentless heat. Let my words give welcome rest to those who are exhausted from lonely battles. Let my words be as healing shade where friends and strangers may find peace and refreshing grace.

Give me a wholesome tongue, O Lord, like a tree of life that bears fruit to feed the hungry and to strengthen the weak. Deliver me from empty words and idle conversation when I am in the presence of someone who, but for my word, might not know the touch of Your love and the substance of Your grace. Guard me always from careless words that could unsettle the faith of another. Give me words that are fitly spoken to bring hope to the discouraged, healing to the sick, and joy to those who are downcast in spirit.

Give me a wholesome tongue, a tongue like the Master's, who spoke with fearless courage and timely truth, yet always with deep, caring love. For then my tongue will be a tree of life, a blessing to others and a glory to God.

For the sake of Him who said, "By this my Father is glorified, that you bear much fruit." Amen.

MOVING ON IN THE LIFE OF PRAYER

We don't normally use our tongues in our personal and private praying. Usually in prayer we are either "listening" in the quiet of our own reflections as we pore over the Word, or "talking" from the depths of our heart. Aided by the Spirit Himself we "talk" with "sighs too deep for words" (Romans 8:26).

But prayer does create in us the motivation and it does point us to doors of opportunity when the tongue can be used as a tree of life. Think about the good side of the tongue. Pray about minding your tongue. Mind your tongue and find a blessing. Mind your tongue and be a blessing.

Day 119

LIVING TO PLEASE GOD

"*. . . How you ought to live and to please God*" (*1 Thessalonians 4:1*).

Read: **1 Thessalonians 4:1-11;** Proverbs 16:7; John 8:29; Hebrews 11:5, 13:16.

WHAT IS GOD SAYING?

One of the goals of "religion" is to be good enough that God will like us. In religion people have to be good to God so God will be good to them. This is totally opposite to the truth of the gospel. Religion, when defined as keeping a set of rules and "toeing the line which the Almighty has drawn," is as remote from the Good News as outright unbelief. Perhaps more so.

Religious leaders in our own time, in the name of religion, have perpetrated acts of vengeance and hatred that are spawned in hell. "Religion" has been the launching pad of murder, bloodshed, and "holy wars." "Religion" is not the gospel. We are not saved *by* our good works, much less by religious zeal that answers evil with evil and commits atrocities in the name of "righteous" anger.

We are *not* saved *by* good works. We *are* saved *for* good works. It is in that vein that our portion of God's Word speaks today. We will want to please God with our lives if we are saved.

We don't need to make God love us by being good. He already loves us. Need proof? Turn to Romans 5:8: "But God shows his *love* for us in that while *we were yet* sinners Christ died for us."

How Does This Apply to Us?

The Good News has a bearing on how we ought to live. The Christian wants to please God as an expression of thanksgiving. When we please God, love is making its answer to Love. In Christ we have liberty and that freedom is one of our great joys. But liberty is not spelled "libertinism." There is a kind of liberty so-called that is really licentiousness. It is a curse, not a blessing. It destroys the welfare of others. It mutilates the family and blights the community. And, not least, it rings down the curtain on the ones who practice it. "God has not called us for uncleanness" (1 Thessalonians 4:7).

We please God when we draw our guidelines for living from Him. There is more. It pleases Him because it is a blessing for us. We "ought to live and please God" because not pleasing God is to die, inch by pleasant inch to the painful end.

Pray with Me

Lord, life is Your gift to me. The way I live that life is my gift to You. Help me turn over to You both my life and the manner of my life.

I must come to see that how I live is even more important than that I live. I must give You my life not in words easily spoken but in deeds faithfully done. Anything less would be unworthy of my high calling in Christ. Anything less would keep me from rising to the full potential of Your full purpose for my life.

Remembering that my life has been claimed again and purchased back, I must also remember that there is a way to invest it that will please You and there is a way that can only bring You pain. I love You, Lord, and I want to please You. In Your mercy, whether in firm denial or in patient forbearance, whether in interrupted plans or unexpected joys, whether in some dark Providence or in the light of convincing logic, let me learn how I ought to live.

Along that path of obedient trust I would discover the joy of "pleasing God." Nothing could ever compare with Your "well done." No glittering but trivial reward should ever entice me away from the hope of seeing Your smile. No lesser goal, no lesser good, no lesser god could ever fill my heart with the satisfaction that I know when I practice the presence of God and seek His good pleasure.

There is a way to live that pleases You. In all the maze of possible ways, make that one way luminous with Your blessing and approval. Let it be before me as the "path of the righteous [which] is like the light of dawn, shining brighter and brighter until full day."

Until that full day which shall be glorious with Your final triumph over evil and darkness, I would live as I ought to please the Lord whom I love.

In the all-sufficient grace of Jesus Christ, my Lord, Amen.

MOVING ON IN THE LIFE OF PRAYER

Prayer is waiting upon God because He loves us. Prayer is self-examination not only under the light of truth in God's Word but also on the foundation of His eternal love. What He wants for us is best for us. Prayer is the time we find out what that is. Prayer is the way we receive both the motivation and the strength for living that pleases God and blesses us.

Day 120

LOVING GOOD + HATING EVIL = GLADNESS

"You love righteousness and hate wickedness. Therefore God, your God, has anointed you with the oil of gladness above your fellows" (Psalm 45:7).

Read: **Psalm 45, 34:15;** Isaiah 3:10; Hosea 10:12; Matthew 6:33; Romans 8:28.

WHAT IS GOD SAYING?

There are good reasons to believe that the forty-fifth psalm is an example of a poet's eloquent and extravagant praise for a king who is about to be married. Was it Ahab? He proved to be a disappointment. But who would find it easy to be married to Jezebel and yet continue long "to love righteousness and to hate wickedness"? He was aided and abetted by one whose very name has been claimed by history to represent evil personified. Jezebel! How could Ahab hold on to "great expectations" with Jezebel calling the shots? So he began to reverse the order: he hated righteousness and loved wickedness.

The immediate occasion for this "royal wedding song" could have been a psalm of praise and fervent hope for a king who looked promising and then faded in the stretch. But with good reason, scholars have identified the subject of this psalm as King Jesus. *He* is "the fairest of the sons of men" (v. 2). *His* is the "divine throne [that] endures forever" (v. 6). *His* is the name to be "celebrated in all generations." *He* is to be praised by peoples "for ever and ever" (v. 17).

How Does This Apply to Us?

Jesus loved righteousness. He knew it to be the only road to happiness. He taught righteousness. "Seek first his kingdom and *his righteousness,* and all these things shall be yours as well" (Matthew 6:33). By His example and by His words He is calling us to the love of righteousness. Jesus hates wickedness. He hated it when Satan suggested an easy way out in the time of temptation. He hated it when wickedness showed up in others. He denounced it wherever He saw it and He did so when it might have been easier to look the other way. He died to bring down the kingdom of evil. He will come again to send it finally and forever into oblivion.

If we would be like the King, we must hate wickedness. The battle is joined but victory is assured. And right now before the end and all the way to the end we will be "anointed . . . with the oil of gladness."

Pray with Me

O God, Your ways and Your thoughts are always right. Your plan for our lives leads only to the gladness of final victory. Help me, therefore, to love the right and hate the wrong.

I profess to love that which is good and in my heart I truly want that which is good. But, to my sorrow and shame, I have not always hated that which is not good. I know that if any man love the world, the love of the Father is not in him. Nevertheless I have allowed myself to accept and even to seek a compromise. My heart has been closed to those sweet influences that can turn my life toward full salvation and peace and gladness. I have failed to realize that only the pure in heart can see God and so experience eternal and unfading joy. I have failed to realize that only in the love of righteousness is there unwaning satisfaction. All that is opposed to such love has upon it the blight of decay. All that makes the love of righteousness and the hatred of wickedness seem out of focus and unimportant has upon it the seal of death.

Lord, possess my heart. Reign there without a rival until I desire and choose to walk only in the paths that lead through righteousness to joy. I would so covet Your anointing with the oil of gladness that I would never falter. Defend me from the kind of doubt that wavers on the brink of dark and evil choice, wondering if the love of wickedness is really all that bad.

Help me to see the things that belong to my peace. Strengthen me in the hour of decision. Let not the grasping of some immediate but fleeting pleasure make me insensitive to the deep and lasting joys which, in Your justice and mercy, surround all those who love righteousness and hate wickedness.

In the Name of Him who died because love of righteousness and hatred of wickedness are so eternally right, Amen.

MOVING ON IN THE LIFE OF PRAYER

We have reason to believe that prayer is entering the palace of the King (Psalm 45:15). Often we agonize in prayer. We are puzzled by unanswered prayers. We are frustrated by plans and dreams that go awry. We are troubled that problems—our own and others'—are not more quickly solved. But when we are privileged to enter the palace of the King, it is above all a reason for "joy and gladness." "Gladness" because we are in His presence. "Joy" because "we know that in everything [even the greatest of problems, or the heaviest of burdens] God works for good with those who love him" (Romans 8:28a).

The King's palace! In prayer we are *shut in* but *never* shut out.

Day 121

RAISED UP WITH CHRIST

"But God . . . made us alive together with Christ . . . raised us up with him, and made us sit with him in the heavenly places" (Ephesians 2:4-6).

Read: **Ephesians 2;** Psalm 119:50; John 5:21; Colossians 3:1.

WHAT IS GOD SAYING?

This is a foretaste of what life is going to be in Heaven and what it can be now. Paul is reminding us that we are not only delivered from death, we are given life. It is like moving from mere existence to exciting, satisfying, beautiful life. Life that is incomparably wonderful now, life right now that is within our grasp because we are in *His* grasp. It is part of God's plan.

At one time we were far off, we didn't want His plan. In fact, the more we knew of His plan, the less we wanted it. Once we were on the side of all that opposes God. "The prince of the power of the air" had us tethered, as it were, by a ring in the nose. We followed when he tugged. We marched to his tune. We were part of a crowd headed for death and worse—aimlessly wandering, unable to think for ourselves, powerless to rise above the swamplands of the world's moral degradation. We blindly followed the course of this world (Ephesians 2:2), the prince of the air (v. 2), the desires of body and mind (v. 3).

But God! How wonderful are those words; dead through our trespasses, *but God* made us alive together with Christ. Headed for the worst, *but God* changed it all into the best. Bewildered and befogged, listless and lifeless, cheerless and hopeless, *but God* rich in mercy, "out of the great love with which he loved us, . . . raised us up with [Christ]." Not reformation but transformation. Not a prize we deserved but grace that He bestowed. BUT GOD!

How Does This Apply to Us?

This great chapter confirms the privilege and the power of prayer. In verse 18 we have it spelled out: "For through him we both [those far off and those who are near] have access in one Spirit to the Father." God who speaks to us in His Word allows us access to Himself through the Spirit. We are no longer strangers (v. 19). Prayer takes on a new dimension when we realize that He wants us to talk with Him as friend to Friend, as child to Father, as disciple to Lord, and even as those who are already sitting with Him—secure, established, and greatly loved, in places (and thoughts) that are heavenly.

We come to prayer with confidence, knowing that the desires of our hearts, the needs of our hearts, and all our requests are of great importance to Him. That's just one more facet of His many-splendored love. Saved to be near Him in heavenly places. Saved to serve Him in earthly places. Saved to share with Him our deepest needs and our highest hopes.

Pray with Me

Lord, I have been delivered from the death that my sin deserves by the riches of Your pardoning grace and in the power of my Lord's resurrection. Now I know the glory of life with Christ . . . not merely life, not merely seeing and speaking and caring, but *life with Him* that sees and says and cares as if with His eyes, His lips, and His heart. This is life with a capital L. I am not merely delivered from death but am given power to live. I do not have life that is austere and lonely, but life that is filled with His joy as with His presence.

Then I am raised up with Him. It is so good to know that the things which have a stranglehold on others do not demand my time or sap my energy or dictate my will. It is so good to know that the petty ambitions that seem so great, the imagined slights that seem so unpardonable, and the popular acclaim that seems so necessary are all beneath me when I am raised up with Christ.

Raised with Him I have new goals to seek, better values to cherish, more useful work on which to spend my energy. I am raised up with Him . . . above the misty lowlands where sight is limited, above the confining valleys where the spirit is cramped, above that jungle where men strive unto death for fame and fortune that quickly vanishes away.

But, Lord, beyond all this, beyond living with Him and being raised up with Him, I have the most exquisite joy of all: to sit with Him in heavenly places. To sit in calm security, to sit in restful enjoyment, to sit in unhurried contemplation of Your majesty and perfection, to know that all eternity is mine to glorify and to enjoy You, Lord. This is the best of all!

Take away every blessing but these and I will still have all.

In His Name whose resurrection glory has made all this and more both possible and real, Amen.

MOVING ON IN THE LIFE OF PRAYER

Even in hard work and busy activity, we can practice the presence of God. We can keep on praying with pressures all around us. We can race against deadlines. We can accept the demands of a crowded schedule and still keep our prayer life intact. Has He not made us to "sit" with Him in heavenly places? Is that a scene of frenzied activity or is it blissful calm? We can listen to God better and talk with God more meaningfully when we remember that we are made to sit with Him in heavenly places. Sit down now and pray with Him. Isn't that heavenly?

Day 122

GOD ALONE IS SUFFICIENT

" '. . . Is it because there is no God in Israel that you are going to inquire of Baalzebub?' " (2 Kings 1:3).

Read: **2 Kings 1:1-18;** 1 Kings 19; James 5:16-18.

WHAT IS GOD SAYING?

Although Elijah's name is synonymous with courage, James says he was a man just like we are (James 5:17). He had moments when his guard was down. He could be discouraged. Or frightened. He could go from the triumph on Mount Carmel to the deep depression of Beersheba almost in the time it takes to tell it.

But it was his success in prayer that caught the attention of James: "The prayer of a righteous man has great power in its effects" (James 5:16). This was the man God used to stand up against incredible evil in high places, rousing the anger of kings, disturbing their comfortable ways enough to send them into a blind rage and in search of irrational revenge. Ahaziah was the last king whose godless reign was so challenged by Elijah. He had injured himself by falling through the lattice in his upper chamber. In his mind, twisted by incessant evil, he thought his wound too severe to be entrusted to the God of Israel. So he sent for the advice of Baalzebub, a god of the Philistines.

God sent a message through Elijah: "Is it because there is no God in Israel that you are going to inquire of Baalzebub, the god of Ekron?" It cut Ahaziah to the quick and he tried to get Elijah, spelled A-N-N-O-Y-I-N-G N-U-I-S-A-N-C-E, out of his way once and for all. So he sent not one, but two companies of fifty men each. All were consumed by fire from heaven. It isn't strange that God got the attention of the third company who begged for mercy and Elijah went with them back to the king. The condemning king was himself condemned. In the end he could not evade the God of Elijah. Ahaziah found, too late, that there *was* a God in Israel, a God who could not be ignored.

How Does This Apply to Us?

Elijah was a man of prayer, a man of courage, a man subject to swings of mood, and yet a man who trusted God to the very end. He knew there was a God in Israel. He had the wisdom to discern His word and the courage to speak that word with unflinching clarity. We want to think that we would do the same, but the fact is there are things in our lives that make it seem as though we really believe there is "no God in Israel."

Pray with Me

Dear Lord, I need to face that question. It is a question I often would but never can avoid. It is Your question to make me stop. It is Your question to make me strong. It is Your merciless way to be merciful. It is the cut of a surgeon's art to show the kindness of a healer's heart.

Is it because there is no God in our nation that we resort to weapons which destroy not only the enemy but the hearts that hate the enemy? Is it because there is no God in our country that we tumble before the threats of those who would tear Him from the skies above and from the conscience within?

Is it because there is no God in our home that we allow ourselves to be encumbered with luxuries while many in the larger family of God suffer great lack?

Is it because there is no God in my mind that I allow it to be cluttered with faithless doubts and soiled with evil thoughts?

Is it because there is no God in my heart that I do not serve day and night for the love of Him who delivered me from the power of death and set my feet on the path of life?

At every point I must own my guilt, God of all righteousness and truth. Yet at every point, I am encouraged by Your willingness and power to enter and make Yourself known. That country, that home, that mind, and that heart which shows even a mustard seed of honest faith will find in You, dear Lord, One who not only is, but is available; One who not only is available but is able to do far more abundantly than all we ask or think.

In faith, I seek. In Your faithfulness, give.

To the glory of Jesus Christ, Amen.

MOVING ON IN THE LIFE OF PRAYER

Do we lack power in our prayer life? Does the mark of recognition that James gave to the great prophet seem too remote a claim for us? "The prayer of a righteous man has great power"—but what about our prayers? Trusting in the righteousness of Christ and offering our prayer in His name, we, too, can have "great power in prayer." The secret: knowing that there *is* a God in Israel. There is a Christ who lives and intercedes for us. There is the very present companionship and guidance of the Holy Spirit. There is a Son at God's right hand. Listen to Him. Pray in His name. Walk in His love. Let us bring Him all the desires, all the longings, all the doubts, all the burdens, all the problems, and then let us leave them there.

There is a God in Israel. There is a Christ who cares.

Day 123

THANKS TO GOD FOR OTHERS

"We give thanks to God always for you all . . ." (1 Thessalonians 1:2).

Read: **1 Thessalonians 1;** 1 John 3:14-23.

WHAT IS GOD SAYING?

In this letter Paul deals with the grandest of themes, the coming again of Jesus Christ. Absorbed in such a theme, it might be easy to forget about others, how we love them, how we need them, how much we owe to them. When our eyes are fixed on the Main Event, we might be tempted to overlook the preliminaries. Not so with Paul.

In 3:13, the apostle refers to "the coming of our Lord Jesus with all his saints." He opens that section with the prayer that the Thessalonians might "increase and abound in love to one another and to all men, as we do to you." He also recognizes how greatly indebted he was to others. God is the source of all blessings, but sometimes, in fact, *usually*, He brings those blessings to us through the hands and hearts of others.

In the prayer which opens this letter, Paul recalls things people did which encouraged him and strengthened the church: "Your work of faith and labor of love and steadfastness of hope." It is easy to understand how all these good things were awakened in their lives, for love awakens love, joy begets joy, friendship reproduces friendship. Prayer to God and appreciation for others flow along the same streambed and, like the water that so flows, they are continually mingled.

How Does This Apply to Us?

We need to ask ourselves a question as an important segment in our practice of prayer: Whom has God sent into our lives to be a blessing? Whom has God given to us as an inspiring example? Who has been touched with the gospel of God through our life and testimony? Are we praying continually in thanksgiving to God for those we have blessed and for those who have been a blessing to us?

Pray with Me

Lord, I thank You for the blessings that come into my life because of people. You are the only source of all that is good. Yet You have brought so many blessings to me through the love and faithfulness of people.

I thank You, Lord, for those whom You have used to guide me through days of indecision. I thank You for those who have put up with me through trying stages of growth.

I thank You, Lord, for those who are bound to me by family ties and who have brought to me the touch of love in human terms that I need and understand.

I thank You, Lord, for friends whose tie to me has come from nothing else than our mutual sense of need before Your throne of grace. I thank You for friends whom You have brought across my path with sudden and unexpected joy, as with a cheering melody or a pleasing fragrance. I thank You for friends who look upon my weaknesses with charity and my aspirations with confidence.

I thank You, Lord, for those who have stood across my path and through whose resistance I have been led to a deeper understanding of myself and of my constant need for You.

I thank You, Lord, for people who do not know me and whom I do not know and yet through whose courage, I have taken courage. I thank You for unknown friends whose written words have given me a new vision of Your splendor. I thank You for unknown friends whose prayers have helped to renew a right spirit within me. I thank You for all those whose unconscious influence has made it possible for me to see a truer life and to choose a better path.

I thank You, Lord, for all people through whom You have entered my life for good.

In the Name of Him who, having given Himself for all people, shall one day reign over all people, Jesus Christ, my Lord, Amen.

MOVING ON IN THE LIFE OF PRAYER

In our conversation with God, other people must come across our minds. They are important. They need our love as we need theirs. There are no more necessary ingredients in prayer than that. Take them to the Lord in prayer. And we must always remember to be thankful: thankful for those who help us, for those who stand across our path when we are headed in the wrong direction, for those who challenge us by their example, for those who speak the truth (that sometimes hurts) in love, for those who quietly bear with our failures. Prayer should always have faces, faces with names—people whom God has given to us to be loved, people whom God has given to us to be loved by.

Day 124

GOD'S LOVE IN GOD'S DISCIPLINE

" . . . *The reproofs of discipline are the way of life*" (Proverbs 6:23).

Read: **Proverbs 6:20-23;** Ecclesiastes 7:5; Psalm 141:5 (NIV); Hebrews 12:5-11.

WHAT IS GOD SAYING?

Solomon wrote three thousand proverbs and over a thousand songs. He built a great temple and ruled over a united kingdom. His words offer down-to-earth help for sound living. Time and again he stresses the importance of heeding what we *don't want to hear* in order to find the life we *don't want to miss.* In preparation for today's prayer time, we should read Hebrews 12:5-11. It puts the discipline God sends into our lives in its true light as summarized in that single, memorable verse: "For the Lord disciplines him whom he loves" (Hebrews 12:6). If we want to walk in the way of life, we must discover that God's will may not be always pleasing. But it is always right.

How Does This Apply to Us?

We don't take kindly to rebuke. Reproof is a bitter pill. We resent it. We do anything to avoid it and wish that others would stop making waves. We want smooth sailing. How wisely the Word of God directs us to accept ways that we would not naturally choose. Ecclesiastes 7:5 (NIV) paints a graphic picture on how and why to take advice: "It is better to heed a wise man's rebuke than to listen to the song of fools." Easy to listen to a song. Hard to listen to rebuke. Yet one is the way of life and the other may be the prelude to destruction. If something has cut across the grain of our lives, we find ourselves resenting the intrusion. That is surely a matter of prayer. Let us ask God to help us sort it all out. Some pain comes into our lives because we are struggling against God's plan. Some pain comes into our lives because of wrong decisions. There is other pain that is meant to bless. Prayer enables God to let us know which is good and wise, and which is wrong and unnecessary. Take the hard things of life to the Lord. In prayer that "listens" quietly and "speaks" honestly, we can discover which trials should be accepted to teach us a lesson and which can be left with the Lord as a burden laid down and mercifully removed.

Pray with Me

Loving Father, lead me to the place where I am absolutely convinced that Your will is right. I need that which does not come naturally. I need to accept the fact without questioning or hesitation that "the reproofs of discipline are the way of life."

Too often I have thought of discipline as a hindrance to life instead of its best ally. Too often I have resented Your reproofs when I should have known everything You do for me, everything You do to me, everything You do about me is meant to bring greater peace and fuller joy. Too often I have thought of Your disciplines as rocks being added to the prison of a restricted life instead of paving stones on the highway to Heaven and freedom.

Now, Lord, I rejoice in knowing that You are the Beginning and the End. Furthermore, You know the end from the beginning. And as I come to realize this, I am more ready to accept the detours and roadblocks that You see are necessary if I am to remain in "the way of life."

I am sorry that I have allowed little irritations to hide Your wise and loving reproofs. I have been too self-willed, too impulsive, too limited in my vision to recognize the loving purpose behind all Your corrections.

Nevertheless, I am willing—no, I am wanting—You to come to me with Your wise and loving firmness. In Your mercy compel me to accept the "reproofs" that prove Your love and the "discipline" that decides my destiny.

In the Name of the Master who calls me to the discipline and to the glory of discipleship, Amen.

MOVING ON IN THE LIFE OF PRAYER

Reproofs will never stop coming, but we know how to handle them when they come. Instead of *resenting* them, in the restless turbulence of a wounded heart, we may keep on *presenting* them to the Lord. Prayer deals with the hard realities of discipline and grows in strength as we realize where we can take these negative things. God will brush aside the useless and needless suffering and allow us to keep the true reproofs of discipline that are the way of life. Prayer becomes a way to life and a way of life.

Day 125

TALKING IS IMPORTANT, BUT . . .

"For the kingdom of God does not consist in talk but in power" *(1 Corinthians 4:20).*

Read: **1 Corinthians 4;** Acts 4:30.

WHAT IS GOD SAYING?

In dealing with the many problems that were continually rising in the Corinthian Community Church, Paul points out this important fact: "Talk is cheap." What counts is spiritual power. What counts is a life of practical goodness. This comment is made against the backdrop of the most important city of Greece in Paul's day, Corinth. Corinth was also an incredibly wicked city with all the problems that have traditionally beset seaport cities. This restless, pleasure-worshiping society spawned controversy that reached into the life of the Christian community itself and left the stains of a careless morality on the newly established Christian church.

The problem surfaced in many ways: Outright immorality; Christians taking other Christians to civil courts; selfishness raising its ugly head on every side; and much, much quarreling

(1 Corinthians 1:11). People used words to promote their self-importance and to establish themselves at the top of the heap. This led to a mood of arrogance (4:18). Paul sends this letter to tell them he will be there very soon (4:19). Then he will find out how much of this is self-serving talk, and how much is real power in terms of the kingdom.

How Does This Apply to Us?

Christians need to be constantly reminded that love is something we do. Jesus uses the words of Isaiah to drive home the truth that we can say all the right things and still have a heart that is far from God (Matthew 15:8). This is especially true when we are engaged in the exercise of prayer.

God's words to us have great power. Let us be on our guard, for our words to God may be lacking in power. Let us try to frame our true desires and our true intent with words that are well chosen and sincere. The Holy Spirit can take our wordless prayers and give them power (Romans 8:26). He intercedes for us with sighs "too deep for words."

But prayerless words are different. There is no power in words that come out disconnected from our minds and our wills. Do we mean what we are praying? Would we be willing to start walking as we are talking, to start being what we are promising, to start doing what we are saying? Talk is cheap. Obedience is costly and productive.

Pray with Me

O God, Your Word is power. You have only to speak and it is done. Thank You for speaking so clearly to me today.

To listen for Your voice in the brightness of morning is a magnificent privilege. To read Your Word while the mind is still sensitive to divine truth and still undulled by contact with the world of men and things, is among life's choicest blessings.

Your kingdom *is* talk—Your talk! But in Your talking there is power. There is no inconsistency between Your speaking and Your doing. You say what You will do and You do what You say.

Yet, Lord, I must admit that in my life, though I am lifted by Your grace above secular mediocrity and set apart for the sacred best, there is much talk that is not power.

Forgive the idle word that nervously fills some vacuum of insecurity. Forgive the angry word that impetuously fills some vacuum of wounded pride. Forgive the boastful word that impatiently fills some vacuum of selfish ambition.

I am sorry for smooth words that disguise insincerity and for hasty words that reveal an unsurrendered self. Let me guard all mere talking until my words are consistent with my works and my works are invested with Your power. Let Your power, the power of redeeming love, patient forgiveness, and unquenchable hope, fill my life. Let the power that is the kingdom of God give strength to my hand and wisdom to my words. Let all my speaking and doing, all my talking and walking, all my professing and practicing be worthy of Your kingdom.

And, O God, let me never forget that to be a true subject of Your kingdom, I may work without talking but I may never, never talk without working.

In the Name of Him who did not merely talk of Calvary, but proved in death the invincible power of love, Amen.

Moving On in the Life of Prayer

Once again, we see the premise of this book shining with clear meaning. Listen to God! His words come with power: power to transform, to heal, to challenge, to awaken, to encourage. Let His "living and powerful Word" guide us into prayer. Then, as it works its way through our lives, His words will become embodied in a life that is power—power to live, to love, to win over temptation, to serve with faithfulness, to be the sons and daughters of God that we were intended to be.

Day 126

Showers of Blessings

"And I will make them and the places round about my hill a blessing; and I will send down the showers in their season; they shall be showers of blessing" (Ezekiel 34:26).

Read: **Ezekiel 34,** 3:16-21; Deuteronomy 32:2; Hosea 6:3.

What Is God Saying?

Ezekiel follows Jeremiah, not only in the biblical order of books, but also in chronological sequence. He was one of the young men taken captive to Babylon while Jeremiah was still prophesying in the terminal days of Jerusalem. Ezekiel was commissioned by the Lord to give words of warning (3:16-21). He did this through parables and signs like the vision of the fruitless vine destined for burning in Ezekiel 15. He was also commissioned to bring words of comfort and hope as he did in the vision of the dry bones in Ezekiel 37, great words of promise concerning the future. It was a case of bad news, good news. It was a thankless task to bring the warning of impending doom. But to bring the news of a great restoration was a joyful privilege.

God will gather the scattered remnants of His people. Note in Ezekiel 34:6, "My sheep were scattered over all the face of the earth, with none to search or seek for them." A glorious age awaits them. Israel will know that the Lord is God, their God, and that they are His people (Ezekiel 34:30-31).

How Does This Apply to Us?

It is of interest to see how many times in this thirty-fourth chapter of Ezekiel God says: "I will." When God says "I will" it is time for us to listen and futile for anyone to oppose or deny it. Now the God who *will* send blessing on the restored people of Israel is the same God who has in His care the lives of individual Christians. We proceed on the assumption that in Christ what God promises to a future Israel is available to Christians alive in the present (2 Corinthians 9:8; Philippians 4:19). Since Christ came that we might have life abundant (John 10:10), we may pray for and receive showers of blessing. If our souls remain parched in the midst of all the riches of Christ available now, we have only ourselves to blame.

Pray with Me

Lord, although I am showered by Your blessings, I can still complain. Although I am engulfed by Your goodness, I still have times of anxiety and doubt. Although I am deluged by Your mercies, I still show myself so often to be ungrateful.

The showers of blessings which You have promised are daily realities. Your mercies are as generous as the sun, as limitless as the oceans, as constant as the hills. If I remain parched in the middle of this abundance or if I count myself poor in the middle of this plenty, I have no one to blame but myself.

Lead me, Lord, from the periphery of pathetic fears into the calm center of full trust. Lead me from the fringes of faltering faith into the center of glad, bold confidence. Lead me from the borders of life where half-faith and half-doubt must be content with occasional drops. Lead me into the bountiful center of faith where You are always sending down showers of blessing.

Then I shall find a greater blessing. Filled, I shall overflow. Blessed, I shall be a blessing. "I will make them and the places round about my hill a blessing." This is the promise You have made and the program in which, fully blessed, I may have a part. I claim the blessing of this larger goodness.

The blessings that fill my cup to overflowing are not just for me. If I believe them to be so, the cup will no longer overflow. So, through me, let Your blessings become blessings for "the places round about."

Gracious Father, You bring showers of blessing. I pray for a more obedient and trusting faith. Bring me into the place of receiving and sharing Your showers.

Through Him who perfectly showed Your love and abundantly showered Your love for all mankind, Amen.

MOVING ON IN THE LIFE OF PRAYER

God's abundant blessings are on tap. We don't have to worry about a diminishing reservoir. We don't have to look at a cloudless sky and wonder. We don't have to sink a shaft deep in the earth only to find it's a dry hole. Prayer is opening the windows of heaven to receive constant, refreshing, nourishing rain. Prayer is simply asking, believing, and receiving. God's supply is never limited. Only our faith has limits. Moving on in the life of prayer should take us from the periphery of pathetic fears into the calm center of full trust.

Day 127

SUFFERING FOR THE RIGHT REASONS

" . . . *But share in suffering for the gospel in the power of God*" (*2 Timothy 1:8*).

Read: **2 Timothy 1;** Acts 5:41; Hebrews 11:25; 1 Peter 2:20.

WHAT IS GOD SAYING?

Paul is taking up his pen for the last time. There would be no more doctrines to set down in Romans, no more arguments to settle in Corinthians, no more heresies to lay to rest in Colossians. But there was Timothy, his beloved son in the gospel. In his cold prison cell, he longed to see Timothy again. Timothy had been such a part of his life. Now, as the days of that life appeared to be running out, he needed to be encouraged as well as to encourage. He asked Timothy to pick up his warm cloak and some of his favorite books and parchments. "Do your best to come to me soon," he wrote (4:9). In fact, "Do your best to come before winter" (4:21).

But whether Timothy, even doing his best, would get to Rome on time, was not the most important item on the agenda. He must be told that he would get his share of suffering wherever he was. On the move or at rest, around strangers or on familiar turf, whether by word of mouth or deeds of life, testifying to our Lord can bring its share of suffering. That is why Paul includes in his letter these words, "Endure hardness, as a good soldier of Jesus Christ" (2:3, KJV).

HOW DOES THIS APPLY TO US?

Our circumstances today are quite different from the ones Paul and Timothy encountered long ago. Had Timothy lived today, he could have sent the cloak and books by Federal Express and Paul would have had them long before winter. He could have commuted to Rome every week after handling the Sunday services.

But even with all the changes that have taken place, one who lives consistently with the gospel will find the going rough in our thoroughly secular, and often godless, society. We will be thought peculiar. We will lose friends (how real were they anyway?). We will not be welcomed in some circles. Even our own family may not understand and may believe Christians are misguided and brainwashed. But in the power of God, we can keep on testifying and we can take our share of suffering for the gospel, wherever that leads us and whatever it requires of us. We can do it in the power of God. That is the secret— "In the power of God."

When the impossible is required, God supplies the power. We have only to be vessels—available, clean, and ready. The most important ability that God requires is availability. He does the rest.

Pray with Me

Lord, I cannot say that on the basis of my own capacity or my own desire I am able or willing to "share in suffering for the gospel." My life has too often proved the opposite.

But today You have led me to a wonderful new discovery. I can suffer and I can be willing to suffer when it is "in the power of God." This kind of suffering does not lead to despair. This kind of suffering does not rob life of its meaning and purpose. This kind of suffering does not drain from the heart its joy nor open the door to misery. This kind of suffering does not nourish the spirit of complaint. This kind of suffering does not build around the soul walls of self-pity.

If it is Your will, Lord, let me take my share of suffering for the sake of the gospel but always and only "in the power of God." Acting thus, in faith, I will discover an open door to glory and life and peace. Let me see the Father's smile beyond the pain of duty. Let me hear the Master's "well done" beyond the burden of toil.

Let me not be afraid of taking my share. Relying on Your strength I would even welcome my share of suffering, if by so doing I could bring the gospel to others. As I do not ask for suffering in my own strength, I cannot ask to avoid it when with that suffering You send Your power.

Help me not to question Your providence. Help me not to doubt Your power. Help me not to miss Your purpose in any suffering which may come upon me for the sake of the gospel.

In the Name of Him who in the power of love divine, suffered to redeem mankind, Amen.

Moving On in the Life of Prayer

It is seldom that we use the word *suffering* in connection with almost anything the Christian encounters today. But when it comes, we can "share in" it through the power of God. As we pray, then, our prayer should very consciously ask for the enabling power of the living Lord. In quiet openness, we receive the Holy Spirit's power. In courageous living and loving service we use the power. In loving the unlovable and in reaching the unreachable, the God of power and the power of God uses us.

Day 128

The Right Place to Rest

"Arise and go, for this is no place to rest; because of uncleanness that destroys with a grievous destruction" (Micah 2:10).

Read: **Micah 2;** Deuteronomy 12:7-10; Leviticus 15:24-25; Isaiah 24:5, 11.

What Is God Saying?

Micah proclaims Samaria, the capital of Israel, a disaster area. God could not let its defiant disregard for His sovereignty and holy laws go unpunished (1:6, 7). Her images and her idols must be destroyed beyond all recycling and the city itself become a heap of ruin in the open country.

A visit to the present site of ancient Samaria is a desolate experience. Furthermore, it is the lament and warning of Micah that the infectious sickness that caused Samaria's demise had spread to the gates of Jerusalem. Judah was not to be spared because Judah was becoming increasingly defiled. The poor were oppressed. Their property was coveted and prized. Women who once had pleasant houses with happy children were driven out into the street. The people of Judah didn't want real preachers with a real message. They would only listen to those who said, "You're O.K., I'm O.K." Or, "Don't worry. Be happy." And all the time the festering wound was accumulating its poisons. The place that used to be home, a place of health and peace and joy, was now a place of "uncleanness that destroys with a grievous destruction." This was no place to rest. This was a place to leave.

How Does This Apply to Us?

Centuries later, Alexander Pope in his "Essay on Man," Epistle 2, wrote:

"Vice is a monster of such frightful mien
  As to be hated is but to be seen,
  Yet, seen too oft, familiar with her face,
  We first endure, then pity, then embrace."

For those who had grown accustomed to and tolerant of the polluted land, the prophet raised his voice in vain. For the others, his warning was loud and clear. "Arise and go, for this is no place to rest."

We can and do allow ourselves to be so tolerant and accepting of that which sickens and defiles our world, that we fail to sense the awful destiny of its constant, steady, downward drag. We live in a civilization that has allowed spiritual values to go under. Sin and sickness are rampant. The media is almost universally polluted.

Christians must be aware that while they are powerless to clean up all the hazardous material and toxic waste of sin, they do not and must not come to rest on top of the dump site. We can arise and go. We can find the right place to rest. God can give us a place to rest when our minds are focused on His Word and our feet are walking in the ways of truth and our spirits are willing to embrace His perfect plan for our lives. He is not willing that any should come to "grievous destruction" but that all should reach repentance (2 Peter 3:9).

Pray with Me

Heavenly Father, I would be deeply assured that I can find no rest except in Your righteousness and mercy. Keep me from ever trying to find rest short of Your will or apart from Your will.

Surely "*this* is no place to rest." Here, where there is "uncleanness that destroys with a grievous destruction," I am called upon to work ceaselessly, to walk untiringly, and to watch vigilantly. To rest in the midst of uncleanness is to become infected. To sleep at the post is to invite the enemy's attack. To imagine that I am beyond the reach of uncleanness and can therefore relax is to lay myself open to costly deception.

Lord, give me a soul-saving restlessness and an unceasing dissatisfaction with the uncleanness of this world. I thank You that there is so much that is good and holy and clean. I know that truth and love are never without their witness. I know that they are never lacking toward me if I am ever looking toward You. Help me, then, to seek rest only in the green pastures of Your perfect love and protecting grace. Help me to find satisfaction only beside the still waters that never run dry or turn bitter.

By faith I will not settle down in peaceful co-existence with destructive uncleanness. I want to work in Your Spirit to subdue it. By Your grace I want to escape it. I will never hope for rest, I will never expect it, I will never want it, I will carefully avoid it, until I find it, Lord, in You.

In the Name of Him whose perfect obedience to the Father's will has made possible our perfect rest in the Father's love, now and forever, Amen.

MOVING ON IN THE LIFE OF PRAYER

God will provide waters that are clean and pastures that are green. He will lead us in paths of righteousness away from the oil spills of immorality that pollute and destroy everything along the shoreline of life, away from the poverty of lust and into the riches of love, away from the sickness of half-truths into the health of His eternal truth, away from prayerless indifference into prayer that cares. We can move on in prayer while resting in the place of God's cleansing and renewing grace.

Day 129

THE POWER AND CURE OF UNBELIEF

"So we see that they were unable to enter because of unbelief" (Hebrews 3:19).

Read: **Hebrews 3:7-19;** Psalm 95:7-11; Proverbs 28:14; John 12:37-43.

WHAT IS GOD SAYING?

The Jewish believers, especially those living in Jerusalem, had been growing discouraged. They were often the objects of ridicule and scorn. Other Jews would say to them, "Look what you are losing. No more altar, no more sacrifices, no more priesthood, no more tradition." These Christians, born into Judaism, were turning their backs on all that. And for what reason? The novelty of the preaching of this Nazarene could hardly stand up against their deeply rooted customs and time-honored rites.

Christian Jews needed encouragement and in Hebrews it came to them. What we have because of Christ is so much better. "Better" becomes the key word of the book. Take as one example, Moses. Now, that's touching a Hebrew to the quick. Moses was a servant of God but Christ was "faithful over God's house as a *son*" (3:6). He is to be followed as an even "better" Leader out of bondage and into the rest and freedom that God has promised. Moses was great, but Christ is greater.

But even today there is the problem of unbelief, or hardness of heart. It was unbelief, fostered by the deceitfulness of sin, that defeated God's purpose under Moses. Unbelief can still keep a person away from Christ. Unbelief can even hold back the hand of God (Matthew 13:58). Unbelief can still block the entrance into the Promised Land of salvation and freedom and rest. The power of unbelief cannot be taken lightly.

How Does This Apply to Us?

Cancer is a subtle, shadowy enemy that has made a shambles of many a life. But what about the cancer of unbelief? When it takes root it can do more far-reaching damage. It can block the entrance to Heaven. It can do for the soul what aggressive cancer cells do to the body. It can bring a different kind of pain, all the more serious because it goes so long unnoticed. It can splinter hopes and shatter dreams.

Unbelief has great power. Only faith has more. Only faith can meet it head on and emerge triumphant. Unbelief is the enemy of all prayer, making God seem unreal and irrelevant. Faith is the foundation for all prayer. Faith believes God is able and available. Only faith can conquer unbelief. In prayer we cast our vote for faith and against unbelief. It is a battle of the Titans. In prayer we choose the winning side.

Pray with Me

Lord, Your people were chosen to be blessed above all others and to be a blessing to all others. Yet, when they hardened their hearts in rebellion against You, they sealed their own fate. Ever since, unbelief has been the only obstacle to keep men's souls from entering into Your promised rest.

Unbelief is the only thing that can keep anyone from receiving God's best and being God's blessed. It is the only reason sinners are unconverted and saints are often unhappy. It is the curse that extinguishes the light of hope. It is the disharmony that garbles the song of joy. It locks the door to bliss and opens the door to sorrow. It blocks the road to peace and paves the road to frustration. It makes us afraid to walk on the narrow road that leads to life. It drives us into the folly of going with the crowd on the broad road to destruction. It makes the best seem poor and the worst seem good. It makes the impossible remain impossible and the easy seem hard. It can even restrain the omnipotent hand of God: "He did not do many mighty works there, because of their unbelief."

Lord, let a new vision of Your eternal glory enable me to break away from the chilling grip of doubt. Let a new understanding of the security and adventure I have as a follower of Christ set me free from imprisoning fear. Let a new awareness of Your steadfast and deathless love, like the sun rising on a new day, drive away the blinding and chilling clouds of unbelief. Lord, "I believe; help my unbelief." By Your grace smite this constant and stubborn foe. Give me the liberty that belongs to those who have entered into the reality of Your redeeming and ever-present love.

In the Name of Him who said, "This is the victory that overcomes the world, our faith." Amen.

Moving On in the Life of Prayer

We will never be free of nagging doubt. We shouldn't be surprised that unbelief is so persistent. Prayer becomes our necessary weapon in a constant battle. But faith gives us the victory, day by day, hour by hour, moment by moment. Faith is nourished by God's glory, God's truth, God's love, and His unspeakable gift in Jesus Christ. Think about those things and unbelief will surrender. Think about those things and prayer will become a source of joy, an avenue of freedom . . . and a habit of life.

Day 130

Are We Trees God Can Use?

"Only the trees which you know are not trees for food you may destroy" *(Deuteronomy 20:20).*

Read: **Deuteronomy 20;** Matthew 7:17-20; Luke 3:9.

What Is God Saying?

It is hard for us to reconcile the warlike actions commanded in this and other portions of the Old Testament with the curse of war as we view it today. Christ has a better solution for dealing with enemies, demonstrated in such a profound and ultimate way by His own death on the Cross at the hands of enemies. But we must first consider the threat which the evil Canaanite customs and their gross idolatry represented to the new nation of Israel.

The Jews were strangers, outnumbered and struggling. They were just emerging from their amazing exodus and wilderness journey. Any confusion of loyalties, any compromise with godless immorality, any countenancing of the disgusting, shameful practices of Canaanite religions would be like inviting a deadly virus to take up residence in their bodies. So God commands utter destruction of all that was in open and defiant opposition to His holy laws and pure worship.

In Deuteronomy 12:1, we note the rationale for this series of instructions, some of them drastic: "These are the statutes and ordinances which you shall be careful to do in the land which the LORD, the God of your fathers, has given you to possess, all the days that you live upon the earth." One such commandment was to refrain from cutting down any trees— even though they were needed by the defense department—if they were fruit-bearing trees.

How Does This Apply to Us?

In modern times conservation of all trees is a growing concern for all of us. Can this renewable resource keep pace with the ever-accelerating demands? But trees that yield fruit are as vital now as they were then. Food is a high priority in these days of growing population and diminishing resources.

In the kingdom of our Lord, fruit-bearing trees and vines are of special importance. Consider the Lord's drastic action in Matthew 21:18-19! He also stresses the importance of having fruit-bearing branches in the parable of the vine (John 15:5ff). The call to be fruit-bearing disciples continues in many other places. Our desire to live for Jesus in fruitfulness and our faithfulness in drawing nourishment and life from Him in prayer go hand in hand. Prayer is the doorway to fruitful living.

Pray with Me

God above all nature, You are the Lord of all nature. Your design is perfect. Your knowledge of all that You have created is without flaw. You have said certain trees are to be saved from destruction because they "are for food." Is this not true also of the souls which You have created? Am I not seeing that only those lives which are useful and productive can hope to abide?

Let it be, therefore, the primary goal of my life to become and to remain a good tree that brings forth good fruit. Let me bloom and bear fruit where I am planted. Keep me from the restlessness and anxiety that makes a person want to move away from the place of Your planting. As a "tree for food" sends its roots down into the ground, so I would hunger for Your love. Let me draw into myself the wisdom, the purity, and the strength of Your Spirit. As the rain washes the leaves, so let Your grace come upon me until I am cleansed. As the rain softens and prepares the soil to do its nourishing work, so let Your grace come upon me until I am yielded and ready for spiritual growth.

Teach me the secret of abiding. Show me the joy of abiding. Give me the victory of abiding. And when, in Your wisdom, You see me growing restless in that one place where I can be blessed and used, break through the clouds with the eternal splendor of Your truth. When I am discouraged by poor results and become envious of the easier and more interesting lives that others seem to have, lay upon my fretful spirit Your hand of healing.

Teach me the lessons of contentment. Give me the joy of becoming and continuing as a food-bearing tree. Here alone, as Your Word says so clearly, is safety and peace, security and enjoyment, lasting usefulness and the promised blessing of God.

In the name of Him who promised that if we abide in Him, He will bear fruit through us, even Jesus Christ, the True Vine, Amen.

MOVING ON IN THE LIFE OF PRAYER

It takes time for the sun and the rain and the soil to bring abundant growth to food-producing plants. It takes time in prayer (listening and responding to God) to produce fruit that glorifies God and blesses others. But the waiting is worth it. "They who wait for the LORD shall renew their strength" (Isaiah 40:31). "Behold, the farmer waits for the precious fruit of the earth, being patient over it until it receives the early and the late rain" (James 5:7). For the cultivation of spiritual fruit, there must be the same kind of patient waiting and the same kind of restful exposure to God's grace in the exercise of prayer. Then, results. Then, fruit.

Day 131

RESCUED FROM AND WELCOMED TO

"That through these [promises] you may escape from the corruption that is in the world because of passion, and become partakers of the divine nature" (2 Peter 1:4).

Read: **2 Peter 1;** Genesis 6:11-13; Romans 1:28-32; Galatians 6:3.

WHAT IS GOD SAYING?

In his first letter Peter comforts those who were being persecuted because of their faith. In this letter he addresses another problem. Like poisonous gas it seeps through locked doors. It circulates through the air-conditioning system. It subtly invades even the Christian community. It is not outright persecution and suffering. It is the temptation to yield to the spirit of the times, or "the corruption that is in the world because of passion" (2 Peter 1:4).

There is a remedy. We not only can "escape the corruption," we can actually "become partakers of the divine nature." Take a sonar reading of the depth of that truth. It won't even show on the screen! To escape corruption on the one hand and to become partakers of the very nature of God on the other hand. The contrast is incomprehensible. Only God could do it. Only believers can receive it. And believers can only receive it by grace. Read and reread 2 Peter 1:3: "His divine power has granted to us *all things* that pertain to life and godliness, through the knowledge of him who called us by his own glory and excellence." That's the secret Peter gives to escape the worst and inherit the best.

HOW DOES THIS APPLY TO US?

We are surrounded, even inundated by evil and corruption. To look around for help is futile. What we need is a life preserver connected to a rope thrown by Someone who can lift us up—up, up, and away. Let the goodness of God make its full impact on our lives. He can lift us out of the quicksand of destruction and into the oasis of love and beauty and life. He can replace faltering weakness with conquering strength. He can exchange certain disaster for life abundant.

The only way to escape the vicious and subtle and universal corruption in the world is to let God live His life through us. Then follows an important sequence of virtues, very attainable and very necessary. They are not building blocks that we place one on top of another until they reach the heights, where we watch them tumble. They are qualities that grow out and up, branch by branch, blossom by blossom, and all anchored to the root of the divine nature of which we are partakers (2 Peter 1:5-7). The end of all that (and all the way to the end as well) is a rich welcome "into the eternal kingdom of our Lord and Savior Jesus Christ" (1:11).

Pray with Me

O God, by Your grace and through Your great, unfailing promises, I may not only escape this world's corruption, but become a partaker of Your perfection. This is beyond all comprehension but, on the basis of Your Word, it is beyond all question. Let it be my joy to discover this today and to rediscover it every day:

Not only to flee from death and defeat and destruction, but to be welcomed into life and victory and salvation;

Not only to be shielded from that which spells my doom, but to be sheltered by that which guarantees my deliverance;

Not only to be kept from the passions that lead to death, but to be kept in the paths that lead to life.

Heavenly Father, my need is to discern and to desire those paths. Let my feet be directed into a walk of faith and virtue. Let my mind be content with nothing less than the knowledge which shines in Your Word. Let my will be ruled by the self-control and steadfastness that rise from a deeper devotion to my Lord. Let my life be filled with evidence of godliness. Let my hands be busy with deeds of brotherly affection. Let my heart be filled with love, divine and pure.

Such is Your path for me. It is the wise man's path that leads to life: away from the corruption of sin and onward to the coronation of virtue; away from the misery of failure and upward to the joy of triumph; away from the pain of past defeats and forward to the prize of Your high calling in Christ Jesus.

O Lord, I thank You that You provide both an escape from corruption and an entrance into life, a way out of shame and a way into glory, an end to despair and a beginning to hope. And, being fully persuaded of Your wisdom and love, I would more and more die to self and live for God.

To the glory of my risen and living Lord, Amen.

MOVING ON IN THE LIFE OF PRAYER

In prayer we should always remember what God wants to take *out* of us and what he wants to put *in* us. We should rejoice in what we have been saved *from* and what we have been saved *to*. Escaping corruption . . . God is engaged in that for us. Only we can prevent it. Partakers of His divine nature . . . The supreme object of prayer is to open the door to that. Prayer continued on that basis leads to a rich welcome—even now—into the eternal kingdom of our Lord and Savior Jesus Christ. "Buy now, pay later." That's one slogan. "Pray now, enjoy forever." That's a better one.

Day 132
THE LOVE OF GOD: A REWARD AND A REFUGE

"*. . . A full reward be given you by the LORD, the God of Israel, under whose wings you have come to take refuge*" *(Ruth 2:12).*

Read: **Ruth 2.**

WHAT IS GOD SAYING?

Ruth was born in Moab. The people of Moab were unrelenting enemies of the children of Israel. They worshiped a degrading god, Baal of Peor, and constantly stood against Israel's ways and customs—geographically near, but far away from the high standards of Jewish monotheism. Only a severe famine could incline a man named Elimelech and his wife Naomi to take up residence even for a little while in such a place as Moab. But he didn't live to return to Bethlehem. The two sons of the widowed Naomi then married Moabite women. After ten years they also died.

One of the young widows was named Ruth. She was given the choice of staying in Moab amid familiar surroundings or accompanying her mother-in-law to Bethlehem. She followed her heart and said to Naomi in those beautiful and oft-repeated words of love: "Where you go I will go, and where you lodge I will lodge; your people shall be my people, and your God my God. . . . May the LORD do so to me and more also if even death parts me from you" (Ruth 1:16-17). In the course of time, in a touching narrative of romance and suspense, Ruth marries Boaz and goes from rags to riches. This is an amazing and beautiful story, as Ruth, a heathen, becomes an ancestress of Jesus, born in Bethlehem many centuries later.

HOW DOES THIS APPLY TO US?

Ruth was drawn to Naomi, to Naomi's people, and to Naomi's God because she felt her selfless love and wanted to be among people who had that kind of a God. The influence of other lives has drawn us closer to God even as Naomi's sincere faith and gracious spirit led Ruth to make her decision. We are thankful for the evidence of God's love we see in the lives of others. They have helped us in making a decision to follow Christ, to receive the reward of forgiveness and the hope of eternal life. We find in Jesus Christ not only the reward of faith, but the refuge of a Savior's love. In Him we receive the reward we could never earn and find the refuge we will never lose.

Pray with Me

Dear Lord, Ruth's faith was simple. Her love was uncomplicated. That is what I want and need. You have brought many people into my life in whose lives I have seen the beauty of Jesus Christ. Just as Ruth saw the beauty of Naomi's Lord in Naomi's life, I have seen the love of Jesus in the lives of His followers. To the light which shone in the beauty of Naomi's character, Ruth responded with loyal love. In the same way I would respond to every revelation of Yourself that I see in the lives of those I love and respect.

Ruth found both a reward and refuge as she followed Naomi to her homeland. Let this be my experience too. In the company of those who believe, I shall enter that land where faith is rewarded and love finds a refuge.

I would leave behind the little prizes of a cautious and selfish existence. I would set my heart upon the rewards that are given to the brave and selfless.

I would forget the things which are behind and press toward the mark for the prize of the high calling of God in Christ Jesus. I would no longer hide beneath the thin covering of a straining self-righteousness. I would seek the refuge of Your great love.

Let my reward be the smile of a Lord whose heart is pleased, and the words of a Master who will say, "Well done!" Let my refuge be the promises of Your Word and the words of Jesus, "Come unto me!"

Give me a heart that follows Your leading with simple love. Give me the will to obey. Give me the wisdom to turn my back on the past with all its mistakes and embrace the future with You and for You. Then, Lord, I shall know completely even as now I am knowing more fully each passing day the reward and the refuge of Your redeeming love.

Through Jesus Christ my Lord, Amen.

MOVING ON IN THE LIFE OF PRAYER

We don't engage in prayer to be rewarded, but when we seek the Lord's will we will be rewarded. We do engage in prayer, without shame or apology, because we need a refuge—a refuge from the storms of life; a refuge from winds that blow across the desert of secularism with searing and tedious monotony; a refuge from our foolish mistakes, which, though abandoned, still linger on to plague us. So in prayer we find the refuge of God's love supremely revealed in the cross of Jesus.

Day 133

FORGIVENESS: A BLESSING TO SHARE

" . . . *But he who is forgiven little, loves little*" *(Luke 7:47b).*

Read: **Luke 7;** Acts 5:31; Ephesians 1:7; 1 Timothy 1:15.

WHAT IS GOD SAYING?

This is a passage of striking contrasts. Here was a meeting of people on the opposite ends of society's scale of respectability: on one hand, a proud and self-righteous Pharisee; on the other, a humble, forgiven, and grateful woman with a shady reputation. Having received new life from Jesus, she couldn't do enough to show her love for and gratitude to Him. The alabaster flask was perhaps her most prized possession, and the ointment was not cheap. She displayed her extravagant love in a way that the rigidly correct Pharisee found offensive.

Was he sorry he invited this popular young rabbi? He muttered to himself, "If this man were a prophet, he would have known who and what sort of woman this is who is touching him, for she is a sinner." He may have gone on to mutter, "Why *did* I invite Him? If He were the real thing, He would not have permitted this disgraceful scene."

Jesus told the story of the two debtors who were both forgiven their debts. The difference was great, perhaps five hundred to one. Quite a difference! Simon had to agree that the one who was forgiven the larger debt would love the creditor more. The conclusion was self-evident.

In the same way, while the sinner who was forgiven her many sins couldn't help but show her great love, while the Pharisee, who felt little need for forgiveness in his eminently correct life, felt little need to love.

HOW DOES THIS APPLY TO US?

We cannot pray effectively if we are carrying on our hearts a burden of unforgiven sin. But when we realize how much God has forgiven us, how much He wants to set us free, how many great compensations He wants to give us in lieu of the trifling idols we give up for Him, then our hearts run over with love. Forgiven much, we have great reason to love.

Pray with Me

Forgiven! O God, it has been called the most beautiful word in our language. I know it is the greatest word in my heart, the strongest support for my spirit, the deepest well of my joy.

God of all truth and mercy, I am forgiven not little but much. Not once but often. Not partially but completely. Not by careful accounting but by lavish generosity. Not according to my merits but according to Your mercy.

Now, Lord, forgiven so much and loved so greatly, I would not miss the next step. If little forgiveness brings forth little love, great forgiveness will bring forth great love. Forgiveness and love are like weights that bring a scale into balance: a heavy weight on one side calls for a heavy weight on the other side.

As Your love for me has issued in forgiveness, so ought my love for You find expression in the forgiveness of others and myself. Forgiveness and love are inseparable.

This nameless woman broke her alabaster flask and poured out its priceless contents as a symbol of her great love. It was a response to Your great forgiveness. May I count no point of pride too expensive, no secret ambition too dear in value, no spirit of revenge too close to my heart to be gladly and freely sacrificed.

Forgiven and loved, may I be forgiving and loving.

Forgive me, Lord, that my love, being so often so little, appears to say that I have not been forgiven so often and so much. Let my love begin to match Your forgiveness. At least, Lord, let it try.

In the Name of Him whose forgiving love was, is, and ever shall be inexhaustible, Amen.

MOVING ON IN THE LIFE OF PRAYER

Forgiven much and loving much: these are pillars that hold up our prayers, and these are the reasons we can hold on in prayer. If we remember how much we have been forgiven, we will be less likely to forget how much we are loved . . . and ought to love.

Day 134

THE FULLNESS OF THE SPIRIT

"And after a while the brook dried up, because there was no rain in the land" (1 Kings 17:7).

Read: **1 Kings 17;** John 1:16; Acts 11:24, 13:53; Ephesians 3:19.

WHAT IS GOD SAYING?

Elijah was an instrument in God's hand. Miracles were a matter of course throughout his spectacular life. He was, at the same time, "a man of like nature with ourselves" according to James 5:17. This statement precedes a brief summary of why he was always being used of God. It is a very simple secret and an all-important addendum: *"He prayed fervently."*

In our passage today, God provides even for his physical nourishment in miraculous ways. He ordered the ravens to feed him with bread and meat in the morning, and bread and meat in the evening—and there was plenty to drink from the brook. First Kings 17:7 refers to the way the waters of that stream— once so abundant— "dried up, because there was no rain in the land."

HOW DOES THIS APPLY TO US?

We have all known times of plenty. We also have had times when there was real want. The flowing brooks had become rivulets which soon trickled out. The sun shone down on barren rocks. The dancing joy of flowing water was no more.

Have we wondered why? Our key verse tells us the reason: "There was no rain in the land." When we watch the streams of spiritual vitality and nourishment dry up, it is because we have not allowed the always-available, heaven-sent, healing rain to fall in the highlands of our souls. There has not been enough stillness nor enough openness for the healing rain to gather there. The stream runs dry and causes our lives to become deserts instead of gardens. Sometimes it is because we have allowed a dam of doubt and willfulness to be thrown across our life of prayer which prevents the fullness of God's Spirit from flowing into and through our lives.

God is able to send the rain. We must be willing to receive it and share it. Prayer brings rain to the land. Our willingness to yield to God's Word and Spirit brings that fullness to our lives.

Pray with Me

With Elijah, Lord, I went at Your command to drink from the brook. In my thirst, I was refreshed. In my discouragement, I was cheered. In my need, I was satisfied. Drinking deeply, my soul revived. It was the place of Your choosing, and the fellowship I had with the living God was sweet.

But, Lord, I have also known what it means to watch the brook die away from great fullness to a small trickle. I seemed to be kneeling beside a creek-bed of hot stones and scorching sands. Before me was bleak and blistering evidence: "No rain in the land!"

O God, send the refreshing rain of Your Spirit to the highlands of my soul. Let it be poured out until the brook is full again.

Yet I should know that the heavens of our loving Father are always full of healing rain, always full and always ready. Emptiness is only possible and always inevitable "out" of Your presence. "In" Your presence there is fullness of joy.

Even as I ask You to send what I need, I realize I must bend to what You command. The barricade is in me. The dam that keeps back Your mercy lies across my own heart. The wheel that turns open the floodgates of Heaven's joy lies within my reach. It wants only the yielding of my will.

O God, I kneel beside the brook and even now it comes to life. You are waiting only for my willingness. The channel that I have allowed to run dry is now being filled with life that You never fail to supply.

For this I am thankful and by this I shall live.

In the Name of Him who is the joy of loving hearts, Amen.

MOVING ON IN THE LIFE OF PRAYER

The fullness of God's Spirit is the secret to joy and victory and it only comes when we wait in quietness and expectation beside the brook. It may seem to be dry and empty now. But remember there is rain in the hills, there is that all-important snowpack in the mountains. We have only to be receptive in our spirits and obedient in our lives. God has enough refreshing grace. Do we have enough faith to submit to His will? "God's love has been poured into our hearts through the Holy Spirit which has been given to us" (Romans 5:5). That's the cure for the dry stream-beds of life.

Day 135

SPEAKING SINCERELY FOR CHRIST

" . . . *In the sight of God we speak in Christ*" *(2 Corinthians 2:17).*

Read: **2 Corinthians 2:1-3:6;** Joshua 24:14; Titus 2:7-8.

WHAT IS GOD SAYING?

Paul is aware that many posed as authorities in spiritual matters, "peddling" the Word of God. It was financially profitable. We might associate this kind of charlatanry with the glaring exposés of religious quacks in our time. We have our share.

But Corinth was busy and crowded, with many strangers coming and going, eager for novelty and willing to buy into anything. The peddlers of God's Word had a field day in a thriving and gullible market. Paul emphasizes that, in God's sight and as God knows the apostle's heart, he is preaching the Word of Christ in sincerity.

HOW DOES THIS APPLY TO US?

We must be sincere when we share the Word of God with others. It is especially important to avoid any impression that we are handling spiritual truth in order to gain material advantage. We received the grace of God in salvation as a gift. God's Word needs to be freely given as it is to be freely received. Our only profit should be the joy of knowing God's Word has brought light to a darkened soul. That's remuneration enough, more than enough.

We know God commends reasonable support for His servants that they might be able to "devote [themselves] to prayer and to the ministry of the word" (Acts 6:2-4; see also 1 Corinthians 9:11, 14). Yet it is equally important for Christians to know that all we say or do is in God's sight. Our whole life is under His constant review. Let this not only keep us sincere but let it also give us encouragement and guidance. The work is hard, the hours are long, the results are often not tangible. But if we "speak in Christ" and live for Christ and share His truth with others, "God sees us" and our compensation will come from Him. The pay is adequate and the fringe benefits, out of this world.

Pray with Me

Lord, how perfectly I am known and how constantly I am seen under Your wise and watchful eye. To be aware of this could bring fearfulness. Let it rather bring reverence. It could be a source of chafing resentment. Let it rather bring gratitude. And instead of impatience, let it find me calmly accepting.

My whole life is under Your constant review. My breakthroughs in righteousness are Your joy. My failures in sin are Your heartbreak. My steadfastness in the way of truth is Your pleasure. My weariness, overburdened with needless cares, is Your concern. You are always seeing. You are always caring.

It is also in Your sight that we "speak in Christ." You know when I speak for Him. You know when, with cowardly denial, I remain silent. You know when I endeavor to speak "in Christ" while living in ways that speak against Him. You know when I speak in pride and anger when I should be speaking in humility and forgiveness.

As You see me in Christ, so let me speak in Christ. As You enable me to speak in Christ, so let me live in Christ.

Continue doing Your gracious and patient work in my life until what You see and what I say and what I am may all be one. I ask for this to the praise of Your name and in the confidence of Your love.

Through Christ, my Lord, Amen.

MOVING ON IN THE LIFE OF PRAYER

Speak *to* Christ in prayer. Speak *in* Christ to others. When we speak to Christ about others, it will not be long before we are speaking to others about Christ—and God sees that. In prayer let us always be confident that God sees us and hears us and, when the love of Christ comes from our lips and shows in our lives, He will be pleased.

Day 136

OUR NEW NATURE, ONCE GIVEN, ALWAYS RENEWED

"And have put on the new nature, which is being renewed in knowledge after the image of its creator" (Colossians 3:10).

Read: **Colossians 3;** 2 Corinthians 5:17; Ephesians 4:24.

WHAT IS GOD SAYING?

The focus in Colossians is all on Jesus. Heresies to suit every taste were breaking out in Colossae like a virus, and the attack was weakening the body of believers. Believers, new in the faith, were being taught that angels should be worshiped, that

Jewish rituals should be added to the simple gospel, that Jesus the Man died but that Christ the Divine did not.

They needed a word then (the proliferation of cults in our day suggests that the word is still needed) that Christ is all and in all. He is the Head of the Church and the reason we labor for the Church (1:24). He gives us freedom from human regulations (2:8). He is the reason for and the power behind all holy living (3:1-25). He is the reason for praying, for preaching, and for godly conduct (4:2-5).

Paul reminds us of two things in the tenth verse of chapter 3. First, the new nature was given to us in the miracle of the new birth. Second, this new nature does not remain static, like a museum piece in a glass case. It is being renewed (growing) in knowledge after the image of its Creator. Since Christ is all and in all (3:11), everyone is included: Greek, Jew, slave, free, circumcised, and uncircumcised. All who have the new nature are being renewed.

HOW DOES THIS APPLY TO US?

In coming to prayer, we need to remember that the God who created is the God who recreates. God's gift of salvation is an act and a process. This is one thing that makes prayer so important. Prayer is based on "listening" to God. Prayer continues as we respond to what God has said. Prayer is having our lives renewed day by day through knowledge of the Word and after the image of its Creator, Jesus Christ, the Giver, the Pattern, and the Architect of the new life.

Pray with Me

God, almighty and all-loving, You created and You are always creating. I thank You for the awareness through Your Word and in the midst of life that the new nature which I once "put on" is still "being renewed."

"Create in me a clean heart, O God, and put a new and right spirit within me." Time and again it comes home to me, each time with the joy of a new discovery: the God who "creates" is the God who "renews." The gift of God is an act and a process, a goal attained and ground still being gained.

Knowing this, Lord, keeps me from discouragement and pride. When the Accuser points to persistent faults and taunts me with the memory of unkept promises, this assurance keeps me from discouragement. When I rest on victories won and look back on my achievements instead of forward to the fuller life You have promised, this assurance keeps me from pride.

It is wonderful to know that my walk with Christ began in the past but continues in the present. It is dynamic, not static. It grows while being grounded.

The Son, who is my Lord and my Savior, reflects the glory of God and bears the very stamp of His nature. Help me, at least in some measure, to become a reflection of His perfection. Help me to exemplify His patient love. Then the new nature which was given shall continue to become until that glorious day when, having finished the race, I shall enter the rest.

Until then I will rest in Your will. I will serve in Your strength. I will conquer in Your name. All the while I will keep on trusting that God who has begun a good work will surely bring it to completion at the day of Jesus Christ.

In whose Name I pray, Amen.

MOVING ON IN THE LIFE OF PRAYER

If our lives seem at a standstill, or as it was called in the old days of sailing vessels, "becalmed," we *can* experience spiritual renewal. The sails of our vessels can be filled with the winds of the Spirit. The first word for Spirit was *ruach*, "wind." Prayer is the act of lifting our sails by faith toward the sky even when there is not a whisper of a breeze stirring . . . and soon, we are moving, for Him. The new life grounded in Christ is the new life growing in Christ. Faith is the key to salvation. Prayer is the key to growth.

Day 137

THE ARM OF FLESH
VERSUS THE HAND OF GOD

" 'With him is an arm of flesh; but with us is the LORD our God, to help us and to fight our battles.' And the people took confidence from the words of Hezekiah king of Judah" (2 Chronicles 32:8).

Read: **2 Chronicles 32:1-24;** 2 Kings 6:15-17; Isaiah 51:12; 2 Corinthians 2:14.

WHAT IS GOD SAYING?

In 2 Chronicles there is good news and bad news. The bad news is that evil kings defied the sovereignty of God and turned their backs on His works and His love. The good news is that there were periods of revival under good kings who gave God the glory. They gave His laws an important place in their own lives and in the nation. Although the nation was "on the skids" toward captivity and humiliation, there were times when the pace slackened and the sun of righteousness broke through. You can count those kings on one hand! One of them was Hezekiah.

Sennacherib was at the gates of Jerusalem. Instead of turning over the keys of the city to this swaggering bully, Hezekiah repaired the walls and secured the water system for a long siege. Then, his own confidence in God convincingly real, he said to his people: " 'Be strong and courageous. Do not be afraid or discouraged because of the king of Assyria and the vast army with him. . . . With him is *only* the arm of flesh, but with us is the LORD our God to help us and to fight our battles' " (NIV).

HOW DOES THIS APPLY TO US?

The anxiety induced by a king from Assyria, with a great army poised and ready, bent on utter destruction and determined to administer humiliating defeat . . . well, that isn't our current problem. But we do have battles to wage.

It may be a personal moral conflict when the wrong seems easy and natural and the right calls for more strength than we can muster. It may be standing alone in a society that has relegated spiritual values to the limbo of non-essential trivia. It may be a family problem or a financial crisis brought on when we would not compromise our principles and personal integrity.

We have our battles. When we rely on human answers or draw upon human resources, we can experience discouragement, paralyzing helplessness, and fear that won't quit. We need to sort things out just as Hezekiah inspired his people to do on the strength of his own confidence. "The enemy is relying on the arm of flesh. But for us the way out to freedom, the way through to safety, the way up to victory is to trust in the power of God and let Him fight our battles."

Pray with Me

Eternal Father, strong to save, I want to rest in the words of faith spoken by Hezekiah. In such trust there is rest. When trust is in something or someone else, betrayal and fear must follow.

The arm of flesh has never truly delivered. Weapons of war, promises of physical aid, human alliances, and boastful pledges, even the strong resolves of honest moral endeavor must at some point yield. They will all be spent before the end is reached and true victory is won.

"But with us is the LORD our God to help us." How different! How completely different are these words. In them we can rest. They have never been spoken in vain. You are the Alpha and the Omega, the Beginning and the End. Before all trouble began and long after all trouble ends, You are God. I will rest in the assurance that underneath are the everlasting arms.

Forgive me for lack of trust and for moments of weakness and faithless panic. Too often I have tried to wage my battles trusting in an arm of the flesh. Overcome the struggles of pride. Conquer the turbulence of fears. Amend the errors of impetuous will.

Lead me to the place of quiet trust and humble faith. The battle I must fight may be moral conflict within or persistent evil without. Nevertheless I will rest in the knowledge that I am a citizen of Your realm and a child of Your family. So long as Your cause is my cause and Your honor my honor, so long will my battles be Your battles.

Lord, You are fighting my battles. How foolish I am when I do not rest. The final victory is Yours and the strength of Your presence all the way to that victory is mine.

In His Name whose ever-conquering grace is my never-failing strength, Amen.

Moving On in the Life of Prayer

Difficulties will arise and obstacles will be thrown across our paths almost every day. To find daily strength for daily problems read Isaiah 51:12-16. With continuing prayer, the arm of flesh against us is weakened and the help of God in fighting our battles becomes stronger. "Thanks be to God, who in Christ *always* leads us in triumph" (2 Corinthians 2:14).

Day 138

Set Free for Good Deeds

" . . . *So that those who have believed in God may be careful to apply themselves to good deeds*" (Titus 3:8).

Read: **Titus 3:1-11;** Matthew 5:16; 1 Timothy 6:18; 1 Peter 2:12.

What Is God Saying?

Titus was the bishop of Crete, not an easy task. But he was a seasoned veteran for this assignment. At Paul's request, he had dealt with the horrendous problems in Corinth. Paul calls Titus "my true son in our common faith" (NIV). He had proven his faithfulness to true doctrine and his ability to speak the truth in love. Now he has another great responsibility to "straighten out what was left unfinished [in Crete] and appoint elders in every town" (NIV).

In this letter Paul stresses the importance of good works. False teachers must be silenced. They claim to know God but by their actions they deny Him. Good deeds are not optional for the Christian. They are as inevitable as fruit growing on a vine. This is practical Christianity based on and flowing from salvation. Read especially Titus 3:4-8. That's the name of the game.

How Does This Apply to Us?

Saved *by* good works? Never. Saved *for* good works? Always. Prayer should open with gratitude to God because of our freedom from sin by His grace. It should then go on with steadfast desire to do good for others because of our freedom from sin and self. Salvation gives us liberty to help others. Salvation gives us the desire to do good and for the best reasons: love and gratitude. St. Augustine saw salvation in its true dimensions when he said:

"I would not work my soul to save,
   For that my Lord has done—
   But I would work like any slave
   For love of God's dear Son."

In prayer let us thank God we are free. Then let us lay out our plans for doing good. Let us ask God, who has set us free from sin, now to set us free for serving. Let us thank God that by His grace He has made us *good enough* to go to Heaven. Now let us ask God to help us do *enough good* on the way to Heaven.

Pray with Me

Believing in You, O God, brings freedom from care and anxiety. Believing in You, O God, is release from bondage and fear. "If the Son makes you free, you will be free indeed."

I don't need to do a certain amount of work for a certain amount of salvation. I am free from that! Faith in Your redeeming power and mercy can swing wide the gates of Heaven! I am glad to know that I don't have to climb back to the heights or crawl back into Your favor as a subdued prisoner. I don't have to "regain Paradise." It is done. It was finished, completely and forever, at Calvary.

Yet I would remember Your Word commands those who believe in God to "be careful to apply themselves to good deeds." To be free indeed is not to be free from deeds. Good deeds can never be the root of salvation, but they must be the fruit of salvation. Released from the carefulness of wondering *if* I am saved, I should assume the carefulness of working *because* I am saved.

Let Your mercy inspire me both to rest on Your promises and to labor in Your vineyard. I am "carefree" because You have been good to me. Now help me to be carefree in goodness that extends to others. Forgive me, Lord, that I have been so often willing merely to consider good deeds and so often unwilling to apply myself to good deeds. Help me to apply myself with carefulness to good deeds, not for my credit and not to my praise, but in thankfulness to Him who has rid my heart forever of every care.

In the Name of Jesus Christ, my Lord, Amen.

MOVING ON IN THE LIFE OF PRAYER

The best way to move on in the life of prayer is to move out in the life of service. The more we show the love of God to others, the more we feel free to claim the continual blessings of His love for ourselves. Prayer is a channel of blessings and not a reservoir. We may take in all we want. We must give out all we can. The Source will never run dry. Pray boldly. Serve faithfully. Live joyously. It *is* more blessed to give than to receive.

Day 139

FROM DEATH IN SIN TO LIFE IN GOD

"For this is why the gospel was preached even to the dead, that though judged in the flesh like men, they might live in the spirit like God" *(1 Peter 4:6).*

Read: **1 Peter 4;** Proverbs 21:16; John 5:24; Ephesians 2:1; 1 John 3:14; Romans 12:2.

WHAT IS GOD SAYING?

Our highlighted verse is found in a passage that is difficult to understand and hard to explain. There are many possible interpretations. Trying to discover the meaning of this passage has carried many sincere thinkers far afield. They have built doctrines based solely on this text which are sharply at odds with the central truth of the gospel. "Preaching to the dead" becomes the debatable point. Is there a second chance? Does this verse prove the doctrine of purgatory? Is there universal salvation? These are the extremes which surface in the troubled waters of heated debate.

The simplest explanation may well be the best one. Jesus *did* preach to the dead. He preached to us when we were "dead": dead in trespasses and sins; dead to the call of God; dead to life set free from all bondage; though living, dead to everything worthwhile. However else this passage may be interpreted, it does have a bearing on those who are dead to the things of God. Christians are free from living in godless ways.

How Does This Apply to Us?

Those who see prayer as a door to blessing and a way of blessing must lay hold of one great fact contained in 1 Peter 4:6: We *can* live in the Spirit like God. Can we think of a greater destiny? Impossible as it sounds, living like God in the Spirit is the plan God has for all Christians. It is the meaning of the gospel. It is the ultimate purpose of the gospel. In the opening verses of his second letter, Peter states it so clearly: "His divine power has granted to us all things that pertain to life and godliness . . . that through these you may *escape* from the corruption that is in the world because of passion, and become partakers of the divine nature" (2 Peter 1:3-4). We were created in the image of God. We can be recreated to live in the Spirit like God. Prayer sets us free from the clamorings of the flesh. Prayer lets us freely ask for and abundantly receive the blessings of the Spirit.

Pray with Me

Heavenly Father, You are the God of salvation. You are the Lord of infinite mercy. You are the Spirit always present and always renewing. I bow in wonder and thanksgiving before the power of the gospel.

The gospel was not only preached to me but by Your grace it reached to me. Not only has it reached me in my spiritual slumber, it has revived me. It has awakened me to the joys of living in and for Christ. It has shown me Your judgment upon all that is contrary to life in the passions of the flesh. Beyond that it has given me the power to live in the Spirit. For the power of the gospel, my only pride, I thank You.

I would go on to a fuller appreciation of why it was preached even to me, even to the dead. "That though judged in the flesh like men, they might live in the spirit like God." Lead me, Spirit of God, away from those things upon which God's judgment must fall. Guide me into the way everlasting where I shall love all that God loves, allow all that God allows, and bless all that God blesses.

To "live in the spirit like God" seems far beyond my capacity. It is. But, Lord, confirm in me the assurance that such living is possible. It is even inevitable, when "it is no longer I who live, but Christ who lives in me." Lead me from false humility that unintentionally casts a doubt on Your greatness by suggesting that I cannot "live in the spirit like God." To doubt this is to doubt You.

Let Your truth light all my path. Let Your love prompt all my thoughts. Let Your life fill all my being.

In the Name of Him whose strength is made perfect in my weakness, Amen.

MOVING ON IN THE LIFE OF PRAYER

Let us not be conformed to this world but rather transformed (steadily, constantly, daily, hourly) by the renewal of our minds. That is the way to tap into the abundance of God's love and the endless blessings he would have us enjoy. When our hearts and our hands are not filled with hollow substitutes, God can fill them with the real thing. Keep on praying. Keep on saying what you want. But, best of all, keep on discovering what *God* wants.

Day 140

REJOICING IN GOD'S SALVATION

"My heart shall rejoice in thy salvation" (Psalm 13:5b).

Read: **Psalm 13;** 1 Samuel 2:1; Matthew 2:10; Acts 8:39; Romans 5:2.

WHAT IS GOD SAYING?

This psalm deals with some heavy things, such as "pain in my soul," "sorrow in my heart," being forgotten by God, losing out to an enemy who crows about it. It also shows the afflicted reader where to turn. It points out a greater kind of rejoicing and for a better reason. "My heart shall rejoice in thy salvation." Our salvation is good reason to rejoice. Hannah rejoiced because of salvation in a song that Mary echoed when Jesus was born and salvation had come. The magi rejoiced when they saw the star that led them to the infant Jesus and salvation (Matthew 2:10). The Ethiopian eunuch rejoiced in the discovery of salvation through Philip's ministry of the Word (Acts 8:39). Christians rejoice in hope and even in suffering since they have peace with God (Romans 5:2-3).

HOW DOES THIS APPLY TO US?

Rejoicing and salvation belong together. The coming of Jesus into this world can never be a matter of academic aloofness or objective study. Because it is real and because it means so much it goes right to the heart to make it leap with joy. It is the emotion felt when a woman finds a lost coin or a shepherd finds a lost sheep or a waiting Father sees his lost son on the horizon (read Luke 15). It is not like a student poring over a book in the library. It is more like a student with a thousand others, rejoicing over a touchdown on the field. It is like oil drillers watching their first wild fountain of black gold after days of hard and fruitless labor. It is a soldier seeing a light in the window or a returning prisoner finding yellow ribbons tied all over the tree. In prayer let us remember all the joy we have drawn from the wells of salvation. It should make quite a list.

Pray with Me

O God, it was in Your loving heart that my salvation was conceived. It was by Your boundless mercy that Jesus Christ came to make my salvation a reality. I am sorry that I so often regard Your greatest gift with academic interest. I am grateful for it with my mind but in my heart there is, sometimes, apathy.

Heaven is mine for nothing except the bringing of a broken and contrite heart. Sin, both its stain on my life and its reign in my heart, is removed in a moment of faith. Doubt that makes every step a cautious and fearful one is replaced by a vision of Your holy will and perfect plan. Death, swaggering colossus on the journey of everyman's life, lies defeated and impotent in the glory of one resurrection morning.

All this is "Thy salvation." All this is Your salvation for me, as if I alone were the special object of Your redeeming grace. Yet the infinite sacrifice of Christ is also for anyone, anywhere, who believes on His name. "Thy salvation" can be shared as water flowing freely and endlessly from the eternal spring of divine love.

If this is not reason to rejoice, if this is not reason to live in glad triumph over all the powers of darkness, if this is not reason to live continuously above the sad confusion and turmoil of meaningless existence, then Your patient love has knocked in vain on the doors of my heart and the Redeemer has never returned from the rock-sealed tomb, and all faith is grounded on history's cruelest lie.

But Deep *has* called unto deep. Love *has* awakened love. His life from the dead *has* meant my life from the dead. I may, I should, I "shall rejoice in thy salvation."

Through Him who intended us to possess His joy, and to possess it fully, Amen.

MOVING ON IN THE LIFE OF PRAYER

We begin and keep moving on in prayer by taking constant inventory of the blessings that stem from *salvation*: having sins forgiven, off-loading guilt, getting ourselves off our hands and being free to love one another, being free to bring another to the throne of grace, having peace with God and the peace of God, being privileged to become an instrument of God's peace, living fully now, and having bright hope for tomorrow. As we rejoice in God's salvation we will be able to rejoice in everything else that has value: true beauty, beautiful truths, unhampered joy in the best things of life, goodness that is not stuffy, hope that will never let us down, and all other good things from the hand of God.

Day 141

FINDING THE COURAGE TO SPEAK

"And the Lord said to Paul one night in a vision: 'Do not be afraid, but speak and do not be silent; for I am with you' " (Acts 18:9-10).

Read: **Acts 18:1-17**; Jeremiah 1:6-8, 17; Ezekiel 2:5-7; Acts 5:20.

WHAT IS GOD SAYING?

Paul was always at the battlefront. He didn't wait until all the conditions were favorable before giving testimony to his faith. That is why the battle-weary soldier has so many Purple Hearts. Read 2 Corinthians 11:23-29. In this instance, while there were many who responded to his earnest message, there were others who wanted him out of the synagogue. The Jews were offended and became so abusive that Paul left. What was he going to do? It was one of the many crisis moments in Paul's life. It was a crossroads.

He wouldn't give up. That was out of the question. But could he do his best here? As it turned out, Paul spent a year and half in Corinth teaching the Word of God. The reason: In a vision the Lord spoke and in obedience and trust Paul obeyed. "And the Lord said to Paul one night in a vision, 'Do not be afraid, but speak and do not be silent; for I am with you, and no man shall attack you to harm you; for I have many people in this city."

HOW DOES THIS APPLY TO US?

What makes us afraid to speak when it is most necessary? Do we want to please men—or God? When God gives the command to speak, He will supply the words to speak. Remember the words of Jesus? "When they deliver you up, do not be anxious how you are to speak or what you are to say; for what you are to say will be given to you in that hour; for it is not you who speak, but the Spirit of your Father speaking through you."

Many are afraid to speak. Afraid that we might say the wrong thing and in the wrong way; afraid that when it comes out, it will sound silly; afraid that what we say will be taken wrong; afraid that we will lose a friend.

The best antidote for fear is a fervent love: love of God and love for others. "Perfect *love* casts out fear," especially the fear of speaking out the truth about how much God loves the world. If anything should unseal our lips and make us eager to speak, it is that. But it isn't always easy. Sometimes in love we must speak truth that hurts, truth that has to hurt if it is going to help. To say the hard word when it would be easier to be silent, we need extra help. That help comes from knowing that God has promised to be with us. When we need courage to speak, we can call upon the Lord to be with us. That is what changes fearful and hesitant testimony into glad and confident sharing.

Pray with Me

Your presence—Your constant, conquering, comforting presence—is the secret of fearless testimony. Teach me to trust in that fact every moment. Help me not to look around for anything else to prop me up. I will receive the encouragement to speak by Your presence. By Your presence I will even receive the words to speak. "Do not be silent; for I am with you."

Yes, Lord, I have found this to be true. It is fear that seals my lips but faith that opens them. It is fear that makes me stammer but faith that makes me stand. It is fear that makes me stumble but faith that makes me strong. It is fear that makes me a coward but faith that makes me a conqueror. "Do not be afraid, but speak."

Lord, in Your perfect love cast out all fear. Why should I be afraid to offer a remedy? Why should I hesitate about bringing someone good news? Why should I hold back from telling someone in pain and distress that there is a solution? Why should I be timid about turning men's thoughts toward You that they may find perfect and permanent peace? Why should I falter in speaking about a Savior and a friend who invites all of us to leave the ways of darkness and death, and love the ways of light and life? Why should I be silent when to speak is to bless? Why?

I can think of only one reason. I have not always been aware of Your presence. I have not always appreciated Your presence. I have not always wanted Your presence.

Come to me in the beauty and strength of the risen Christ, O God, and ever abide. Then I will put aside all frightened silence and receive the gift of enlightened speech.

To the glory of Jesus Christ, Your living, perfect, eloquent Word, Amen.

MOVING ON IN THE LIFE OF PRAYER

Pray for a more constant awareness of God's presence. He is always with us: in the post office, in the bank, at a service club, in a Sunday school class. Always, yes, always God hears the inaudible prayer. But others need to learn of His love through audible words fearlessly spoken and through the convincing evidence of a consistent life. His love gives us the reason to speak. His presence gives us the power to speak.

Day 142

THANKS FOR THE MEMORY

"I thank my God in all my remembrance of you" (Philippians 1:3).

Read: **Philippians 1;** Colossians 1:12; Acts 28:15; 1 John 1:7.

WHAT IS GOD SAYING?

Philippians is a letter without shadows. It is all rejoicing, all light, all thankfulness, all good memories. There are no heresies to be put to rest. There are no personal conflicts except a reference to a minor disagreement between Euodia and Synteche, and even this closes with the assurance that *their* names are in the book of life. And then, following immediately, "Rejoice in the Lord always; again I will say, Rejoice."

This letter rises out of the deep affection Paul had for the Christians who were the first to meet him when he brought the gospel to Europe. It was a "giant step" for Paul and he always had a special thankfulness in his heart as he remembered these people. He was thankful for their partnership in the gospel from the first day until now. He cannot remember them without being thankful (1:5). He cannot pray for them without joy (1:4).

HOW DOES THIS APPLY TO US?

Paul had special people in mind because God had sent them into his life to meet special needs. It is possible to have hearts filled with the love of God for all the world. It is also inevitable that some people should rise to the top of our grateful memories. We don't love others less because we love these others more. Love embraces all. But God, in His mercy, allows us to be especially close to certain people in whose face we have seen the joy of the Lord and from whose lives there has flowed the goodness of the Lord. It is not wrong to come to the Lord in prayer with thankfulness for special people. It is not wrong. It is all right.

Pray with Me

Dear Lord, when I am thankful, I remember. When I remember, I am thankful.

Only the proud and thankless heart can forget. You have filled my heart with Your goodness. Through all my days I have known either the cleansing grace of Your sunshine or the refreshing mercy of Your rain. I have never awakened to a day, however dreary its prospect, when I have not seen evidence of Your love. I have never come upon a day, however burdensome its duties, when Your strength has not surged into my being. Your love is brought to my remembrance when I am quiet in prayer, when I am busy with good and happy chores, and when I listen again to Your beautiful, reassuring promise, "Lo, I am with you always."

But Lord, I also remember the blessings which are mine because of others. "I thank my God in all my remembrance" of parents who cared for my needs before I could respond to either them or You. I thank You for their sacrifices and for their confidence that seeds which they planted would bear fruit.

"I thank my God in all my remembrance" of friends who have remembered me in prayer and sustained me by counsel. I thank You for their loyalty when others might have given up and for their understanding when the better self was slow to surface.

"I thank my God in all my remembrance" of wife and children whose response in human love gives meaning to life's most tender and beautiful relationships. I thank You for their patience in the face of unintended wrong and for their optimism in the running tide of hardship.

For all that I have because I have You, I would remember to be thankful. For all that I have because You have showered Your love on me through others, I would remember to be thankful. And above all, for all that I have because of Your unspeakable Gift, Jesus Christ my Lord, I would remember to be thankful.

To His glory, my praise; in His Name, my prayer, Amen.

MOVING ON IN THE LIFE OF PRAYER

If we count the blessings that have come to us through the faithfulness and love of others we will have the stuff of which real prayers are made. Let us thank God every time we remember what someone means to us because God sent him or her to help with the load, to cheer our spirits, or to shed some light along our path. That will keep us busy in the exercise of prayer. It will also make prayer for us what is was for Paul: "*always* in *every* prayer . . . with joy" (1:4). Prayer was never a drag to Paul. It doesn't need to be for us.

Day 143

GOD IS KNOWN TO MEN THROUGH MEN

" *'I will open your lips among them. Then they will know that I am the LORD'* " *(Ezekiel 29:21).*

Read: **Ezekiel 29;** Luke 21:12-19; 1 Corinthians 1:4-9; 2 Corinthians 8:7; Colossians 4:3-4.

WHAT IS GOD SAYING?

In this section of his prophecy, Ezekiel is declaring the judgment of God against the nations who had evil plans against Israel. The judgment of God against nations who have been a curse to Israel has been going on ever since He first let it be known that "I will bless those who bless you, and him who curses you I will curse" (Genesis 12:3). Egypt was to be next as it became dust beneath the feet of Nebuchadnezzar, king of Babylon (Ezekiel 29:19). The fate of anti-Israel forces has a modern ring to it, as well. Take, for example, the fall of the Third Reich. No nation can touch Israel without getting burned. That's history.

Ezekiel had a hard commission, however. He must "set [his] face against Pharaoh king of Egypt, and prophesy against him and against all Egypt." This assignment would rate as high on the popularity scale as telling a striking union that no raise would be coming their way. But it needed to be said. "I will make a horn grow ["horn" symbolizes strength] for the house of Israel" (29:21, NIV). Tell Egypt that for all their boasted strength, "I will make the land . . . a ruin and a desolate waste" (29:10, NIV). Not easy, Ezekiel, but you must do it. Then they will learn that I am the Lord.

How Does This Apply to Us?

Who is in need of words from *our* open lips to learn the truth of God's judgment? Who is weary of the struggle and in need of the strengthening grace of God's Word from *our* open lips? Who is lost and needs to find the way with direction from *our* open lips? Who is at the end of his or her rope and needs to hear from *our* open lips that God still cares and that "man's extremity is God's opportunity"?

Our lips should be open with clarity and they need even more to be open with charity. All this is in order that others may know that God is the Lord and there is no other. Our lips should be open in order that others may know Him, whom to know is life eternal. Let us pray that God will set a guard over our mouth and keep watch over the door of our lips (Psalm 141:3) that they may speak of love not pride, of hope not fear, and of conviction not compromise. Lord, open our lips for all the right reasons, but also keep them closed for all the right reasons.

Pray with Me

Loving Lord, You have chosen to make Yourself known to men through men. May I be counted worthy to be one whose lips are open among men for You.

Open my lips that I may speak of truth and power. Open my lips that I may speak of love with persuasiveness that comes from real experience. Open my lips that I may lift the discouraged and cheer the sad. Open my lips that I may warn the wicked, awaken the slumbering, and enlighten the ignorant.

Sometimes my lips are opened by pride and fear. Sometimes I have complained when I should have praised. Sometimes I have not spoken the whole truth for fear that it might affect my own comfortable pattern of life. Sometimes I have taken to verbal sparring with those who have touched the quick of my pride. Sometimes I have been quick to retaliate when selfish interests were disturbed. In all those ways and more, the evil one has opened my lips. I know this and I confess my weakness.

From now on, Lord of my life, be in a special way the Lord of my lips. Open them to speak with courage. Open them to speak with conviction. Open them to speak with clarity. Open them to speak with love.

Let the opening of my lips always have the effect of making You known. Let not the reflection of Your truth and love be disturbed by hasty speech or cowardly silence. As a pebble can mar the whole surface of a pool, so the single word that is not "fitly spoken" may keep someone from knowing that You are the Lord.

Set a guard upon my lips. Let them be closed when to speak would bring shame to my Master. Let them be open when to keep silent would keep Your glory from men. Make and keep my heart so right with You that my lips will never be open except to bless and never be closed when they can speak of Your love to others.

For the sake of His glory who is the Lord of my life—and lips, Amen.

MOVING ON IN THE LIFE OF PRAYER

We pray in order that we may know when our lips should be open to be a blessing or closed for the same reason. The warning of James is to the point, "From the same mouth come blessing and cursing. My brethren, this ought not to be so" (James 3:10). Prayer helps us to see that it doesn't happen. When our hearts form words in prayer for the blessing of others, they are not likely to do anything else when they are open in daily conversation. This, too, is the power and the purpose of prayer.

Day 144

JESUS IS NEAR . . . IN THE MORNING WE'LL SEE

"Just as day was breaking, Jesus stood on the beach" (John 21:4).

Read: **John 21;** Luke 5:1-7; John 14:18, 17:24; Psalm 30:5; Hebrews 13:5.

WHAT IS GOD SAYING?

The crucifixion was over. Christ was buried. The chapter was closed. His disciples waited until the third out in the bottom of the ninth inning. And then Peter, always the first to put into words his feelings, always the first to get moving, said, "I'm going fishing. That's my job and how better can I take my mind off this sad turn of events?" It was failure there, too. They toiled all night long and caught nothing. Things were bad all over!

But as dawn brightened the sky to the east, the shoreline to the north became distinguishable from the water, and then— what is that?—a form, not a post, not a shadow, not a piece of driftwood but a form, a person, a person with a voice. It said: "Throw your net on the right side of the boat." John, who seldom spoke until he was sure, was the first to realize it. "Peter, it is the Lord!" After the long and frustrating night, Jesus was there, waiting on the beach. Glad reunion. Hope restored. Life worth living again.

HOW DOES THIS APPLY TO US?

We have all had sleepless nights. Fears are exaggerated. Problems mount up. Crazy solutions float across our minds and few of them can stand the light of day. Wakeful nights can be so long and so lonely. We know the problem. The disciples knew it too. Their hope was at its lowest ebb and all their accustomed labor had proved useless. They found little comfort in their activity and no fish in their nets. *But* they found Jesus waiting on the beach at daybreak. He was *already* there. He had words that changed the fruitless night into a miracle of plenty.

So He can deal with despondency and pointless labor in our lives. He can do it and He will. He is standing on the shore at daybreak. Trust in that through the night. "Weeping may tarry for the night, but joy comes with the morning" (Psalm 30:5).

Pray with Me

Lord, I have known sleepless nights. I have known times when labor seemed all in vain. I know what it means to go through motions that seem pointless. Fishing in empty waters, I have become discouraged. Discouraged, I have grown tired. But I have never known a night so long and so dark that it did not, at last, yield to dawn.

When such nights come, O Lord, teach me to wait on You. May I have the faith of the psalmist who sang: "My soul waits for the LORD more than watchmen for the morning." May I have the reward of Peter, who "just as day was breaking" saw Jesus standing on the beach.

Waiting for the Lord, let me discover He is waiting for me. After the darkness of night, beyond all restless waves, and through the morning haze, He will be there, always and dependably and patiently there.

"Just as day was breaking . . . ," Lord, when I become aware of Your constant presence, that is the breaking of day even in the middle of the night. To be aware of Your presence, O Sun of righteousness, is to live in perpetual day. The fears and fruitless labors of doubt's dark night are only mine when I take my eyes away from the reality of Your risen glory.

Let my life be forever lived on the margin of dawn. I would always be looking toward Jesus. Simply and abundantly I will be blessed with the joy of His presence. Then I will bring those who doubt to the Savior's living presence. I will bring the discouraged to the bright dawn of faith.

When Jesus stood on the beach, He was waiting for those He loved to come to Him. He is waiting for me. At the breaking of day, I come.

In the Name of Him whom to know is to possess the dew-spangled freshness and the rain-washed fragrance of God's "Good Morning," Amen.

Moving On in the Life of Prayer

Prayer is coming to Jesus in the assurance that He is waiting for us. He is waiting to bless us with encouragement and instruction as He did for those who had worked all night in vain. Our prayer may be in the midst of trial, when it is nighttime in our souls. Fear stalks like animated shadows. Discouragement weighs down our spirits. Doubt surrounds us as an impenetrable fog. Nevertheless, on the beach Jesus is waiting. Whatever time it is, in prayer, day is already breaking. With the coming of daybreak, Jesus is there. When Jesus is there, daybreak has already come. We can pray at any time. With the Lord, it is always the break of day.

Day 145

POOR IN THE WORLD; RICH IN FAITH

"Has not God chosen those who are poor in the world to be rich in faith and heirs of the kingdom which he has promised to those who love him?" (James 2:5).

Read: **James 2;** Proverbs 22:22; Deuteronomy 7:6-8; Psalm 4:8; 1 Corinthians 1:26-29.

What Is God Saying?

Faith and works belong together as roots belong to fruit trees. We are grateful to James for helping us keep the balance. Concerning Abraham whose faith was reckoned to him as righteousness (2:23), he also says, "Faith was active along with his works, and faith was completed by works" (2:22). The author gives another analogy at the end of this chapter: "For as the body apart from the spirit is dead, so faith apart from works is dead" (2:26).

James does not take away the all-essential quality of faith as the sole source of salvation. He simply says that faith, when it

does not result in works, is not real in the first place. In fact, it's
dead. One of the areas in which faith should be evidenced by
works has to do with showing favoritism to the rich and neglect
to the poor. Faith shows its good works by being impartial to
everyone. That is why James writes at the opening of the chapter, "Show no partiality as you hold the faith of our Lord Jesus
Christ, the Lord of glory" (2:1). To show partiality is to commit
sin (2:9).

HOW DOES THIS APPLY TO US?

While the purpose of James is to show the sinfulness of
partiality, James 2:5 has a penetrating message that can be
applied to every Christian, rich or poor. To be poor in the world
is not to be deprived of the riches that count. To be rich in the
world does not necessarily mean to be poor in faith. It is only
harder to be rich in things *and* rich in faith. But all are heirs of
the kingdom which is promised, not to those who are poor or to
those who are rich, but to *those who love God.*

Thank God the promised kingdom does not depend on
our status in the world or the accounts we have in the bank. It
does depend on the reality or the riches of our faith. But we
need to guard against the deceitfulness of riches: "The cares of
the world and the delight in riches choke the word, and it
proves unfruitful" (Matthew 13:22). Let us all decide (if the
choice must be made) that we would rather be poor in the
world and rich in faith—and not the other way around.

Pray with Me

Thank You, Lord, for the discovery that to be chosen by
You is to be rich because of You. I have been blessed more than
most in the riches of the world. But when and if the choice must
come, I would rather be poor in the world and rich in faith than
to be rich in the world and poor in faith.

I will not fear the loss of position nor chafe when my
personal prestige is imperiled. As Yours is the kingdom so mine
is the kingdom. It is a gift of Your love to me and a sure reward
of my love to You.

I thank You, Lord, for the strength of those words *chosen*
and *promised.* Here are the facts which the best bliss of earth
cannot dim nor the strongest whispers of doubt erase.

"Chosen . . . to be . . . heirs of the kingdom which [You
have] promised." I am chosen and the kingdom is promised. As
surely as the kingdom is promised, just as surely am I chosen.
The same wonderful, omnipotent God has done both.

But for my part, Lord, let there be a willingness to be poor
in the world. Nothing will displace my love for You. When I seek

the riches of this world, I am weighted down with its cares. When I seek its honors and praises, my hope is set on something less than the glory that God gives and shares. When I crave its securities and its comforts, I am trusting in something less than Your inexhaustible riches in Christ. When I am surfeited with its pleasures, my love for You grows weak and faith seems to be a useless relic.

Refresh my heart with the boldness of Your promises. Let no temptation remove my zest for the kingdom. Let me see how surely the riches of this world pass away. Let me see how eternally Your kingdom of love and peace survives.

I have been chosen for what You have promised. I choose to love You for all You have done, for all that You are, and for all that will be mine as an heir of Your kingdom.

In the Name of Him through whose poverty I am rich, Amen.

MOVING ON IN THE LIFE OF PRAYER

We must keep in mind that we are heirs of the kingdom God has promised to those who love Him. In prayer our renewal of love toward God should be constantly in our thoughts. On the human level, those who are in love cannot say it too much. Toward our Father and Jesus, our loving Shepherd, we can certainly not say it too often. Our minds should turn regularly to all the promises of God. But more often than any other, let us rejoice that we are heirs of the kingdom. The riches of this world *all* pass away. The riches of the kingdom last forever and should be the greatest reason for our continuing thanksgiving and rejoicing in the life of prayer.

Day 146

HANDING DOWN THE FAITH

"And you, Solomon my son, know the God of your father, and serve him with a whole heart and with a willing mind" (1 Chronicles 28:9).

Read: **1 Chronicles 28;** Hosea 6:3; John 23:24; Acts 17:27; 3 John 4.

WHAT IS GOD SAYING?

David was nearing the end of his long reign, getting ready to pass on the responsibility of leadership to Solomon. In verses 4 through 10 he shares with his son his deepest secret. They are the words of a conscientious father to a promising son. And they can be the substance of a heartfelt message from any Christian father and mother who want the best for their sons and daughters. It is a forerunner of those touching words John spoke near the end of his life: "No greater joy can I have than this, to hear that my children follow the truth" (3 John 4). "Solomon my son, know the God of your father and serve him with a whole heart and with a willing mind."

HOW DOES THIS APPLY TO US?

How many parents there are who have known and walked with God, failures notwithstanding, in paths of righteousness! What better heritage could they leave, what better quality of life could they hope to see continued, than that their children would know the God of their fathers and mothers? They can pass on jewelry, the deed to a house, ownership of a business, equal shares of an estate. There are so many things that are worthwhile, but none approaches the importance of knowing the God of their fathers.

Since that is the best thing we can pass on to our children, it is of supreme importance that it comes to them without a blemish or breakage or loss. We must make sure that our children *want* to know the God of their fathers. What do they see in our lives that makes the option of knowing God the most attractive item on the agenda, the most important treasure in the inventory? Is it possible that the parents' reflection of God is blurred or distorted? Do they ever sense that knowing our God and serving Him with a whole heart and with a willing mind wasn't really all that important to us? That's how this passage applies to us, and the true reflection of God's love and goodness to our children should be the highest thing on our list of priorities in prayer.

Pray with Me

God of my fathers and my God, I thank You for the faith triumphant and the knowledge of Your love which have come to me because those who went before served You with a "whole heart and a willing mind."

Help me to see that I am a link in the chain. I have no choice. I may be a good link or a bad one. I will pass along some impression of the importance of faith. It will be true or false, strong or weak, convincing or confusing. But it will be something.

Lord, I want to turn to my sons and to others and say without embarrassment, "and you, my son, know the God of your father." May they want to know the God of their father because they see that knowing God has done something worthwhile for him. May they want to know the God of their father because they see that knowing God has brought meaning into their father's life. From the springs of such deep, clear knowing will flow the service of a whole heart and a willing mind.

O Lord, let there be nothing in me that would keep others, especially those who are younger, from knowing You and serving You. If there is a root of disobedience or faithless doubt that would keep me from the service of a whole heart and a willing mind, remove it. Remove it now. Remove it completely. Remove it forever. If there is just a crack in the surface of my devotion to You, heal it by the touch of Your transforming grace.

Then, with convincing confidence, I will turn to others and say, more by my life than by my lips, "know the God of your father, and serve him with a whole heart and with a willing mind."

For the sake of Him who has made God the Father perfectly known and whose own life inspires the service of the whole heart and the willing mind, even Christ my Lord, Amen.

MOVING ON IN THE LIFE OF PRAYER

Prayer should always focus on how our lives are being read by others. Are there things in our lives that should be changed or removed so that our profession becomes believable? This is truly a matter of prayer with regard to the impact of our life on all others. But it is supremely essential that we pray about the effect it is having on the best earthly gifts that God has given to us, our children. This alone would keep us moving on in the life of prayer.

Day 147

CLOSER THAN A BROTHER

"False brethren . . . slipped in . . . that they might bring us into bondage" (Galatians 2:4).

Read: **Galatians 2;** Acts 15:1-4; Proverbs 18:24; John 15:15.

WHAT IS GOD SAYING?

The cornerstone text of Galatians is, "Stand fast therefore in the liberty wherewith Christ hath made us free" (5:1, KJV). Today's highlighted verse refers to "false brothers." These were Jewish teachers who had come into Galatia, a rural district without many scholars. They were doing their best to convince relatively unschooled people that if Christianity had any validity at all, it should not do away with the rite of circumcision and the works of the law. In other words, if the Jewish converts had found some hope in the message of salvation by faith in Jesus Christ, it was wrong to circumvent the ancient traditions and laws, the very thing that made them Jews. They were becoming Jewish *Christians*, but in doing so they should and must remain *Jewish* Christians.

The seedbed of Christianity is undeniably Jewish. But to insist on a continuing bondage to the Law, observing a religion of works, would be like spraying a deadly herbicide on the tender shoots of freedom. Those who taught that one has to be *first* Jewish and *then* Christian were, indeed, false brothers.

How Does This Apply to Us?

Our intent in listening to Paul's advice concerning false brothers is to contrast those who would bring men into bondage with Jesus Christ, the "True Brother." Our loving Savior leads men into freedom; away from the bondage of sin, away from the minute observance of laws and ceremonies as the means of salvation, to the acceptance of what God made possible in His unspeakable Gift. Salvation is made possible by what God has done, not by what we must do.

There are all kinds of false brothers who would lead us away from the goodness given, the joy bestowed, and the victory won in Jesus Christ. This makes us cleave all the more closely to the Brother, the Friend, the Lord who is true. We have all kinds of "true-false" choices to make in the course of our lifetime, but none is more important than that of knowing who is our True Friend "who sticks closer than a brother" and who are our false friends and brothers who would lead us away from the freedom so dearly bought in Christ's atoning death.

Pray with Me

Dear Lord, when there are so many brothers who are false, I am thankful for Jesus Christ, the Brother who is true. He is far more than a Brother, but he is truly a Brother. By grace that I cannot comprehend, I have been made joint-heir with Him of Heaven's treasures.

Brother Christ, how true You have been and are! You have loved my soul. You have conquered my passions. You have subdued my will. You have pardoned my sin. Through the holy presence of the Comforter, You have cleansed my heart from deep-festering injuries and strong-rooted disloyalties.

You have won for me independence from the agony of self-accusation. You have opened to me a door into the fold of Your own love where I have both freedom and safety. From the sad, dark bondage of the past into the glad, bright freedom of the present, You are leading, always leading.

I claim the love of One who sticks "closer than a brother." I believe in that love. I lean upon it. I live by its power. I walk in its joyous hope.

Because the love of my true Brother is so real, I can recognize and resist "false brethren" who would lead me back into bondage. My true Brother brought me to freedom. False brethren are powerless to trap my conscience in little laws I have broken or in stuffy traditions I have failed to keep.

My true Brother holds me to Himself in holy and life-transforming love. Therefore I will not yield to the tempting voice of false brethren who would lead me into the snares of impurity and into the bondage of lust.

Lord of life, true Brother, kindest Friend—draw me to Your side by the beauty of Your holiness. In the joy of Your freedom so dearly bought on Calvary, keep me from the bondage into which false brethren would lead me.

For the sake of Your own glory, O Christ, hear this prayer and assure me of Your saving presence, Amen.

MOVING ON IN THE LIFE OF PRAYER

The false in life slips in. It seldom knocks at the front door. It finds an unsecured door or a slightly open window, then quietly, surreptitiously, it slips in. Our main thrust in the continual and growing life of prayer is to let Jesus in at the front door and to see that all other doors and windows have their alarm system in the "on" position. Let us stand fast in the freedom and pray fervently in the joy that is ours in Christ.

Day 148

FIGHTING THE RIGHT BATTLES

"... *For the LORD will certainly make my lord a sure house, because my lord is fighting the battles of the LORD*" (1 Samuel 25:28).

Read: **1 Samuel 25:1-44;** Psalm 40:2; Isaiah 54:14; Colossians 2:6; 2 Thessalonians 2:17.

WHAT IS GOD SAYING?

Abigail was the wife of Nabal. His name means "fool" and he lived up (or down) to his name. David had come to him with overtures of peace. Nabal, playing the fool, answered the good-will gesture with defiance and caused David to answer him with the threat of force. This would have accomplished little for

David except the immediate and brief satisfaction of revenge. It was the wrong battle for the wrong reasons.

Abigail made her way secretly to David, hoping to appease his mounting anger and prevent him from doing something he would later regret. Going through with his plan would cause only suffering to all concerned. She persuaded David that the kind of getting even he was planning was beneath his dignity. The beauty of her person, the strength of her character, the plausibility of her argument all impressed David. He said, "You are right. Praise the Lord, your good judgment has kept me from engaging in this petty skirmish. It would have done no good and much harm. May you be blessed for your good judgment."

As it turned out, Nabal's life was to be gone within hours. God fought the battle in the right way and at the right time. Only Nabal, the fool, was taken and David was spared the needless cost of a quick and pointless revenge. In a tender sequel to this aborted vendetta, Abigail became David's wife.

How Does This Apply to Us?

As David was dissuaded from fighting in the wrong way for the wrong reason, so let us be led of the Holy Spirit to fight in the right way for the right reasons. Find out what God is for and get on that side. Find out what God is against and join the attack. In prayer we can sort this out. In prayer we can see which side needs our support. In prayer we can make the strong, wise, quiet decision to be counted on the side for good and love and peace. In prayer we can find the strength to be counter to evil and hatred and revenge.

Pray with Me

Lord, as Abigail persuaded David not to fight in the wrong way and for the wrong reasons, so let Your Holy Spirit guide me into fighting in the right way for the right reasons.

I claim this promise from the distant past. It will be a reality for me in the living present. When I stand with the Lord against the enemies of the Lord, I am secure. May I never fear for my own security or for that of my house so long as I am engaged in the cause of my Master. He is most secure who for the sake of the Lord is most willing to give up security. It is in waging the battle that we are least open to harm. Fighting the good fight of faith leads to resting on the strong arms of Hope.

Lord, make me a "sure house." Teach me the secret of true security. I am tired of the false hopes and vain promises that are the stock-in-trade of the world. The pleasures of temporal comforts are empty and fleeting. It is only in moving on and moving out for You that I keep the sense of unfailing grace. It is only in losing myself for Your sake that I find myself.

May I have real knowledge of when and where Your battles are fought. I would not be so quick to call my battles Your battles, that I fail to see that it is Your battles, only Your battles, that should be my battles. Then give me a willing heart that, having seen the place of service, I may not hold back in fear and doubt.

I do not despise protection. I need it. I am not ashamed to confess the need. I am lost without it. But, Lord, let it be Your grace that covers and Your love that shields.

Let me find my true security in bold advance for I will never find it in fearful retreat.

In the Name of Him who as the Pioneer of our salvation, fought and won the world's great battle on Calvary's lonely hill, Amen.

MOVING ON IN THE LIFE OF PRAYER

The way God gives us a "sure house" is through our submission to His will and our willingness to be counted on His side. When we are enlisted on His side, He fights the right battles for the right reasons at the right time and we enter into the spoils of His victory. Let us not be too sure that our battles are always the Lord's battles. But let us make very sure that the Lord's battles are our battles. Moving on in the life of prayer is knowing *when* to fight and *why* and above all, *how*. Prayer is discovering "I can do all things in [Christ] who strengthens me."

Day 149

CONTENTMENT

"There is great gain in godliness with contentment" (1 Timothy 6:6).

Read: **1 Timothy 6;** Proverbs 15:16; Philippians 4:11; Hebrews 13:5.

WHAT IS GOD SAYING?

Paul spent a greater amount of time sending down the roots of the gospel and establishing the church in Ephesus than anywhere else. It was an important base for the Christian mission and was situated in a large and sophisticated center of the Roman world. It was the chief place of worship for Artemis of the Ephesians. A temple constructed in her honor was listed as one of the seven wonders of the ancient world. It was in

Ephesus, strategically located in this thriving area of the Roman Empire, that Timothy was given the task of supervising the Christian community. He would need all the support and advice he could get.

In this celebrated outpost of Rome, at its best and worst there were all the evils that plague any society sold out to pleasure, greed, and lust. Few people were ever content. There was the scramble for wealth, the love of money, a morbid craving for controversy, rampant and ceaseless envy. Even Christians were wandering from the faith through their hankering for money. They were finding out too late that the god of mammon is a hard taskmaster and brings more pain than gain to his worshipers. In that climate Timothy needed to know that godliness with contentment is gain.

How Does This Apply to Us?

This message should not be lost on us who live in a world awash in greed and luxury; in a world sold out to the hollow, barren excitement of pleasure and wealth at any cost. As the planets outdistance the moon, so our age has surpassed the days of Roman paganism with its godless and restless discontent. More than ever, we need to learn the lesson and make it the aim of our prayers. Godliness with contentment is an attainable goal. With it comes gain, the sacred "pluses" of God's peace, God's approval, God's "well done," and a conscience void of offense toward all.

Pray with Me

Lord, there are times when I feel I am fighting a losing battle, when others fail to understand. Sometimes the ground I have gained seems to be lost because others are impatient to criticize. Help me over these rough places, Lord, by this truth: "great gain" only comes through absolute contentment in You.

Fill all my horizon. Let Your glory and honor become the keenest longing of my heart. Let me be obsessed with the beauty that I see in Jesus. Then I will live above the obstacles that block my path.

Whether surrounded by friends or enemies, I would be conscious of all the beautiful, positive things that come to me through faith: Your unfailing providence, Your unslumbering watchfulness, Your peace that passes all understanding.

Help me, Lord, to be content in whatever state I find myself, whether I am around those who have found content- ment in You and so are patient toward me or those who, finding no peace in God, show no patience toward others. In Your love may I be filled to the singing point with blessings, even though I may be called to walk a hard and lonely path of unsought duty. Whether I sail with favoring winds or fight contrary gales, whether I abound or am abased, grant that I would find, cherish, and never cast away contentment in You. Help me to do all things, to bear all things, and to be all things in the strength of Him whose redeeming power and deathless love can never fail.

This is great gain. To strive for less is to lose. To set one's heart on anything less than God is to fill the heart with fears, anxieties, and frustrations.

As I have found in Christ my salvation, help me, Lord, to find in godliness my contentment.

To the praise of His glory whose indwelling presence is the only secret of continuing contentment, Amen.

MOVING ON IN THE LIFE OF PRAYER

If we want to prosper our financial investment, we look for a reliable company with a good earning record. If we want gain in spiritual well-being, in contentment, and in the joy of the Lord, we need to invest more time—our best time—in prayer at the throne of grace whose earning record is sound and whose dividends never fail. Godliness, contentment, gain; they go together and they grow together—especially in prayer.

Day 150

GOD—EVER RULING AND OVER-RULING

"This is the word that the LORD has spoken concerning [Sennacherib] . . . 'Because you have raged against me and your arrogance has come into my ears, I will put my hook in your nose and my bit in your mouth, and I will turn you back on the way by which you came' " (2 Kings 19:21, 28).

Read: **2 Kings 19;** Deuteronomy 4:39; 1 Chronicles 29:10-13; Psalm 135:5-6; Daniel 2:20-21; 1 Timothy 1:17.

WHAT IS GOD SAYING?

Sennacherib was nearing the end of the line. Like most people blinded by hatred and revenge, he was unaware of the predicament into which his arrogant assault on Jerusalem had brought him. Hezekiah, fortified by prayer and the wise counsel of Isaiah, stood his ground. Against enormous odds he held the city. He chose to believe the Word of the Lord through Isaiah that in attacking the people of God, Sennacherib was signing his own death warrant.

Isaiah sent a message to Hezekiah which we find in today's highlighted verse. It is a dramatic scene. Hezekiah praying, Isaiah prophesying, Jerusalem inhabitants trapped, and a defiant enemy waiting at the gate. And one more thing, on Israel's side, not contained or restrained by any walls of any city, God overruling, God in control. "That night the angel of the Lord went forth, and slew a hundred and eighty-five thousand in the camp of the Assyrians" (2 Kings 19:35). Then, having limped back to Nineveh, Sennacherib, while worshiping *his* god, was murdered by his own sons. God ever rules and God overrules.

How Does This Apply to Us?

Other enemies may be camping at the gates of our life, laying siege to the citadel of our hearts. They may cause us great alarm as at times we feel ourselves outnumbered and defenseless. We don't wrestle against flesh and blood Sennacheribs, but we are standing up against all the flaming darts of the Evil One. We come to prayer with the confidence that the same God who "put a hook in the nose and a bit in the mouth of Sennacherib" is on our side today.

Pray with Me

Holy One of Israel, You are the everruling and overruling God. When someone has been confined to a stuffy room, he welcomes the opportunity to fill his lungs with the limitless fresh air of all outdoors. With that same eagerness to be refreshed and satisfied, let my mind be filled with the knowledge and let my heart be filled with the trust that You are causing all things to work together for good.

A beast is easily turned and tamely led by a hook in his nose. In the same way You are able to subdue the pride of unbelief. You are able to lead into captivity all that would enslave Your people and cause them shame.

Help me to know that You do not only exercise this power over the enemies without but also over the enemies within. When pride inflates the ego with empty notions of self-importance; when hatred, anger, and envy force me to some irrational act later regretted; when unbelief sits on my spirit like a cold fog; come, Lord of hosts. Say that one word, shed that one beam of light, take in Your Hand the reins, and peace will be restored.

Too often I have let the beasts of passion put the hook in my nose and the bit in my mouth. By Your grace and under Your authority, I will control and not be controlled. I will turn and not be turned. I will rule and not be ruled.

In the name of Him who tamed raging seas and drove out demons, I claim the victory. Let my heart be His throne. Let my hands be His tools. Let my feet move without fear or hesitation where He directs.

Grant it, merciful and mighty God, for the glory of Your Son. For He is Your loving answer to mankind's haunting fears, and the unconquerable Master over all that opposes the will of God.

In His great and wonderful Name, Amen.

MOVING ON IN THE LIFE OF PRAYER

Hezekiah prayed fervently. He also listened to the advice of Isaiah. He heard the Word of the Lord. He chose to believe it even in the face of overwhelming opposition. He came out on top. He listened to the Word and he prayed to the Lord. There is no better pattern for effective prayer.

Day 151

FAITH IS THE VICTORY

"*. . . And this is the victory that overcomes the world, our faith*" (*1 John 5:4b*).

Read: **1 John 5:1-15;** John 16:33; Luke 22:32; Romans 10:17; Revelation 3:21.

WHAT IS GOD SAYING?

John addresses his first letter to Christians—any Christian at any time, anywhere. There is no salutation given and no place specified. Its intent, boldly stated in the first sentence, is to take the things John had seen and heard and touched and through them to proclaim "the word of life" (1:1). This has to do with the gift of eternal life (1:2), the great fellowship we can have with each other as we grow in fellowship with the Lord (1:3), making our joy complete (1:4). It recognizes that we face many problems in the world and because of the world. The same apostle John writes in his Gospel: "In the world you *have* tribulation"—not probably, not maybe, not perhaps, but *you do have* it— "but be of good cheer, I have overcome the world" (John 16:33).

Having captured that quotation of Christ in his Gospel, John now confirms it in his letter. It is faith in the same overcoming Jesus that gives us victory over the same world. By faith we share in His victory.

How Does This Apply to Us?

To put our faith in anything less than Christ is to put our faith in a losing cause. Faith in the world is a constant source of disappointment and frustration. The world cannot save us. It can't even win its *own* battles. Locked in the grip of the Evil One, it needs to be saved. It cannot do any saving.

Our faith is not in the world or in anything in the world: not in the sporadic efforts to clean up its act, not in the dreams of philosophical minds or the advocates of self-improvement, not in repeated efforts to limit nuclear weapons and control nuclear waste, not in treaties and solemn assemblies, not in the beauties of nature. As a young man I felt close to God in the scented, soaring pines and beside the awesome canyons of Yellowstone Park, but one summer lightning fire turned it into a raging beast.

Our faith in Jesus Christ is usually *in spite* of the world. That is the faith that can give us hope and love. Our hope is not in vain and our love, it seems, is the only sane thing that is left in a world ruled by hatreds and jealousies. As temporary residents in such a world, we choose faith. Faith wins. Hope survives. Love triumphs. This is the victory, the only victory that overcomes the world.

Pray with Me

Lord, You are the Author and Finisher of our faith. Faith comes from You and leads to You. From beginning to end faith cannot be complete apart from You.

Today I want to know more about the power of faith. With ever firmer grasp, I would lay hold upon this unconquerable resource. It has power to overcome the world. I want to see this gift of Your love in its true dimensions.

Faith against the world! Faith invincible! Faith victorious!

When I am disturbed by the futility of faith in the world, give me that saving hunger that cries out for faith in spite of the world. You make even the wrath of man to praise You. Let me be filled with quiet assurance as I accept and use Your gift of faith.

Let faith be the ideal that inspires, the light that guides, the strength that sustains, and the hope that cheers—until every fear is conquered and every foe vanquished.

Help me to find and to hold this faith, not as a general mood of optimism and good will but as specific knowledge in the saving power and person of Jesus Christ.

He alone can give the final and lasting victory to my soul for He alone has won it. He alone can help me overcome, for He alone has overcome. I simply enter into His victory. To eternity I will praise Him who has made His victory my victory, His peace my peace, and His Heaven my Heaven.

In the Name of Him who has made faith a way of life through this world, to Heaven, Amen.

MOVING ON IN THE LIFE OF PRAYER

To have continuing and growing confidence in prayer, let it be based on faith at every turn. Never a request but that which believes that God can, if God wills. Never a sin confessed without believing that God wants to forgive us and is faithful and just to forgive us. Never a problem submitted without believing that God gives wisdom to all men generously and without reproaching (James 1:5).

Day 152

BEGUN BY OUR FAITH; FULFILLED BY GOD'S POWER

". . . That our God may make you worthy of his call, and may fulfill every good resolve and work of faith by his power" (2 Thessalonians *1:11*).

Read: **2 Thessalonians 1;** 1 Corinthians 1:26; Ephesians 1:18; 2 Timothy 1:9; 2 Peter 1:10.

WHAT IS GOD SAYING?

Paul's second letter to the Thessalonians is meant to clarify the main message found in his first letter: "Christ is coming again!" All that is said points to 1 Thessalonians 5:23 in the prayerful hope that these believers would "be kept sound and blameless in spirit and soul and body at the coming of our Lord Jesus Christ."

This precious doctrine ought to produce steady comfort. Yet there were many who were "shaken in mind" because some deceivers were stating that "the day of the Lord has already come" (2 Thessalonians 2:2). Others were "living in idleness, not doing any work" (3:6, 11). Why work if Jesus is coming back? "No," says Paul, "work and wait until He comes."

And as long as it is necessary to wait, says Paul, make sure that you allow God by His power to fulfill every "work that faith inspires." That is still the way we become worthy of our high calling. When Jesus does come again—and He will—He will be glorified by who we are and what we are doing. What a humbling, yet ennobling, thought! Part of the glory of the returning

Christ is in our hands, just as a teacher's glory is in the scholars he or she produces. That's the way to wait for Jesus' return.

How Does This Apply to Us?

Meanwhile back to our calling. Our calling is a top priority. What may *not* be so evident to us is that we become worthy of this calling through the power of God, working in us. That is the deep, rich, accurate meaning of the closing words of 2 Thessalonians 1:11: *by His power*. We can hinder His power. We can doubt His power. We can live without conscious dependence on that power. But if we let Him, it is God who makes us "worthy" of our calling. We would take these words to heart. We would ask the Holy Spirit to keep them indelibly on our minds: "He who calls you is faithful, and he will do it" (1 Thessalonians 5:24).

Pray with Me

O Lord, all power is given to You, and Your kingdom is everlasting. I thank You for the joy of this discovery: it is God who does it all. God makes me "worthy of His call, and fulfills every good resolve and work of faith."

Supported by this I can shout it from the housetops and whisper it in the quiet of my open heart: No more the ups and downs of humanly-based good intentions. No more the heavy steps of faltering faith. No more the sapping of finite energy. No more the sagging of human resolve. It is Your power that counts. It is Your power that continues. It is Your power that conquers.

Let me not, therefore, be afraid to make the good resolve. Let me not hesitate to start the work of faith. Yes, I have often failed before. Results do seem little and few. But from now on, every good resolve and every work of faith will be laid in the channel of Your power.

Forgive me for tearing it away from Your omnipotent Hand. Forgive me for not resting in the almightiness of God.

Forgive me for choosing rather to struggle through the underbrush, when, lifted by everlasting arms, I might be soaring through the skies.

And, when through repeated failures I have grown cynical about the value of any good resolve or any work of faith, melt that hardness of heart with a vision of Your eternal splendor. In the light of eternal truth and goodness, the good resolves I make and the works of faith I begin will have Your blessing.

If by my obedience they are begun, then by Your omnipotence they will be fulfilled.

In the Name and by the power of Jesus, risen and returning King, my Lord, and my God, Amen.

MOVING ON IN THE LIFE OF PRAYER

Since it is God who both calls us and gives us power to be worthy of that calling, it ought to run through our praying as a stream runs through the desert. Such a stream, when it is both constant and abundant, makes the desert rejoice and blossom. When we trust that the Lord "is *at work in [us]* both to will and to work for his good pleasure" (Philippians 2:13), when we know that it is by *His* power that we become worthy of our calling, prayer takes on a new meaning. Prayer is letting Him fill the heart as a vessel He has molded. In choosing us, God has called us to a great life. In calling on God, we receive the power to make that great life a good life——to His glory.

Day 153

GODLY REVERENCE IS NO TRIFLING MATTER

"I will show myself holy among those who are near me, and before all the people I will be glorified" (Leviticus 10:3).

Read: **Leviticus 10;** Exodus 3:5, 29:43-46; Psalm 29:2, 89:7; Romans 3:18-19.

WHAT IS GOD SAYING?

According to Exodus 29:9, Aaron and his four sons were consecrated to the priesthood by a perpetual statute. In verse 20 of that chapter we read that the blood of the ram was placed on the tip of the right ear of Aaron and each of his sons. It was also placed on their right thumbs and upon the great toes of their right feet. This elaborate attention to anatomical detail had a purpose: it was symbolic of the dedication of the whole man to God's service. From "head to toe" each was God's man.

That is why, whatever irresponsible and presumptuous action may have been taken by two of Aaron's sons, Nadab and Abihu, whatever the expression "unholy fire before the LORD" means (Leviticus 10:1), these two sons were doing something with impetuous disregard for God's command. They made light of the sacred importance of their consecration. They forgot so soon. Reveling in their newfound importance, they may have decided to do things their own way. They might even have been under the influence of drink (v. 9). In any case, "fire came from the presence of the LORD and devoured them" (v. 2). Five consecrated priests and now there were three. God took drastic action.

How Does This Apply to Us?

Our instant reaction may be to deplore this act of God. The punishment doesn't seem to fit the crime. But when the dust settles, one eternally valid truth stands out. God means what He says. His commands cannot be tailored to suit our fancy. Godly reverence is no trifling matter.

The sin of Aaron's sons is not so remote from Christians in our own day. It is not so remote from any of us who confess that Jesus is Lord and who accept His commandments. How many Christians sing "Holy, Holy, Holy" with their minds in neutral? We want to honor God, we sing His praise with gusto, we want to be counted among those who are "Marching to Zion." But still there is that insistence that we find so hard to shake: "I'll go where You want me to go, dear Lord, but not for the time being, not in this way, not here, not yet. Let's talk it over, Lord. Here are the conditions under which I would like to honor You."

Nadab and Abihu's sin—to be avoided at all costs—was the wish that God would be pleased with what *they* did when they should have done that which would please *God*.

Pray with Me

Lord, let the error of Aaron's sons be to me a perpetual restraint and an unanswerable argument. Let me not suppose that their sin was great and that mine is less.

Let me not think that they deserved their reward and that I deserve a kinder justice.

Your Word does not bend to accommodate passing customs. Your Word is unchanged by the hardened consciences of men. That Word has said: "I will show myself holy among those who are near me, and before all the people I will be glorified."

Having accepted the demands of discipleship, I lay claim to the blessings of Your love in Christ. I am one in whom You have chosen to show Yourself holy. As Your Word is unbending, so Your grace is unending. That is my great hope and my only consolation.

Forgive me when I allow in my heart the sputtering of an unholy fire. Extinguish all fire except that which is ignited by Your truth and mercy. Subdue all burning except that pure love for You and for all Your children. Let the shining forth of Your holy love through me not be hindered by noncombustible pride nor obscured by clouds of doubt.

Fire came from Your presence to devour the sons of disobedience. Let it now come forth from Your presence as I wait before You. Let it devour all unbelief. Purge away all indulgence. Put to rest all poor excuses. Melt down all resistance.

Remove the "me" that is devoted to me in order that I may become the "I" that is devoted to You.

Then I will be numbered among those who are "near" You. Then through me "before all the people You will be glorified."

Make me grateful for the privilege and sensitive to the responsibility which they have who are "near to You."

In the Name of Jesus Christ, Amen.

MOVING ON IN THE LIFE OF PRAYER

God still sends "fire from His presence." As we pray, let that fire burn, not to destroy our lives but to give us life, fire that will get rid of the rubbish to make room for the important, fire that will consume the barriers of disobedience and clear the way for a life of obedience, fulfillment, glory, and love. It costs to be "near" God but the price we pay is not worthy to be compared with the glory that shall be revealed in us.

Day 154

HOW MUCH MORE WILL THE FATHER GIVE

"I tell you, though he will not get up and give him anything because he is his friend, yet because of his importunity he will rise and give him whatever he needs" (Luke 11:8).

Read: **Luke 11:1-13;** Genesis 18:23-33, 32:24-36.

WHAT IS GOD SAYING?

The disciples asked Jesus to equip them for ministry. At the top of the list was prayer. "Lord, teach us to pray." Note, it was not, "Teach us how to perform miracles," or "how to preach," or "how to give intelligent and penetrating answers to hard questions." It was simply, "How should we pray?"

Jesus shows them that they have asked the right question. They have understood the top priority of discipleship. He first gives them a model prayer. Called the Lord's Prayer, it is really the Disciples' Prayer. Through history no words have been more often on the lips of Christians than this prayer. It will continue to be heard until God draws the curtain on time and Christians know in fact what they have prayed in confidence and hope: "Thine is the kingdom and the power and the glory *forever*."

The first example that Jesus gives on the subject of prayer, following the great pattern of prayer, is one that deals with importunity. When the answer to our earnest praying seems long in coming, it is of first importance that we should not grow discouraged. It is a moving illustration. Persistence wins over a reluctant friend.

You can almost hear him muttering to himself: "With friends like this, who needs enemies?" But remember that God is *not* reluctant to answer. It is contrast that is being brought out here. The balance of the passage proves this (vv. 9-13). If an unwilling friend will finally give in, how much more will God the loving Father supply his children's needs and answer their requests.

How Does This Apply to Us?

The point must not be lost. There should be earnestness, intensity, and faith in our prayers. If there is ever a time when we should "hang in there," it is when we pray. We don't have to overcome God's reluctance. If we receive no answer, it is not because God is like the unwilling friend who resents having his sleep interrupted at midnight. It means God has some better thing for us. He may deny us what we think is good to give us what He knows is best.

Pray with Me

Help me to become more importunate as I pray for spiritual graces, for moral victories, for a loving heart, and for the souls of others. When I pray, let my first longing be for Your glory and honor. Let my continuing desire be the coming of Your kingdom. Let my greatest ambition be the knowledge of Your will. Let me become insistent about the things that count and the things that last.

As I grow in my insistence upon the things which can be sought in the name of Jesus, I will find great answers to prayer. Miracles will come as a matter of course. Unimagined joys will spring into life. Living power will fill my being.

I would remember that quality of life and character, and destiny itself, are all determined by the things over which we grow insistent: "For he who sows to his own flesh will from the flesh reap corruption; but he who sows to the Spirit will from the Spirit reap eternal life."

From now on I will be importunate. I will come to the throne of grace with unwearying determination. I will come until the likeness of Christ is stamped on my being. I will come until my heart beats with His love. I will come until my hands move, as His, in quick response to human need.

This is the path of life. This is the way everlasting. This is the one answer to prayer that brings an answer to all prayer.

This is the answer I shall keep on seeking and keep on finding until, released from the burden of the flesh, I shall be in the glory of Heaven's perfect and final Answer,

Even Jesus Christ, my living and ever-interceding Lord, Amen.

MOVING ON IN THE LIFE OF PRAYER

We keep on praying because it is our privilege. We keep on praying because it is the road to victory, the receiving of peace, the finding of answers. God wants us to be persistent. Halfhearted and hollow prayers mean that we don't really mean it. Mere words cannot claim mighty grace. Earnest, persistent, importunate prayers reach the throne of grace. If we really mean what we ask, determined never to give up, we will receive what we want—or something better, far better.

Day 155

GOD IS OUR REFUGE

"These were the cities designated . . . that any one who killed a person without intent could flee there . . ." (Joshua 20:9).

Read: **Joshua 20;** Deuteronomy 19:1-10; Numbers 35:6-15; Psalm 62:7-8; Hebrews 6:18-20.

WHAT IS GOD SAYING?

The "cities of refuge," three on each side of the Jordan, were set aside as places where anyone who caused the death of another by accident, or without intent, could come to receive asylum and protection. Although the avenger (who was the next of kin) might be in hot pursuit to dispense justice in the heat of anger, it was possible for the one who killed to be protected until he had a chance to state his case before the congregation.

The right of asylum is an ancient custom and continued through the Middle Ages when cathedrals served as "cities" of refuge. There is, at this distance in time and place, a little bit of humor in the "Sanctuary Door Knocker" of the Durham Cathedral in England. A mythical figure made of bronze is holding in his mouth a metal ring which is the door knocker. And there it is, a deep, round hole left by an arrow intended for a sanctuary-seeker. Missing its victim, it left its mark in the skull of the bronze figure. A fanciful story? Perhaps. But the Church was "sanctuary" and people thought of the house of God as the place to find understanding, protection, and justice. This was the exact purpose of the six cities of refuge.

How Does This Apply to Us?

It is unlikely that one who has committed a homicide is reading this. Should there be one, however, all sin and any sin (except one, Matthew 12:24-37) may be forgiven through repentance and God's merciful pardon. But it is sadly true that most of us have done other kinds of killing with or without intent.

When we have carelessly quenched the spark of faith in someone else's heart or spoken a thoughtless word to shake the confidence and "kill" the hope of another person, when we have shown a gross inconsistency between what we *say* with our lips and *show* in our lives, causing another to stumble, or in a moment of anger have snuffed out the enthusiasm of a babe in Christ, all of these can be considered forms of "killing" which call for repentance. Thank God there is a "city of refuge," a place for forgiveness, a time to forget past mistakes, a time to press on to future victories. God is our refuge: He forgives the past, comforts in the present, and guides into the future.

Pray with Me

God of mercy, I thank You for restraining grace. I have never brought physical death to anyone. Yet I need to wonder whether in another sense, I have sometimes "killed" without intent or even knowledge. It is possible to "kill" without anger or violence or criminal intent. I might have killed someone's hope. I might have quenched someone's newborn interest in Your kingdom. I might have undermined someone's simple trust. I might have destroyed someone's confidence in Christ.

You know, dear Lord, when I have walked with destructive mood and careless steps into the life of another while knowing and even intending to do so. Forgive this sin. I confess my wrongdoing. I want to conquer the things I know I am doing and should not do. I want to start doing the things I know I am not doing and should. Yet beyond all knowledge and intention, I am sure the shadow of my life has fallen across the path of others. I have spoken the careless word. I have committed the thoughtless deed. I have used with selfish unconcern my personal liberties and brought death to another's faith or to another's struggle against evil.

Thank You, Lord, that as there were "cities of refuge" in the days of long ago, so today there is a place of refuge for all who come with earnest faith. Thank You for sanctuary provided at the foot of the Savior's Cross. His death cancels all sin for all time and for all believing hearts.

Undo in Your mercy all the evil which I have caused, knowing or not. Then let mercy received become mercy given. Let me go on, shielded by Your merciful pardon, to lead others who are wounded and weary, hunted and haunted into the sanctuary of Your holy and bountiful love.

In the Name of Him who offers to all mankind the sanctuary of His redeeming love, Amen.

Moving On in the Life of Prayer

Prayer brings many blessings, many assurances, many seasons of refreshing. It is a multifaceted jewel in our treasure chest of Christian graces. But nothing glows more brightly than the realization that in prayer we have a "city of refuge." God gives us refuge from a tormented conscience and a restless spirit. God gives us refuge as He brings us renewal. God gives us refuge because He is our Refuge. Read Psalm 62:8. Read it and trust it.

Day 156

Giving Beats Getting

". . . *Remembering the words of the Lord Jesus, how he said, 'It is more blessed to give than to receive'* " *(Acts 20:35).*

Read: **Acts 20:13-38;** Proverbs 11:25; Ecclesiastes 5:13; Matthew 10:8; Luke 6:38; Hebrews 13:16.

What Is God Saying?

On his last missionary journey, Paul was conscious of the fact that he would probably be saying farewell to his greatly loved friends for the last time. Of course, he knew that Christians *never* say goodbye for the last time, for we all have the gift of eternal life. To be with Jesus in the place He has prepared for all of His own means that we will be with each other. But there is a poignancy about these "farewells."

The Ephesian church leaders wept and embraced Paul, "sorrowing most of all because of the word he had spoken, that they should see his face no more" (20:38). This is the only address we have in the Book of Acts which was given to Christians only. Paul was sharing his deepest feelings, the sacred memories, the great hopes, the earnest warnings, and every word was wrapped in love. Paul knew that the infection of the world's greed and selfishness was never far away. For that reason he closes his farewell message by a saying of Jesus, quoted only here, "It is more blessed to give than to receive." That seems to say it all. When these nine simple words were spoken, "Paul knelt down and prayed with them all."

How Does This Apply to Us?

"What's in it for me?" That's the first question that rises from the lips of a materialist who has had no experience of God's liberating love in Christ. It is the world's agenda. It is the world's theme song. "The only riches that count are the riches you can count," in the bank or on the ledger sheet. Such riches act like a thick curtain to hide the true riches of the spirit.

We need to put these memorable words of Jesus to the test. To do so calls for courage because those who are blind to the grace of God call it crazy. It must have great importance or it would not be the last thing Paul would say to Christian friends he didn't expect to see again. This is what he wants them to remember: when they think of him, when they return to their work, when they live out their simple, honest lives, he wanted them to remember "the words of the Lord Jesus, how he said, 'It is more blessed to give than to receive.' "

Pray with Me

O God, thank You for the gift of memory. It bridges the distance to the past. It lets the heart linger in the garden of friendship. It strengthens the will to know that heights once gained and burdens once lifted may be conquered again. It calms the fretful spirit to know that God who has never failed shall never fail.

I use that gift today, Lord. I remember all those whose lives and sacrifice of life have made my life full and satisfying. I remember the quiet act of mercy, the wakefulness of a parent, the guiding hand of a brother, the counsel of a friend—all like tiny streams that flow into a continuously cresting river of blessing.

Above all, I would remember the words of the Lord Jesus for they shine from the past, on the present, and into the future. I would remember His words, for what He said and what He did were always one. I would remember His words for they live and make alive. Especially I would remember these words: "It is more blessed to give than to receive."

I want this secret to apply to my life. In a world so marked with greed and malice, I need to remember these words of life. Infected by the very atmosphere of a world that is at enmity with God, it is easy for me to slip into perilous forgetfulness. Therefore, I deliberately choose to remember these words of the Lord Jesus.

Let them guide my steps and move my hands today. Let me claim the joy of those who have no fear except the loss of You. Let me know this blessedness of which the Lord Jesus spoke. Let the memory of what He said, what He did, and what He was become the pattern and the power for all that I say, all that I do, and all that I am.

For the sake of His glory, Amen.

MOVING ON IN THE LIFE OF PRAYER

In our world of getting and spending, in our world of crass materialism and self-indulgent greed, we can all get infected with the virus of "What's in it for me?" God has a better idea, a more blessed way, a healthier life for us to live. Remembering the words and the example of our Lord, we move out in faith to discover that for real happiness, it's the only way to go. And the first step of this journey of faith is usually taken when God lays it on our hearts in prayer to get ourselves out of His way so that He can work through us. God knows and we will come to know that giving *is* much more blessed.

Day 157

FOR THE MASTER'S USE IN THE MASTER PLAN

"Shall the axe vaunt itself over him who hews with it, or the saw magnify itself against him who wields it?" (Isaiah 10:15).

Read: **Isaiah 10:5-19,** 40:15-17; Jeremiah 18:1-11; 1 Corinthians 15:24-25.

WHAT IS GOD SAYING?

In this portion of Isaiah we are being reminded of God's absolute supremacy. According to Isaiah 10:5, Assyria becomes a tool in the hand of God: "Ah, Assyria, the rod of my anger, the staff of my fury!" Assyria couldn't do a thing without God's oversight and control. Note, "I [God] send him [Assyria]" and "I command him" (10:6). *By My command and as My agent,* God is saying, *Assyria will raid and destroy the idols of Jerusalem as he did the idols of Samaria . . . and it needs to be done. Still it is I who send him and command him.*

Flushed with success, the king of Assyria makes arrogant boasts and struts around with haughty pride (10:12). He is unconscious that he is but a tool in the hand of God. He begins to assume that the God of Israel is a helpless idol, like all the others he has destroyed. It is then that God lets it be known that, having used him, He can also set him aside. Having built him up, He can bring him down. That is the context in which our highlighted verse appears: "Shall the axe [Assyria] *vaunt itself over him* who hews with it, or the saw *magnify itself against him* [the God of Israel] who wields it?" God is the Lord of history. If Assyria, having been God's "axe and saw," prides himself on being greater than the God of Israel, he is in for a rude awakening.

How Does This Apply to Us?

The application to our lives is light years away from God's use of an Assyrian army. Who wants to be numbered with them? Who needs it? But all of life is under God's control. Yes, the scene changes, the instruments for carrying out God's purpose are different, the way God can use the energies and skills of our lives are far removed from a godless army bent on proud superiority. But God has absolute control.

For us, Jesus is now the Lord. He uses us and controls us. We want Him to do so. He commands us and sends us on missions of love and mercy, although along the way we might destroy an idol or two. We are tools in His hand. We are agents of His purpose. We are on the winning side. Read 1 Corinthians 15:24.

Pray with Me

Father, I am glad that my relationship with You is not just that of an axe or a saw in the hand of a craftsman. I am not a mindless, lifeless tool. You have created me in Your own image. You have made me for fellowship with You.

Yet, as You are the Lord of the universe, the Maker and Owner of everything, so it is Your right to command and to use. Help me to see that I am Yours. Taking things into my own hands, regardless of Your will, may have broken our relationship. Sin, like a cloud, may have obscured Your face. I still belong to You as much as the prodigal son belonged to the waiting father.

Help me to offer up every self-willed impulse. Help me to lay my whole self at the foot of the Cross, that being dead to sin, I may live to righteousness. Grant that I may surrender all claim to myself until I am as available to Your hand as the axe is to the laborer and as useful to Your plan as the saw is to the builder.

You have given a great privilege to man. The privilege of choosing to give His life to You and of living His life for You. Your way is always right. Only the fool will refuse to be Your tool.

I would be as an axe and a saw in Your hand that by my life as well as by my prayers, Your kingdom shall come and Your will be done. As the axe and the saw cannot vaunt themselves above the workman, as they never direct but are always directed, as they never use but are always used, as they do not understand the design but are always used to bring about the design, so am I in Your hands.

By Your grace keep the cutting edge of my witness sharp and true. In the love and constant praise of Your Son, keep me near at hand, available for the Master's use in His master plan.

For sake of His glory, Amen.

MOVING ON IN THE LIFE OF PRAYER

A Christian knows how much he has been blessed. In prayer we come to say "Thank You" to our loving Father. But we also take the next step. God has blessed us to make us a blessing. So let our prayer be not only thanks *for* great blessings but discovering how we may *be* a great blessing. The tool doesn't tell the builder what and how to do the job. The tool rests in His hand. In prayer our lives rest in God's hands, ready to do His will. Prayer is not a tool to get what we want. Prayer makes us a tool to do what God wants.

Day 158

LOST AND FOUND

"Now . . . the sinners were all drawing near to hear him. And the Pharisees and the Scribes murmured, saying, 'This man receives sinners . . .' " (Luke 15:1, 2).

Read: **Luke 15;** Matthew 9:11-13, 15:2-6; John 5:41-43.

WHAT IS GOD SAYING?

Chapter 15 of Luke is known as "the chapter of the lost." It is also the chapter *for* the lost. Jesus gives us three of His best remembered parables: the lost sheep, the lost coin, and the lost son. Each of them is strong encouragement for those who have lost their way and feel the need of God's redeeming love. God loves the lost. God seeks the lost. God finds the lost. Note how each of the parables ends with rejoicing (15:6, 15:9-10, 15:23-24). But only repentant sinners can know this truth and experience this joy. That is why it was "sinners" who were always drawing near to hear Him and only the "religious elite," the proudly self-righteous, who stood back and complained.

Publicans and sinners who know they are lost respond with joy to these parables. They can relate to being lost through folly as sheep who nibble themselves lost, or being lost by carelessness as a coin is lost, or being lost by willfulness as a prodigal is lost. The super religious who don't know they are lost cannot relate to these parables. They can only stand on the periphery and criticize.

How Does This Apply to Us?

These "stories of the lost" are lost on all who feel they are not lost. The proud cannot know the joy of being found because, in their mind, they were never "missing" in the first place. The elder brother missed all the joy of reunion because he had neither love nor pity for the brother who failed to live up to his standards. Those who are judgmental always miss the joy.

God loves us enough to search for us, as the shepherd searched for the one lost sheep. Coming to Jesus, feeling the touch of His love, and going in search of others for His sake is far better than standing back and finding fault. Those who have tasted His grace can never be critical of those who are lost or of Him who does the finding.

Pray with Me

No, not "this man," Lord. It is the living and loving God who is receiving sinners. Thank You, Lord, that sinners are welcomed in the presence of Your holy love. Thank You for receiving sinners. Thank You for receiving me.

"God be merciful to me a sinner." With these words and in the company of all those You have come to seek and to save, I draw near to hear. I will not run away in order to be spared the pain of hearing. I will not hide in the shadows of fear when, in a moment of decision, my heart may be lifted into the warmth of Your love. I would rather be among the sinners who can hear than among the self-righteous who cannot hear because of their own complaining.

Lord, remove from me all selfish and foolish pride. Pride can only murmur. It can only criticize. It can only complain. It can only miss Your saving words, Your healing touch, and Your redeeming love.

I choose the better part. I will draw near—through the low door of humility, across the strong threshold of faith, along the joyous path of forgiveness and into the beautiful and restful garden of divine fellowship.

And when in the weakness of my flesh I cannot draw near to You, dear Lord, please draw near to me. Then I will look up and see my salvation. Then I will be within range of Your voice. Then I will hear the word *reconciliation*. Then, like shadows before the rising sun, fear will disappear in the glory of Your presence.

The Pharisees complained: "This man receives sinners . . ." Their complaint is my praise. Their murmuring is the mighty anthem of my soul. Their dissatisfaction is my peace. Their bitterness is my blessing. Receive me, O redeeming Lord. I lay and I leave the burden of my sin at the foot of the Cross.

In the Name of "this man," this more than a man, this redeeming God, my Lord Jesus Christ, Amen.

MOVING ON IN THE LIFE OF PRAYER

The very complaint of the religious leaders is the basis of our hope and confidence in prayer. "This Man—this living and loving Lord—receives sinners." Knowing our need and owning our need in prayer brings us to the joy of being found. In prayer Jesus receives us. In prayer Jesus finds us. In prayer Jesus gives us new direction. In prayer Jesus fills our hearts with the very joy of heaven. Prayer grows strong on the nourishing truth that God loves the sinner and that heaven rejoices over one sinner who repents.

Day 159

WHO AM I? I AM HIS

". . . *Who am I, O Lord* GOD, *and what is my house, that thou hast brought me thus far?" (2 Samuel 7:18).*

Read: **2 Samuel 7;** Genesis 32:9-10; John 15:12-15.

WHAT IS GOD SAYING?

David was the greatest of kings. He was also the greatest of warriors. This had its glory and its price. Because he was a man of war who "shed much blood and have waged great wars" (1 Chronicles 22:8), God gave the building of the temple, David's greatest dream, to his son Solomon, a man of peace. David, however, had the great vision of a temple to God's glory. He drew up the plans (1 Chronicles 28:11ff) and gathered many of the needed supplies (1 Chronicles 22:2ff). Yet he was denied the honor of building it.

God had not rejected David in doing so. He had a greater honor reserved for him. In 2 Samuel 7:16 God promises David a house and a kingdom that will be forever. Could there be a greater honor than to have as one of his descendants the promised Messiah, the Savior of mankind? Jesus was born in Bethlehem, David's birthplace. Jesus' mother, Mary, was told by an angel that her Child would be given the throne of David and that His kingdom would literally *never* end (Luke 1:32-33).

Little wonder that David asked, "Who am I?" The humility was real. The thankfulness was earnest. Disappointed in his fondest dream, the temple, he was fulfilled beyond all dreams in his forever kingdom through Jesus Christ.

How Does This Apply to Us?

If David asked the question as an ancestor of Christ, how much more should we, as inheritors of that kingdom, ask the question, "Who am I?" We know that with Jacob we are not worthy of the least of all God's mercies (Genesis 32:10), yet we have been given by the grace of God the greatest of all blessings, eternal life. We are part of our Lord's eternal kingdom. What have we done to deserve it? Nothing. What can we do to show our thankfulness? Obey the commandments of Jesus and share His love with others. "Who am I?" I am something very important, "I am His!"

Pray with Me

Thus far, dear Lord, You have brought me. An unknown road lies ahead. It may be long or short, hard or easy, bright or dark. But at its ending I will still be able to join David in saying, "Thus far thou hast brought me."

Jesus Christ is the same yesterday, today, and forever. I am content and secure in that knowledge because He who never changes never forsakes. Every day I can awake to this trustful awareness, "Thus far Thou hast brought me."

Yet, Lord, the thought is humbling and even overwhelming: I, the undeserving, am undeserted. Forsaking, I am not forsaken. Willfully wandering, I am patiently sought. Condemned by my failures, I am comforted by Your victories. Loveless, I am loved. Hurting, I am healed. Hiding, I am found. "Who am I, that Thou . . . ?"

Please don't let my feelings of unworthiness lead me to self-demeaning despair. Rather let it reveal the glory of Your grace. Instead of always asking, "Who am I?" let me be glad for the assurance of "Who You are!"

Lost in the wonder of Your love, I am set free from enslavement to self. I don't know why I deserve such favor and protection. I just want to become so identified with Him who was willing to become identified with me in the death my sins deserved, that instead of asking, "Who am I?" I will simply say, "I am His!"

Then I will know why I am chosen though undeserving and why I have been brought beyond all danger and disaster and defeat by the providence of a merciful and mighty Lord.

To the praise of Him who leads all who are willing to follow in paths of righteousness and through valleys of shadow to eternal glory, Amen.

MOVING ON IN THE LIFE OF PRAYER

In prayer it all comes into focus. It is *not* "look at who I am." It is, rather, "look at who God is!" In prayer we look at what we may become because of who He is. Prayer is the climate in which God cultivates the new life He has given us in Christ. "Who am I?" Good question. "I am His!" Best answer. And as Paul wrote to his greatly loved friends in Philippi: "I am sure that he who began a good work in you will bring it to completion at the day of Jesus Christ" (Philippians 1:6).

Day 160

EVERYONE'S INVITED

"Every one who calls upon the name of the Lord will be saved" (Romans 10:13).

Read: **Romans 10;** Joel 2:28-32; John 1:11-13; Acts 2:21, 10:42-43; 2 Peter 3:9.

WHAT IS GOD SAYING?

Paul is writing this passage in deep anguish of heart (Romans 9:2). His own people, God's chosen ones, the Jews, were privileged above all other races. God spoke to them in special ways and gave them great advantages. They had the glory of the covenants, the giving of the Law, bright promises for the future and, above all, "according to the flesh, they were given the Christ" (Romans 9:4-5). But so many of them refused to believe in their own promised Messiah. As a race, they regarded their salvation as a reward to be paid to them because they kept the Law.

Paul agonized over this. No one is good enough to make it solely on the basis of keeping the Law. Grace is the only answer. But this liberating truth, this blessed gift, the reason Christ came, this amazing grace of God fell on deaf ears and unresponsive hearts. Still Paul pleads, even using a verse from their own sacred Scripture, (Joel 2:32) "all who call upon the name of the LORD shall be delivered." Jews and Gentiles have all sinned. In Romans 3:10, Paul again quotes from their Scripture, Psalm 14:3 and 53:3: "None is righteous, no, not one." Everyone has sinned, but anyone may be saved. Salvation is free—not cheap, but free. Simply call upon the name of the Lord and you will be saved. That's what makes the Good News so good.

How Does This Apply to Us?

There is so much in Romans 10:13. It applies to everyone. We don't have to climb up a ladder or spend agonizing hours in penance. We don't have to be good enough for God to like us or give us a passing grade. It is not doing a lot of work, nor is it a rigorous program of spiritual fitness, just a call of faith, a simple prayer, a sincere invitation to Jesus to come into our hearts and take control.

We call upon a Person, a loving Person who has a name. We don't call up and point to a set of rules which we have kept with a few lapses here and there. We don't call out to an idol of stone or a lifeless image. We call upon a Person with a name, a name above every name. And having done that, we have assurance. Romans 10:13 says "*will* be saved." Not maybe, not perhaps, but *will*! How wonderful for Christians to know with equal assurance that we *have* been saved!

Pray with Me

Everlasting praise to that name and to Him who bears it! Jesus is mighty to save. He is able to scatter the darkness in every corner of every heart when it is turned toward Him. He is able to change cowards into heroes. He can turn lust-driven weaklings into love-driven conquerors. I call upon this name and in a single moment and on through every moment, I am saved.

I thank You, Lord, that this is an all-inclusive invitation. Everyone means everyone. Everyone means me. I can and I do call upon the name of Jesus.

I thank You, Lord, that it is simply a call and not a lifetime of penance nor the dread of future punishment. It is simply calling upon Your name that saves.

I thank You, Lord, that it is a name, the name of a Person. It is the name, for all its abuse and dishonor in the world, that has become the dearest treasure of my heart. A Person with a name, the Person of that name, can stoop and rescue and lift and hold. I do not call upon an idol of stone or wood. I do not call upon a lifeless creed or a code of ethics. I call upon a Person who responds to human need because He knows human need.

I thank You, Lord, for the certainty that all who call upon Your name "will be saved." It rings with confidence. It sings with joy. It is neither wistful longing nor wishful thinking. It is Your own word of promise. It is as sure as creation. It is as real as light. It is as certain as seed-time and harvest. Such is the promise of salvation to Him who calls upon the name of the Lord.

I call on You now, O Strong Deliverer. Let me continue in such constant fellowship with You that Your grace which always saves shall be the grace I always have.

In that Name upon which no penitent and believing heart has ever called in vain, Amen.

MOVING ON IN THE LIFE OF PRAYER

The essence of prayer is "calling upon the name of the Lord." We may call on that name after salvation and receive blessings that exceed all we could ask or think. We may call on that name in the full knowledge that He who knows our real problems has real solutions. He knows where and when and how we are weak and in prayer provides us with strength that is made perfect in weakness. His power becomes our power. The ultimate power of prayer is His power working in us.

Day 161

OUR BODIES, GOD'S TEMPLE

"For now I have chosen and consecrated this house that my name may be there for ever; my eyes and my heart will be there for all time" (2 Chronicles 7:16).

Read: **2 Chronicles 7;** Romans 12:1-2; 1 Corinthians 3:16-17.

WHAT IS GOD SAYING?

Solomon saw his father's fondest dream come true. It took seven years to build the great temple with a work force of 30,000 Israelites, plus 150,000 Canaanites. It was all accomplished without the sound of a hammer or any tool (1 Kings 6:7). At the time of the dedication, Solomon prayed that it would indeed be the "resting place for the LORD God, that here his priests would be clothed with salvation, and that here his saints would rejoice in the goodness of God" (2 Chronicles 6:41).

God responded to that prayer by sending down fire from heaven to consume the burnt offerings and His glory filled the temple. When all the people had gone to their homes, God had a further word for Solomon. God appeared to him with the message that is found in today's highlighted verse. The temple is the place that God has "chosen and consecrated; his eyes and his heart [his seeing and his caring] would be there for all time" (2 Chronicles 7:16).

How Does This Apply to Us?

Perhaps it will be in the night time, but it could be any time when, through prayer, we discover what this verse means to us. When God "appears" to us personally and privately and communicates His will for our lives in ways too deep for human words, it suddenly dawns on us that *we* are the temple of God and that His Spirit is dwelling in us right now. We are God's temple, His chosen and consecrated dwelling place. Paul writes: "God's temple is holy, and that temple *you are*" (1 Corinthians 3:17).

Now consider the meaning of God's word to Solomon about the great temple. It also applies to us. Like the temple of Solomon then, we are chosen and consecrated now; God's eyes and heart were to be in that temple for all time. Could this be the ultimate meaning of "for all time"? Are we not chosen and consecrated, are we not the ones through whom God's eyes now see and through whom God's heart now cares?

Pray with Me

Eternal God, let the consecration of my life be as real as the consecration of the temple which Solomon built to Your glory. I am encouraged to believe on Your Word that the big and costly temple counts no more with You than the broken and contrite heart.

Let my heart, even as that temple, be the place where Your name shall be forever. With that name on my lips in love, I shall speak the kind and true word. With that name undergirding my will, I shall do the pure and honest deed. With that name to open and close each prayer, I shall see the path to follow. With that name as my assurance I shall claim the promises in faith.

Let my heart, even as the temple of Solomon, be the place where Your name shall be forever. Let me never try to hide from You. Let me not suppose that anything can be concealed from Your all-seeing wisdom. You know the careless thoughts that are artfully concealed from the sight of men. But You also see the little nameless acts of love which go unnoticed, unpraised, and unappreciated. You see, but more than just seeing, You care.

So, let my heart, even as that temple of old, be the place where Your heart shall be forever. All-seeing God, all-caring Father, how wonderful is this union and how perfect is this blending. My heart is the residence of Your holy presence and the channel of Your loving compassion. Your heart, Your mysterious, wonderful, unfathomable mercy, dwells with me and within me forever.

Your name, Your eyes, and Your heart are always to be the blessing of the consecrated temple. Let my life be touched by Your holiness, illumined by Your wisdom, and filled with Your love.

Through Jesus Christ in whom, perfectly blended, there is purity, truth and compassion, Amen.

MOVING ON IN THE LIFE OF PRAYER

We never come to prayer without remembering the wonderful status that God has given to us . . . our bodies, our minds, our souls are indwelt by the Spirit of God. This lifts us up when we are down. This brings us back to the way and to the joy of righteousness when we have strayed from the truth. This helps us to see others in need and to care about others in need, because His eyes and His heart are in us right now. Prayer is discovering what He sees in others and how much He cares for others. Prayer is cultivating His presence, "listening" for His words, and obeying His will.

Day 162
"ME FIRST" NEVER BLESSES AND IS NEVER BLESSED

". . . *But Diotrephes, who likes to put himself first . . .*" *(3 John 9)*.

Read: **3 John;** Matthew 23:12; John 5:44.

WHAT IS GOD SAYING?

Diotrephes is a thorn between two roses. In this brief letter by John, there are two bright lights and one dark shadow. The contrast is immediately obvious.

John mentions three people by name. *Gaius* the beloved comes first and is the one to whom the letter is sent. He is a younger man who extended hospitality to the messengers John had sent as "fellow workers in the truth." *Demetrius* is mentioned last and according to the word that came back to John, he, too, was prompted by selfless love. But the one in the middle is the thorn! It is his attitude that prompted this letter. *Diotrephes* wanted to be the top man on the totem pole. He had to be the one in charge at any cost. Maintaining his own position of authority was more important than getting on with the real business of the church. "He loved to put himself first."

The itinerant missionaries sent by John and rejected by Diotrephes represented a threat to the program of the local congregation over which he exercised control. He was a strong-minded elder with an unloving and uncaring heart. His kind still live on and, held captive by their icy grip, churches still grow inward and shrivel and die.

How Does This Apply to Us?

"Me first" people are always basically insecure. They cannot recognize the needs and rights of others because they are so busy building little guardrails around their own places of power and positions of authority. They cannot lose themselves in the larger cause. They are great on order, especially the order they can control. They are lacking in love and thoughtfulness and compassion because the needs of others and the work of the Lord are all washed out beneath the blinding light of their own needs for self-importance.

We cannot reach out to others when our hands are busy gathering in to ourselves. We cannot think of others when our minds are tethered by our own selfish interests. If we are so important that *we* take up all our time, God can hardly use us as instruments of his blessing. "Me first Christians" are always taking in and seldom giving out. That is life's surest formula for death. Ask the Dead Sea.

Pray with Me

O Lord Jesus, You are the One whose name is above all others. You are the One at whose name every knee shall bow. You are the One whom every tongue will confess to be Lord. Yet You were willing to gird Yourself with the servant's towel and wash the disciples' feet. The Master becomes the Model. I would learn from You the lesson of selfless love and the secret of abiding joy. Diotrephes, "who likes to put himself first," has many followers in the world. He will not be my model.

Yet, as I search my heart, I see the problem of Diotrephes showing up again and again. Honestly, I find it hard at times not to put myself first.

Help me, Lord, to fill my eyes with the vision of Your glory and to fill my heart with the wonder of Your love. Lead me, gracious Spirit, until I am lost in the adoration of the risen and reigning Christ. Help me both to possess and to be possessed by the love of Jesus. Let Your will be my one desire. Let Your Spirit of outreaching love be my supreme responsibility. Only then can I remove the hard-dying root of pride.

A servant of Christ, far wiser than the little known Diotrephes, once chose the better way: "He must increase, I must decrease." I would follow Him. I would follow Him although the world would call it nonsense. He has found the lowly door to abundant and purposeful living. I would follow His example though it leads to imprisonment and shame and even death. Only in the imprisonment of self am I released. Only in the shame of the Cross am I exalted. Only in the death of pride am I led to eternal life.

Through Jesus Christ who, now exalted, once emptied Himself and took the form of a Servant, Amen.

MOVING ON IN THE LIFE OF PRAYER

When we get right down to the business of praying, its effectiveness usually depends on whether we are followers of Gaius or Diotrephes. If we find ourselves praying for others, we will find ourselves being blessed. If our prayer is frequently or even exclusively for ourselves (or ours), we may be following the lead of Diotrephes on a road that is neither blessed nor blessing. It is right that we pray for ourselves. It is a privilege. It is a blessing. We are lost without it. But having done so, a greater blessing comes when we pray for others.

Day 163

THE SECRET OF GLADNESS

"Thou dost make him glad with the joy of thy presence" (Psalm 21:6b).

Read: **Psalms 20, 21;** 16:8-11; Proverbs 3:13-18; Acts 14:17.

WHAT IS GOD SAYING?

Psalm 21 is one of two consecutive "royal psalms." They were sung to and about a king, certainly a king of Judah, and perhaps King David. Psalm 20 was a litany used before the king went into battle. Psalm 21 is a song of triumph to welcome his return. Verses 1-7 express thanksgiving for victory which comes from God. Verses 8-13 speak of confidence that God will continue to triumph over all enemies.

God subdued the king's enemies in this battle. But He is not through. Neither is the king finished with wars. There will be more to come. Though "they plan evil against you . . . they will not succeed" (Psalm 21:11). "God will put them to flight" (Psalm 21:12). There is reason to be thankful, glad, and confident because God is always with you. That is the meaning of of Psalm 21:6: "Thou dost make him glad with the joy of thy presence." This is a psalm of thanksgiving, gladness, confidence, and victory.

How Does This Apply to Us?

This is still the mosaic of a Christian's life. It was real for David the king. It was real for David's Lord, Jesus Christ. And it is real for us. We have battles to wage. We have enemies to subdue. But we have reasons to be thankful. The secret of all our gladness, in good times and bad, is found in the "joy of God's presence."

Sadness and gladness: the words sound so much alike yet the difference is so great. We can go from the depths to the heights, from the nighttime of fear and anxiety to the daytime of confidence and gladness, from thinking all is lost to knowing all is well by discovering the great secret of this verse. "Thou dost make him glad with the joy of thy presence." "If God be for us who can be against us?" If God be with us how can we be sad?

Pray with Me

Lord, all my gladness has its beginning and fulfillment in the joy of Your presence. I have tried to find gladness in other ways and in other things. I have hunted for it, bargained for it, and schemed for it. But, like a mirage, it has always been just beyond my reach. Thinking it was mine and that I could hold it in my hands, it was like embracing a cloud . . . no substance, no permanence, no warmth.

True gladness only comes when I covet and claim and cherish the joy of Your presence. To court gladness by avoiding the joy of Your presence is to ask for honey without sweetness, flowers without fragrance, a day without sun. To seek gladness along paths where I cannot expect the joy of Your presence is to find sadness.

Your presence never leaves. It can be grieved or pleased. It can be ignored or honored. But it is always there. Let my life be so lived that I may know the joy of Your presence rather than the judgment of Your presence.

In the future I would look for and trust in the gladness that comes from the joy of Your presence. Let my gladness consist of partnership with You in the work of redemption and healing. Let my gladness come from seeking and finding the lost. Let me be glad in the task of bringing home hearts that are lonely and wandering. Let me be glad in the privilege of binding up and healing the wounded in spirit. Let me find gladness in sharing everything, even the last crust of bread, as if mine were the inexhaustible riches of Heaven.

Then, as a flower crowns the end of a stem, so gladness will blossom and continue to draw its unfading, living beauty from the joy of Your presence.

Through Him who, by His death on Calvary, has taken the sting out of death and the penalty out of judgment and left me only with the joy of the Father's presence, Amen.

MOVING ON IN THE LIFE OF PRAYER

In prayer we constantly "listen" to what makes God glad and we discover what makes us glad. Sin forgiven, hearts repentant, faith renewed, God's will made clear, love for our "self" which God is still making, concern for others who have great needs and finding ways we can help them . . . these are all steps that lead us into God's presence where there is fullness of joy. Prayer is a path of gladness that leads to more gladness. In its purest form prayer is becoming aware of God's presence. And *that* is the true secret of gladness.

Day 164

EVIL IS STRONG; JESUS IS STRONGER

"But when one stronger than he assails him and overcomes him, he takes away his armor in which he trusted, and divides his spoil" (Luke 11:22).

Read: **Luke 11:1-28;** Matthew 28:18; Romans 1:4, 8:31, 37; 2 Corinthians 4:3-4; Ephesians 3:20-21, 6:12; 1 Peter 3:22.

WHAT IS GOD SAYING?

Jesus has just cast out a demon. There was no denying the miracle. The evidence was there. A man who was dumb now speaks, and the people marvel (Luke 11:14). Since in the face of this concrete proof it was pointless to deny the validity of the miracle, there was just one thing left to do. They would try to discredit Jesus before the people by saying, "It happened, but it was really Satan who did it. He gave his miracle-working power to this impostor."

Their blasphemous accusation is an indication of their desperation. Jesus was winning the people. Their vaunted power over the people was waning. Desperate situations call for desperate measures. "It happened," they said, "but the Devil helped Him do it." Jesus shows the absurdity of this by pointing out that a "kingdom divided against itself is laid waste, and a divided household falls" (Luke 11:17). He then turns the spotlight back on them, saying that since they also claimed to cast out demons, by whose power did *they* do it? But since Jesus is doing this as "by the finger of God" (Luke 11:20) or by divine power, they and all who witnessed the miracle should know that "the kingdom of God had come upon them."

In fact, Jesus goes on, far from being in league with Satan, he is the mortal enemy of evil. Not only is He opposed to him, He has subdued him. Instead of being Satan's tool, He is Satan's nemesis. Satan is a strong man guarding a house with formidable weapons. But Jesus has invaded the strong man's palace. He is stronger than the Evil One. He has stripped him of his armor. By a miracle of grace He has freed those who are held hostage. Satan is strong but Jesus is stronger.

How Does This Apply to Us?

Satan does not relinquish power easily. He is like a strong man who, fully armed, maintains peace. Souls of men are the contents of his house and under his "protection" the contents are content. All is at peace. It is only when Satan's authority is challenged by a stronger Power that trouble rises. Those who are held hostage by evil *seem* to be at peace. But they have an inner restlessness, a longing for true contentment, a hunger for real freedom. When Jesus, the "Lover of our souls," disarms the "strong man who guards imprisoned souls," they lose their chains, they walk out of the palace dungeon and exchange their false peace for real freedom. Evil is strong. Jesus is stronger.

Pray with Me

O God, I thank You for Him who is stronger. Jesus, my Lord, is stronger than all opposition. He is stronger than darkness settling on a doubting heart. He is stronger than fear stalking its prey in the shadows of the unknown. He is stronger than worry striking and pitching its tent in the long succession of tomorrows. He is stronger than error whose poisonous thrust is veiled by what seem to be garments of light. I thank You for Him who is stronger. I thank You for His all-sufficient grace and His all-conquering power.

Let my hope be grounded in Him. Let my heart be given to Him freely and fully. For then I will have no fear of that "strong man" who, fully armed, has held me as part of his spoils. Christ has come and Christ has conquered. By the power of the Cross He has entered the palace of the strong man. He has assailed him, overcome him, and taken away his fearful armor. "O death, where is thy sting? O grave, where is thy victory? Thanks be to God who gives us the victory through our Lord Jesus Christ."

I would live as one who has been set free by a stronger hand. I would love as one who has experienced a love that is stronger than death.

Because He is stronger, so am I. Because He is Conqueror, so am I. May this be a day in which I will truly experience the joy of having a stronger Hand beneath me, a stronger Love beside me, and a stronger Hope within me.

In the Name of my Lord whose deathless love is stronger than all the powers of evil, Amen.

Moving On in the Life of Prayer

Let all our praying be done in the confidence that a stronger Lord has charge, a stronger Purpose prevails, a stronger Love is beside us and a stronger Hope is within. Great answers are on the way. As Jesus is stronger than every evil, so He is able to bring us every good "beyond all we ask or think."

Day 165

God's Unquenchable Love

"Many waters cannot quench love . . ." (Song of Solomon 8:7).

Read: **Song of Solomon 7:10-8:14;** Jeremiah 31:3; Luke 7:47; John 3:16; Ephesians 2:4-5; 1 Corinthians 13:7; Jude 21.

What Is God Saying?

Solomon's beautiful song celebrates conjugal human love. It deals chastely with the intimacies of human relationships. Human love is one of God's great gifts even as its abuse is one of Satan's subtle invitations to misery and frustration. When human love is realized within the bounds of God's laws and grows beneath the sunlight of his blessing, it is true that "many waters cannot quench it." Problems that might divide and conquer a casual relationship only bring the marriage partners who truly love each other closer together. Hard times and having to adjust to unwelcome circumstances could drown the ardor of those who are uncommitted, but true lovers are drawn all the closer. This is how it is when love in marriage has God's blessing and is guided by His truth.

How Does This Apply to Us?

We are justified in seeing beyond this pure and placid celebration of human love the far greater love of God. Human love, at its best, is but a shadow of divine love. God's unquenchable love is the prototype of all true human love. It gives without demanding. It sacrifices without counting the cost. It never gives up. "Love bears all things, believes all things, hopes all things, endures all things" (1 Corinthians 13:7). So the truth suddenly dawns: if any love is unquenchable, if there is any love that cannot be drowned by troubles or extinguished by adversity, it is the love of God.

Jeremiah, whose faith was tested beyond all reasonable limits, heard the Lord and believed the Lord when He said: "I have loved you with an everlasting love; therefore I have continued my faithfulness to you" (Jeremiah 31:3). That was His conclusion. That is also the unshakeable foundation of our prayers. God's love is everlasting. "Many waters cannot quench it, neither can floods drown it." Prayer responds to that love. Prayer counts on that love. Prayer claims that love.

Pray with Me

O God, my comfort is this: You are eternal love. God is love. Love always was. Love always is. Love never fails. Your justice is without flaw. Your truth is without end. So also is Your love. As man will never sound the depths of Your power, so he will never see the end of Your love. How wonderful to realize that divine love cannot be overcome and will never be exhausted.

I want to be more willing to share this love, knowing that the Source of its blessing will never run dry. Let my life be as a cup running over because it receives from a cup that is running over. Since nothing can quench Your love to me, let nothing quench my love for You and for others. The real test of real love is this: it cannot be quenched.

I regret the things I have done, the thoughts I have harbored, the words I have said or left unsaid that might have quenched a lesser love. With words of promise on my lips, I have cherished compromise in my heart. I have said, "Thy will"; I have meant, "My will." I have been with You in the glory of the upper room, I have rested in the strength of Your redeeming love, I have tasted the goodness of Your presence, only to turn back to the shadows of some unyielded affection. Still Your love is not quenched. The many waters of my imperfect love for You have never quenched Your love.

I want to keep in such close fellowship with You that my love will also be an unquenchable love. If I would have Your love, I must have it for others. It is only as I live in the sunshine of Your love that I can learn to hate all that is opposed to God. As I give unquenchable love I will be counted worthy as a disciple of Him whose love was more than conqueror over the many waters of hate and enmity and jealous pride on Calvary.

Let the ideal become the real.

In the Name of my Lord and in the spirit of His love, Amen.

MOVING ON IN THE LIFE OF PRAYER

Prayer in Jesus' name is prayer in the love of God. That is why in the prayer of faith we can come with our greatest burdens, look for our greatest deliverance, live in greatest freedom, and receive God's greatest blessings. The secret lies in knowing that God's love is unquenchable. In prayer we go in to be renewed in that love. In service we go out to share it.

Day 166

WHAT DO YOU SEE IN JESUS?

"And they watched him . . . so that they might accuse him" (Mark 3:2).

Read: **Mark 3;** Matthew 10:34, 22:15, 27:12; Luke 8:36, 11:53-54, 14:1, 20:20.

WHAT IS GOD SAYING?

In this early chapter of Mark, we find that Jesus and the VIPs of the religious community were at odds. The proudly orthodox were so suspicious and jealous that they "watched" Him. Is it possible that He would desecrate the Sabbath by performing a work of compassion and healing? Jesus wanted to be a blessing to all who suffered anywhere anytime. They wanted to catch Him in the act.

They were there in the synagogue—in the front seats of course—not to worship, not to learn, but to accuse, to criticize and to keep the people from being misled. That was their responsibility and they brought to it a fanatical devotion. To the Jew all work was forbidden on the Sabbath. To heal was to work. Even a fractured bone could not be attended to on that day. A cut finger might be bandaged but no ointment could be applied. On the Sabbath an injury might be kept from getting worse but it must not be made better. This was the kind of legal trivia that assumed such important dimensions to the "fact-finding commission." Such was the awful crime of the compassionate Healer.

They saw in Jesus someone who might break the Sabbath. Jesus saw in the man with the withered hand someone who might be helped. It all seems trivial to us. Much ado about nothing. Yet it called for great courage in Jesus. And God's great love triumphed over man's petty jealousies and pathetic self-importance. It always does.

How Does This Apply to Us?

We all see something in Jesus. Those who want to trap Him—or His followers—will watch Him to see some flaw. That would make it easier to consign Him to the role of an innocuous do-gooder or a misguided guru. They would discredit His flawless love. We watch Him for different reasons. We watch to learn. We watch to rejoice. We watch to receive inspiration and blessing. That is what we see in Jesus. We see One whose love brings help to the troubled of body, mind, and spirit. One who looks beyond man's faults and sees his need.

What *do* we see in Jesus? Are we among those who watch suspiciously or those who believe implicitly? Is our priority the keeping of little laws or the sharing of a great love? Do we stress correctness over compassion?

Pray with Me

Lord, in the beauty and strength of love You walked among men. With great compassion, You healed the sick. You lifted from tired spirits the burden of pain. You removed from sightless eyes the curtain of darkness. Yet "they watched in order to accuse."

It is hard to believe that religious people should care so little when it is God's way to care so much. It would take a heart of stone to "watch" the Lord at the work of love "in order to accuse."

Let the example of this unbelievable suspicion move me away from all uncaring pride. These little souls lay on life the chains of heartless legalism. Teach me it is mercy You require and not sacrifice.

They watched in order to accuse. I would watch in order to imitate. To them Your love was a threat to power. To me Your love will be the source of power. To them Your caring was a roadblock to thwart their prejudices. To me Your caring will be a trail blazed, a road cleared, a way whose end is peace. To them Your healing of a withered hand meant the raising of their good hands in judgment. To me let the sight of a hand restored constrain my own hands to selfless service.

Then, Lord, as You had to deal with the barb of suspicion and the indignation of jealous little souls, let me take heart that for Your sake, and engaged in Your work, I will encounter misunderstanding and resistance and disapproval even when I am trying to do good.

Let others watch to accuse, Lord, so long as I may know that You are watching to approve. In this I will find my strength to go on. In this I will find my joy in going on.

For the sake of Him who one day will speak the words I am waiting to hear:

"Well done, good and faithful servant," Amen.

MOVING ON IN THE LIFE OF PRAYER

Prayer is the time we "look unto Jesus." His example helps us run with patience the race that is set before us. His selfless love is the inspiration for all our relationships. The same touch that healed the withered hand causes our withered spirits to grow and blossom. Prayer is when we seek and find in Jesus the answer to all our needs, the source of all our hope, the reason, the substance, and the goal of all true life.

Day 167

WHY TRADE EVERYTHING
FOR NOTHING

"Ephraim is oppressed . . . because he was determined to go after vanity" (*Hosea 5:11*).

Read: **Hosea 5;** Job 15:31, 31:5-8; Jeremiah 2:5; John 6:27; Acts 14:15.

WHAT IS GOD SAYING?

This time it was the North seceding from the South. Israel, also called Ephraim (the largest and most central of the Northern tribes), set up a kingdom of its own with deep hostility toward the two tribes in the south. The great days of David and Solomon were past. The northern tribes did bask for a while in the afterglow of the united kingdom, but dark clouds were gathering on the horizon. Sin and idolatry were the order of the day. The glory was rapidly departing. Elijah and Elisha were sent to warn the rebellious nation but it remained obdurate and determined to go its own way. Still God yearned for their return.

He sent Hosea to plead with them: "How can I give you up, O Ephraim! How can I hand you over, O Israel!" (Hosea 11:8). These words of the Lord are deeply moving. "When Israel was a child, I loved him, and out of Egypt I called my son. The more I called them, the more they went from me" (11:1-2). Hosea called upon Israel to repent. They might yet be spared, even though "loving shame more than glory" (4:18), their fate seemed to be sealed. "The wind" had wrapped them in its wings (4:19) to carry them off to a land of captivity. That is why Hosea says "Ephraim is oppressed because he is determined to go after vanity." He is giving up everything for nothing. "Ephraim's glory shall fly away like a bird" (9:11).

How Does This Apply to Us?

We are far removed from the wicked idolatries of Ephraim, but his rebellion against the God of his fathers has a modern ring. Ephraim's determined choice to spurn the yearning love of God and to look for help from other sources could, with different names and places, be found in this morning's paper. Now, as then, nations and individuals are still trading everything for nothing. Time-proven standards of morality with their harvest of joy and fulfillment and security are disdained in favor of "do as you please," "don't get caught," "sow the wind" now and worry about "reaping the whirlwind" when and if it comes.

Belief in God, obedience to His commandments and respect for the truth—all these are excess baggage from a previous era when people were less scientific and chose myth over reality. It should all be trashed.

We are still giving up everything for nothing. We must invite God to take control and we must accept His love as it still yearns for our return.

Pray with Me

Were it not for Your intervening grace, dear Lord, along with all Your other children, I would be determined to "go after vanity." There is no use ignoring it. The disposition to do so is always there. When the wise restraint of Your love is brushed aside, my inner bent surfaces and leads me into trouble.

As with Ephraim, when I go after vanity, I find oppression. When I walk away from the riches of Your favor, I walk into the poverty of human pride. When I turn from the freedom of Your will, I ask for the bondage of sin's control.

In Your great compassion, Lord, come into my heart to take and keep control. Help me to be as determined to go after truth as I have been determined to go after vanity. Let my life be known for its determination to know Your will. Let me always heed Your Word. Keep my feet walking in Your way. Let such determination sweep before it all lesser ties as a living, bubbling spring refuses to be choked.

Oppression is the fruit of vanity. I am determined to see that. Freedom is the fruit of faith. I am determined to see and to act upon that. Let me not be brought, as Israel was, to the saturation point of sorrow before I can recognize the things that will make for real freedom of soul and peace of heart. Satisfy me just now with Your goodness. I claim the promise that "they that wait upon the Lord will renew their strength."

In the conquering name of Jesus, I declare my independence from vanity's oppression. With determination I enter into the peace and the joy of His fellowship.

Going after Him, I will have neither time nor desire to go after vanity. Being filled with the glory of His love, there will be no room for the debris of wanton desires. Make this, Lord, a constant reality to the praise of Your own glory and power.

In Jesus' Name, Amen.

MOVING ON IN THE LIFE OF PRAYER

Let God show us in prayer that the fruit of vanity is bondage while the fruit of faith is freedom. Prayer is making a deliberate choice to keep the "everything" of God's promises and love while letting go of the "nothingness" of everything else.

Day 168

ALONE—WITH JESUS

". . . *Jesus withdrew again to the mountain by himself"* (*John 6:15b*).

Read: **John 6:1-15;** Matthew 6:6, 15:29, 17:1-8; Luke 5:16; Genesis 32:34; Jeremiah 9:2.

WHAT IS GOD SAYING?

Each time Jesus leaves the lowlands and seeks the solitude of the hills, He has been expending His physical and emotional energies. In the miracle of the loaves and fishes, feeling compassion for the hungry, hearing the cries of children, and just seeing that every one of the five thousand was fed, must have been a draining experience. Then, because He had given them what they wanted and did so under dramatic circumstances, they saw in him the King, the Messiah, for which every Jew was waiting. He had been healing them and now He was putting food in their mouths. Did they need further proof?

They pressed in upon Him and would have lifted Him then and there to a throne. This was not the time or the place or the way or the reason. It is exhausting to deal with a mob, even a friendly one, when it is insisting on its own way. To the hills, then, to be alone, to be with the Father, and to renew His mental and physical strength.

After His longest recorded journey to Tyre and Sidon (Matthew 15:21-29), weary from traveling, He went up again to the hills. Having heard the breakthrough of his disciples' faith, "You are the Christ," and having realized that this was His time to take the last journey to Jerusalem (Matthew 16:16-21), he took the inner circle, Peter, James, and John, to a "high mountain apart" to be alone with them and with the Father.

How Does This Apply to Us?

If Jesus, with inexhaustible resources, human and divine, needed to get away from it all, how much more do we need to shut out the world and be alone with God! As we turn *from* the world with its clamoring and insistent demands, we turn *to* the Lord to listen to His Word and to be renewed in body and spirit. It is just as necessary as turning off the freeway on a long drive in order to fill up at a gas station. If we don't stop, we can't go on! To go on with Jesus, bringing His love in practical ways to a spiritually hungry and physically needy world, we must stop and spend time with Him. Isn't that the ultimate meaning of "Be still and know that I am God"?

Pray with Me

With You, dear Lord, I want to withdraw from the pressing problems and cares of life until I find the calm of hills above. Out of these lowlands where life is drained of spiritual energy and covered with the dust of the commonplace, I would be lifted into Your holy presence. There I find clear vision and deep, healing rest.

I would be with You, for until I am beside You I must always be "beside myself." You chose Your disciples for the purpose of being with You. I am redeemed. I am bought back and I am brought back to live with You. May I see how much I need to withdraw to the hills of high inspiration and quiet calm.

Help me to withdraw. Let it be a conscious act of the will. Let it be a decision to leave the shallow comforts of half-way discipleship and half-hearted following. Let it be a decision to believe that God has better things to fill our hearts than the trivial and the ordinary. Let it be a decision to go upstream against the downward drag of all that caters to the flesh. O Christ, Your loving Spirit is ever present. Draw me that I may be with You. Let this be my withdrawing.

Help me to withdraw to the hills. To drift is easy. To climb is hard. But as there is no energy expended in drifting, so there is no vision given in drifting. Only those who climb the hill can claim the thrill. Only those who seek the heights will see the sights. There in the cleanness and the quiet of hilltop prayer, "be Thou my vision, O Lord of my heart."

Help me to withdraw again to the hills by myself. Yet never by myself. For You are already there. You are always there. You always wait for my coming. It is Your hand that swings open from within the gate to prayer's garden. It is Your love that beckons from the hilltop like a beacon. It is Your presence that lingers on the hilltop as a benediction.

For the sake of Him who leads the way, let me withdraw, again and again, to the hills by myself.

In His Name, I pray, Amen.

MOVING ON IN THE LIFE OF PRAYER

Disciples, then and now, see the transfiguring glory of Jesus and hear the voice of God speaking out of the cloud (Matthew 17:1-8) when they are alone with Jesus in a quiet place, away from pressures, distractions, and interruptions. It may not be, it need not be, far away or on an actual mountain. Jesus said in Matthew 6:6 that it could be our own room so long as we "shut the door." Any place is the place for prayer when we are there "alone—with Jesus."

Day 169

IS MY LIFE A GIVEAWAY FOR CHRIST?

"And when any of the fugitives of Ephraim said, 'Let me go over,' the men of Gilead said to him, 'Are you an Ephraimite?' When he said, 'No,' they said to him, 'Then say Shibboleth,' and he said, 'Sibboleth' for he could not pronounce it right; then they seized him and slew him at the fords of Jordan" (Judges 12:5-6).

Read: **Judges 12:1-7, 8:1-3;** Matthew 5:13-16, 26:27; John 13:35; 2 Corinthians 3:2-3.

WHAT IS GOD SAYING?

Judges is a chronicle of the worst of times. The book is characterized by anger, jealousy, mistrust, and violence. Occasionally God would raise up leaders to straighten things out. They were called judges. They were men (and one woman) who believed in the God of Israel, and who, in obeying Him, exemplified courage and honor. But for the most part it was four hundred years of chaos. "In those days there was no king in Israel; every man did what was right in his own eyes" (21:25).

Ephraimites considered themselves to be more important than the other tribes. Strategically located in the central highlands and having the great sanctuary at Shiloh, they felt they deserved more recognition. When Gideon fought against the Midianites, they were miffed because he did not ask *them* to fight. They wanted a piece of the action and a share of the glory. The same situation developed when Jephthah subdued the Ammonites and again they were not invited to the party. So they tried to soothe their offended spirits by taking on Jephthah. How could he do such a thing as to overlook *them?*

In the ensuing battle, Ephraim lost. Jealousy opens the door to stupidity—and disaster. There was wholesale confusion as the Ephraimites beat a hasty retreat. But the Gileadites stood at the ford of the Jordan and told every man who tried to cross to say "shibboleth." Every fugitive Ephraimite said, "Sibboleth." It was a dead giveaway, and dead is the right adjective. The casualty list reached forty-two thousand.

How Does This Apply to Us?

Shibboleth in the Hebrew means "an ear of corn" or a "stream," but it has come to mean a test or a watchword. It is a give-away. It lets others know to which side one belongs.

What is there about our lives that gives us away as followers of Christ? An Ephraimite could not disguise his identity. A Christian's life should give him or her away to others. As those who are living for Jesus and enlisted on His side, let our speech *and* our acts be a dead giveaway that we belong to Jesus.

Pray with Me

Lord, I have placed You on my heart's throne. There You are as a spring breaking forth in the desert. It is Your Lordship that brings joy instead of sorrow. It is Your authority that gives me freedom instead of bondage. It is Your love that leads me in paths of service instead of on a treadmill of self-serving. It is Your blessing that surrounds my day with peace instead of strife. The presence of life is seen where there are springs in the desert. So Your life in me should be clearly seen in the way I live.

The Ephraimites gave themselves away because they could not say, "Shibboleth." May the telltale traces of the Christ-life in me consciously—and even more, unconsciously—give away the fact that I am Yours and You are mine.

That is a giveaway that leads to life, not death. Everywhere people are looking for answers to their doubts, light for their darkness, and a way out from under their anxieties. As they see my life and as they ask the logical questions: "Is it real? Does it work? Do I want it? Can I have it?" let my life be the dead giveaway that shows them life and the One who brings it. Let them see the pattern of Your Life traced in my convictions, in my conversation, and in my conduct.

Do Your work so completely, Lord, that even when in moments of weakness and fear I may try to say the "Shibboleth," it will only come out as "Sibboleth."

Be my Lord, O Christ, until habits that are unconscious and deeds that are unpremeditated and reactions that are involuntary will join in the praise which now, in conscious joy, I raise to Your name, O Christ, Giver and Lord of Life.

In Your triumphant Name, Amen.

MOVING ON IN THE LIFE OF PRAYER

One of the reasons for prayer is to develop and strengthen the qualities that give us away as Christians. In the ways we think and talk, in the ways we work and walk, others will come to know that we belong to Jesus. Prayer is the time we become better give aways for Christ.

Day 170

FIRMLY BOUND, FOREVER FREE

" 'All things are lawful for me,' but not all things are helpful. 'All things are lawful for me,' but I will not be enslaved by anything" (1 Corinthians 6:12).

Read: **1 Corinthians 6:12-20;** Romans 12:1-2; 2 Peter 1:3-8.

WHAT IS GOD SAYING?

Corinth of Paul's day was almost a synonym for "anything goes." It was one city which, perhaps more than any other, could compete with our own civilization as we watch the rapid decay of moral standards. The dictionary defines license as "freedom that is used with irresponsibility." The Corinthians confused freedom with license. They maintained that we should throw off all restraints. There is nothing wrong with satisfying hungers, any kind of hunger, any time. It comes with being human. This applied then (and now) especially to sexual license.

Paul states that he is also free but he is not going to allow that freedom to make a slave of him. He is free, not to do as he likes, but as he should. Phillips's translation of 1 Corinthians 6:12 makes it all very clear: "As a Christian I *may* do anything, but that does not mean that everything is good for me. I *may* do everything, but I must not be a slave of anything." The body is important. As the concluding verses of this same chapter assert, the body is the temple of the Holy Spirit and must not be abused or given free rein. We cannot sin with the body and leave our souls untarnished. Contrary to the thinking of some Corinthian Christians, Christian liberty cannot become an excuse for immorality.

How Does This Apply to Us?

There is only one way to be truly free. Submit voluntarily and totally to the lordship of Jesus. We belong to Him. He paid the price of our redemption. To be totally free, to enjoy the best of life, here and hereafter, to live above the clamoring hungers of the flesh, and to be independent of the kind of freedoms that lead to bondage, we must own Jesus as Lord.

The Lord is for the body. He made it. He wants us to use it without abusing it. He provided guidelines for its well-being.

The body is for the Lord. It is His needed instrument. He owns it. He lives in it. His wise control and loving directions can make it function as it should. A body that is functioning as it should is free. The way to freedom is along the path of obedience. The way to enslavement is along the path of self-indulgence. We are free to choose, but we are not free to choose the consequences of our choice.

Pray With Me

If the Son makes you free, you shall be free indeed. I will walk in this light. I will claim this at every turn of the road. I will let this make me bold in the many decisions I must make every day.

Because I belong to You, I am free: I am free from the power of desire for wrong things. But I am also free from right things which, unwisely indulged, can lead me into bondage.

Since this is my New Birth right in Christ, O God, make me constantly aware of it. Let it rule my spirit. Let it inform my mind. Let it move my will.

Lord, Your grace is always at hand and always sufficient. Let me draw upon it now and through all the moments of this and every day. Then I will be set free from the tyranny of lawful things: habits from the past, broken but not quite dead; present and persistent trivialities; all the pressures of social correctness, vain and showy pretense, empty customs that fill our days and from which we dare not break lest we seem ridiculous.

There are some things which the law allows that are not helpful. But let my life become filled with those many things which grace provides that are always helpful: praying for the enemy, blessing for the persecutor, love for the unlovely, peace within when storms rage outside, light that glows strongly in the gray dusk of an immoral world, humility which, bending low, is lifted by grace while pride in its stilted stiffness is stumbling.

"Firmly bound, forever free." These are only words, neatly phrased, yet they can lead to the Lord, greatly praised! So be it, Lord, until in the face of all that is so lawful but so empty, I, too, can say: "I will not be enslaved by anything."

In the Name of Him who led captivity captive, Amen.

MOVING ON IN THE LIFE OF PRAYER

We are all exposed to a hyperactive and multi-faceted media. Do we spend as much time in prayer as we do in front of the TV? Do we dare to answer? Are we victimized by its subtle invitations to indulge the flesh? "It's okay. Everyone deserves to be pampered." Are we exposing ourselves to a constant flood of persuasive voices that condition us for the dangerous philosophy that "anything goes"? In prayer we turn from the vanities of the passing parade and become tuned to the will of the eternal God. Prayer is when we tune out the world and spend uninterrupted moments on a frequency where God is speaking, the world is silent, and we are "listening."

Day 171

AFRAID OF THE DARK?
GOD IS THERE

"The LORD has set the sun in the heavens, but has said that he would dwell in thick darkness" (1 Kings 8:12).

Read: **1 Kings 8:1-21;** Psalm 139:9-12; Haggai 2:5-9; 1 Corinthians 4:6; Revelation 21:23.

WHAT IS GOD SAYING?

After years of waiting and sacrifice, the temple of Solomon was completed. The ceremony of dedication was marked by solemn jubilation as the Ark and all the holy vessels were placed in their proper location. Then came the moment, so long awaited, when Solomon would offer the prayer of dedication.

The priests came out from the Holy of Holies, but the cloud was so thick they could not see to go on with their duties. It was the Shekinah glory of the Lord. It was the same "presence" that led the Israelites through the wilderness as a pillar of cloud by day and as a pillar of fire by night; the same cloud that rested on Mt. Sinai; the same cloud that hovered over the first tent of meeting; the same cloud that covered the tabernacle, dark by day and luminous by night; and now, as the temple is dedicated, it comes again to fill the temple. It was a glorious and awesome moment. One wonders how Solomon could even speak.

The effect of the temple-filling cloud was so moving that Solomon's first words were lifted up to the God of Light: "He set the sun in the heavens but has said that he would dwell in thick darkness."

How Does This Apply to Us?

God is everywhere present. The psalmist knew that he could not escape the divine presence. However far or fast he might flee, God is already there (Psalm 139:7-9). If he tries to hide under cover of night even the night shall be light about him (139:12).

But there is another sense in which to think of God's presence in thick darkness. Not only is He there when we are trying to hide from Him, He is also there in the darkness *when we need to find Him.* By faith we can know that God is present even when the eye cannot see Him nor the mind understand Him. When the darkness of some trial or sorrow, when the nighttime of doubt and despair settles upon us, when we feel forlorn of spirit and have lost the way, there is a "kindly Light that leads amid th'encircling gloom."

He has said He will dwell in thick darkness. In the temple, that darkness was the proof of His presence. In the journey of life, on our way home through the wilderness, the clouds that surround us could mean, not that He is missing, but that He is closer than ever. Trust Him in thick darkness. He said He would be there.

Pray with Me

Lord, I thank You for the simple and wonderful gift of light. I thank You for the many blessings that flow from it. It is the source of all energy and warmth—and even life itself. The sun is the work of Your hand, the evidence of Your power, and the proof of Your unfailing love.

I thank You for the days when clouds that seemed so heavy and the night that seemed so long are changed by divine artistry into fresh creations of breathless beauty. I thank You for the bright sun at noon, in which we do our common work, oblivious to the greatness of the blessing of this, Your common light. I thank You for the rich and always varied splendor of the evening sky when the sun, in going, gives its flaming benediction. I thank You for showing Yourself in the blessings of common light.

Yet, Lord, there is a deeper truth I need to learn. You are near at hand even when Your presence is not obvious. You are strong to deliver and ready to uphold even when all seems lost and the path is covered with thick darkness. Let me be aware of Your presence, Father, in times and places where the eye cannot see nor the mind understand.

Let me discover You not as a man groping in the dark might happen to find a rail. Rather let my discovery be that "In thick darkness You are dwelling." The cloud filled the temple and priests could not stand to minister. It is a harder prayer to offer. It is a bolder step of faith to take. But it leads to a joyful discovery: thick darkness, as well as the clear shining of the sun, can be evidence of Your glory and assurance of Your power.

Above all, Lord, as You have set the sun in the heavens, so set Jesus Christ, the Sun of righteousness in my heart, that even in thick darkness I may walk in the confidence that I am never forsaken. That is the joy the world cannot take away.

To the praise of Your glory, Amen.

MOVING ON IN THE LIFE OF PRAYER

We won't be afraid of the dark. God is there. We won't stumble and fall when there is no light. God's hand is there to guide. We won't lose our way when clouds close in. God is above and also in the clouds. Let our praying be the spiritual equivalent of radar by which God sees where we are and can bring us safely through all our dark nights and heavy seas. Trust Him. He said He will dwell in the thick darkness. Fanny Crosby, the blind hymn writer, said it for us all:

"Bright cloud, indeed, must that cloud be,
    When Jesus only the heart can see."

Day 172

THE WORD OF LIFE, KNOWN AND SHOWN

"The life was made manifest, and we saw it, and testify to it" (1 John 1:2).

Read: **1 John 1;** Luke 1:2; Acts 1:8, 5:32, 10:39, 13:31; 2 Peter 1:16.

WHAT IS GOD SAYING?

At the time of John's letters, more than a half century probably had passed since Jesus was on earth. There were many who scoffed at this new faith. There were others, known as the Gnostics, who tried to introduce elements of thought to suit their own tastes and to make the business of religion more intellectually defensible for the intelligentsia. It distinguished between the "spiritual" (which is pure) and the "material" (which is evil). They counted themselves to be the spiritual aristocrats of the religious community because no ordinary person could know the truth about God as well as they. They were on the inside track.

As such they were the self-appointed cleansers of the Church. They must get rid of the deadwood, such as the teaching of Jesus' incarnation. It was no idle threat and all the more dangerous because it came from within. If spirit alone is good and matter is completely evil, the incarnation would be impossible and the great fact that "the Word became flesh and dwelt among us" would be rendered null and void. For John, that price was too high. Jesus, God incarnate, really lived. His real (material) body could be seen and touched. And those who were with Him can and must testify to that great essential truth. If Christ did not become man to die for human sin, there is no Christian faith.

How Does This Apply to Us?

We were not eyewitnesses of Jesus in the days of His flesh. But God, who once appeared clothed in human flesh, has promised through His Holy Spirit to be present with us always. Jesus was known then and shown then by eyewitnesses. Jesus is known to us now through the eternal Word of Life but He is shown now in our day-by-day lives. If the same Jesus who became flesh and dwelt among men is alive in our hearts, we can and must be His witnesses now.

Pray with Me

Lord God, out of the impenetrable silences of infinity, You have spoken. It is wonderful to hear Your still, small voice, when doubt and fear are silenced. It is good to know that beyond that curtain which our minds can never lift there is a presence. Your presence is sometimes disturbing, sometimes comforting, but always disturbing in order to comfort.

I have heard Your voice in the sea and on the wind, in the stirrings of the forest, in the falling of the rain, and in the song of birds. I have heard Your voice in prophetic utterance and in the imperturbable march of history. But most wonderful is it to know that Your very life has been manifest for men to see and to share, to possess and to declare.

"The life was made manifest, and we saw it, and testify to it." It is shown to be known. Let nothing hinder me from knowing what has been shown. Remove all doubt. Let Your calm, sure light drive back fear and uncertainty. Awaken the slumbering conscience. Smite the sheer, dead weight of mental laziness until I give myself to the holy and beautiful contemplation of Your life manifest in Christ.

Then, Lord, as Your life was shown to be known, so let it also be known to be shown. I ask Your forgiveness for the many times I have withheld the glory of Your saving love and truth. Forgive the times when unyielded desires and unblessed liberties have caused the image of the Christ to be obscured in me. God, forgive and remove those flaws, born in moments of disloyalty and nourished by hours of carelessness, which have caused the Christ I have known in grace to be shown in disgrace.

Lord, this is no light and whimsical yearning. It goes deep. Without it I seem to live but really die. With it, I seem to die but really live. As He has been known, so may He be shown . . . in all my words and all my ways, through all my deeds and all my days,

To the glory of Jesus Christ, Amen.

MOVING ON IN THE LIFE OF PRAYER

We read the Word of God that His truth may shine in our hearts. Then we pray for grace to take the truth that God speaks and let it become visible in our lives. He has touched us with love; are we sharing that blessing with others? We have been comforted; do we become comforters? We have been forgiven; are we now forgiving? This is the prayer that counts and it leads to a life on which God can count. God, in Jesus Christ, is known to be shown.

Day 173

GOOD NEWS, RECEIVED AND SHARED

"And they stripped him (Saul) and took his head and his armor, and sent messengers throughout the land of the Philistines, to carry the good news to their idols . . ." (1 Chronicles 10:9).

Read: **1 Chronicles 10;** Isaiah 40:9, 52:7, 61:1; Luke 2:10; Romans 1:16, 5:1-2.

WHAT IS GOD SAYING?

The rise and fall of King Saul is one of the Bible's sad and tragic stories. He was so promising and so disappointing. Perhaps 1 Chronicles 10:13-14 is enough at this point to summarize the elements of his downfall. Saul is not the first nor is he the last who "did not seek guidance from the Lord," and, going his own way, failed. His life was a fireworks rocket, rising in power, bursting in splendor, and then falling to earth like a spent and dying ember.

His death was "good news"—to the Philistines. He was a great warrior and the symbol of authority in a nation they hated. So, flushed with victory, the Philistines sent messengers with the good tidings. Their idols would be so happy to hear the news! Of course their lifeless idols could neither hear their jubilant cries nor wear a smile of approval. But that mattered little, the "good news" had to be shared, first with the gods, and then with those who kept the home fires burning.

HOW DOES THIS APPLY TO US?

We also have Good News. The Philistines took the report of their triumph on Mt. Gilboa to their dead gods. We receive our Good News from the living God through the triumph of Christ on Mt. Calvary. Notice the eagerness with which the Philistines spread their story of a conquered king: "They sent messengers throughout the land to carry the good news to their idols." A fallen king was their good news! A risen King is our Good News! Yet how eager are we to share our Good News "throughout the land?"

Ours is a living and loving God who is not willing that any should perish, and those who could hear our Good News are not lifeless idols in a shrine. They are living (and dying) people in the post office and the bank and the supermarket. This illustration, taken from an instance of humiliating defeat and tragic failure long ago and far away, says something to us. We have far more reason to carry the Good News, we have a far greater victory to celebrate, we have the message of a far greater King who not only died to bring us salvation but rose to give us eternal life.

Pray with Me

Lord, I thank You for Jesus Christ through whom the Good News of Your saving power has been brought to the world. I thank You that it was the desire and plan of "the only wise God, our Savior," to bring Good News to us.

What a poor religion it is when a man must carry to some inferior deity of his own making the good news of his victory! How pathetic to shout the song of triumph before an idol whose ears will never hear! How empty to share the gladness of victory before a face whose expression can never change!

The good news of vengeance and bloodshed was carried by living Philistines to their dead gods. It is far better—day compared to night—when the Good News of redemption is brought from the living God, through the risen Christ, to those who are dead in trespasses and sins.

Let the knowledge that You have brought to me good news fill my heart with deep love for You. Help me to share the Good News with others who have never been convinced that God lives and loves and cares. Then the good news that I will bring to You, loving Father, will never be that of pride cruelly revenged or of opponents violently subdued. My good news to You will be that, through Christ, I have been subdued and others for His sake have been loved into the kingdom.

You have not brought Good News to me in order that I may keep it in a safe, secret place. I am to share it with conviction and joy. Then I will return to You with that good news that can make even the angels sing. Here, Lord, is one grateful and forgiven sinner who has been found and rescued by hearing and believing the Good News of the blessed God.

In the Name of Him whose deathless love is the everlasting Good News, Amen.

MOVING ON IN THE LIFE OF PRAYER

The light that shines on our souls with a lingering benediction as we pray; the song that puts a melody in our hearts when we lift them in prayer to God; the peace that floods our being as we contemplate the powerful and deathless love of Jesus; the grace that is sufficient for us in every trial; the truth that gives us a steady step; the love that gives us a willing hand when we rise from prayer—*is* the Good News. We are justified by faith, we have peace with God and we rejoice in our hope of sharing the glory of God (Romans 5:1-2). That's Good News. Let's share it.

Day 174

LOVING OBEDIENCE

"If you love me, you will keep my commandments" (John 14:15).

Read: **John 14;** 13:34; 15:10, 14; Psalm 119:97.

WHAT IS GOD SAYING?

In these great, rich chapters of John 13-15, much is said about love and just as much is said about obeying. Love is not an emotional satellite swinging around in an orbit of fantasy. It is not out of touch with the practical matters of earth. It is related to such mundane things as obeying commandments. Jesus makes much of this.

In Chapter 13, He washes His disciples' feet, then rises from the lowly but necessary task with the words, "do as I do." "As I have loved you, love one another" (13:34). Loving Jesus and obeying His commands go hand in hand. Chapter 14, perhaps the best loved chapter in the Bible, continues with the theme that love is something we do. The test of love is not only what it does to us but how it motivates us to do something for others for Christ's sake.

Jesus talks about love, the Father's love for Him, His love for us and our love for Him as expressed in our love for others. He talks about the untroubled heart (14:1, 27). He talks about peace that the world can neither give nor take away (14:27). He talks about the Father's house with its many rooms and the place prepared for us (14:2). But these wonderful promises are not spoken in a vacuum of noninvolvement. They are all intertwined with things that need to be done. Heaven is coming but obedience is now. No heart can be at peace in itself unless it shares that peace with others. No one can come to the Father through Him who is the way, the truth, and the life (14:6), without wanting to help others find that way, learn that truth, and receive that life.

HOW DOES THIS APPLY TO US?

Christ, the living Word, and the Bible, God's written Word, show us the love of God. "God so loved the world that he gave his only begotten Son . . ." (John 3:16). Love was something God did. And the same Word—living and written—spells out in clear detail that love is doing what Jesus commands. We don't obey because we can earn God's approval. We don't obey because we are afraid that something bad will happen if we don't. We simply obey because we love. We obey Him because we love Him.

God, in Christ, has given us both the command and the example. He tells us what to do and draws a picture of how it's done. We are without excuse—but if we love Him, we won't be looking for an excuse.

Pray with Me

Lord, You are both holy and loving, and in Your love You have given us law.

I thank You that my hope is not based on perfect obedience to the law. In the weakness of my flesh, I have not kept it. In the waywardness of my thoughts, I have not loved it.

I am determined not to ignore or despise the kindly disciplines of divine law. Restraining, they guide me safely. Holding in, they lead me on. Denying license, they give me liberty. I would find it in my heart to praise You with the psalmist: "O how I love thy law."

Today, dear Lord, lift me by Your Spirit to a far better understanding of law and love. I want to keep Your law for no other and no lesser reason than because I love You. Let love be the force that inspires and controls. Let love be purposeful steps on the road of obedience and not the wispy cloud of a fleeting emotion. Let it be as real and as simple as saying: "Here am I, Lord; send me."

There are those who keep Your commandments because they fear Your anger. Others keep Your commandments because they are proud of their righteousness. I would keep Your commandments because I love You. I would keep Your commandments because I know You first loved me—and because I know You love me forever.

Forgive me for ever supposing that man's love for God and God's law for man could ever live apart. Let the keeping of Your law be on the plane of love. Nothing else is worthy. But let all love for You be on the plane of obeying Your will. Nothing else is real.

In His Name who, though He were a Son, yet learned obedience by the things He suffered, Amen.

MOVING ON IN THE LIFE OF PRAYER

Prayer is the time to be renewed in our love for God. Think of all the gifts we have received. Think of the days of sunshine and blessing. Think of the cup that overflows with the joys of health and family and loving companions. Think of the times that love warned us and, to our good, we heeded the warning. Think of the open doors we might never have entered without the gentle and persistent nudge of God's love. Think of all the riches that love has deposited in our account. Think! Think and thank! But there is more. Prayer will pinpoint the times and the places we can show our love for Jesus in the things we do for others.

Day 175

THE PRAYER GOD HEARS

" 'As I called, and they would not hear, so they called, and I would not hear' says the LORD of hosts" (Zechariah 7:13).

Read: **Zechariah 7;** Psalm 81:11-16; Proverbs 1:24, 28; Jeremiah 7:13-19; James 4:3.

WHAT IS GOD SAYING?

Joel said it first and Peter opens his Pentecost message by quoting him: "Your young men shall see visions" (Acts 2:17). Zechariah was a young prophet who saw visions. He encouraged his people by telling them of the bright future God had in store for them. There are eight visions in the first six chapters of his book. All of them point to prosperity and blessing for Israel.

But, as we read in the closing verse of chapter six, all of this is contingent upon their "diligently obeying" the voice of the Lord (6:15). *IF* is the big little word written across Israel's destiny. In chapter eight, the message of hope is repeated: Old men and women sitting in peace and children safely playing in the streets (8:4, 5). "They shall be my people and I will be their God" (8:8). But in chapter seven there is the stern warning of what will happen if Israel does not diligently obey the voice of the Lord.

Zechariah is answering a question posed by a deputation from Bethel about the validity of fasts. He points out that fasts have no meaning unless those who fast obey the Law of the Lord. Faithfulness, sincerity, and obedience are of primary importance. "To obey is better than to sacrifice" was the counsel of an older prophet (1 Samuel 15:22). "To obey is better than to fast" is the pungent counsel of the young prophet.

HOW DOES THIS APPLY TO US?

We saw in yesterday's meditation that love and obedience go hand in hand. If we love the Lord, His commandments will not seem burdensome. They will be liberating. They do not fence us in. They set us free. Love is the root and obedience is the fruit. Now we see that obedience to God's holy laws is not only an index of the genuineness of our love, it is also a condition that determines whether God will hear us.

God hears the earnest cry of repentance. But if we have no sincere intention of obeying, our prayers may be lifted in vain. A heart that is adamant against the law and the words God has spoken (7:12) is an iron-clad guarantee that God will not hear us. It comes to this: if we turn a deaf ear to God's Word, he must turn a deaf ear to our formal, half-meant, and shallow praying.

Pray with Me

Heavenly Father, You have never turned away the prayer of those who come in faith. You have never withheld Your mercy from those who try to walk the path of obedience. When I am troubled by what appears to be "unanswered prayer," let me look at my heart under the revealing light of the Word to which Your Spirit has led me today.

To believe that I will be heard when I call to You, even though I am unwilling to hear Your voice calling to me, is blind and unreasoning audacity. May the fuzzy half-obedience of an unyielded heart snap into focus until I am more concerned about hearing Your call than I am about Your hearing my call. O Spirit of God, silence the static of a life that is not quite tuned in on Your frequency. Keep me from listening partly to God and partly to anti-God and really hearing neither one.

I can count on answered prayer when I fulfill the simple requirement of a listening and obeying heart. Lord, supply the missing ingredient. In all the confusion of competing interests, through the din, the dust, and the distraction of earthquake, wind, and fire, let me hear Your still, small voice.

Listening for that voice, I will concern myself less with getting things in answer to prayer. I will be more concerned with becoming Yours in a walk of faith. In tune with Your will, I will not be so much demanding answers as supplying answers. I will not waste time trying to bend Your will to my notions, and I will see the wonder of answered prayer as I bend my notions to Your will.

Call, and I will hear, Lord. Then in Your wisdom, in Your way, and by Your grace, You will hear when I call,

In the Name of Christ my God, Amen.

MOVING ON IN THE LIFE OF PRAYER

"Listening *and* obeying" make up the true essence of praying. The prescription for prevailing prayer is not only to hear but to heed. God will listen and God will answer in wisdom and justice and power when the prayer that is lifted is linked to a life that obeys. Let us spend more time supplying answers *to* God than in demanding answers *from* God.

Day 176

THE RIGHT KIND OF PRAYING

"Draw near to God and he will draw near to you. Cleanse your hands, you sinners, and purify your hearts, you men of double mind" (James 4:8).

Read: **James 4;** Psalm 73:28; Proverbs 8:17; Jeremiah 4:14; Hebrews 10:22; 2 Timothy 2:21; 1 John 3:3.

WHAT IS GOD SAYING?

Today's highlighted verse is taken from a passage that depicts a great and incessant conflict. The battle line is drawn. It is time to choose: God's way or the world's. They are not only opposites, they are opponents. To be a friend of the world is to be an enemy of God (4:4). These are clear, unmistakable, stinging, stabbing words.

Christians must be especially on guard. We can be caught up in the spirit of covetousness and desire without realizing it. These are the world's highest priorities and the media is always in front of us with the subtle persuasion that "we deserve it." We can even find ourselves praying for what the world counts important. That is "asking wrongly" (4:3). We must not overlook the place of prayer in this ceaseless conflict. "War," or life that is not at rest but in constant turmoil, results either from no praying (4:2), or wrong praying (4:3). The only answer is found in verses 7 and 8: "Resist the devil." He is no friend. Put him in his place. Then "draw near to God and he will draw near to you."

HOW DOES THIS APPLY TO US?

James gives us consecutive sentences (4:7 and 8) that go together like the red and green lights at a traffic intersection. "Stay away from the devil and he will stay away from you." "Draw near to God and he will draw near to you." Trouble, even catastrophe, comes when we fail to stop at the red light and fail to move at the green light. All of us are drawn into the traffic patterns of the world. But God has given us clear instructions on how to get home safely. Wait for the red light— "Resist the devil." Move on the green light— "Draw near to God."

Pray with Me

Lord, here is a promise that is certain. It is Your own Word. Here is a gracious promise. It speaks to my deepest need. Here is a changeless promise. It is, like Christ who makes it possible, the same yesterday, today, and forever.

It is good to know that when I turn toward You in sincere desire, You are already turned toward me with the yearning love that I have seen in the face of Jesus Christ. How good to know that for every tiny step I take toward You in faith, You are taking giant steps toward me in love. The gap is being bridged from both sides. Faith is not the search of a desperate heart for a withdrawing God. Faith is not a frantic effort to recover a vanishing dream. It is simply drawing near to the Father, who, in the Son, draws near to me. Nothing gives more satisfaction to the empty heart. Nothing gives more peace to the troubled heart: "Draw near to God and he will draw near to you."

Yet what keeps me from drawing near, O God? Surely it is not so much doubt. For that I would gladly leave. It must be something else. In truth it is double-mindedness and a lingering attachment to things You can neither approve nor bless. Let me, therefore, not turn a deaf ear to the whole counsel of this verse: "Cleanse your hands . . . purify your hearts."

The Holy Spirit has given the prerequisite for "drawing near to God." He has given it in the sweet song of David. He has given it in the stern word of James. "Who shall ascend the hill of the Lord? . . . He who has clean hands and a pure heart."

O Holy Spirit, You have given this counsel in the beauty of song and in the clarity of simple truth. Help me to obey promptly. I want to find the God who is already seeking. I want to draw near to the God who is already here.

Through the mercy of Jesus Christ who has brought God to man and man to God, Amen.

MOVING ON IN THE LIFE OF PRAYER

When we come to prayer, it might be helpful for us to pronounce "priorities" as "pray-orities." Then we will have the singleness of purpose, the cleanness of heart and the humility of spirit that God can bless and honor. It is the door to effective prayer. It is the way to blessed living.

Day 177

RUNNING FROM OR RESTING IN GOD

"Flight shall perish from the swift . . ." (Amos 2:14).

Read: **Amos 2:6-16, 9:2;** Deuteronomy 4:39; Psalm 139:7-12; Proverbs 15:3; Jeremiah 23:23-24; Romans 2:3.

WHAT IS GOD SAYING?

Amos had two occupations, both of them humble. He followed sheep across the hillsides southeast of Jerusalem. On a lower level of that wild terrain, he dressed sycamore trees. He had no religious training. He was not enrolled in a school of the prophets. He had no credentials as a priest. He was an unlikely candidate. But God has often taken a liking to the unlikely. They do his bidding with less bargaining and quibbling. They live simply and speak plainly. Amos was God's man for this hour.

He traveled the twenty-two miles from Tekoa to Bethel, the religious capital of the north, where the king's sanctuary still took pride in the two golden calves set up by Jeroboam I. Amos walked the land without fear, even though Bethel was dangerous territory for a prophet of Jehovah. His message comes out loud and clear. First, there is God's judgment on six heathen nations. Many Israeli heads nod in agreement. Then the spotlight rests on Judah. Heads are still nodding. Next, pulling no punches, Amos tells Israel that God has *them* marked for punishment and doom. Now the heads are not nodding in approval but wagging with anger and resentment.

Privilege, Amos tells them, must be accompanied by responsibility. Israel had taken the privileges and forsaken the responsibilities. And God was displeased. Israel is not clever enough to find a way out. Israel is not fast enough to get away from nor strong enough to stand up against the judgment of God (7:14).

HOW DOES THIS APPLY TO US?

Have we ever tried to get away from God? Have we become lost in a busy round of duties or pleasures really intended to keep God at arm's length? Have we, perhaps, shown a nominal interest in spiritual things like attending church and going through the motions of a religious life? And is it just a facade? Our real agenda leaves out God. We hurry on to other activities where we will not be constantly reminded that Jesus is Lord. We keep perpetually involved with programs that do not call our consciences to task. In a word, we try to get away from God.

No use! "Flight shall perish from the swift." God is inescapable. He is at the end and way beyond the end of our swiftest, farthest flight. So let us rest in Him and not run from Him.

Pray with Me

O God, it is foolish and impossible to fly from Your presence. "If I take the wings of the morning and dwell in the uttermost parts of the sea, even there Thy hand shall lead me and Thy right hand shall hold me." Halt these flying feet. Hold this willful heart. By the authority of Your never-yielding love cause all flight to perish.

As I reflect on the willfulness of my spirit, I am aware that flying on swift feet has become a practiced art, a settled habit, even a source of pride. Others may not be swift enough to elude the grip of justice. They may lack the agility to dodge the arrows of conscience. They may not be able to outrun the sounds of pleading love. But as for me . . .

Now, dear Lord, let the knowledge that I can never run fast enough or far enough to out-distance Your love cause all flight to perish from my heart. Let the running cease and the resting begin. As You are the end, and way beyond the end, of my swiftest flight, so be with me in the midst of these flying days. Even now let the peace of eternity govern all my goings.

I have run in pride, now let me walk in humility. I have fled in fear, now let me hold on in trust. I have sought to avoid You by swift escape; now let me embrace You by swift obedience.

Then, O Lord, I will discover with great joy that swift as evil is to accuse and to destroy, You are swifter to justify and to save.

My hope once lay in my flight from You. Now, O loving God, my hope lies in Your flight to me,

In the wonderful grace of Jesus Christ, my Lord and Your beloved Son, Amen.

MOVING ON IN THE LIFE OF PRAYER

God cannot be outdistanced by our running nor can He be ignored in our busy schedules. Prayer is the choicest of times, the greatest of privileges, the most meaningful of appointments in any hour of any day. It is the time when, above all, our running away stops and our resting in God's goodness begins. Prayer is waiting upon God. It is the time when all flight perishes and all the promises of God come alive.

Day 178

CHRISTIAN FAITH: FORM OR FORCE OR BOTH?

"Holding the form of religion but denying the power of it" (2 Timothy 3:5).

Read: **2 Timothy 3;** 1 Samuel 15:22; Hosea 6:6; Daniel 12:9; 2 Peter 5:3-4.

WHAT IS GOD SAYING?

We are now in a portion of the Word which spells out in exact detail the apostasy and corruption that will be rampant in the "last times." One does not need to be a date-setter to feel that our current conditions are as a mirror held up to Paul's writing. Paul's catalog of wickedness personified hits amazingly close to home. The picture rocks us back on our heels. We scarcely need to repeat Paul's list in 2 Timothy 3:1-7. It is found in news items and television programming *ad nauseam* every day. Feeling the impact of evil so accurately described, we join the chorus of Christians who say of Jesus' promised return: "Even so, come, Lord Jesus."

One of the aspects of these troubled and godless times is that "religion" will keep going on with its forms and traditions, and still be void of power. Services are held in churches, people go through the motions, traditions are duly honored, but the Holy Spirit is absent. The form is present. The power is absent. And it sounds a lot like today.

HOW DOES THIS APPLY TO US?

The *form* of religion (in the King James version, "the form of godliness") has its good points. Organized "religion" has been responsible for immeasurable good through the centuries. But it has also written some of history's darkest pages. It has been, and still is, the creator and perpetrator of war and vengeance, such as the loathsome excesses of Islam's "holy wars." That is a form of religion.

But we are indebted to the works and writings of sincere believers across the centuries who have been deeply involved in "religion." Their forms, their prayers, their creeds, their great places of worship have made us rich in faith and grounded in love. But form is not enough. A good illustration is that of a steam locomotive and the power that is generated by the steam in its boiler. The engine is the form. The steam is the power. The engine without the steam is dead. The steam without the engine is pointless. True Christian faith is not form *or* force. It is both.

Pray with Me

O God, we have been called to worship You in the beauty of holiness. I am thankful for the form of religion. I thank You for the beauty of temples made with hands. I thank You for prayers that have risen from sensitive hearts. In their written form, they still live . . . to bless. I thank You for the boldness of ancient creeds. I thank You for the majesty of deathless hymns. I thank You for the form of religion.

Nevertheless, keep me from the danger of growing too fond of form. It is a poor substitute for the living power of a personal relationship with Christ. If I hold the form of religion, uplifted by its beauty and strengthened by its order, let me not forsake a constant communion with Your Holy Spirit. Your promised companion, O Christ, is pure and purifying. He is vital and vitalizing. He is holy and sanctifying. Without his assistance, all form, however beautiful and cherished, is empty and vain and even deceitful.

Lord, I want to maintain such fellowship with You as will keep alive in me the living power of true faith. I would permit no obstacle in the way of Your will for my life. I am tired of having often denied the flow of Your power in me and through me. Inspire every desire. Control every impulse. Guide every thought until my life displays and does not deny Your power.

Replace mere form with mighty force. Fill ancient prayer with living power. Let the good become the best, until, living by the power of faith, I shall hold in true perspective its worthy and cherished form,

To the glory of Jesus Christ, Amen.

MOVING ON IN THE LIFE OF PRAYER

Prayer must never become just a ritual. It is good that we have forms that provide direction in prayer. We should be grateful for written and classical prayers, *if* they help us to express our own true feelings and needs. They are worse than useless if, in repeating them, we are mouthing empty words. The habit of praying is good but if praying is only a habit it is bad. The best form of praying is to pray that Christ may be formed in us (Galatians 4:19). There is our power. That is how mere form is transformed into mighty force.

Day 179

My Life, God's Vineyard

"When I looked for it to yield grapes, why did it yield wild grapes?"
(Isaiah 5:4).

Read: **Isaiah 5;** Matthew 21:33-45.

What Is God Saying?

To bring home the truth of God's yearning love for His wayward people, Isaiah uses many parables and illustrations. In chapter five he even uses a song which has come to be known as "The Song of the Vineyard." The theme of rejected love reaches people where they are. It is hard to go on when love is unrequited on the human level. In this song he wants them to sense how God must feel when His, the greatest of all loves, has been met with ingratitude and contempt.

The God of Israel planted His people as the choicest of vineyards. He placed the vineyard on a fertile hill (5:1). He cleared it of stones. He planted choice vines and set up a watchtower. His people had every advantage and protection from all harm. God had a right to expect a good harvest. He had done His part. What more could He do? (5:4) But when He looked for it to yield grapes, it yielded wild grapes.

Later in the chapter, Isaiah speaks of the judgment God would bring on them because they failed to treat their privileged status with respect and gratitude. They took so much and gave so little. The promising vineyard yielded the wrong kind of fruit. God had no alternative. He would remove the hedge and let sin reap its own dread harvest. First, desolation, waste, clouds without rain, and diminished harvests. Then, the crushing blow of heathen kings and captivity.

How Does This Apply to Us?

Since we have all been the recipients of God's love, we must all examine our own hearts to see whether we are truly honoring that love. If we love Him we will obey His commandments. If we obey His commandments, we will have fruitful lives. God has made us His vineyard. He has given us every advantage and has every reason to expect a good harvest. The privilege, the honor, the love belongs to us but so also does the responsibility of yielding good fruit. We are responsible if the harvest is wild and bitter. We cannot blame it on the breaks of life or the irresponsibility of someone else. May God never have to say to us, "I looked for the vineyard of your life to yield grapes. Why did it yield wild grapes?"

Pray with Me

Lord, let me not dodge my personal responsibility for yielding the good fruit of holiness and virtue. The harvest of wild and bitter grapes is also the result of an undisciplined life. It is bound to happen. And I am responsible when it does happen. It cannot be laid on any other doorstep.

You have the right to expect good fruit. As "Your beloved," I am a vineyard planted on a fertile hill. Everything has been done by Your omnipotent hand. Every good gift has come from Your heart filled with love. Every circumstance has been arranged by Your perfect providence. The lack that brings about a disappointing harvest does not have its origin in You.

Nor can I blame other people or the breaks of life. The failure is mine. When I know bitterness in my heart and show it in my life, it is because my relationship to You, the Source of all life and good, has broken down. When wild grapes grow within and show without, it is because communion with You in prayer has been despised. It is because service for You has been neglected. I have chosen not to abide in the true Vine. I have chosen to draw my life from some other source.

Restore to me the joy of Your salvation. Let Your pardoning grace surround me as nourishing soil. Let the magnetism of my Lord's example draw me forth as the sun and rain bring fruit that buds to the harvest that abounds. Then there will not be any room for grapes that are wild. Let the strength of a settled faith keep me from sin's withering blight. Then You shall look for and You shall find good fruit which will be to the praise of Your own eternal love,

Through Jesus Christ, my Lord, Amen.

MOVING ON IN THE LIFE OF PRAYER

Prayer is the nourishing soil that produces good fruit. In prayer we choose to be quiet before God and let the sunshine of His love bathe our souls with cleansing and renewal. Prayer is a time for knowing God's will and growing where He plants us. Prayer leads us to the strength of a settled faith. Prayer provides the way to a harvest that pleases God, the Owner of the vineyard, and the Lover of our souls.

Day 180

THE PATIENCE OF
AN ESTABLISHED HEART

"Behold. the farmer waits for the precious fruit of the earth . . . You also be patient. Establish your hearts, for the coming of the Lord is at hand" (James 5:7, 8).

Read: **James 5;** Hebrews 6:11-12, 15; Colossians 1:11-14; 2 Timothy 3:10-11; Revelation 3:10-11.

WHAT IS GOD SAYING?

James gives us two examples in this portion of his letter to bring home two great essentials of our faith: *patience* and *prayer.* Job is our model for patience. Elijah is our model for prayer. Patience and prayer are closely tied together in James's letter. In life they flow together down the same stream bed. Prayer and waiting for God's timing is like the "farmer" (a third example) who sows the seed and waits for the "precious fruit of the earth" (5:7). This is why prayer is so often regarded as "waiting on the Lord" (Isaiah 40:31, Psalm 27:14, etc.).

The ability to wait with patience for God's answer to prayer depends upon whether or not our hearts are "established" (5:8). The "established heart," in turn, is derived from "being rooted and grounded in God's love" (Ephesians 3:16, 17). Having that, we have the patience to wait for God's answer to prayer and for Christ's return in power and glory. Patience in prayer, patience in tribulation, patience in everything is the fruit of a heart which is "established in God's love."

HOW DOES THIS APPLY TO US?

In this day of agribusiness, most of us seem far removed from farming. Still it is good for us to remember that even machine-sown and machine-harvested crops require patience during the growing period. "The precious fruit of the earth" *will* come. The fields *will* be white unto the harvest. Prayers *will* be answered. Jesus *will* return.

When we pray, when we sow the seed, when we claim the promises with hearts established in God's love, we must wait through the sunshine of joys and through the raindrops of tears, until the time is right and the harvest is ripe. This calls for patience and patience comes from the established heart.

Pray with Me

Eternal God, Source of all good and only good, give me the patience of an established heart. Let me trust that You are working out Your purpose in my life and in the world. Let me believe that You are doing this according to Your timetable.

When my heart is established in Your love, it will have the patience to accept Your purpose and Your timing. When my heart is established in Your love, it will experience the joy of Your presence in everything and in spite of everything.

To know beyond all doubt, to believe beyond all fear, to accept Your promises with unquestioning trust, this is what I want. By Your Spirit bearing witness within, this is what I want. By Your Spirit bearing witness within, this is what I may now have. Established in this truth, I can be patient to the very end of any long, dark corridor into which Your permissive will ordains that I should enter.

O Christ, King of kings and Lord of lords, I look for Your return. I long for Your appearance. Ever since You came to my heart in that first dawning of faith, I have been waiting for Your coming to the world in glorious triumph. Seeing evil deeply entrenched and securely enthroned in the hearts of men and nations, I have often prayed: "Even so, come quickly, Lord Jesus."

Nevertheless, today I pray for the established heart that can wait with patience until You come. In that patience I know I shall discover Your peace which passes all understanding and possess that divine strength which is made perfect in human weakness.

Come quickly, Lord Jesus, but until You do, give me the patience of an established heart.

For the sake of Your own glory, Amen.

MOVING ON IN THE LIFE OF PRAYER

Every time we listen for the Father's timely word in prayer and every time we raise our petitions to Him, we should feel that we are coming closer to "the established heart." Prayer is when we share our joys and lift our praise. Prayer is when we ask for miracles and look for thrilling answers and they have often come. Prayer is also the time when above all else, beyond all else, and through all else, we find the established heart. Do we have the patience of an established heart? It is one of prayer's great byproducts. Don't miss it.

Day 181
STRONG IN THE LORD

"Finally, be strong in the Lord . . ." (Ephesians 6:10).

Read: **Ephesians 6:10-20;** 1 Kings 2:2; Isaiah 35:4; 1 Corinthians 16:13-14; Philippians 4:6; 2 Timothy 2:1.

WHAT IS GOD SAYING?

Paul wrote this letter as he was chained to a Roman soldier. Night and day, a fully armed soldier was at his side to make sure that this "terrible criminal" would not escape. As he brought his letter to a close, he probably stopped and looked up. There it was. His closing remarks. His clinching illustration. The soldier was wholly armed, ready to take on far more dangerous enemies than Paul. Yet he was ready. Should not Christians be wholly armed for their warfare? The belt, the breastplate, the sandals, the shield, the helmet, the sword . . . and one more, the secret, the invisible, and the greatest weapon, prayer.

HOW DOES THIS APPLY TO US?

It is no accident that Paul's exhortation to Christian soldiers opens with "finding our strength in the Lord" and closes with "praying at all times." It is also no accident that hearing or "listening" to the Word of God (6:17) comes immediately before "praying at all times" (6:18). "The sword of the Spirit," then "praying in the Spirit." That is what it is all about! *"Listen* to the Word—*then pray."* Result: Strong in the Lord.

This passage reminds us that we are engaged in a spiritual conflict from which there is no retreat. Spiritual warfare calls for spiritual weapons. And while there is no retreat in this struggle, there also need be no defeat. The shield of faith can quench all the flaming darts of the evil one (6:16). And with the whole armor of God, having stood our ground, we will still be standing when the battle is over. "Having done all, to stand" (6:13). In the "whole armor of God" there is not a single piece to protect the back. We can stand up to the enemy. We can conquer the enemy if, "praying at all times" (6:18), we are "strong in the Lord" (6:10).

Pray with Me

Lord, when all is said and done, when the student leaves the School of Calvary to set his feet on the walk of daily Christian love, it is the joy of Your presence that cheers him. It is the strength of Your presence that sustains him.

How often I have sought the support of a friend and leaned upon his understanding and encouragement. And I am grateful for friends. They are often a blessing direct from You. Yet I am so eager to have these friends agree with me. I go to great lengths trying to be appreciated. I have often looked for support in someone other than You or in something short of Your grace.

Lead me, strong Redeemer, truest Friend. Lead me in a walk of courageous faith which counts on nothing but Your Word. Help me to listen for nothing but Your command. Let me seek no glory but Your "Well done." Let me be alone with You, and if necessary, let me dare to be with You alone. Let me choose to abide with You when others have forsaken the shining goal and forgotten the greatness of our calling. Let me dare to stand alone in the hour of some lonely moral choice. Let me discover that in standing alone, I am never alone.

"Strong in the Lord." Apart from You I am never truly strong. In the midst of people, occupied with duties, busy with cares and pleasure, when the sun is high and my hands are busy, I think I can be strong apart from You. But when the busy world is hushed and my thoughts are free to roam . . . when the tools are returned to the shelf and my hands are idle . . . then, looking into the unruffled depths of my being, I can see that ultimate and triumphant strength is found only in the Lord.

Help me to live now and through each passing moment as though this ultimate and final strength were my only strength. And it is.

In the Name of Him who has made us "more than conquerors," Amen.

Moving On in the Life of Prayer

As we bring our six-month exercise in prayer to a close, we too can say "*finally*, be strong in the Lord." Just to live in this kind of world, we need the whole armor of God. Truth to counter falsehood. Righteousness to overcome evil. Peace to replace restlessness and turmoil. Faith to overcome cynicism and unbelief. Salvation to assure us we are not losers.

These are all needed and these are all effective. But when all is said and done, it is knowing that God is with us and that we are with Him that helps us finally to be strong in the Lord. And this comes through listening to God's Word and praying at all times in the Spirit. Our bodies grow strong and stay healthy by physical exercise. Our souls stay strong in the Lord and glow with the joy of spiritual well-being by the exercise of prayer.

Finally, that's the way to be strong in the Lord.